MATTERS OF FACT

Margery Fisher

matters of fact

ASPECTS OF NON-FICTION FOR CHILDREN

 BROCKHAMPTON PRESS

ISBN 0 340 03577 3

First edition 1972
Published by Brockhampton Press Ltd, Salisbury Road, Leicester
Filmset by Keyspools Ltd, Golborne, Lancashire
Printed and bound in Great Britain by C. Tinling & Co. Ltd, Prescot
Text copyright © 1972 Margery Fisher

Contents

To Norah Enderby, Lettice Loughnan and Esther Nicholson,
who taught me to enjoy learning

Acknowledgments

I ACKNOWLEDGE gratefully the help of the Superintendent and staff of the British Museum Reading Room and of the County Librarian and staff of the Northamptonshire County Library, and the Leicestershire County Library.

The section on Atoms would have been impossible to compile without the generous help of Dr John Ashworth, lecturer in biochemistry at the University of Leicester. His advice on particular points and his illuminating review of the background made it easier for me to assess books which I had to approach as a beginner.

I am grateful to Ann Beneduce of Thomas Y. Crowell Company, for her encouragement and help; and to those present and former members of the staff of Brockhampton Press who worked on the book – especially, Janet Bord, who checked the reading lists; Peter Ducker, the designer of the book; Suzanne Jarvis, for researching and collating the illustrations and captions; and Vivienne Robertson who corrected the proofs and compiled the index.

My warmest thanks go to Antony Kamm as my friend and editor over many years. His terse and often tart marginal comments on the various drafts of MATTERS OF FACT have been most stimulating and I could not have done without his sound advice and encouragement while I was collecting, sorting and arranging the material.

MARGERY FISHER *Ashton, 1972*

1 | *Introduction*

THE names of Farjeon, Coatsworth, Pearce, Ransome are current coin in any assembly owning the slightest connection with books for children: the names of Wymer, Adler, Boswell Taylor, Unstead are not. The first group are writers of fiction, the second of non-fiction. This cannot be explained by the assumption that there are more readers of fiction than of non-fiction: statistics suggest otherwise. The belief is still current that one acquires more merit by reading about facts than about imagined scenes and people. Despite this, the writers of non-fiction for children are not universally thought of as writers in the same way as authors of junior novels. Peggy Heeks makes the point emphatically:

> There is a magic about the creation of even a mediocre work of fiction which is missing from the assembling and ordering of facts. Sneakingly, a number of us believe that with a fortnight of peace and a couple of encyclopedias we could put together an outline for children on some subject that interests us. To hold the detailed threads of plot, conjure up characters and find voices for them needs an effort of a different kind.
> "Getting at the facts", in *The Times Literary Supplement*, 2 July 1970, p. 721

Because of an unexpressed feeling that information books are not "creative", they are far more often reviewed for their content than for their total literary value. Today hundreds of books are available to help children to satisfy their eager curiosity about the world of past, present and future, but up to now there have been few attempts to suggest guide-lines to the assessment of non-fiction. Book reviews are more often concerned to point out mistakes of fact than to

consider the way an author has presented those facts. In this book
I hope to suggest ways in which certain types of information books
might be defined and discussed.

What is non-fiction? As a composite word it has official though
not yet published existence. So far it has been traced back to 1909,
and examples of its use are being collected currently for the next
printed supplement to the Oxford English Dictionary. It is still not a
term that can stand up to close examination. For that matter, neither
can "fiction". Historical novels are normally classified as fiction,
when they are neither wholly nor materially so. Even if we call them
"stories" rather than "fiction", it is still clear that they have some
right to be classified as information books. The haziness of verbal
definition made it possible for a Silver Medal for non-fiction to be
awarded by the magazine *Elizabethan*, in 1969, to C. Walter Hodges
for his historical story THE OVERLAND LAUNCH.

The distinction between fiction and non-fiction is no clearer if
we use the terms "information books" and "stories". A great many
fact-books make use of incidental fiction, and who could argue that
fiction had no element of fact? The distinction between fiction and
non-fiction is blurred and constantly shifting, but we still use it and
need it. We have to accept the convenience that lies behind this
naïve generalisation for very young readers:

> There are shelves of books in a library. The story books are called
> fiction. Other books, not stories, are called non-fiction. These are
> books about history, nature and hobbies.
> BUILDINGS AND PEOPLE, p. 15

Like so many general terms, "non-fiction" represents a compromise
with some sense in it.

As a commercial distinction, it is necessary to help with the
marketing and the library classification of commodities available in
enormous numbers. It is irrelevant that the category of non-fiction
is often rendered meaningless for various reasons by authors, critics
and readers. In a more important sense, the terms fiction and non-
fiction express *intention* in a broad way. It is true that some children
may look for and extract nothing but facts from a novel by Cynthia
Harnett, while others may become so deeply involved in a history
of the invention of the wheel or of church music that facts become a

springboard for emotion. Looking at it from the writer's point of view, however, we can see that there is a distinction, a very flexible one, between writing a story and writing an information book. In a novel the story – the fiction, perhaps I should say – comes first and has priority: facts, of whatever kind, exist to support it. The writer of an information book sets out to help towards knowledge, and the techniques he uses, which may well include story-telling, will be subordinate to this end.

Accepting then a broad validity for the terms "fiction" and "non-fiction", do we need also to distinguish, as the book trade does, between juvenile non-fiction and school text-books? "Text-book" too is a fluid word. As one writer remarks, "Books on dress, make-up, birth control and career guides can be called text-books in schools, but they can be sold like gramophone records or Penguins in the market-place."*

It is often asserted that text-books are giving place to "individual guided reading", but I cannot see any formal difference between the graded questions in a Latin grammar and those in one of the innumerable information books which are put on a school shelf for supplementary reading but which contain questions referring back to the text, to be answered in class. Both kinds of book can be used by a teacher as an aid to teaching: equally, a child interested in history need not be considered unnatural if he takes a class history book home just to read.

All text-books are information books but not all information books are text-books. Are they, then, for home or school consumption? Though a very high percentage of information books is bought by schools, parents will and do buy them for their children, and children even buy them for themselves. Certain types seem more at home in the classroom, certainly. A general review of Blackwell's *Little Learning Books* contains an interesting point:

> They are essentially books to be read and talked about. Although the basic content in all cases is simple, with a vocabulary carefully controlled to aid the child reading it by himself, one is aware of an underlying principle that young children need to *talk* about what

*J. R. C. Yglesias. "Has the textbook had its day?" in *Books*, September/October 1966, no. 367, p. 181.

they have read and to link it with their own experiences. For those
who are reading, the simple questions at the end of each booklet
could be answered in written form.

As I see it, their value lies not only in the information actually
offered – sound though it is – but also in what on-the-spot discussion, with reference to the pictures, will lead to.

E. Bowker in *The School Librarian*, vol. 17, no. 2 (June 1969),
p. 218

There is no reason why parents should not be involved in discussions
with their children about the books they read, and of course they
often are so involved, but a group of children with an interested
and interesting teacher is likely to produce a greater diversity of
opinion.

It is the writer's business to provide a book which a child *can* use
himself, whether in private or in the atmosphere of a classroom, to
discover something new or to confirm what he already knows. The
fact that the reader is young will impose certain limitations and
responsibilities. Beyond the literary obligations which any writer
faces in regard to any kind of readership – obligations to be accurate,
to be clear in explanation, to be stimulating, to pursue a logical
arrangement of his material – he must be aware of the age and
aptitude of his readers in a broad way, just as a teacher or a parent
selecting books must take into account in a relative way a writer's
choice of vocabulary and of facts, as well as the illustration and
design of a book as a whole.

But there is more to an information book than its technical aspect.
Each one should contain fact, concept and attitude. Any book that
is not a mere collection of facts (and many of them are only this) has
an end in view, a generalisation towards which the facts are arranged.
This final concept might be a statement of the result of victory or
defeat, in a book of historical fact, or the definition of the end-
product of a process and its use in a book of technology; it might be
the summing-up of the purpose of an institution or a public service,
or the pronouncement of an abstract idea.

Behind the generalisation that concludes, or should conclude, an
information book lies the attitude of the writer. In some cases this
may be a visible partisanship – as for instance in Frank Knight's
THE DARDANELLES CAMPAIGN or Bruce Catton's study of the

American Civil War, THIS HALLOWED GROUND. The enthusiasm of an expert discernible in a book on a sport, a pastime, a hobby, is in itself an attitude. Flatness of style, perfunctory writing, flabbiness in generalisation, all denote the lack of an attitude and promise ill for any book. A writer's conviction has an immediate effect on the reader, whether it is to invigorate and stimulate interest or to communicate a prejudice.

A writer's attitude is often revealed in his terminology. Natural history books provide a useful example here. In any index of this category certain words are likely to recur – Wonderful, Marvellous, Oddities, Miracle, Secrets. What attitudes do these indicate and how should we regard them?

Anyone who chooses to write about natural history has the responsibility for communicating a scientific attitude. To indicate that nature is "wonderful" is to suggest that to the writer the world of nature, in which he properly includes his own existence, is something that excites him and something that he feels could excite the reader. The child's sense of wonder is two-fold. He notices with a lively interest and he also wonders – that is, he wants to know and he asks questions. Whether his interest is stimulated by reading a book or by using his eyes when he is walking in city or country, "wonder" implies an attitude that is potentially active. It leads to discovery and knowledge. "Wonderful" is a word that denotes the observer and his state of mind, not the observed; it need not interfere with a scientific attitude.

But—"marvellous"? What does this imply? Surely, that there is something inexplicable in nature, something involuntary, something different. Such an attitude is basically unscientific. Whether it is devoted to a single subject (spiders, a cat having kittens) or to a region of behaviour (animal navigation), the business of a natural history book is to relate facts to a pattern of life in which humans participate as animals and which they should understand because they are part of it. However informal the approach, however simple, a natural history book for the young belongs to the science of biology. To suggest that the food-catching mechanism of a mussel or the egg-depositing behaviour of a cuckoo is "marvellous" is to make nonsense of the whole process of evolution. This pre-Darwinian attitude is discernible today also in the words "miracle" and "creature", though these may be used without any conscious intention. Words like this are enough to lead a young reader to accept the author's anthropomorphism as a matter of course.

An equally dangerous attitude may be detected in the *avoidance* of certain words. Scientific principles and terminology need not be daunting to young readers. It does not make it easier to see the natural world in perspective, for instance, if the term "animal" is used for "mammal", as it almost invariably is in information books. Alan James in ANIMALS (1969) even goes so far as to explain that

Carol Barker's jacket for QUEST FOR PREHISTORY (Dobson/John Day) suggests by its design that the search can be varied and exciting.

"usually when we say 'animals' we are talking only about *Mammals*" but he still decides "we shall use the word 'animal' all through the book". His reasoning eludes me. It is not pedantic to suggest that the proper terms should be used in the simplest book. Children read books like this to sort information, and to sort properly they must be given the proper categories and terms to work with.

Formally or informally, an information book sets out to teach. To conceal this entirely natural aim, authors writing in many categories use the ubiquitous word "fun" as a smoke-screen. In this respect, trends in non-fiction have followed trends in education, not always with advantage. The move away from a captive audience and set classroom lecturing, healthy though this move certainly is, can lead to trivial studies as easily as to original and exciting work. A superficial permissiveness in the classroom is reflected in the throw-away manner of some information books. An advertisement for a junior travel series announces "a series of guides for young people with a completely original approach. The books are fun to read and the authors have concentrated on amusing the reader, while the educational aspect is left to look after itself."* The book advertised on this occasion was LET'S LOOK AT AUSTRIA by Gwynneth Ashby. I wonder how the partition of Austria in the past or her fate in World War II could be made to seem "amusing"; in fact, the author does not try to fulfil this promise except by being evasive at this stage of her survey.

Children are invited to have fun with coloured paper and with time, with collage and with palaeontology. How disconcerting for them to discover that a book recommends them to *use* mind or hands, and how surprising, too, to open a book like MR BUDGE BUYS A CAR and to find that Gareth Adamson has made technicalities into fun without saying so and without demeaning himself or his readers.

Learning has always been fun in the sense of exciting, invigorating, stimulating and entertaining, but it has never offered to be effortless. The delight in discovery goes far deeper than "fun". A title that uses the word "quest" or "discover" or "look at" picks up and uses the energy which boys and girls are ready to exercise if they are helped to do so. The writer who respects his readers will call upon them to

The Bookseller, no. 3158 (2 July 1966), p. 28.

exercise their minds as well as their hands; no better exercise-machine for the intellect has yet been devised than a book. A teacher wrote recently:

> Activity can too easily mean filling jam jars with water, weighing sand, measuring the playground, making cardboard models of Jerusalem or papier-maché models of this year's school camp. Why so frightened of books? They are friendly things, willing to be picked up or discarded at any time without reproach, able to be copied, absorbed, read and reread, looked at, skipped, pondered over – are completely at the disposal of the user. They do not cut one's finger as scissors can, nor stick one's cuffs with paste; they do not form gritty patches on the floor like sand, nor wet messes like water. The world's books contain the world's knowledge. Surely it is worth everyone's while to help children to learn how to use them.
> Robin Bateman. "Children, teachers and librarians", in *The School Librarian*, vol. 18, no. 2 (June 1970), p. 139

This demurely humorous rallying call to teachers may be extended to writers, publishers, reviewers and readers. I write in the belief that for learning, as for teaching, books are still and always an irreplaceable tool.

Reading List

Adamson, Gareth. MR BUDGE BUILDS A HOUSE (*Brockhampton* 1963) *Chilton* 1968, MR BUDGE BUYS A CAR (*Brockhampton* 1965) *Chilton* 1968. Illustrated by the author.

Ashby, Gwynneth. LET'S LOOK AT AUSTRIA. Let's look at . . . *Museum Press* 1966. Illustrated by photographs.

Catton, Bruce. THIS HALLOWED GROUND (*Doubleday* 1956) *Gollancz* 1957. See also page 12.

Darling, Louis. THE GULL'S WAY (*Morrow* 1965) *Constable* 1966. Illustrated by Lois and Louis Darling. A notable example of one man's long, precise observation of a sea-bird colony, proving that wonder and delight can be expressed without negating a proper scientific outlook.

Gibbons, Irène R. (translator). ANIMALS OF TUNDRA AND ICE-LANDS
Private Lives of Animals. (Italy 1968) *Warne* 1970. Numerous compilers and
illustrators. The use of the term "private lives" in the series-title is borne out in
the text of this book, in which subjects are arranged in random rather than
scientific order and are explored mainly for attributes that are strange or
exciting to human eyes.

Hafslund, Per. MARVELS OF NATURE (Norway 1964) *Evans* 1964. MIRACLES OF
NATURE (Norway 1964) *Evans* 1965. Photographs in colour and black and white
by the author. In these two books the exclamatory, jocular captions interpret
animal behaviour in human terms and contradict the effect of superb photography.

James, Alan. ANIMALS. Learning Library. *Blackwell* 1969. Illustrated by Jennifer
Robbins. Colour photographs by L. Field Marchant.

Knight, Captain Frank. THE DARDANELLES CAMPAIGN. *Macdonald* 1970.
Illustrated by F. D. Phillips.

Selsam, Millicent. BENNY'S ANIMALS AND HOW HE PUT THEM IN ORDER.
I can Read Science Books. (*Harper & Row* 1966) *World's Work* 1967.
Illustrated by Arnold Lobel. A book for very young readers which introduces
simply but firmly the value of systematics.

Selsam, Millicent. THE BUG THAT LAID THE GOLDEN EGGS. I can Read Science
Books. (*Harper & Row* 1967) *World's Work* 1969. Photographs by Harold
Krieger. An exercise in identification that proves natural history can be treated
in proper scientific terms without being dull.

Smith, David and Newton, Derek. BUILDINGS AND PEOPLE. Our Wonderful
World. *Blackie* 1970. Illustrated with photographs in colour.

2 | *Foundations*

Facts are formidable playthings for the young. While an adult may use them to buttress his preconceptions – building either a bridge or a well depending on his openness of mind – the child feels no obligation to erect anything other than delight. Without the grown-up drudgery of need to express an opinion he can collect facts simply for the fun of doing so, absorbing or rejecting as the mood flashes. Information is still an astonishment.

Tom Hutchinson. FACTS FOR CHILDREN, in *Spectator*, 29 May 1971

2 | *Foundations*

CHILDREN collect facts when they read, look or listen, as naturally as they collect shells or tea-cards. In their junior years, books can help them in two ways, providing them with facts and showing them by example how to store them and relate them together, as they would store and classify a collection of fossils. The child who accumulates general knowledge at random needs discipline. A short simple book on a particular subject may offer him some facts he knows already, some which need confirming or expanding, some which are new; he should end with the confidence and flattery of proper knowledge. In LITERATURE AND THE YOUNG CHILD (1967), Joan Cass wrote:

> Children will find amongst the books they enjoy many that deal mainly with facts, books of information concerned with such things as pond life, stars, railways, plants, numbers and a host of other topics. Such books are a useful addition to any child's collection and factual knowledge can give boys and girls a feeling of security; the known is less frightening than the unknown.
> op. cit., pp. 79–80

Joan Cass defines these subjects as "topics" and I propose to use the term "topic book" in a general descriptive sense, to denote the type of information book planned for children up to the age of eleven or twelve and concerned with a single, isolatable subject. In the present climate of children's reading, books of this kind are more often used in school than at home and many of them are produced specifically for school use, either as supplementary readers or as source books for project work. For this reason, the books I shall discuss will be "topic books" also in a stricter and more directly classroom sense. This need not necessarily mean that they must be evaluated in two ways, for school and for home use. The impact of a writer's personality, opinions and knowledge need not differ according to the reading context. An intelligent child can follow up suggestions for further activity or research as readily at home as at school, unless these suggestions involve equipment only available at school. Whether the bias of a book is towards one environment or the other, the qualities one looks for will be the same.

The child who has just begun to read topic books is starting on the bottom rung of the ladder with the simplest pocket-sized pamphlets or toy books; they will lead him finally to specialist books on a single subject. Pocket-sized books for the really young are not new, but in recent years many of them have been standardised and J. C. Gagg has usefully labelled them "sixteen-pagers", hailing them as "a small revolution . . . among books for infants and lower juniors".* These versatile little books are essentially *collections* of fact. They approach learning as a form of play and perhaps for this reason they are occasionally viewed doubtfully by teachers – but not often. It seems a pity that the public is not more aware of the alternative retail editions which exist for many of the series, for although an intelligent child will quickly want to move to more advanced books, a dull one might well be persuaded by the attractive presentation and neat pocket shapes to take a new interest in his surroundings. Gladys Williams's phrase "books of awareness" neatly suggests this function.†

Information books on single subjects are often grouped under a general title which helps to correct inevitable limitations. Some subjects are in themselves mixed – the study of a particular country, for example, can involve, in the simplest book, history, geography, art, industry, technology and so on. On the other hand a universal commodity like bread may be treated in isolation but will be more relevant and interesting if it is grouped with other related subjects, in a pattern of milk-bread-cheese-apples, for instance. In this way, too, a writer can compensate for a small word allowance. But whether or not his book is to be read with others in a group, he

*J. C. Gagg. "The sixteen-pager", in *The Times Educational Supplement*, 16 February 1968, p. 537.
†Gladys Williams. CHILDREN AND THEIR BOOKS (1970)

A quarter of a century ago Otto and Marie Neurath of the Isotype Institute and J. A. Lauwerys, in consultation with Lancelot Hogben, devised a Visual History of Mankind for use in primary schools. The spread shown here comes from Book One of the series, LIVING IN EARLY TIMES (Parrish). With a clever combination of strip-cartoon, diagram and formalised description, the artists illustrated certain concepts or stages of historical and geographical change so simply that with a little initial help from teacher or parent a child could understand how man established himself in his environment. The questions attached to each spread were not meant to be restrictive. I used many of the Isotype books to teach my own children between the ages of five and seven and found that the pictures suggested a great variety of queries and lines of thought. The Isotype method of illustration has been developed over the years and is still used in history and science picture-books by Marie Neurath.

Man comes on the Scene

1
Which of the pictures shows th that happened perhaps 10(years ago? Millions of years Thousands of years ago? Hund of years ago?

2
Which animal is a dinosaur' mammoth? What other animals you spot?

3
When was the climate coldest?

4
Look at other charts in this boo see whether you can find any in them that is like scenes on chart.

5
What other chart in the book you whether the men could killed the mammoth or the bea

6
Why is it that trees seem t getting fewer?

7
Between which two periods di number of men alive grow quickly?

will serve children best if he aims for completeness rather than finality, if he casts round widely for his material and by flexibility of style, by allusion, reference or anecdote gives his book the appearance of being fuller than it can possibly be. The really good topic book, if it is quantitatively small, is qualitatively large.

Even a sixteen-pager can lead a young reader somewhere. In the earliest stage he is being helped to collect information and to arrange it in his mind in an orderly way. A good book will make him want to collect more facts more purposefully – it will make him want to learn. Topic books often contain suggestions for further action on the part of the reader, who may be asked to answer questions, to experiment, to play a record, to choose from a reading list, to visit a place or a person. Such suggestions are not likely to be accepted unless the book is persuasive – or unless a compulsory class exercise is involved.

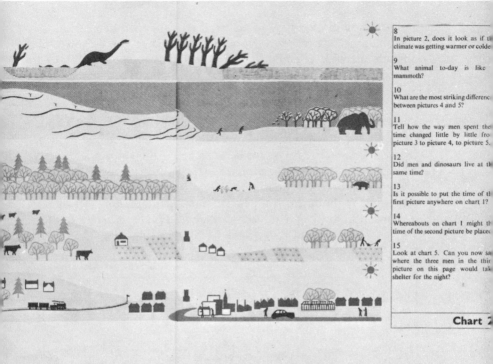

8
In picture 2, does it look as if th
climate was getting warmer or colde

9
What animal to-day is like
mammoth?

10
What are the most striking differenc
between pictures 4 and 5?

11
Tell how the way men spent the
time changed little by little fro
picture 3 to picture 4, to picture 5.

12
Did men and dinosaurs live at th
same time?

13
Is it possible to put the time of th
first picture anywhere on chart 1?

14
Whereabouts on chart 1 might th
time of the second picture be place

15
Look at chart 5. Can you now sa
where the three men in the thir
picture on this page would tak
shelter for the night?

Chart 2

A topic book can be either a starter or a stopper. A starter gives a clear and vivid outline of a subject so that the child wants to pursue it further. A stopper can be quickly skimmed and will be as quickly forgotten because it gives that deadly impression of being self-contained and yet incomplete. Whether a book is a starter or a stopper does not always depend entirely on the writer. An outline within the capacity of an average junior will never give all the facts he wants to know; it will, however, offer teacher or parent a convenient summary of information as the start of further reading or activity. In a sense a topic book at its simplest is a substitute teacher or parent and may at any time be supplanted either by more directly visual teaching methods or by an energetic question and answer session between parent and child.

Even if a book serves only as a starting point for other methods of learning, it must always be analysed as a book, on its own merits, and as a complete entity. Most of all its value will depend on the personality of the author. He is being asked to do a simple but difficult piece of compilation in a field where he may not be a specialist and so may not have the special impetus of the obsessive. Still he must be interested and his interest must show; he must have, as P. L. Travers has put it, "an individual glint of a piercing eye that is different from any others".* It is just as important for a child to feel in touch with the writer in a book of fact as in a story. For the youngest readers this can be achieved if the subject is directly related to them; this is the excuse for the "you" approach in junior information books (though no excuse for using the device coyly or clumsily). Without this simplest personal identification – when, for instance, the study of a subject is made in a plain sequence of fact,

*Bookbird 4/1967, p. 7

It is wet!

This page from WATER (Lutterworth Press) by Denis Wrigley shows an amusing visual corroboration of a single stated fact.

with no fiction element or aside to the reader – the author often adopts an expository tone and loses touch with his reader. It may be because he is not himself really interested in what he is writing about; it may be that he has not a real style of his own.

Children deserve to have books of fact which, however simple they are, are still individual, strong, alive. The author is obliged to be simple but he need not be banal. A few paragraphs of a topic book by Louis Slobodkin, Mary Cockett, Boswell Taylor, Jeanne Bendick, to name but a few, will show how individuality may be communicated by the choice of words or by a characteristic sentence rhythm or an ingenious argument.

For the writer of a junior topic book, the problem of selection is as important as that of simplification. We may take it for granted that he has studied his subject in enough depth to be accurate and,

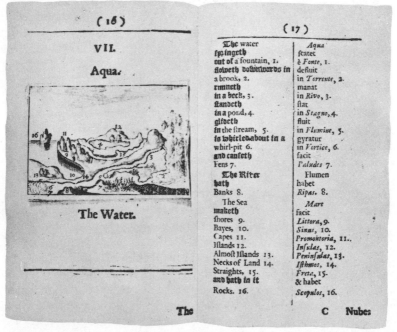

Spread from ORBIS PICTUS (1659) by John Amos Comenius, by courtesy of the Trustees of the British Museum

as far as possible, up to date. He must now decide how much knowledge he can assume in his readers and how much must be left out. J. C. Gagg has said:

> ... we need to remember that there are different levels of meaning-difficulty. A simple narrative story is no strain on a child beyond the recognition of the words. But a book which conveys a succession of facts – however interesting they are – calls for considerable thought over and above the physical reading-process.
>
> "The sixteen-pagers" in *The Times Educational Supplement*, 16 February 1968, p. 537.

The writer must be mindful of the order of his facts so that he does not create confusion and so that his arrangement can positively help the young to learn as well as to absorb specific information. Above all, he must establish himself as the invisible but ever-present teacher, friend, adviser, explainer – the person who through the printed word speaks to a child with authority and with comradely enthusiasm. Whether his book is used for communal study or private reading, he must contrive to suggest to each child that he is addressing him personally.

The subjects of topic books are, obviously, chosen for their relevance to the lives and interests of children. This section of MATTERS OF FACT is based on six subjects, each of them likely to be familiar one way or another to the young, and all of them treated in a variety of books covering pre-school to middle school ages. Each subject sets special problems for the writer. *Bread* and *The Postal System* challenge him to make the obvious fresh and interesting. Books on *Holland* show how far the post-war changes in communication have brought corresponding changes in our ways of writing about other countries. *Honeybees* illustrates the problem of explaining alien forms of behaviour in precise terms which are still simple enough for children to understand. Anyone who writes about *Cowboys* has a ready-made audience, but this circumstance has inherent dangers for the writer. Finally, in the books about *Time* we shall see how authors have explained abstract and scientific concepts, or have tried to avoid doing so. It is possible to arrive at criteria for judging information books of every kind. In the long run, however, each book is the expression of a personal point of view and must be considered as a unique source of basic fact for the enquiring child.

Reading List

Cass, Joan. LITERATURE AND THE YOUNG CHILD (*Longmans, Green* 1967) *Humanities* 1968.

Gagg, J. C. "The sixteen-pagers", in *The Times Educational Supplement,* 16 February 1968.

Hoare, Robert J. TOPIC WORK WITH BOOKS. *Geoffrey Chapman* 1971. The author offers a definition of this elusive term, and not only suggests subjects for topic work but also indicates gaps where books, or better books, would be welcome.

Williams, Gladys. CHILDREN AND THEIR BOOKS. *Duckworth* 1970.

2a | Bread

bread, *pain* [F.]; staff of life; bread-stuff; white bread, dark bread, whole-wheat bread, rye bread, pumpernickel bread, graham bread; sourbread, sourcake [dial., Eng.]; unleavened bread, matzoth [Jewish]; loaf of bread, tommy [Scot. and dial., Eng.]; ashcake, hoecake [South, U.S.]; damper [Austral.]; toast, Melba toast, French toast; crust.

Roget's THESAURUS

2a | Bread

NOBODY could call the making and baking of bread a complicated or difficult subject to make clear to the young, provided the sequence of facts is arranged in an orderly and logical way. The preface to John Rimington's BREAD (1960) sums up the demands of this kind of topic:

> Learning about any new subject is rather like laying bricks to build a new house. You cannot start in the middle or on the top floor – you have to lay the bottom bricks first, and then work your way upwards.
>
> A loaf of bread is such a familiar thing that you might be tempted to think you know nearly all about it already: but it is not quite so simple as that. Before you have bread you have to have flour, and before you have flour you have to grow wheat and put it through a mill – so there are several stages to go through before you arrive at your familiar, simple-looking loaf.
>
> In this book the first chapter is the bottom brick, and the other chapters are the other bricks that have to be laid one above the other to bring you to the top floor. So even if you are impatient to watch the baker at work, do start from the bottom brick first. You will find it all very much easier to follow and, although it may take you a little longer, you will know a lot more about it in the end.
>
> BREAD, Introduction

What is our first brick? We may assume that readers will know what a loaf looks like, but to assume any more may mean leaving out an essential point in the sequence. A country-bred child in a wheat-growing district might laugh at such elementary statements as:

The flour was ground from grains of corn.
This corn is wheat.
Flour for bread is usually made from wheat.

A town child might find the description of a baker's van unnecessary, or a discussion of his day's work, if he helped a baker in the holidays. A child accustomed to helping his mother in the kitchen might skip over simple instructions for making a wholemeal loaf. It is the writer's business to see that the young reader is pleased and not irritated when he meets facts he knows already. This is bound to be difficult in a first topic book of a few thousand words – and simple words at that. There is not much room – but there is some – for personal warmth, humour or idiosyncrasy of language.

Bread in history and literature; in legend and religion; chemistry and dietetics; the working of mills and granaries; export and world distribution of grains – all these aspects of the subject can help to make a book interesting; but most of the topic books for juniors on bread are restricted to a bare account of harvest and manufacture. In these little books, as a consequence, there is often a curiously bleak contrast between the rich feel of harvest and the greyness cast over the mechanical processes – verbally and in illustration. This exaggerated division between natural and mechanical processes can only be corrected if humans are effectively brought into the picture. All but two of the chapters in a very simple pamphlet on WHEAT have a personalised heading – for instance, *George, the English farmer; Gordon, the Canadian farmer; Douglas, the van-driver; Peter, the baker.* The young reader is reminded at the end that "Before we can get things made of wheat, a team of people must set to work", and is invited to make a list of "the people who are part of this team".*

A topic book designed for school use need not be impersonal and remote even if the teaching element is explicit. Blackwell's *Learning Library*, which includes BAKERS AND BREAD by S. A. Manning, has the following general aim:

*Eric J. Barker and Alec Mayland. WHEAT (1959)

These books are produced and planned to help children to begin
learning for themselves. Once children are able to read, the whole
world of books is available to them; but while this reading ability
is developing, they need books which give them information in
specially clear and simple style, supported by careful illustrations.
The books in this series are written to supply that need. They
cover a wide range of topics and may be used for "study learning"
by children of various ages. They should prove particularly useful
to the younger children who are just beginning to know the
excitement of "learning from books".

   Needless to say, the editors presume that the children who use
these books will be writing a great deal as a result of what they
read, and that they will follow up the topics in many ways.

Manning's BAKERS AND BREAD (1964) follows such earlier
pamphlets as Gwen Cross's A LOAF OF BREAD (1949) and FLOUR
by E. L. Gaylard (1957) in putting direct questions to the reader.
The teaching element in the more modern book is certainly more
relaxed. Gwen Cross's A LOAF OF BREAD, for instance, reflects the
period when a teacher could ask pupils to "Write in two columns
the singular and plural of each of these words – sheaf, leaf,
wheat, valley, country" or "In what country do oxen thresh the
wheat?"

   If this approach seems laborious, the book has one feature which
its modern counterparts might well copy. A special vocabulary at
the end, arranged formally under nouns, adjectives, verbs, includes
such words as chaff, protein, edible, ferment, winnow. The question
of technical terms will arise with any subject, especially when it is
treated for the really young. Many later topic books use only such
simple terms as will be known already; for example, one sixteen-
pager lists sheaves, threshing, combine-harvester, yeast, dough.*
The author of the *Learning Library* book, BAKERS AND BREAD,
seems bent on sparing his young readers any exertion which might
increase their vocabularies:

   Some of the good things that are in bread have long names, which
   you may learn one day. One of them gives you energy. You

*O. B. Gregory. BREAD (1962)

would not be able to run, jump or ride a bicycle if you did not
have enough energy.
BAKERS AND BREAD, pp. 10–11

Though in fairness I should also quote two more sentences from
these over-simple pages:

> In every slice of bread there is also something that is called
> "protein". Girls and boys must have this, so that their bodies
> grow properly and work well.

In spite of the friendly, almost chummy note of these junior topic
books, their effect as a whole is didactic and, for so homely a subject,
oddly divorced from real life. Talking about loaves, the writers
rarely get close to a loaf. Certainly Gaylard offers a recipe for a milk
loaf and suggests experiments in growing wheat grains. In a small
pamphlet on BREAD (1963), E. S. Bradburne suggests:

> Thresh wheat grains in your hands and grind the grains into
> flour between two stones.
> Make some bread from the flour you have ground.

and then, facing facts, he concedes "add some wholemeal flour if
you cannot grind enough".
    With what relief, however, one finds in ALL ABOUT A LOAF OF
BREAD by W. Worthy (1962) the downright statement "The best
way to learn how bread is made is to make some yourself", followed
by a proper recipe with explanatory details; for instance, when the
kneading stage is reached, the author explains what yeast is and
exactly what it does. This sensible approach is likely to be more to a
child's taste than the more distant advice in BAKERS AND BREAD:

> If you live in the country, you will be able to ask a farmer politely
> questions about wheat. If you live in a town you may be able to
> visit the countryside during your summer holiday, to see the
> wheat being harvested.
> op. cit., p. 58

The passage quoted from Worthy is one of many, too, in which

he has fitted skilfully and relevantly details of one or another stage
or process, always using the correct technical terms. In arrangement
his book is conspicuously neat; he avoids the plod of an undeviating
forward sequence of facts without losing the clarity of his exposition.

None of these little books is likely to please children as much as
Olive Burt's LET'S FIND OUT ABOUT BREAD (1966), which at the
time of writing is not available in England. There is nothing startling
about the brief, caption-like text, which follows a wheat grain from
the field through to the baker's shop and then to the home, emphasising the variety of cakes, doughnuts, muffins and hot-dogs available
for snacks. But this piece of plain exposition is fluent and spontaneous in its effect. This is to some extent due to the pictures, gold
and black, with their strong design, great sense of movement and
dashing style. Not only do they extend points made in the text,
but they do this through people – a farmer looking at his crop, a
combine-driver with a hired hand carrying a scythe, workers in
factories, cattle-sheds, bakeries, the proprietor of Sam's Delicatessen
making sandwiches, a girl baking corn-bread, a cheerful youth

Illustration by Mimi Korach from LET'S FIND OUT ABOUT BREAD (Franklin Watts)

eating a hot-dog, a stout boy and his mother eyeing a mound of pancakes and a syrup tin. Gay, alive, not specially idealised, the pictures should communicate to a child that bread is a part of life.

Good design and lively drawing can find a place in the smallest school pamphlet, but the illustrations in the examples I have discussed are pedestrian and unimaginative, from the small yellow and black tractor, windmill, corn ears, depicted in Gaylard's book to the uninteresting photographs and marginal drawings in Bradburne's. If books are to be used to introduce this particular topic to children, they must have some intrinsic appeal *as books*; they must do something which only the written word can do, something which cannot be supplied by an afternoon in the kitchen, a visit to a bakery or the making of a scrapbook. Two books which refuse to be pigeon-holed enforce this point.

THE BREAD WE EAT by Margaret Fisher (1944) belongs to a now defunct series, *How Things Are Made*, and contains the usual sequence of facts: but the intriguing scheme puts the book within the reach, and the interest, of a small non-reader and a child of around eight at the same time. Designed as a whole, the book has variations of type and a layout so designed that the child can move from the simplest facts to broader general terms. At the beginning he is told:

This is the story of sowing and growing reaping and threshing weighing and sending grinding and sacking sifting and mixing kneading and raising shaping and baking shopping and eating.

Below a drawing of a child at table eating a piece of bread he finds the following instructions:

When you read this book, begin by looking at the pictures and reading only the big print at the top and bottom of each page.
    Look at the pictures right through the book.
    Then read it the other way round: look again at the pictures from back to front, and read everything between the big lines, to get the full story of our bread.

The child embarks on the blue type and finds a sequence of questions and answers, beginning "Please mother may I have some bread

for my tea", "Yes, when it has been fetched from the baker".
The processes of making bread are described in order, but in reverse
– baker, oven, shaping loaves, mixing dough, loading flour at the
mill, sacking, sifting flour, mill machinery, corn being brought to
the mill, grinding, threshing, sowing, ploughing. The cumulative
pattern of the questions has the reassuring sound of nursery rhyme:

> Please will you reap the wheat and thresh it to be sent to the
> miller to be ground into flour for the baker to make a loaf so
> that mother can give me a slice for my tea.

The answer is, "Yes, when it has grown and ripened." When the
child has reached the last answer – the ploughman's "Yes, I will
do it" – he may work back through the black-type explanatory text,
which is simple in style but covers a great deal of ground and
includes details of the import of wheat, the chemistry of yeast, old-
time methods of reaping and threshing, and so on.

There is a told-to-the-children sound in the book which reminds
us that it was written almost thirty years ago:

> Watermills sometimes looked very pretty and the sound of the
> water rushing down from an artificial waterfall on to the huge
> wheel and the clattering of the wooden blades that turned it were
> nice too. Click-clack, click-clack, went the wheel. The weight of
> the falling water gave each of the horizontal blades a little jerk
> down and then hit the next one. Click one, click another, click
> the next – that's how the wheel turned and the axle turned the
> millstone and the millstone ground the flour.
>
> THE BREAD WE EAT, p. 26

It may be noticed, though, that the passage contains useful and
accurate terms, and the book as a whole has a style not always
found in similar books today. One page shows the intelligent
arrangement and choice of words:

> All grain has to be milled, that is broken up and ground. Primitive
> peoples used to pound the meal on a flat stone with another stone,
> and they found it easiest to grind it evenly by a rotating movement.
> That is what people did many thousand years ago. Then the

millstone was invented. It consists of two big disks of stone rotating round an axle and crushing the grain between them. Most millstones are made of Buhrstone, a kind of Quartz. This very hard stone is found in huge blocks and cut out in big cylinders which are divided by a special method: grooves are cut at distances of about eighteen inches, the thickness of the millstone. Wooden wedges are driven into the grooves and soaked with water to swell the wood. By this means the stone will split into disks. The surface of the millstone is slightly chiselled and patterned to roughen it. The grain runs down into the centre of the stone from a wooden container. A bell is tied to this which tinkles to warn the miller when the container is emptied.

ibid., p. 24

The thought that has gone into this book speaks well for the designers (Adprint Ltd), for the photographers who worked in the field (for instance, at a mill in Essex and a bakery in East Finchley), for the author who sorted the facts and saw to it that they were accurate, cheerful and interesting. This is essentially a home book and a very pleasant one. A child could hardly help learning from it, but without any feeling of obligation. It makes good sense of the phrase "Learn with fun" that proves deceptive in so many series titles.

The topic books of today are smarter, better produced, more sophisticated than those of the past, but forty years ago, when writers seem to have been less self-conscious in their attitude to the young, there was more room for style and individuality. THE STORY OF BREAD by Elizabeth Watson was published by Harper of New York as early as 1927, in a series *City and Country*. The aim of the series, set out in a general introduction, sounds a familiar note:

Here at last are some books designed to answer the endless queries of children about the everyday things of everyday life. . . . This series is designed to fill a long-felt need, the need of children to find out in graphic and dramatic words the whys and wherefores of life around them. The modern schools make trips to the dairies, the milk laboratories, the telephone exchange, the wharves, the printing plants and so on, a part of the curriculum. They feel that there they will find the best basis for civics and geography. And these books fill in the background for these visits, and give the little readers a sense of the romance in subjects they are apt to take for granted.

The phrase "fill in the background" is significant. This is a good starter book with a robust and sensible acceptance of its limitations. At the end of the volume, after a short list of books used, the author advises:

But the most interesting thing for you to do, is to visit a mill near your home, and see how wheat is made into flour, and to visit a big bakery and see how flour is made into bread. And perhaps, if you have bread made in your own kitchen, you could learn to make bread all by yourself.
ibid., p. 48

If the book is intended primarily for schools, it has a zest and a personal care in expression that commend it for private recreational reading too. It is in fact too anecdotal to present that logical description of processes which a topic book on bread should ideally provide. But it has one quality which the books so far discussed have not been able to include (for lack of space certainly, but perhaps for less understandable reasons too). It has a sense of history.
   Very simply the author draws a contrast between bread made in America by the earliest settlers and the machine-made bread of the twentieth century:

Corn saved Great-great-grandfather's grandfather's life, as a little boy, when his family first came from England to live in America. He told my Great-great-grandfather about it when he was a very little boy.
ibid., p. 8

And so in an almost naïve style we read how the first crops failed and the ships did not come from England and the settlers were starving when a "friendly Indian" brought some of *his* grain to the white people:

None of the white people knew this new kind of corn, but after

the Indians taught them how to use it they liked it very much. The first thing the Indians showed them was how to grind it between two stones and make a kind of flour. The whites soon called this Indian meal and learned to make a bread of it, baking it before the open fire. Today we call this kind of corn bread Johnnycake.
ibid., p.11

This piece of domestic history leads to a description of the modern processes of making bread. But the contrast is not spoiled by a nostalgic sigh nor yet by a pat on the back for the machine age. The book ends with some welcome common sense:

Baking bread is, as you see, a pretty complicated affair today, compared with the simple way families used to raise their own grain, grind it at home, and make their own bread. *But if the farmer* keeps on raising good wheat, and the *miller* goes on grinding good flour and the *baker* can make good bread and the *workers* keep on helping them, we need not be sorry that our own families do not do everything the way they used to do.
ibid., p. 47

History as it is used here would hardly fit into the strict word limit of the modern topic books, but what an enlivening effect just a morsel of historical detail might have had there, and how special to a child is the appeal of a detail that is somehow felt to be *extra*. Moreover, the use of "Great-great-grandfather's grandfather" gives that fireside touch that lifts the book into real life. School-children doing a project, for instance, would find interest in asking very old people in their town or village about gleaning, breadmaking and the Sunday joint taken to the bakehouse. Something of the immediacy and intimacy of the past can be captured on the printed page.

At an early stage of reading, facts are more assimilable than ideas, but ideas there must be. Topic books could suggest, for instance, that bread does not grow but is made, and that many people and processes are associated with the making of it; but the point must be made alive somehow for the reader if he is to accept it as an idea. In the course of her narrative, Elizabeth Watson suggests how and why the manufacture of bread evolved from a family affair to big business. Her picturesque descriptions of the Festival of the Corn, of the iron plough and the saddlestone grinder and the early watermills, lead to the development of steam power and to the important basic idea, which she makes crystal clear, that specialisation in industry meant that foods like bread could now be made in quantity.

Now she has taken her bread from the settler's hearth to the factory and she continues, "Have you any idea how many people it takes to make a loaf of bread nowadays?" She names farmer, agricultural expert, Weather Bureau official, harvest hands, cook, wharfies, factory workers. The list widens the horizon of the book so that there is no feeling that the subject is treated in isolation. The making of bread from earliest times is linked with the well-being of a simple community and the smooth working of modern life. There are many ideas suggested or illustrated in this book, none of them baldly or didactically. THE STORY OF BREAD passes that first test of the good topic book; it arouses interest in something familiar but only partially known.

In its scope this long-forgotten book lies midway between the simple early topic book and one or two studies for older children which deal with a group of related commodities. THE PICTURE BOOK OF GRAINS by Anita Brooks (1963) belongs to a series *Picture Aids to World Geography*. Ella Northfield's THE STUDY BOOK OF FOODS (1960) is one of Bodley Head's familiar series. Either book could be equally well called a school book (supplementary to text-books) or one for reading at home. THE STUDY BOOK OF FOODS, while lively enough to make acceptable private reading, leads naturally to further projects of a kind most easily embarked upon at school, and ends with a list of many common foods not included in the text which children could investigate empirically and through the printed page. The foods discussed are fish, beef, sugar, bread, cocoa, rice, tea, margarine, salt, pepper, coffee and sago. Obviously these have been selected to add to geographical knowledge first of all, and a careful use of place-names helps in this, though there is – surprisingly – no map. The sections are short and simple and the book as a whole could be used by a child of seven, but it is far more than a mere recital of facts. Each section shows a marked sense of cause and effect. Points are made where necessary about climate or about the kind of labour or machinery used to produce the various commodities.

The plan of the book makes compression essential; there is no unnecessary detail. The section on bread begins:

> Bread is made from the wheat which you can see growing in the fields during the summer. The golden grains of corn grow in clusters at the top of the corn stalks. These are called wheat ears. The miller buys the corn from the farmer and grinds it into flour in his mill.
>
> The miller sells the flour to the baker who makes it into bread. He mixes water, salt and yeast with the flour to make dough. This is left to rise before being put into the oven to be baked.
>
> THE STUDY BOOK OF FOODS, pp. 22–23

The author compensates for a small word allowance in two ways. She is alert to see how peripheral information can be introduced. A sentence like "The Canadian farmers have huge cornfields where once the Red Indians hunted animals" offers something to the imagination. More obviously, illustration can provide additional

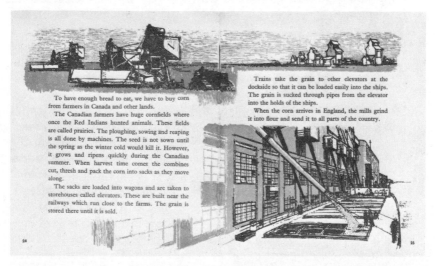

To have enough bread to eat, we have to buy corn from farmers in Canada and other lands.

The Canadian farmers have huge cornfields where once the Red Indians hunted animals. These fields are called prairies. The ploughing, sowing and reaping is all done by machines. The seed is not sown until the spring as the winter cold would kill it. However, it grows and ripens quickly during the Canadian summer. When harvest time comes the combines cut, thresh and pack the corn into sacks as they move along.

The sacks are loaded into wagons and are taken to storehouses called elevators. These are built near the railways which run close to the farms. The grain is stored there until it is sold.

Trains take the grain to other elevators at the dockside so that it can be loaded easily into the ships. The grain is sucked through pipes from the elevator into the holds of the ships.

When the corn arrives in England, the mills grind it into flour and send it to all parts of the country.

This spread from THE STUDY BOOK OF FOODS (Bodley Head) shows how Margery Gill's illustrations help to enforce important points.

material. This book is outstanding in the quality of its illustrative
material, which is by Margery Gill. Her marginal and inter-text
drawings, coloured grey-blue or red-buff with black, are carefully
and accurately supplementary to the text, but they have the graceful
Gill look as well. They are placed exactly in relation to the text
and in some cases provide an extension to it. The illustration seen
on p. 41, matched with a verbal account of Canadian wheat
exports, may serve as an example. This admirable book helps
children to grasp the idea early in their lives that single subjects are
interrelated.

THE PICTURE BOOK OF GRAINS, with a longer text and a slightly
more advanced vocabulary, perhaps needs a slightly older reader –
eight upwards. Anita Brooks aims to show the world at work and
to stress the interdependence of the different countries. There are
general sections on *The land* and *The harvest* and particular discussions of wheat, rye, oats, barley, rice, wild rice, millet, maize
and durra. A map shows plainly which countries exchange cereal
products. Erosion and crop-spraying, warehousing and storage,
the processes of harvest, threshing, milling and so on are discussed
comparatively and there is an interesting account of the farm
machinery and traction animals used in various parts of the world.
With a great variety of photographs, sensibly and adequately
captioned, the book puts the familiar loaf into perspective for a
child who has got beyond the elementary stage and can grasp a
wider picture. The kind of picture he will absorb may be seen in the
final paragraph of this lively account:

Our "daily bread" has many different forms, but is eaten by all
peoples of the world. It may be a loaf of rye or white bread.
It may be an enormous, round, dark loaf from Hungary, or the
thin, long French or Italian breads. It may be paper-thin wafers
from Arabia, folded like a book. You eat a page at a time. It may
be Norwegian bread, looking like a pancake or a large biscuit.
It may be flat cakes made of rice or maize. It can be cereal (hot
or cold). It may be twisted rings like these in a basket in Portugal.
It may be tortillas of maize, or it may be macaroni, or spaghetti.
It may be different kinds of noodles. Whatever form it takes,
grain is still man's most important food.

THE PICTURE BOOK OF GRAINS, p. 94

Portuguese Information Bureau

Our "daily bread" has many different forms, but is eaten by all peoples of the world. It may be a loaf of rye or white bread. It may be an enormous, round, dark loaf from Hungary, or the thin, long French or Italian breads. It may be paper-thin wafers from Arabia, folded like a book. You eat a page at a time. It may be Norwegian bread, looking like a pancake or a large biscuit. It may be flat cakes made of rice or maize. It can be cereal (hot or cold). It may be twisted rings like these in a basket in Portugal. It may be tortillas of maize, or it may be macaroni, or spaghetti. It may be different kinds of noodles. Whatever form it takes, grain is still man's most important food.

94

Page from THE PICTURE BOOK OF GRAINS (Weidenfeld & Nicolson Educational)

The page as a whole (see p. 43) illustrates better than any verbal analysis how much the success of books like these depends on an intelligent and discriminating choice and arrangement of detail, in words and pictures.

If the admirable paperback series of Puffin Picture Books had been multiplied by a thousand or so, parents would now have available a permanent, accessible, reliable and attractive multi-part encyclopedia which could hold its own against any compendium. THE STORY OF BREAD (1964) by H. J. Deverson, with Ronald Lampitt's illustrations, shares with others of a similar kind like Harry Ballam's STORY OF A THREAD OF COTTON, the advantage of its basic design *as a picture book*. Pictures are used sometimes to complement, sometimes to add to the text. Inset pictures like the impression of Chaucer's Miller or the diagram of Vitruvius's windmill help in the easy and useful accumulation of general knowledge at home. Other pictures directly related to the text give the words a lift by their appearance – pictures like one of an Egyptian grinding corn, the public punishment of a cheat, the armorial bearings of the Bakers' Guild. Others again help to clarify a sequence of fact – for instance, a tabulated account of the commercial baking of bread today has a useful diagram to accompany it.

Historical detail is carefully considered in the book. In pictures of Egyptians making bread, Greeks banqueting, Saxons threshing, there is some feeling for racial physiognomy as well as costume. In the main this is a survey of what bread has meant to various periods and countries, but it is worth noting that, alone of all writers so far mentioned, this author has included a discussion of Mendel's work on wheat-growing. Manufacturing processes are certainly not neglected, but tables and diagrams are extensively used to save space for facts depending more closely on the written word.

It would be absurd to suggest that a child was likely to work his way through graduated topic books on the same subject consistently during his primary school years, unless he needed a group of them for a project. In such a case it might be a matter of luck whether or not he found the passages of unusual interest in each book. A more recent topic book, THE STORY BEHIND A LOAF OF BREAD by Charles King (1966), treats the subject in a somewhat impersonal way but includes some of the legends and superstitions connected with bread and asserts its importance in an arresting passage:

According to botanists, wheat, oats, barley and other grains belong to the order of Grasses; nobody has yet found the wild form of grass from which wheat, as we know it, has developed. Like most of the wild grasses, cereal blossoms bear both male and female elements. The young plants are provided with a store of food to ensure their support during the period of germination, and it is in this store of reserve substance that man finds an abundant supply of food . . .

When ancient man discovered a food which would keep through the winter months, and could be multiplied in the summer, it could be said that civilization began. He might have a reasonably safe store of food to carry him over, which would give him time to develop other useful skills beside hunting, fishing and cattle-herding.

op. cit., pp. 1–4

This is the kind of concept that must be put into words for children if their collections of facts are ever going to be significant as a whole.

For a project, again, it would be worth looking at Colin Clair's BREAD (1954) since, although old-fashioned in format and dull in style, the book has a remarkable range of photographic illustration. An enterprising reader might even look into the main source for this and other information books, John Ashton's fine antiquarian study, THE HISTORY OF BREAD (1904), published more than half a century ago, or the interesting STORY OF BREAD by Ronald Sheppard and Edward Newton (1957), where he would find aspects of the subjects which have not yet found their way into books for the young – bread in wartime, for instance, and bread and politics (with descriptions of bread riots at various times). He would find John Rimington's BREAD (1960) a lively account, with useful paragraph headings ("You can see a loaf four thousand years old" or "And now for the bread of today") which emphasise the direct school-masterly approach; and he would probably enjoy those passages where exposition is helped by references to particular people – Mr Wheeler who serves in the baker's shop while his son Harry deals with deliveries, Mr Walsh the plant manager who takes a young visitor round the factory. This book, indeed, provides an imaginary tour for those whose school has not happened to arrange a real one.

When they want to find out about a subject, children deserve to be helped to the full and accurate facts. No book on bread that I have found suitable for the middle years covers the chemical and botanical aspect of wheat and its dietetic properties more clearly and fully than L. F. Sheppick's THE STORY OF OUR DAILY BREAD, published over twenty years ago. Yet the careful and uncondescending way the material is used is at variance with the strangely sentimental preface, which epitomises an attitude fatal to any book of information. Quoting from Tennyson – "Little grain, did I know what you are, Then I would know what God and man is", the author goes on to say:

I cannot believe that we shall ever understand the cycle of the wheat grain. In this cycle are wrapped up the mysteries of nature, and yet it is a thing that is with us from the cradle to the grave; it is so common, we accept it.

THE STORY OF OUR DAILY BREAD, p. 4

"I cannot believe that we shall ever understand . . ." and yet the child of today, as of yesterday and tomorrow, deserves to understand everything that we can understand, of fact. This book, with its timid approach, making facts easy for "both child and busy man", has a notably dignified conclusion. The last page is headed *Bread is blessed*, and the text beneath reads:

Now you know something about the common loaf of bread, from the field to the table. It is worth knowing, if only to enhance your respect for bread. Men have wept for it, fought for it, and died for it. Jesus blessed it.

ibid., p. 59

A child uses information books to assemble what he knows, what he feels, what he sees, as well as to collect new facts. His reaction to something as ordinary as a loaf may be, at one time or another, one of wonder, excitement, interest, aesthetic pleasure, physical satisfaction, curiosity. He needs books which combine warm individuality and clear exposition, a mingling of words that colour the subject and words that clarify it, a recognition of past as well as present. He seldom finds such books.

Reading List

Ashton, John. THE HISTORY OF BREAD: FROM PRE-HISTORIC TO MODERN
TIMES. *Religious Tract Society* 1904. Illustrated with drawings.

Barker,.Eric J. and Mayland, Alec. WHEAT. Our Everyday Needs. *Evans* 1959.
With drawings, diagrams and a map.

Bradburne, E. S. BREAD. Everyday Things. Huddersfield, *Schofield and Sims* 1963.
Drawings by Joyce Johnson, and some photographs.

Brooks, Anita. THE PICTURE BOOK OF GRAINS. Picture Aids to World Geography.
(*John Day* 1962) *Weidenfeld and Nicolson* 1963. Illustrated by photographs.

Burt, Olive. LET'S FIND OUT ABOUT BREAD. Let's Find out About . . .
Franklin Watts 1966. Illustrated by Mimi Korach.

Carey, M. C. THE BAKER. *Dent* 1938. Illustrated by Nora Lavrin. A pleasantly
domestic account for home reading, now almost a period piece.

Clair, Colin. BREAD. The Things we Need. *Bruce and Gawthorn* 1954. Illustrated
by photographs.

Cross, Gwen. A LOAF OF BREAD. Things we Use, in Tropical library. *Longmans,
Green* 1949. Illustrated in two colours, and with a map.

Deverson, H. J. THE STORY OF BREAD. The Story of . . ., in Puffin Picture-books.
Penguin 1964. Illustrated by Ronald Lampitt.

Fisher, M. THE BREAD WE EAT. How Things are Made. *Collins* 1944.
Drawings by Patric O'Keeffe, colour photographs by Douglas Glass.

Gaylard, E. L. FLOUR. How? Why? Where? *E. J. Arnold* 1957. With two-colour
pictures.

Gregory, O. B. BREAD. Read About it. *Wheaton/Pergamon* 1962.

King, Charles. THE STORY BEHIND A LOAF OF BREAD. The Story Behind . . .
Cassell 1966. Illustrated by the author.

Kohn, Bernice. OUR TINY SERVANTS: MOULDS AND YEASTS, Modern World
Series. (*Prentice-Hall* 1962) *Muller* 1966. Illustrated by John Kaufmann. A simple
account of the chemistry of certain foods, which should help children to
understand how bread rises. The book ends with a recipe for a home-made loaf.

Manning, S. A. BAKERS AND BREAD. Learning Library. *Blackwell* 1964.
Illustrated by F. T. W. Cook.

Northfield, Ella. THE STUDY BOOK OF FOODS. Study Books. (*Bodley Head* 1960).
Illustrated by Margery Gill.

Petersham, Maud and Miska. THE STORY BOOK OF WHEAT. *Wells, Gardner,
Darton* 1948. Illustrated by the authors. A simple, friendly survey of the history

of man's staple food, with a strong story element and dainty coloured pictures.
Similar to the Puffin Picture-book discussed in the text (see page 44, and under
Deverson).

Rimington, John. BREAD. How Things are Obtained. *Ward Lock Educational* 1960.
Illustrated by photographs.

Shannon, Terry. ABOUT FOOD AND WHERE IT COMES FROM. Look, Read and
Learn. (*Melmont* 1961) *Muller* 1967. Illustrated by Charles Payzaut. The brief
discussion of some fifteen familiar commodities should help a child to see bread
in perspective.

Sheppard, Ronald and Newton, Edward. THE STORY OF BREAD. (*Routledge and
Kegan Paul* 1957) *Fernhill* 1957. Illustrated by John L. Baker.

Sheppick, L. F. THE STORY OF OUR DAILY BREAD. Liverpool, *Northern
Publishing Company* 1947. With drawings, diagrams and photographs.

Thrupp, Sylvia. A SHORT HISTORY OF THE WORSHIPFUL COMPANIES OF
BAKERS. London. *F. A. Mostyn* 1933. Illustrated by photographs and prints. For
those who enjoy sidelines, this book contains unusually interesting illustrations
and a good deal of fact about the adulteration of bread and the resulting
punishments, besides other material not easy to find elsewhere.

Watson, Elizabeth. THE STORY OF BREAD. City and Country. *Harper and Bros.*
1927. Illustrated by James Daugherty.

Worthy, William. ALL ABOUT A LOAF OF BREAD. All About . . . *Longmans, Green*
1962. Illustrated by W. G. Morden.

2b | *The Postal System*

. . . they continue their dreams;
And shall wake soon and long for letters,
And none will hear the postman's knock
Without a quickening of the heart,
For who can hear and feel himself forgotten?
W. H. Auden. "Night mail"

2b | The Postal System

THE move from first books on this subject to those for older children could be defined as the move from The Postman to The Postal Service. For children up to seven or eight The Postman, a figure as familiar and recognisable as Father Christmas: for older readers, an insight into an *activity* involving people, machines, needs, ideas.

However simple the concept of The Postman may be, there is a basic idea to be conveyed to the small child, as there is with Father Christmas. The Postman helps the community to work efficiently. Any book for young children must convey the idea that The Postman is not one individual but is multiplied through town and country. Together with The Policeman, The Fireman, The Milkman and others, he is an essential character in any baby picture anthology or infant collection of tales about Men at Work. For a young child he is probably a tripartite figure. He may be Our Postman; one of the postmen at the local Post Office; Mr Brown next door, who happens to be a postman. Coming to terms with these changing identities may be an undetectable process in a child's mind, or it may show itself in endless questions. To reach a satisfactory conclusion on this, as on other simple aspects of daily life, the child may resort to observation, question and answer – or books.

Whatever else, the postman will be a person; and a person whose activities have a bearing on the child's life. So, first books on this topic do best to start with the direct egotism of the child – "The Postman is going to bring *me* a letter" or "I am going to post *my* letter to Daddy". It is going to be possible to supply a good deal of detail under the guise of talking about the young reader; he will most easily absorb details about the postman's duties in relation to

himself. What happens to his letter, going or coming, is a continuous
and fairly complicated process and whatever you do about it, in a
book or in family exposition, you are bound to bring in a story-
telling element. "The postman takes your letter out of the box and
then . . ." Because we have adopted for the sake of convenience the
phrase non-fiction, and know just what we mean by it, we hardly
suppose that there is such a thing, any more than there is a kind of
writing called "non-fact" (though occasionally one feels there may
be). All the same, certain subjects come to life best with a judicious
mixture of fact and fiction, and the postal system is undoubtedly
one of them.

To a small child, obviously, the despatch and delivery of mail is
not interesting as a process but as the activity of someone (or two
or three people) whom he sees regularly and accepts as part of his
life. Once past the picture-book stage, where a postman is a kind
of fairy-tale figure like any other, curiosity is still very personal.
As one sixteen-pager has it, "We all know the postman who delivers
our letters and parcels at certain times of the day."*

This domestic aspect is allowed for in an interesting series
published by Blackie in 1963 – JOHNNY AND THE POLICEMAN,
FIREMAN, VET and POSTMAN. Modwena Sedgwick (author) and
Diana John (illustrator) devised a persuasive medium for passing
on a small amount of selected information, to children in school or
at home. Two pictures to a page, in red and black, are linked by a
"story" (a block of text beside each picture) in very simple language;
as in any strip cartoon, the pictures exactly correspond with the
caption text and to some extent tell the story by themselves.

The author has involved Johnny most plausibly with these group-
heroes. For instance, he is already friendly with the local policeman
when he finds a brooch outside a jeweller's shop and seeks his advice
– thus finding out a little about the policeman's job; his own puppy,
hurt by a car, involves him with a vet kind enough to take him on
an afternoon's round; the overturned petrol lorry causes a fire
near where Johnny and his cousin happen to be standing. As for
the postman, he is an essential part of Johnny's life when he goes
to stay with Grandma while his mother is having a baby. He writes
to his mother twice and one of his letters is improperly addressed.

*Jean Wilson. THE POSTMAN (1964)

This of course gives two bites at the cherry and author and artist make the most of it.

In describing a process like the transmitting of a letter from sender to receiver, certain inaudible questions must be answered. Where is the letter posted? Who moves it from there, and in what? Where does it go then? How is it separated from other letters? How many stages are there on its journey before it reaches its destination? How many people (or machines) handle it? There are stages in this sequence where the author has to make a choice of detail. For example, when dealing with the first post-office stage in a letter's journey, he may not necessarily mention facing or segregating, but he must surely mention sorting. He may save himself space by choosing a short journey for the letter – from, say, village to local G.P.O.: but he will then lose the chance to describe the role of the railway, to many children the most exciting part of the story. If he is wise he will compensate for lack of words by using diagrams or tables, so that the process of taking a letter from A to B is in some way or another shown in all its possible stages, even in the simplest early book. Ancillary services – telephone, telegraph, savings and so on – can well be left for longer, more substantial, books.

Modwena Sedgwick has made a carefully considered choice of material in her strip-story. Johnny's second letter (the one which Grandma addressed in full) is followed from pillar-box to collection by postman, to local post-office, to van, to station, to T.P.O., to London G.P.O., to sorting machine, to van, to local post-office, to postman on his walk; while the letter which Johnny impetuously posted before Grandma had completed the address is seen being opened at the local Office, readdressed and despatched back to the sender.

The process is explained clearly and every essential stage is mentioned – yet by the strip-technique, the constant reference to Johnny's own letter and to the domestic nature of the pictures, the story has a boomerang effect; it goes out from the child and returns to him again. Contact is never lost. Modwena Sedgwick and her illustrator have satisfied the need for a clear, adequate explanation of what happens to Johnny's letters. They have also contrived a book in which you feel their interest, sympathy and closeness to the child all the way through. With its offhand modern idiom and friendly domestic atmosphere, JOHNNY AND THE POSTMAN is well suited to the pre-school years. Conveniently gathering up facts for a parent to explain and enlarge upon, it serves primarily as a help to identification; things the child has already observed fall into place and are confirmed.

Vera Southgate's THE POSTMAN AND THE POSTAL SERVICE (1965), in the *Ladybird* series, is more ambitious in material and approach, but it still belongs most of all to the home. The *Ladybird* series as a whole have a random educational value – perhaps the best kind for the early school years. More often than not the books are chosen by accident and they often lead to a genuine interest in a subject. Vera Southgate's book might well be chosen in the first instance for its cheerful cover, with the familiar red pillar-box and friendly-looking postman, but the text should soon catch attention. The prose is clear in meaning but far from monotonous in effect. The general statements stand up to scrutiny. "Five hundred years ago, not many people in this country could read or write"; "Every post-boy on horseback carried a post-horn which he blew three times in every mile." A longer extract shows the reassuring effect of a series of compact, confident statements:

> Along the main roads, there were inns where travellers could eat or sleep. The post-boys on horseback needed fresh horses every twenty miles. They used to stop at the inns, to eat and to change horses.
>
> The inns where the post-boys stopped were called post-houses. They were about twenty miles apart. A post-horn over the door showed that an inn was a post-house.
>
> The innkeepers of the post-houses became postmasters. The post-boys left some letters with the postmaster and collected other letters from him.
>
> THE POSTMAN AND THE POSTAL SERVICE, p. 8

This book also has the advantage of a consistent theme. With a limited space for explanation, the author has not bewildered her readers by trying to mention all the sub-divisions of her subject. In what is really an extended essay on the postal system (the title "postman" being the label most likely to attract readers), she has arranged her facts largely round the evolution of methods of transport – that is, broadly, historical changes in the way mail is moved from one place to another. Post-boys, mail coaches, high-waymen, pose dramatically at intervals. There is no scope here for Dockwra or Rowland Hill; for the purposes of the book, such pioneers are taken for granted. With this deliberate selection of detail, the author has been able to stress change and progress in an uncomplicated and racy way.

Incidentally, the G.P.O. Public Relations Department has made particularly effective use of the theme of transport in seven wall-charts which are designed for primary school use but would be interesting to a good many individual children at home. The charts are entitled *Foot messengers, Horses, Horse-drawn vehicles, Trains, Miscellaneous conveyors, Motors, Aircraft and ships.* Each contains a small piece of boxed text and numerous coloured illustrations by Michael Heslop, attractively arranged and chosen to cover a surprising amount of history. These charts form an exhilarating alternative to books on the subject, and they serve their purpose a good deal better than the two G.P.O. pamphlets, POSTMEN THROUGH THE AGES and A BRIEF HISTORY OF THE POST OFFICE, which overlap to some extent in material, though Gaynor Chapman's pictures in the first mentioned pamphlet are very attractive.

To return to Vera Southgate's book, this is not exclusively con-cerned with transport. In the latter section of the book she moves from mail-carrying to the more immediate work of the G.P.O. in sorting, cancelling and so on. Understandably, there is no room for any mention of ancillary services. Less reasonable, I think, is the impression that the postal service is essentially manual and personal. There is a brief mention of machines for sorting letters, but a book written in 1965 could be expected to go further than this, for all children like to move with the times and would surely be interested in the working (though perhaps not the purpose) of coding, for instance.

This book represents a stage later in a child's reading life than the stage when he could listen to the tale of how Johnny posted a letter. Still, the simplicity of Vera Southgate's scheme puts the book within the range of a very young reader – it is, after all, part of an Easy-to-read series. John Berry's pictures, straightforward repre-sentations of a stage coach, a Victorian letter-box and so on, in bright Christmas card colours, are as unalarming as the text – even, in their way, pleasant to look at. But behind this book, as behind

Modwena Sedgwick's, strip-cartoon story, is the assumption of
"my letter" which must surely be the key to any book for a child
much under ten. The idea of a public service can only be suggested
at this stage – as it is in the last paragraph of the book:

> We all love to see the postman delivering Christmas mail to our
> houses. We wish him a "Happy Christmas" and thank him for
> delivering our mail safely during the year.
> ibid., p. 50

The difference between this book and the *Johnny* series is that the
Ladybird book is impersonal: that is, there is no story of an actual
child posting an actual letter. This is perhaps the reason for keeping
the book till the child is willing to externalise and move away from
his own personal concerns to those of others. However, as a substitute for the warmth of domestic familiarity there is the interest,
so well brought out, of the past history of post-office methods,
brought *towards* the reader by the choice of familiar folk-figures
and objects (coachman, postilion, highwayman, engine driver and
of course postman).

The most noticeable characteristic of the *Ladybird* books is their
homeliness, which makes them very reassuring to children in whose
home life books are not taken for granted. The rather more sophisticated *First Library* started by Macdonald in 1970 offers very much
the same mixture of history and technical explanation, in shorter,
more forthright sentences. It is interesting to compare the methods
of THE POSTMAN in this attractive series with those of the *Ladybird*
volume. The latter sets out by a gentle, friendly approach to *create*
a climate of learning, however simple – the former, assuming that
the child is ready to learn, offers the facts unadorned and with a
greater proportion of technical terms. This is the only book for the
early stages of reading which deals with mechanical sorting, and
very clearly:

> Not all letters are sorted by hand.
> This machine sorts the letters into 144 different pigeon holes.
> A man who sits at a "typewriter" works the machine.
> The typewriter is called the coding desk keyboard.
> The man reads the postal code and taps the keys.

Then the machine puts special dots on the letter.
You cannot really see the dots, but the machine can.
The machine "reads" the dots and sends each letter along a track
to the correct pigeon hole.
THE POSTMAN, pp. 10–11

The illustrations of this process are particularly good in ensuring that this account is absolutely clear: visualising a process from words alone is something that children often find difficult.

The folk-aspect of teaching – the seizing of well-known figures to represent concepts or processes – can help a child to make journeys in imagination beyond the four walls of his immediate surroundings, and to move towards some idea of society and its complexity, simply by understanding what a postman does and why (or, equally,

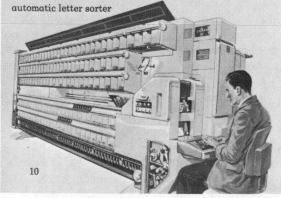

Not all letters are sorted by hand.
This machine sorts the letters into 144
different pigeon holes.
A man who sits at a 'typewriter' works the
machine.
The typewriter is called the coding desk
keyboard.

automatic letter sorter

10

Page from THE POSTMAN (Macdonald)

a greengrocer, a teacher, an astronaut). In topic books for juniors the personifying tendency (*The* postman) and the useful element of fiction (*My* letter) are important and useful.

Before classroom topic books got properly under way, many small books of information were produced for middle-class families. M. C. Carey's THE POSTMAN (1937) has the look of a gift-book, with a neat, square shape and simple, cosy pictures in clear colour. The author is not trying to explain logically how a letter is posted, but is giving a domestic example in which certain facts may be naturally included. Her book has a straight turn-around plan. The first part describes how John received a letter from his uncle in Canada; the second tells how he answers it. The intimacy of the pictures (Cook finding fleece-lined gloves in a birthday parcel, Johnny talking to the postman) is maintained in the way the boy and his letters are kept in the forefront of the story. Most cunning of all, the uncle who writes a letter "all about adventures in the snow with his sleigh and team of dogs" returns in the final paragraph:

> In the picture you see his uncle with his sleigh and team of dogs, racing home across the snow.
> He is his own postman, and he has John's letter safely tucked into the pocket of his fur coat.

John is the link character in a group of books by this author which includes THE BAKER, THE MERCHANT-SEAMAN and THE SOLDIER. In appealing to the curiosity of her fictional hero, the author appeals also to any small reader. Who would not feel his unspoken questions answered when, in THE ENGINE-DRIVER, M. C. Carey explains that the cleaners "had used $3\frac{1}{2}$ lbs. of oil, I lb. of vaseline, I lb. of emery paper, and many sponges and 'waste rags'."

Books like these have gone underground to come up again either as stories describing real life (like WIND, WATER and other little books by Jenny Joseph and Katharine Hoskyns) or as supplementary readers for infant and junior classes – sixteen-pagers, in fact. Kenneth Nuttall's *Services We Use* series, for instance, includes LETTERS BY POST (1964), which opens on a personal note:

> Here is Jane. She is eight years old. She is very busy writing a letter to her Grannie.

She tells Grannie all the news and asks her if her cough is better. At the end of the letter she writes her name.

Jane has written her letter in good, clear writing. Grannie will be able to read it easily.

Jane lives at Watford. Grannie lives at Leeds. It is a long way from Watford to Leeds.

Jane is looking at a map. She is trying to find out how far her letter will travel to reach Grannie.

op. cit., pp. 1–2

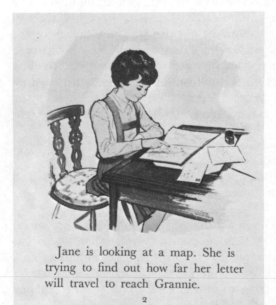

Jane is looking at a map. She is trying to find out how far her letter will travel to reach Grannie.

2

W. G. Morden's picture of Jane tracking the route of her letter on a map in LETTERS BY POST (Longman) adequately illustrates the point, but it is artistically dull. A more lively visual approach is badly needed in the sixteen-pagers as a whole. Who will take up the challenge of providing in them stimulating, attractive and exhilarating pictures?

Simple practical details of collection and sorting keep Mr Wood the postman, his colleagues Mr Smith, Mr Green and others, in the forefront of the picture, and the narrative ends with Grannie at Barton Road, Leeds, so that a list of "Things to do" and "Things to find out" seems very much in the family. This pamphlet is noticeably more lively than THE POSTMAN in W. and R. Chambers' *Book Corner* series, which combines a few simple statements of post-office procedure with small coloured pictures, or POSTMEN in Blackwell's *Little Learning Library*, which compares past and present (the book being a much simplified version of the junior information book discussed on page 61).

From these little books, which are less concerned with teaching than with accustoming children to using books for finding out, we move to more purposive, though still simple studies. Here, as so often happens, the glossy and stylish productions of today, like the rosiest apples, are not always the most satisfying. A school pamphlet of some years ago, WHAT HAPPENS WHEN YOU POST A LETTER by Laurence French (1951), belongs to a series which also explores the workings of the fire service, police, railway, canals, docks and sewers (the last engagingly entitled WHAT HAPPENS BELOW MANHOLES IN THE ROAD). Compact pamphlets of about 2,500 words, they are collected under the series title *Our Daily Life* and are described as a "citizenship series of books designed to tell the young reader, in a simple manner, how some of our essential services operate". The word citizenship is a good deal too ponderous for surveys which are civilised and interesting and, in their general effect, conspicuously domestic.

The plan and purpose of WHAT HAPPENS WHEN YOU POST A LETTER is firmly stated at the outset:

> When you send a letter to a friend, you just put it in a pillar box. What becomes of the letter when you have posted it?
> Let us see what happens when John Smith, of Cheapside, in the city of London, sends a letter to his cousin Mary Brown at Liskeard, Cornwall, which is in the west of England on the way to Penzance. It will have nearly 240 miles to travel.
> WHAT HAPPENS WHEN YOU POST A LETTER, pp. 2–3

As the reader follows in the wake of the letter, he is told about collection, facing, cancelling, segregating, sorting van to station, Travelling Post Office, Underground railway, wayside standards, stamps, re-sorting for the postman's walk. At the same time brief remarks on Henry VIII's official post, Cromwell's Postmaster General and Rowland Hill, and on air mail, transport methods and so on, all widen the scope of a very short survey which covers a surprising amount of ground.

Laurence French writes with confidence and ease; we feel that

he knows a great deal more than he is writing down and that he
expects his readers to realise that there is more to learn. A feeling
of leisure, space to breathe, is to be valued in a short first book of
this kind, and so is the human warmth which can oblige the author
to find room, among the technical details, for the following:

> By the way, even cats work for the Post Office; they were first
> introduced in 1868, but not many are employed today. They help
> to keep down mice and rats, and the Post Office permits a weekly
> allowance of a shilling for each cat's food.
> ibid., p. 12

I cannot resist adding to this pleasant statement, which may have
come from a book for the general reader called POST HASTE, by
I. Halstead (1944), a book nicely salted with anecdotes. The author
describes how in 1870 application was made to the Money Order
department for permission to put in a claim for the maintenance
of post-office cats; the reply was:

> Three cats may be allowed on probation. They must undergo
> a test examination and should, I think, be females. It is important
> that the cats be not overfed and I cannot allow more than a
> shilling a week for their support. They must depend on mice for
> the remainder of their emoluments and if the mice be not reduced
> in number in six months a further portion of the allowance must
> be stopped. Can any statistics as to mice be furnished from time
> to time?
> POST HASTE, p. 62

I have searched in vain for this gem in some of the books for older
children in which it might well have found a place. The lack of
humour (one suspects largely due to a lack of sense of humour) is
one of the surprising and unfortunate features of information
books as a whole.

Considering the restricted scope of Laurence French's pamphlet,
it does have something of the stamp of an individual on it, if only
in the "Things to do and find out" listed at the end, which include
looking for old pillar-boxes, making a map of the air route to
Calcutta and designing a special stamp to commemorate the first

landing on Mars. It is, you might say, a cheerful and alert schoolmaster whose voice is heard here.

Another schoolmaster's voice delivers some 8,000 words in a firm, friendly, didactic tone in the volume POSTMEN AND THE POST OFFICE (1961), in Blackwell's *Learning Library*. Five chapter headings take us through How the post began; You post a letter; How your letter travels; The telephone service; Your own post office. In spite of the familiar "you", there is no direct fiction. This is a practical book. No time is wasted and the pictures (mainly inter-text or full page drawings, with four colour photographs) do as much work as the text. The clean uncluttered pages with their large type, the many short paragraphs, the direct style, all fit the present aim of the teaching profession to come off the dais, but the book, like its junior version, is basically academic in character. There is a good deal of instruction on how to use the post-office or the telephone and how to send a postal-order; indeed, the word *use* may be said to dominate the book as the word *transport* dominates most of the others. Lacking any individual style, without any "story" and without an interesting formal scheme, the book seems really to be a collection of facts and no more.

Is it chiefly the personal element that is lacking here? Another pamphlet for young readers, Mary F. Moore's OUR POST OFFICE (1970) uses people to weld her explanation of how the Post Office deals with a letter. Susan, John and Paul Hammond arrive in a Cotswold village for a holiday. Paul is to be seven next day and his father has promised he shall sign his Savings Book himself. The post-office is in the village shop and Mr Rayne (village-like, ready to waste time agreeably in talk) explains about pensions, postal orders, licences, insurance stamps in a most natural way. The local postman, dropping in midway, invites the children to go to his cottage later to look at photographs connected with his job. Through him, just as naturally, the author explains collection, segregating, facing, sorting and so on, and the exposition is broken up by remarks like "here's a picture that helps to explain a stamp cancelling machine".

We all know that people do not naturally talk in informative paragraphs, but the device can work if its artificiality is decently disguised, as it is here. After John has asserted that if he had mis-stamped a letter he would just get it back, he is corrected:

"Oh, no, you couldn't," Mr. Rayne said promptly. "Nothing can be taken back once it has been posted, or handed in, even if you can prove that you are the person who sent it. You may not have it back even to add something, or to put more stamps on." He went on, "On my side, I'm not allowed to give information about letters or postal packets, except to the person they're addressed to. And I mustn't inform people of anything I know is private."

OUR POST OFFICE, pp. 51–2

The topic books so far mentioned have been dealing with the accumulation of facts, more or less arranged in order. There has been little or no attempt to convey general ideas, to steer the facts in the direction of a concept. The idea that mail is private and that the Post Office has the responsibility of keeping it so is certainly not too advanced for a young reader to understand, and it is, after all, the cardinal point of the system. Children could be told, too, that the postal system is a service as well as a job. John, the oldest of the children in Mary Moore's book, notices that Mr Rayne and Jem Ridings are "both very keen on the Post Office" and asks, "Are all post office workers like that?" The answer comes from Mr Rayne:

"I suppose most of them are . . . You see, the keen ones have a sense of tradition – that is, they want to carry on and improve the work that others have started. We are proud to belong to a team.

He paused, and then said, "I'm sure that the Post Office has more to do with just ordinary folk, like you and me, than any other branch of the Civil Service . . . And its great aim is to serve the public as well, and with as little expense, as possible."

ibid., p. 56

A book for children cannot be cynical, but sooner or later they may begin to question its assumptions. Mr Rayne's words on the Post Office may suggest many reservations in the minds of an adult reader and I would certainly hope that some children at least might challenge the postmaster's enthusiasm with comments on wage disputes, inefficient service, the implications of automation and

THE JOURNEY OF A LETTER

HOME TOWN

1 Posting

2 Collecting

3 Facing and stamp cancelling

4 First sorting

5 Second sorting

6 Delivering to the railway station

7 Travelling post office and wayside apparatus

DISTANT POST TOWN

8 Sorting to the village

9 Delivering to the post office

10 Sorting for delivery

11 Delivering the letter

Pictures vividly summarise text in a spread from the G.P.O.'s pamphlet, OUR POST OFFICE.

so on. Certainly some of them might notice, also, in recent topic books, the surprising lack of up-to-date facts I have already mentioned.

Even if a junior topic book allows little space for details about the use of phosphorus in coding, the zip code system should surely be mentioned. Mary Moore's official pamphlet explains briefly how it works, and in an earlier version published fourteen years ago, she suggested that some kind of "special codes of a few letters and numbers (which the Post Office would give them) on their notepaper and envelopes" would help to speed the work and save money and staff; the later *Learning Library* book is content with drawings of a cancelling machine and a teleprinter and the comment that "Machines for sorting are now being made, but only a few very big sorting offices have them so far." The Macdonald book already discussed (p. 55) has the advantage of having been written at a time when postal codes had become more widespread, but this does not alter the fact that many books written in the last ten years or so *are* oddly old-fashioned. Apart from topic books for beginners, many more substantial studies for the ten-to-twelve age group are timid about the whole subject of mechanisation. Nancy Martin's book for secondary school pupils, THE POST OFFICE (1969), written with direct help from the organisation, is a striking exception, with its very up-to-date survey of every branch of the service, including satellite communication. With this book and the shorter, more specialised MODERN COMMUNICATIONS by Charles King (1970) dealing with telegrams, telex, data, radio and satellites, a technically minded child would certainly feel that he was reading about a service as it is now. He would also find two G.P.O. publications, POST OFFICE RAILWAY and PROGRESS OF POSTAL CODING informative, but he would have to accept a considerable degree of propaganda.

The printed word does not exist solely for passing on information. In none of the works just mentioned will a young reader feel he is communicating with an individual; they are detached and dry in manner.

One of the earliest series of topic books, Hamish Hamilton's *Look* books, includes J. D. Scott's very lively LOOK AT POST OFFICES (1962). This is in fact a long essay divided into chapters but preserving a continuous forward movement all through. The author does not try to be complete; his book is essentially a starter, offering samples from a wide range of knowledge. The production of the book follows a series pattern which now seems a little drab and crude; the few drawings, sensible and sometimes amusing, are lacking in any artistic spirit. What captures the attention is the style – vivacious, flippant at times, casual, intimate, unobtrusively skilful.

This prose style sets the tone for the whole book. It is easily recognisable from J. D. Scott's novels, for he has not tried to write "for the young". Touching on a number of aspects of the subject, from the transporting of a letter to telephone and telegraph services, savings banks and postal history, he makes an intimacy of style work for him. As in most junior books, the emphasis is on children using the post-office. "It's a machine that anybody can make use of, and every time you post a letter this great machine is working for you." The procedure (stamping, sorting, delivery) is seen in relation to certain situations (a child sending out invitations to a party, a holiday postcard, a pen-friend in Africa).

When this method is not appropriate, examples are chosen which a child can appreciate. The fact that the postal service is one with a great responsibility is illustrated by reference to World War II and to the floods of 1960 in Wales and the western counties. The author shows a personal interest in the facts he uses:

Who decides what kind of cloth postmen's uniforms will be made of? Who decides what brand of petrol will be used in post office delivery vans? Who arranges with the Government of Nepal for special deliveries of letters to an Everest expedition? If Britain established a base on the Moon, how would we send letters *there*? To all these questions and millions of other questions, there is someone at St. Martin's-Le-Grand who would be expected to find an answer.

So that when you go to your own post office, that not-very-important-looking place in the village or in the next street, and post your invitation, you are, in a way, rubbing a magic lamp, for you are calling into your service an immense organization, which is also an immense business, one of the biggest businesses in the world – and all working for you for the 3d. stamp that you put on your letter.

LOOK AT POST OFFICES, pp. 95–6

The few pages allowed for the early history of the postal service are used with economy. In an outline like this, it helps the reader if facts are related to a general idea; here the author has suggested the reason why posts developed at all and has emphasised the importance of communications as a part of modern life. He respects his readers and invites them to accept a mixture of fact and idea, with a disarmingly simple mode of address:

> When Charles II came to the throne he stopped this reading of letters, and later a law was passed which said that nobody was allowed to read letters going through the post. This is still the law of the land. What you write in a letter is completely private, and if, when you are inviting Mary to your party, you put in a piece saying: "But I'm not inviting Wilhelmina, because she cheated in the egg-and-spoon race last year", you know that no spy is going to open the letter and tell Wilhelmina what you have said. (Of course you and Mary may quarrel, and then Mary may tell Wilhelmina herself, but that has nothing to do with the post office.)
> ibid., pp. 46–8

An elementary book can be entertaining and stimulating at the same time. The author of LOOK AT POST OFFICES, prepared to be amusing, even jolly, is not prepared to make nonsense of his subject or to waste time on jokes with no purpose. He avoids the type of humour which serves so often to disguise thin knowledge or a nervous desire to be popular – a humour usually betrayed by an excess of exclamation marks. Humour that passes current in the classroom can wilt or coarsen when it is written down. Many information books, even some not written by school-teachers, have the teacher's voice in them, but this is usually the expository, not the conversational voice. All the more praise to Boswell Taylor, whose voice comes through the words of his many information books with the variations of tone of a good school lesson – admonitory, cheerful, blunt, wise-cracking, patient, digressive, speculative. We sense all through his carefully arranged explanations the questions of his pupils; at times he will even, as it were, interrupt himself, to give the effect of a teacher allowing red herrings if they are not too stale.

Boswell Taylor's HERE COMES THE POST! (1964) belongs to the *Walrus* series, designed for primary and early secondary use in a format which is business-like but also persuasive. Clear large type with generous spacing, plenty of paragraphs and plenty of pictures, an informative and dramatic cover – all these things work insensibly on the reader, to put him in the right frame of mind for accepting and even remembering some of the details.

This is frankly a teaching book. Each section has a list of "Things to do", ranging from composing telegrams to working out postal routes on a map or on the floor; each chapter ends with a summary of "Facts to remember"; each short sub-division has a heading practical as well as inviting – "Rogues of the road"; "Engines instead of sails"; "The Royal Mail takes to the air". None of these devices need discourage the child from taking the book home from the library to read; he might enjoy following the suggestions.

The skill in the book can be seen particularly well in the way the author deals with "The story of the Royal Mail", his central section. Here is a far more comprehensive view of past history than in any of the books mentioned so far. That it is also the most interesting outline is due to the choice of examples and the skilful use of contemporary documents and visual material. A quotation from one of the Paston Letters, an extract from Post Road regulations of 1583 and, to match the text, maps of post roads as organised by Thomas Withering in the seventeenth and Ralph Allen in the eighteenth centuries, Dockwra's poster *A penny well bestowed*, and a notice of reward for a thief who attacked a post-boy at York in 1822 – such illustrative details liven up the narrative.

Once or twice the author drops into the historic present – for instance, describing Robert Carey's ride "post" from London to Edinburgh with the news of Queen Elizabeth's death. Apart from the actual examples chosen, the book gains from the author's lively and very concrete vocabulary and the vivacity of his narrative.

It is dark when he comes at last to Scrooby. A blast on the post horn brings the postmaster, William Brewster, to the door. He holds a lantern in his hand. Yes, he can serve a hot meal within the hour and the best bed in the house will be made ready.

One hundred and sixty miles has Robert Carey travelled in the single day. But there are still two hundred and fifty miles ahead.

Robert Carey eats his meal and then throws himself fully clothed upon the bed. He rests his head upon his mail pouch with the precious letter safe inside.

HERE COMES THE POST! p. 35

Boswell Taylor has selected facts that will help him to plot the course of the postal service's evolution and to state its underlying principles. He is the only writer to emphasise one particularly interesting aspect of the service. A boy gets a letter from Italy:

The letter was written in Italy and sent from an Italian post office. The sender bought an Italian stamp. An Italian aeroplane brought the letter to Britain. Then a British van took the letter to the station, and a British train brought the letter to London, and Mr. Tonks has brought the letter to David. Now who gets the money – the Italian post office or the British one?

... One of the first decisions made at the Universal Postal Union Congress was that countries would deliver letters from other countries free.

So the British post office gets nothing at all for delivering the letter from Italy. At the same time a letter is being delivered in Italy with a British stamp. So it is fair to everyone in the end.

ibid., pp. 92–3.

Louis Slobodkin illustrates an unusual way of protecting confidential mail in READ ABOUT THE POSTMAN (Franklin Watts).

This leads naturally to a summary of the history of the Universal Postal Union and to the salutary conclusion, "There are no boundaries for letters. Mail bags travel from country to country without anyone trying to stop them."

The boy who had the letter from Italy provides the two outside sections in this well-arranged book, headed "Outward" and "Inward" respectively. As the book opens, David writes an airmail letter to his father in Australia and posts it at a small post-office, where Miss Tonks is interested in a neighbourly way. The author slips easily into an explanation of the processes by which the letter travels from Miss Tonks to David's father. The last section, Inward, is planned round David's birthday, and the postcards, telegrams, telephone messages and letters that come to him, as well as an airmail letter from his father, cover a good deal of postal routine.

There is too little space given to the mechanisation of postal processes; for instance, we are left to assume (from text and pictures) that all letters are sorted by hand. Apart from this, however, the various stages and methods of transport are covered briskly and clearly and there is a good firm ending:

What a collection of mail there is in Mr. Tonks' post bag every day!

Birthday cards, newspapers, letters from lovers, letters to friends, angry letters, jolly letters, funny letters; letters from Italy, Germany, Switzerland, the Equator, the Arctic; letters that have travelled on great ships, on little ships, in the air, in special trains, in local trains, in vans, on bicycles. The mail bag is full of mysteries, and each letter, if it could speak, could tell such a wonderful tale of adventure.

But none of the letters will speak – unless they are addressed to us. They hold secrets, and they keep their secrets to the end of their journey, wherever that may be.

ibid., p. 93

The child of an age to read Boswell Taylor's book with enjoyment and understanding is of an age to accept the ramifications of a subject. This is a book that mentions in passing many of the ancillary services of the G.P.O. It is comprehensive though not definitive. Besides, the author shows that the postal service *evolved*. His history, brief though it is, is not merely a series of dramatic episodes but of facts chosen to show (though not really by direct statement) how communications and people grow side by side.

The author of an information book, faced with having to encompass a wide subject in a small allowance of words, does sometimes forget that a system becomes efficient only by constant change. In the context of the Post Office, only Boswell Taylor mentions Dockwra's Penny Post, though it was as remarkable as Rowland Hill's reform. Only Boswell Taylor shows post-roads *at different dates*.

One of the sidelines of postal history often neglected in topic books is the snatch-system by which mails are picked up and dropped from the Travelling Post Office. This device, which is already being superseded, has had a varied history which could be illustrated by prints of the past century and earlier, showing a postilion taking a bag from a landlord at the upper window of an inn or an old lady handing a bag up on a stick as the coach slows down. F. G. Kay in ROYAL MAIL (1951) explains that as early as 1838 the Postmaster of an area would throw letters into the train "while the guard simply threw the letters sorted for that area out of the window", and he points out that at this date the train would be travelling at less than twenty miles an hour. The primitive net used then was improved by John Ramsey and later by John Dicker, a mail coach inspector. A quotation from Auden's "Night mail" (a poem popular with most children for its active rhythms) would stress the interest of this special system of distribution.

It is surprising not to find this process included in Robert Page's THE STORY OF THE POST (1967), since this is by far the most comprehensive *history* of the Postal Service for top junior readers. Children who react strongly to the visual aspect of a book would appreciate the emphatic paragraphing and the placing of the numerous illustrations in this very lively book. For pleasurable and easy reference it is perhaps to be preferred to any other, but it is not a book with personality. It can hardly fail to interest a child already alive to the excitement of finding out about a particular subject, but it shares with most others an impersonal tone never livened by humour or acerbity.

Colour, not lacking in the illustrations of modern topic books, is conspicuously absent from the texts of most of them. To the

Picture of London's first pillar box, 1855, from THE STORY OF THE POST (A & C Black), by courtesy of Illustrated London News.

colour of interesting facts we could add the colour of unusual presentation of fact. Few writers nowadays would use fantasy as unselfconsciously as R. F. Robinow did in PETER IN THE POST OFFICE (1934), a charming curiosity with an unexpectedly tough attitude to information. As Peter is looking at a stamp through a magnifying glass, the dolphin on it comes to life and takes him on a tour of post-office departments, where he sees sorting and deliveries, the underground railway, parcel sorting at Mount Pleasant, an airmail posting box, a telegraph office, a telephone exchange, a steamship. In each place Peter and his guide are seemingly invisible and the guide delivers rapid asides about what is going on. The fantasy is pleasing and, though it does not allow for a really full treatment of the subject, the bold white outline of the dolphin, superimposed on photographed scenes, links a satisfactory outline.

For boys and girls of practical bent, another topic book published some time ago used fiction in an exceptionally effective way. This booklet prepared "by authority of the Post Master General,

London" in a series of *Men and Women at Work*, is not in fact specifically for children, but one example at least, G. A. Campbell's OUR LETTERS IN THE POST (1938) could well be given to school-children to read. "The simplest way to understand what happens in the post", writes the author, "is to follow a letter from the time it is written until the time it reaches the person to whom it is addressed." This hackneyed formula is unexpectedly rejuvenated when John Harben, a shopkeeper in Marandellas, Southern Rhodesia, writes to Lawrence and Thompson of Manchester ordering sixty yards of white cotton cloth, and enclosing a money order. The letter is followed on its travels till it reaches Manchester, when the money order is dealt with. Telegraph and telephone are neatly brought into the story, postal orders and their international cousins, money orders, are explained, and the parcel is pursued on its outward journey, seen through the customs and across the sea, till the shopkeeper is able to display the goods for sale.

In production and style, the book would make little appeal to a young reader today, if it were not for the way it opens up the world and shows communications in action. Here we see a piece of trading which depends on the post, and we glimpse by implication an idea not usually included in books for children – the distinction between the Post Office as a service and as a business. The conflicting points of view should be brought to the attention of the young, just as they can be told (but seldom are) that the Post Office is not consistently and continuously a model of efficiency. The context for this kind of comment might well be a description of modern attempts to improve the service's efficiency. For juniors, as for everyone else, a subject like the Postal System is not to be described in the idiom and with the facts of ten years back; yet this is the situation nowa-days, when so many simplified books ignore mechanisation, satellite communications and the developments which can be most confidently trusted to interest the young. A proper study of post office machinery is the logical end of the ascending scale of books which started with the simple figure of The Postman. But the Postal System remains, ultimately, in the hands of human beings. If books for the young are to offer a complete and honest picture of the system, they must be prepared to be as explicit about wages and working conditions in the 'seventies as they are about such matters in past centuries.

Reading List

Adams, H. POSTMEN AND THE POST OFFICE. Learning Library. *Blackwell* 1961. Illustrated by Anyon Cook.

Briant, F. Heathcote. THE POSTMAN. People's Jobs. *Educational Supply Association* 1951, *Ward Lock* 1959. Illustrated by photographs.

Campbell, G. A. OUR LETTERS IN THE POST. Men and Women at Work. *Oxford University Press* 1938. With photographs and one or two small drawings.

Carey, M. C. THE POSTMAN. *Dent* 1937. Illustrated by Mary Shillabeer. See also THE ENGINE-DRIVER *Dent* 1938 by the same author.

Crow, Duncan. THE POST OFFICE. How it Works. *Her Majesty's Stationery Office* 1962. Originally written for the Overseas Information Services organised by the Commonwealth Relations Office, this pamphlet is a model of clarity and simplicity. It gives a practical view of the Post Office and has many unexpected and interesting illustrations.

Downing, J. G. THE STORY OF THE POST. Communications series. *Wheaton* 1967. Illustrated by David Harris. An undistinguished pamphlet with an imaginative cover using a montage technique.

Fawkes, Leslie. THE GPO AS A CAREER. *Batsford* 1964. For older school leavers, but younger children might find ideas in it.

French, Laurence. WHAT HAPPENS WHEN YOU POST A LETTER. Our Daily Life. London, *Factual Books* 1951. With photographs.

Gagg, J. C. POSTMEN. Little Learning Library. *Blackwell* 1968. Illustrated by Kathleen Gell.

Halstead, I. POST HASTE: THE STORY OF THE POST OFFICE IN PEACE AND WAR. *Lindsay Drummond* 1944. Illustrated by photographs.

Hyde, J. W. THE ROYAL MAIL: ITS CURIOSITIES AND ROMANCE. *Blackwood and Sons* 1885, *Simpkin, Marshall* 1889. Illustrated by photographs and prints. Chapter headings like "Singular coincidences" and "Shipwrecked mails" may give some idea of the range of this civilised and witty book, a useful quarry for the writer of today.

James, Alan. THE POST. Past-into-Present. *Batsford* 1970. Illustrated by photographs and prints. A very compressed survey, stiff reading for children under ten. Notable for numerous and illuminating quotations from all periods.

Joseph, Jenny. WHEELS. *Longman Young Books* 1966. WIND and WATER. *Longman Young Books* 1967. Illustrated by Katharine Hoskyns.

Kay, F. G. ROYAL MAIL: THE STORY OF THE POSTS IN ENGLAND FROM THE TIME OF EDWARD IV TO THE PRESENT DAY. *Rockliff* 1951.

King, Charles. MODERN COMMUNICATIONS. Tricorne Books. *Harrap* 1970. Illustrated by the author.

Martin, Nancy. THE POST OFFICE: FROM CARRIER PIGEON TO CONFRAVISION. *Dent* 1969. Drawings by Charles Green, and some photographs.

Moore, Mary F. THE POST OFFICE AT WORK. Social series. *Macmillan* 1957. Revised as OUR POST OFFICE, *G.P.O.* 1970. Illustrated by photographs.

Nuttall, Kenneth. LETTERS BY POST. Services we Use. *Longmans, Green* 1964. Illustrated by W. G. Morden.

Page, Robert. THE STORY OF THE POST. Junior Reference series. (*A. and C. Black* 1967) *Dufour* 1967. Illustrated by Denis Wrigley; also by photographs, engravings and portraits.

Robinow, R. F. PETER IN THE POST OFFICE. *Bodley Head* 1934. Illustrated by Tom Seton.

Scott, J. D. LOOK AT POST OFFICES. Look at . . . *Hamish Hamilton* 1962. Illustrated by Lewis Hart.

Sedgwick, Modwena. JOHNNY AND THE POLICEMAN, POSTMAN, FIREMAN, VET. *Blackie* 1963. Illustrated by Diana John.

Slobodkin, Louis. READ ABOUT THE POSTMAN. Read About . . . *Franklin Watts* 1966. Illustrated by the author. A rapid, racy survey of postal history in the United States and elsewhere, enlivened by tiny, comical marginal two-colour illustrations; to whet the appetite of an eight-year-old. See picture, p. 68.

Smith, G. R. HALF A CENTURY IN THE DEAD LETTER OFFICE. Bristol, *W. C. Hemmons* 1908. Illustrated by photographs and prints. A book worth hunting for because of its entertaining and unique illustrations and for the author's first-hand experiences.

Southgate, Vera. THE POSTMAN AND THE POSTAL SERVICE. Ladybird Easy Reading Books. *Wills and Hepworth* 1965. Illustrated by John Berry.

Staff, Frank. THE PENNY POST 1680–1918. *Lutterworth* 1964. A scholarly, adult book, extremely valuable as a source for junior histories.

Taylor, Boswell. HERE COMES THE POST! Walrus Books. *University of London Press* 1964. Illustrated by photographs and prints.

Wilson, Jean. THE POSTMAN. Our Book Corner. Men and Women at Work. *W. and R. Chambers* 1964. Illustrated by Sally Michel.

Zilliacus, Laurin. FROM PILLAR TO POST: THE TROUBLED HISTORY OF THE MAIL. *Heinemann Educational* 1956. A provocative and forthright book, emphasising the question of the privacy of letters and the struggle between profit-making and service in the postal system. Children would do well to progress from simpler surveys to this book in their 'teens; it should make them think.

—— THE POSTMAN. Macdonald First Library. *Macdonald Educational* 1970. Illustrated by photographs in colour.

—— A BRIEF HISTORY OF THE POST OFFICE. *G.P.O.* 1970. Design and illustrations by Edgar Longman.

—— POSTMEN THROUGH THE AGES. *G.P.O.* 1970. Design by Edgar Longman, illustrations by Gaynor Chapman.

2c | *Holland*

The Hollanders are distinguished from other nations by their peculiar cleanliness, industry and economy.
A PEEP AT THE VARIOUS NATIONS OF THE WORLD, a chapbook of the early nineteenth century.

. . . as for the canals – this morning the Nassaukade had stunk like an overripe Camembert. Not surprisingly – he had reached the Singel – "Look at that; like soup." Full probably of rusty old prams; our delightful Amsterdammers, nearly as undisciplined as Parisians and quite as dirty, thank God. He disliked Dutch cleanliness. Who wanted clean water anyway? They got on without it in Venice.
Detective Van der Valk in GUN BEFORE BUTTER (1963) by Nicolas Freeling

2c | *Holland*

NO child is ready to visit a foreign country until he has some generalised idea of his own land, the confidence to leave his familiar environment, and such acquaintance with the country he is going to visit as he can find in books and elsewhere. To a child beginning to read, Holland will probably first be represented by a series of justifiable clichés. No doubt it is as tiresome for the Dutch to be epitomised in china windmills and ashtrays decorated with carousing burghers as it is for us to see tourists collecting plastic beefeaters or Cornish pixies. Yet such symbols are as relevant to the national character as an international saucepan or brief-case, and of course far more easily recognisable.

It would be useless to show a child as his first glimpse of the Dutch a business man in city clothes or a gang of workmen on a polder. Such types could make little impact if the word Holland did not already arouse some picture in a child's mind of windmills, storks or tulip fields. This child needs first books with plenty of pictures of typically Dutch people and scenes – but there must be no note of patronising insularity in the way the scenes are introduced. Sixty years ago it was possible to publish a book with the title QUEER QUAINT HOLLAND. Sixty years ago it was possible to include in a junior information book the following description:

> The Dutch people, dressed up like quaint dolls with their gay little houses, their little canals, and their bright green fields cut up like a chess-board, live in a country that is for all the world like the most delightful toy; everything is so neat, so well arranged, and so regular. It is not surprising that their favourite flowers are the gorgeous, tidy, conventional tulips.
> Beatrice Jungman. HOLLAND, p. 25

The broader view which we should expect for children nowadays is suggested in a passage written in our own time:

> Chances are you know Holland chiefly by its familiar emblems: windmills, wooden shoes, baggy pantaloons and lace bonnets, tulip bulbs, the Flying Dutchman and the boy with his finger in the dike. It is also the multifaceted country of pastries, fish and cheese, superb diamond cutters, dynamic enterprise and stoic calm, a mosaic of floral colour reflecting the artistry of Rembrandt and Vermeer.
>
> Blending the centuries, ancient moated castles may be observed along with huge industrial centres, young farm settlements, the coal mines of the south and the meadows rich with cattle in the north. Besides being the flower, fruit and vegetable garden of Europe, Holland happens to be a leading supplier of dairy products, a great ship-building nation and a growing industrial power, producing everything from nuclear reactors to vitamins and varnishes.
>
> LET'S TRAVEL IN HOLLAND, p. 10

The charm of Lucy Fitch Perkins's book, THE DUTCH TWINS, can be enjoyed as an example of the style of sixty years ago, but its pictures of storks, windmills and cupboard beds need to be balanced, as do Meindert De Jong's reminiscent tales also, by contemporary descriptions.

Two world wars and the advance of communications systems have not entirely put an end to pretty-pretty studies of foreign countries for children purporting to be accurate for our own time. THE DUTCH BOY by E. M. and C. R. Vann (1952) has end-papers showing a fisherman in pot hat, baggy trousers and wooden shoes talking to his wife and children, who are also in national costume; it shows a windmill by a canal, a field of tulips, skaters on ice, a dog pulling a cart. Nowhere is there a factory, a city street or an airport. The clichés, necessary as an introduction, are neither enlivened by context nor made really relevant to the insipid characters in a stilted story.

It is a relief to turn from this lopsided view to a series of primary assignment cards, ALL OVER THE WORLD, in which the four pages concerning the Netherlands, intended as a starting point for topic

These three objects were also made in Holland. Write about them in your work books. Dutch school children wearing wooden clogs must leave them outside the classroom. They make such a clatter that their Dutch name is KLOOMPERS.

These two items from the assignment sheet, THE NETHERLANDS (Blond Educational), show how sensibly traditional and modern aspects of Holland are combined to give children a reasonably broad introduction to the country.

The boy in this picture is wearing festival costume. What shoes is he wearing? Can you draw a picture of his sister in her holiday costume?

work, include Van Gogh and wooden shoes, docks and tulips, coinage and smoked eel.

At first sight Irene Dark's sixteen-pager HOLLAND (1964) seems a superficial picture, for the author is unabashed at mentioning the most obvious aspects of the country. Her book ends:

> We both hope that one day you will come and visit this land of sea, canals, bulbs and windmills. Bring your bicycle. You will not have any hills to climb, but you will have plenty to see.
> Perhaps you will take back a pair of clogs to wear, as well as two dolls like us.

The last four words give the clue to the attraction of this pretty little book. Being dolls, at one remove from the children who will read about them, Hans and Wilhelmina may legitimately be used to convey a playful picture of their country. The book escapes being commonplace by this presentation of fact. Besides, it makes important points about Holland – about Old Masters, the Dutch love of flowers, the importance of water. Finally, the series as a whole is brilliantly designed (by W. Lewis of the Birmingham School of Design) to capture the interest of children for whom books are not yet a necessity.

Another sixteen-pager shows how the careful choice of words and ideas can refresh familiar points. Soft-covered, plentifully illustrated, MY HOME IN HOLLAND (1961) has nothing original about it (the pictures, indeed, are somewhat banal) but its few hundred words have been chosen to illustrate the two aspects, the familiar and the foreign, and to relate them clearly. Rita, who is seven, wears a pinafore skirt and jersey, but she lives in Delft, by a canal, and her father is a potter. When she goes on holiday she goes to Amsterdam, and as they leave the city again a street-organ plays *Zilvervloot* and her mother sings the song to her. A table set for a meal occupies one page, another shows a canal scene with an arched bridge and seventeenth-century houses. Each detail is relevant not to a picture-book Holland but to the country with past and present existing side by side, and with two typically Dutch elements, clay and water, in a natural conjunction.

Little books of this kind attract children with their bright pictures even if the standard of illustration is not very high but, for a veracious view of a country, photographs in colour are likely to be better in most cases. In recent years the "Day in the life of", illustrated photographically, has become a popular medium for the introduction of a foreign country. The texts of such books are alarmingly variable. Often words will be arranged to suit a previously chosen set of pictures. The Swedish series *Children Everywhere* is notable for the balance between text and pictures. Astrid Lindgren's DIRK LIVES IN HOLLAND (1963), with photographs by Anna Riwkin-Brick, is a particularly good example of this type of simple recognition book. To a child the verbal and pictorial description of a day's trip (journey, household, chores, visit, whatever it may be, the mood is always one of play) is at once attractive and easy to follow. For an adult, who may well be required to read or to paraphrase the text for a child not yet reading, the extreme, almost naïve naturalness of children and scenes can be very pleasing.

Astrid Lindgren's charm of manner survives translation, and the two thousand words of her story about Dirk and his friend Elleke are full of grace and a light-hearted realism. Like the photographs, her words have been chosen to show one small but typical corner of Dutch life. Dirk lives in a small fishing town. He longs for a bicycle; he wants to see the Queen's yacht passing. Bicycle, water, monarchy – three clichés perhaps, but providing a good framework for a journey, snatches of chatter between the children, glimpses of people in everyday clothes as well as national costume, of walls and rooftops, cows and ships. So immediate is the effect of the pictures that their fine-textured black and white leaves no room to wish for colour.

CHILDREN OF THE BARGES by H. C. James (1959) belongs to the series *This is our Country*, in which sets of coloured photographs are linked by a skeleton story, interspersed with straight facts, with two children at the centre. In this book, a pictorial map on the end-papers shows the system of waterways in Holland and the photographs are arranged to illustrate a journey along the Amsterdam-Rhine canal, as Jan and his skipper father take a cargo from the city to the customs post at Lobith on the German border. The departure from Amsterdam gives an opening for comments on the Palace, the Church of the Coronation, barrel organs, herring stalls, bicycles and the Skipper School; the last most relevant fact leads to a delightful sequence of pictures showing how the skipper pays his toll when he comes to a drawbridge. Other details – for instance, the rope and crane device to keep small brother Piet from falling overboard or the fatherly promenading of Hector the dog – relate the story to the home life of a young reader.

Not all the pictures have as clear a relation to the journey or the characters as this. It is reasonable enough for Jan to explain to his younger brother how locks work, but hardly to offer a lesson about the war with Spain in the sixteenth century. It is reasonable to include a description of floating shops but less so to expatiate on the floral business of Aalsmeer, since it operates on another canal. Children do notice when facts are dragged in willy-nilly and any author should respect his readers enough to be sure that the photographs in this kind of book are properly related to the narrative.

Which is more important in these two books – story or photograph? Neither book could exist without a text; pictures tell only part of the story and would have little appeal to young children without that story. The popularity of television serials like "Belle and Sebastian" with its Swiss scenery or "The white horses" with Viennese and Hungarian scenes suggests that a child of six or seven coming to terms with a strange environment can do this more easily if he can identify himself with a character in the fiction. Whether he sees this environment within the time limits of a television programme or in the more leisured and private enjoyment of a book is his own affair – if he is wise, and if it is possible, he will do both. But story there must be, so far.

These short books have all been predominantly domestic. There has been little or nothing in them of Holland as an important economic neighbour to Britain, a country with great social and political problems. However, the skipper in CHILDREN OF THE BARGES hinted at a break with the past as he pointed out the factories on the banks of the river Waal. "Today we are a country of builders", he tells his sons, and the author adds:

> What he says is true. Everywhere there are new buildings and bridges and locks. Many of the buildings are in the red brick which the Dutch people love so well, and some of the brickworks still use horses to pull the trolleys backwards and forwards from the works. But there is, too, much modern machinery designed by clever engineers.
>
> CHILDREN OF THE BARGES, no page numbers.

How soon can a writer afford to introduce the idea of the *complexity* of a nation? If he can expand the conventional image in describing for juniors how a barge captain or a potter get their living, when should he go further and discuss the way Holland is changing today? Two major problems are especially interesting to English readers – control of the sea and of population, the two issues being closely related. Since we owe some of our best farming land to Dutch engineers of three centuries ago, and have a problem akin to theirs on our reclaimed east coast, it would seem natural to introduce at the earliest stage of children's reading, if only in the simplest statements, the idea that a large part of Holland depends for its existence on control of the sea and that the Dutch, with a dangerously increasing population, can only find room for it by stealing land from the water. The sixteen-pager by Susan Howard already mentioned introduced the idea of the importance of water indirectly; Peter Buckley's JAN OF HOLLAND (1956) goes further.

This outstanding book belongs to the series *Around the World Today*, designed for readers from about eight, and using photographs to illustrate a continuous story of a child in a situation appropriate to his particular country. JAN OF HOLLAND, with its well planned narrative and workmanlike, compact style, should make readers curious to look further into the pattern of life in Holland, for the author is so manifestly interested in the family he has chosen to illustrate the country's special problems.

His setting is the village of Urk in the Ijsselmeer. Like Vollendam and Marken, Urk was once an island in the Zuider Zee. The building of the Afluitsdyk turned this enormous inlet into an inland lake with polders, some reclaimed and some still under process of reclamation; and it turned Urk into a small town on what is now the North East polder of the Ijsselmeer. Whereas Vollendam and Marken, nearer to Amsterdam, have become show places which, as Karel Capek remarked dryly many years ago, "do not make their living from fish, but from trippers and painters (especially of the low-brow kind)", the inhabitants of Urk have either changed from sea-fishing to a trade in fresh-water fish, especially eels, or have taken state help and training for a move to the new farming land on the polders. Obviously this is no simple matter. Peter Buckley illustrates it through the fortunes of the de Vries family.

Great-grandfather Adriaan is the centre of the home. A noted fisherman, his stories have guided the boy Jan's interests all his life and when old Adriaan is lost while helping with rescue work during the great 1953 flood in Zeeland, the obligation on the boy to follow a fisherman's life or to train under his grandfather Klaas, a tug-boat captain, becomes very strong. But some of Jan's relations are farmers and his holidays with them have turned his thoughts in another direction. One spring day as he helps his father to set eel traps, he wanders on to the land that has been raised from the sea bed:

He stayed in one spot for almost an hour, full of wonder at the small world around him. He ploughed fields with his fingertips, and used white pebbles as seeds to plant. He picked blades of grass and called them his first harvest. He watched the bees and knew they would help his garden to grow. He built a polder of his own by piling rocks around a puddle, and he drained the water away in canals he dug with a twig. From an old log he built a farm beside the field he had ploughed, and he put green beetles in the barn instead of cows. He made a world of his own on the land, and he was happy.

JAN OF HOLLAND, p. 59

A chance meeting with the burgomaster, who explains how the new polder land is apportioned, sets Jan on the path to agricultural college, with the idea of ultimately applying for a farm near his home.

So the two typically Dutch industries of fishing and agriculture are plausibly linked, and in family conferences and fireside chats the problems of controlling the sea, of preserving the best of the old and creating new spheres of work, of literally making new land for the most densely populated country in the world, are aired naturally in a way that should be understandable to a young reader. This is a far cry from the wooden shoes and baggy trousers description, yet nothing of the real Holland, the accepted Holland has been lost. This is especially clear in the photographs, for each generation of the de Vries differs slightly in dress, in physiognomy and in expression. Here are fishing boats and cupboard beds, a navigation lesson at school, the favourite tobacco pipe, the new pumping station and the locks on the great dyke. This *is* Holland –

Photograph by Peter Buckley from JAN OF HOLLAND (Chatto & Windus)

an aspect only but, because it is both vital and picturesque, one of the best to use in a book for children.

A dry analysis of the plan of this book hardly does justice to the author's power to create character. Certainly the members of his fictional family have been chosen to illustrate a thesis – the father who resents the blow to traditional fishing methods, the grandfather whose tug is employed on a dyke to enclose the Eastern Flevoland polder, old Adriaan who looks back to the earliest plans for the Ijsselmeer under Dr Lely and who has a wise grasp of the whole issue, the boy trying to understand every point of view, teased at school for deserting the fishing trade but holding firm to his ambition. Yet there is nothing mechanical about the way the characters are drawn.

Loaded conversation is not easy to write. JAN OF HOLLAND goes as far as a book of this kind can towards natural talk, so that our interest in the de Vries family is not inhibited by the necessary insertion of fact. Most striking of all is the passage where the author includes the vital point of information, the great Delta Plan, without losing anything of the affection between boy and old man or of the impending danger which quickens his narrative:

> "It is very late. You have eaten too many biscuits, and it is time for bed. You know now why the new land exists, and you know why many Urker men think that I am a strange de Vries fisherman because I love the new land and my country more than my small island. We must build, build for the future. The southern pincer of the sea still threatens in Zeeland. On a stormy night like this it could destroy us. Good night, Jan, good night."
>
> The wind whistled outside. Jan put his arms around Great-grandfather Adriaan's neck and hugged him. As Jan left, Adriaan picked up his Bible and started to read.
>
> Later on that same night, as Jan lay asleep, a message full of terror came over the radio. The sea had once more attacked. High spring tides and furious winds of hurricane force had swept down from the North Sea. In Zeeland the waves had broken through dykes as high as two-storey buildings. The greatest flood in five centuries attacked Zeeland on that night of January 31, 1953, as the sea tore at the heart of the country.
> ibid., p. 22

Excellent in its use of fact, its mood and character interest, this book has a welcome unity, for the author has used his own photographs and his neat plan really works. The last paragraph in the book shows Jan standing on a half-built dyke and looking out to sea. "Some day I'll live there . . . on the land, somewhere under those waves", he thinks; and the reader believes that he will.

JAN OF HOLLAND has something to offer the junior reader and the child of eleven-plus as well. The popular "We go" formula can also be used over a wide span of reading ages. A writer can have the best of two worlds by introducing English or American children into a foreign family. The visitors can plausibly ask questions about matters which the inhabitants take for granted and can expect sensible and accurate answers, and with a little contrivance the author can provide a junior tour as well. These considerable advantages may or may not outweigh the inherent artificiality of conversations and journeys designed ultimately to convey information. This is how it was sometimes done thirty years ago:

"It looks like a checkerboard, doesn't it, Dotty?"

"That's just what it looks like, Jimmy. The canals are very pretty, Mother. I just love those boats filled with vegetables and cheeses."

"It is pretty," said Jimmy. "I never saw such flat-bottomed boats, and I never saw boats painted in such bright colors. And don't the skins of those red cheeses shine, Mother?"

"The red skins shine because they are polished carefully."

"I guess that makes them sell better," cried Jimmy.

"So it does, my little business man," said Daddy!

Dorothy Gordon and John J. Loftus. KNOWING THE NETHER-LANDS, p. 17

This book is relentlessly domestic, and Dotty and Jimmy go home having seen cows, street markets, flowers and dykes but no art galleries, no factories, no shops and next to no people.

Children nowadays deserve more robust and sophisticated versions of the touring family. There are ways of avoiding the extreme artificiality of the informative conversation. The dullest reader might be expected to notice the absurdity of making a young

schoolboy on a visit to Holland comment like this while driving
over the Ijsselmeer dyke:

"What a marvellous achievement it has been to make a fertile
land emerge from an enormous bog! Those parts of the country-
side that have been reclaimed from the sea are called *polders*, and
this land has been turned into cornfields and fertile meadows
where sheep and cows may graze."
SALLY AND STEVE VISIT HOLLAND, p. 22

Steve owes his improbable narrative style to the ambiguity with
which the author is more or less obliged to let even her asides come
apparently from him. Besides, translation must take some of the
blame for the forced note in this book. SALLY AND STEVE VISIT
HOLLAND (1962) belongs to a series originating in Germany with
a text by Ilse Kleberger that is manifestly built round a set of
photographs – excellent and extremely natural – by Liselotte and
Armin Orgel-Köhne. For purposes of international publication,
Sally and her brother have been virtually de-nationalised and their
host counterparts in the various countries are like paper dolls
on which are hung, by folding tabs, the appropriate national
costumes.

By contrast, the young narrator of PETER GOES TO HOLLAND
(1969) certainly does not lack character. Indeed, I find this brash
Canadian lad altogether too natural in his idiom and too explicit
in his reactions:

"I have to tell you here that wine isn't all that great. Raspberry
juice is better. I drank my whole glass of wine anyhow, and it
made me feel silly-sneezy."
Ria Postma-Stolk. PETER GOES TO HOLLAND, p.86

All the same, the author has given a convincing account of a boy
visiting Holland, bringing his prejudices with him and discarding
some of them, sometimes bored, occasionally disappointed, usually
interested, describing his experiences in a jocular style which we
guess will be slightly toned down when he gets back to school and
gets his assignment scrapbook ready to show the Principal.

Moreover, the author has accepted that the children who read

her book will have eclectic tastes and that the Holland she knows
from inside is not precisely the Holland that shows herself to the
outside world or can be shown to exiles overseas. So here are
explanations of dyke-building and its past history, here are windmills and the cheese market and the tulip fields, but here also is
everyday life on a Friesland farm, legends that Dutch children hear
at bedtime, a Golden Wedding anniversary and a neat description
of the Variomatic car and, all through the book, constant cross-
reference between the attitude of a visitor, a Dutch reader overseas
and a Dutchwoman at home.

The broad interpretation of the travelogue formula in this book
is explained by the special circumstances of its publication. The
foreword explains:

> This book is published on the occasion of the tenth anniversary
> of "Wereldcontact", a Dutch association for families of immi-
> grants overseas. Wereldcontact tries to strengthen the ties
> between the old and the new world. Special lines are drawn to the
> cultural and educational fields in the countries in which Dutch
> immigrants have settled . . .
>
> The book PETER GOES TO HOLLAND describes the visit of a
> boy of Dutch origin to the old country. He discovers that country
> and the people in their way of life.

Although the manner of the narrative might not suit English
readers – at the very least they would find Peter rather odd – the
material in this book is exceptionally varied and interesting, and
the general feeling of relaxed attentiveness is unusual in this kind
of writing. A briefer and less informative pamphlet, CHILDREN
OF HOLLAND (1969), prepared by the New Zealand Department of
Education as a bulletin for schools, is notable in that the author,
Ingeborg Brown, has arranged facts in the framework of visits
within Holland, as Carla from Haarlem on the west coast goes to
stay with the Dijkstra cousins in Friesland and then entertains
Riemke in her own town. The interlocked stories are simple and
natural and give a good idea of what a child living in Holland today
might notice and what she might take for granted in her own
surroundings.

The travelogue needs some device that will give coherence to the random and not always interesting impressions which fictional young travellers gain from the lands they visit. Liesje van Someren treats the travel formula with unusual briskness and point. THE YOUNG TRAVELLER IN HOLLAND (1948) has two virtues still most desirable today. First, her central character, fourteen-year-old George, is on a *long* visit, to the family of Mr Jansen, his father's business friend. The book can therefore include a more than cursory look at Amsterdam, where the Jansens live, a motor tour in the south as a reward when Jan and Miep pass their exams, and a visit to Mr Jansen's family farm in Friesland. George has time to live in Holland as the Dutch do, reaching the stage when their domestic habits are no longer a surprise. His remarks are neither ignorant nor naïve, yet he still has plenty to find out and since Jan and Miep are fourteen and fifteen respectively, questions and answers can be pretty intelligent (though the book as a whole remains within top primary reading range).

Secondly, for part at least of the book the author has *grouped* her information round certain interesting events. For example, when Jantje the servant is married in Friesland, social custom is not merely described *in vacuo* but is seen in action and the author even tries to explain the uniquely Dutch rural custom of *Noaberschap*. Again, Holland in winter is seen actively; George is allowed to join a group of children who follow the entrants in the Eleven Towns race until their strength gives out.

Of course this is not pure narrative. The story serves as a repository for numerous facts. Still, there is a degree of selectiveness in the book and a leisurely pace which help to make the fiction of George's visit acceptable. It is especially noticeable that the author is balancing old with new so that the young reader is not merely looking at a tourist's Holland. When the party visits Utrecht and Jan tells George about St Michael's chapel and the famous bells, his father reminds him of Utrecht's importance as a railway junction, as a university town with a leading medical school and as a business and trade centre with a famous site for international commercial exhibitions. From time to time, also, the author lets her own feelings show through the words of her character; for instance, when they drive through Zeeland, Mrs Jansen tells George that the islands were deliberately flooded during the war as a move against the enemy:

"We shall soon be coming to a part where everything has been lost and instead of big trees you will see only saplings. If you had seen it just after the liberation, you would have felt you were travelling through the land of the dead," she added. "Nothing was living. The top of the dyke was the only bit of green on the island sand that indicated the water level of the inundated land."
THE YOUNG TRAVELLER IN HOLLAND, p. 83

If any book with the *We go* formula deserved to survive, it is this one, although events move so quickly that it is now in some respects out of date. It is far more useful than Liesje van Someren's later ANN AND PETER IN HOLLAND (1959), which belongs to *The Kennedys Abroad* series. Here is an interesting hybrid of junior tour and junior thriller. In each of the books about the Kennedys abroad, a mainly domestic impression of a country is formally incorporated in a mystery story. In ANN AND PETER IN HOLLAND, a brother and sister on a short visit to the Wassinks in a village near Rotterdam help to find lost jewels which will transform the lives of their troubled neighbours. The formula is not a very successful one. If the mystery plays the dominant part, information must be cut down. In this particular book, the fate of Lientje's father and the jewels is constantly interrupted by visits to the bulb fields, to an Indonesian restaurant, to Utrecht for bird-watching and to Amsterdam by canal. Vivacious though the writing is, the story is not arresting enough to stand on its own nor is the information wide enough in range to prolong the life of the book.

One other *We go* book does deserve perhaps a few more years on the library shelves – again, top primary for choice. Sylvia Corbridge's WE GO TO HOLLAND (1957) belongs to a series which has supplanted *The Kennedys Abroad* with its more flexible and generalised travel plots. Children ask questions, various people reply, including Father (who has been doing his homework). The fact that she is using a formula has not prevented the author of WE GO TO HOLLAND from choosing her material thoughtfully and arranging it with intelligence. Facts are grouped as they reflect major issues or institutions important to Holland, and for each group of facts she finds a suitable exponent. Han Boek, a bulb dealer of Amsterdam, saved Father's life at Arnhem: a chance meeting in London leads to a visit, and it is natural for Mr Boek to talk mainly of Holland's recovery from the effects of war. The children get into conversation at the airport with a business-man, van Hilton, who is able to take them on a trip; he naturally wants to show them factories and talk about housing. Mrs Boek's mother is devoted to the Royal Family and loves showing her collection of photographs and postcards; a woman from Zeeland is ready to describe the 1953 flood and talk about the Delta Plan; while Jo's collection of postcards and souvenirs usefully accounts for such typically Dutch institutions as the cheese market at Alkmaar or the Amsterdam canals. As formula books go, this is a reasonably good one, though it has no distinction of style and no strong personal feeling behind it. But do we need these story/fact hybrids?

To answer this we must ask what they are trying to do. Is their first objective to give a geography lesson, that is, to acquaint the young reader with "Holland" as with "the Norman Conquest" or "Winston Churchill", using Holland as a subject among others and not expecting pupil or home reader to be personally involved? Or are these fictional tours designed to fire a child with a desire to see the world for himself and to understand people of races other than his own; and, in the act of reading, to feel that he *is* in Holland?

We may still need books that can be thought over and reread for the purpose of learning (though they will have to be a great deal more interesting if they are to be reread). But if the true object of the junior tour is to be actively used, as a guide-book, perhaps the *We go* formula has had its day. A series of television programmes linked with pamphlets of photographs properly captioned would serve the purpose better than most books. Alternatively, the young reader might find what he needs better in fiction.

A story like Hilda van Stockum's KERSTI AND ST NICHOLAS will take a young child straight to Holland in imagination, and a reader as young as seven would quickly feel in sympathy with the brothers in THE SKATING RACE, a vivid tale of the Eleven Towns race by A. Rutgers van der Loeff. Hundreds of children in past generations entered Holland with Hans Brinker and now use Meindert De Jong as their passport and guide, through such books as THE WHEEL ON THE SCHOOL and FAR OUT THE LONG CANAL. In more serious vein, Margaretha Shemin's simple story, THE LITTLE RIDERS and the more mature tale by Leonard de Vries, THE LAND IS BRIGHT, describe the fortunes of ordinary folk in the Second World War A sympathy with the boys and girls in these stories will help a young reader to appreciate the innocent and honest introspection of the universally valid DIARY OF ANNE FRANK.

Books like these seem to be the natural opposites of the direct book of fact: travelogues must be very personal and vital to earn a place on a child's list of favourites. To take another subject, statistics and tables are needed to show Holland's problem of sea control as a whole, but for the young this is not as a rule the right dimension. For them it is best to relate facts and figures to individual persons and places, and this means a predominance of fiction. Reading stories of the Zeeland floods of 1953, for example, especially A. van Rhijn's THE TIDE IN THE ATTIC, children can really appreciate the dangers which made the huge dyke plan necessary even though it would disrupt so many lives. A Dutch writer who lived for many years in Zeeland, Gertie Evenhuis, discusses this second aspect of the problem by implication in a book called LOCKED HARBOR. A dyke is shortly to be completed across the harbour at Zelle. Fishing families must find another centre, and the children, understanding only their own limited aspect of the crisis, are inevitably hostile to the young son of the chief engineer when he appears at the local school. To see the perplexities of the adults through the children's eyes is to reach a working understanding of the situation.

Though nobody would suggest that information books must concentrate on Holland's struggles with the sea, it is probably the most dramatic aspect of the country for a middle-school reader, and two writers of information books have chosen to use this as their single subject. The child who is interested in people first and technicalities second may prefer, of the two, the American BATTLE AGAINST THE SEA by Patricia Lauber (1956), a striking treatment of the subject. Occasional purple passages do not blur the firm plan of the book. From an outline of geology (to explain Holland's coastline), and some discussion of early races in the Netherlands, the author traces Dutch plans to master the sea from the first prehistoric mounds in Friesland through the great floods of the Middle Ages and later engineering to the building of the Afluitsdyk and the aftermath of the 1953 flood. There is plenty of practical detail here, and in particular an excellent description of the building of a dyke, but the mood of the book is predominantly exciting and flood provides a natural climax:

> Dike after dike fell open, like doors smashed inward by a giant's hand.
> The greedy sea rushed through the doors, ripped at the sides of the breaches, and made the holes bigger and bigger.
> Roaring hungrily, the sea raced in, gobbling polder after polder. It swept over farmhouses, snatched up barns and threw them down again. On, on, it ran – through village streets, spreading into houses, sweeping up people, chairs, roofs, shutters and carrying them forward in its vicious race. In the darkness of night, 20-foot waves towered up and crashed down upon defenceless houses.
>
> BATTLE AGAINST THE SEA, p. 31–2

In a way this book is a compromise between stories like THE TIDE IN THE ATTIC and the expository school-book in which events are inevitably followed by reasons. For this particular subject the compromise seems a useful one.

But for the boy or girl of practical bent, Alan Jenkins' THE GOLDEN BAND (1967) is essential. The theme of the series entitled *The World we are Making* is man's conquest of his environment; other volumes concern the Snowy River dam, irrigation in the Indus Valley and so on. The sub-title of Alan Jenkins' book, "Holland's fight against the sea", speaks for itself. His title is taken from a medieval Dutch document which promises:

> ... that we Frisians shall establish and control a sea-fortress, a GOLDEN BAND that shall encircle all Friesland, in which each portion of dyke shall be the same as the next and against which the salt sea shall thrust both by day and by night.

Represented in this book are those parts of Holland directly affected by this "fight against the sea" – Rotterdam, Wieringen, Marken, the new polders which may eventually become a twelfth province of Holland. But the author does not interpret his brief too narrowly. Reclamation of land is as important as defence against water, and the reader needs to know *why*. Loss of colonies, population increase, urbanisation – all these aspects are as thoroughly dealt with in the book as the new dykes, the Delta Plan, the engineering methods used. The precise, detailed account of how a dyke is built may be just what is needed to encourage boys of middle school age to take an interest in something outside their own experience. This is a very clear-headed book, its points economically made. Here, for example, is a paragraph which starts with a reference to Holland in the seventeenth century:

The tiny Netherlands, with a population then of about one million, began the process of founding an empire seventy times its own size. But empires and colonies are notoriously difficult to retain, as everyone from the Romans to the British has discovered. In the course of time the Dutch empire overseas melted away. The most enduring and rewarding colonization the Dutch

Brushwood mattresses and rubber ballast reinforcing underwater foundations of the Ysselmeer dyke. Photograph from THE GOLDEN BAND (Methuen), by courtesy of the Royal Netherlands Embassy.

eventually achieved was carried out at home. They set about colonizing the sea that had caused them so much trouble.
THE GOLDEN BAND, pp. 35–6

From the literary point of view, THE GOLDEN BAND seems to me superior to any other book I have found for the reader of ten upwards – better written, better organised and in particular with that occasional quirkiness of style that shows an individual is writing and not a computer. A search for books of more general scope for this age is not encouraging. In the main they are introductory studies, covering a variety of subjects without detail or depth, having regard to the supposed limits of a child's staying power at ten or so. It is perhaps unjust to complain that they are snippety, since they are in fact aiming to give snippets on many subjects; but it is reasonable to wish for better writing, better arrangement of material and far, far more personality.

The most recent of these junior study books, Anna Loman's LOOKING AT HOLLAND (1966), is immediately attractive for its agreeably spacious layout and admirable pictures. The clue to the book lies in the series title, *Looking at Other Countries*. Here is, in fact, another tour in disguise – a tour in which we stay briefly at a few of the principal cities, watch the progress of a dyke, look inside a prosperous Dutch home, see Queen Juliana accepting flowers on her birthday. The book (by a Dutchwoman) gives a fair picture so long as one accepts that it is a picture for the outside world and necessarily generalised. There are no rough edges – no poverty, no price lists, little suggestion of the difficulties of living in a crowded country, no hint that invariable neatness and meticulous state organisation may produce neurosis as well as satisfaction.

Are such depths suitable for the middle school years? I would suggest that when a child has reached the age of twelve he may be expected to *hear* exceptions, doubts and complexities, even if he cannot fully understand them. On another level it can be said that the invariable note of approval in such books (symbolised by the persistent sunshine in photographs) offers little that is stimulating. LOOKING AT HOLLAND is visually most attractive. The photographs are interesting, well chosen and exactly placed in relation to the text; indeed, the design of the book is really an expansion of the collection of captioned photographs.

Attractive, yes; comprehensible, certainly; provocative, no. No more so is Angelo Cohn's THE FIRST BOOK OF THE NETHERLANDS (1962). This is a less decorative volume, illustrated mainly by black and white photographs and serious in intention. It offers the usual rapid survey of a number of aspects of Holland, and a glance at the chapter headings suggests that the author is trying to introduce contemporary Holland – headings like "Steel at the seashore", "Scientific fisherman", "Old and new houses", for instance. But again the book is disappointing in its total lack of impact. The first page or two raise the hope of a strong theme, for the author defines Holland as a watery country and offers a clear analysis of the Delta Plan as engineers and as ordinary folk might see it. But the theme is quickly lost as town succeeds town and subject subject; the book becomes dippable rather than authoritative.

Nowhere is the lack of purpose more obvious in these two books than in their treatment of Dutch history. History is not just a series of facts, and the history of another country, for which the reader lacks familiar associations, is hard to enjoy if it has no guide-lines. Surely it is less important for a boy or girl to learn who William of Orange was or what he did than to learn how his actions are related to modern Holland. Why are the Dutch what they are? What have they made of their environment and what has it made of them? Such questions are neither implied nor answered in these junior books, and the rapid sequence of dates, battles and reigns is not likely to make much impression on the memory. Will this matter? Not in so far as we do not expect children to use such books primarily for learning facts. What matters is that they are not likely to be interested as they read, and so it is hardly worth the effort of reading. For younger children it would be possible to make history interesting by using that unique model town Madurodam, with its replicas of houses, railways and streets, as the basis of a fantasy which could bring some of the principal events of Dutch history to life. But for older readers there must be a real connection between past and present, made in a way neither too didactic nor too impersonal. A. J. Barnouw's HOLLAND AND HER PEOPLE (1961), belonging to the American *Portraits of the Nations* series, fulfils these conditions at least in part.

This book has the virtue of confidence. I do not imagine that every Dutchman would agree with the author's generalisations, yet he would be grateful for generalisations made with such sense and strength. Here is a man who can see the way the country works and can explain his chosen details in terms of politics or engineering or national psychology. There is nothing scrappy about his book. He does not jump from a paragraph on food to another on costume, but uses detail in an orderly way. Moreover, he sees Holland not as a closed community but as part of the world. His discussion of the loss of Indonesia or of the increase in Holland's industries in the past twenty years asks for intelligent reading:

> These country people are not bumpkins. They receive good schooling and are acquainted with city ways and manners. No rural district is very far from a town. Great distances do not exist in little Holland, so each urban centre radiates its light of culture on its environs. As a result there is little that distinguishes the townsman from the countryman. They wear similar clothes and furnish their homes with unimaginative similarity. Television has entered most farmhouses nowadays, the four stations available in Holland, Belgium and Germany being widely used.
> HOLLAND AND HER PEOPLE, p. 15

There is enthusiasm in the book, and humour too. The comment on one cliché about Holland should be especially appreciated:

> Hollanders have nothing but ridicule and contempt for what they call the silly story of the little Haarlem boy who stopped a leak in the dyke with his finger. Unwieldy bags of sand, each much heavier than that little fellow, are the only protection on which the Dutch farmers rely for stopping a breach in the dyke.
> ibid., p. 29

If the purpose of reading a book about Holland is still, at middle school level, primarily to achieve some understanding of Holland, then Barnouw's book has a great deal to commend it. It might be balanced by Liesje van Someren's HOLLAND (1962) which gives a more lively and individual view. Within the framework of a tour, starting in Friesland, the author introduces many towns, describes villages, landscapes, with the intention of defining the nature of each province and describing, too, the people as they live in it, whether they are retreating into their past in Schaphorst or meeting a cosmopolitan world in Rotterdam. With its lively historic present, this is in a sense a guide-book but a very personal one. National pride has been sharpened by the war years to an acute observation. On the way to Friesland, by the Wieringermeer polder, the author pauses for comment:

I can remember the time when all this was nothing but water. This part of the Zuiderzee was drained in the later 'twenties and early 'thirties, and immediately put under cultivation. During the last war it was flooded by the Germans, and for a while reverted to its former Zuiderzee self. After the war it was again drained and re-cultivated. Whenever I travel through here I like to remember the millions of worms and birds which had to be imported to help refertilise the soil.

HOLLAND, p. 25

Deeply concerned with the past, she relates it to the present enough to be able to explain in terms a young person could understand the essential feel of each province. Here is a paragraph describing the northern province of Giethorn:

People have lived in the Giethorn area since the early Middle Ages, when, for reasons of their own, they left Northern Italy and wandered for years through Switzerland, Germany and Holland. Nobody wanted them except the Dutch, who, even in those days, did not wish to turn refugees away. The then Count of Holland presented them with a stretch of land – in an isolated part of the country, admittedly, but much better than nothing. The wanderers settled, and their descendants have stayed ever since, earning their livelihood in their adopted country. As they were isolated for so many centuries, their habits and customs have been preserved. One of these characteristics is "noborschap" (neighbourliness), which is particularly notable three times in a person's career – at birth, marriage and death. On these important occasions the neighbours take over responsibility from the next-of-kin. The custom survives not only in Giethorn, but also in many parts of Eastern Holland.

ibid., pp. 52–3

Well handled, the travelogue can give an impression of immediacy, and a relaxed style and an easy pace, such as one finds in this book, go a long way to building deeper associations with the word "Holland" than any child may originally have taken from first books. With something of the verve of a television programme, Liesje van Someren's HOLLAND also allows that time for reflection, for checking and rereading, which books alone can provide.

What books do not provide, for the 'teens, is a frank appraisal of social anomalies (overcrowding, for instance, or the acknowledged permissiveness of Amsterdam in its role as an international city). In general, the protective attitude assumed by anyone who writes specifically for the young leads to an ever-increasing gap between "the news" which they find in the mass media (and which is not *necessarily* distorted) and the descriptions of places and peoples offered to them in books. What is the solution? Not all boys and girls in the early 'teens are ready for adult books and yet the world they live in makes it necessary that they should be ready to exercise a sense of proportion on unpleasant or challenging aspects of that world. If books are still going to be couched in special terms for the 13–15 reader, they must be conceived in bolder, broader and more honest terms than they are at present.

Reading List

Barnouw, Adriaan J. HOLLAND AND HER PEOPLE. Portraits of the Nations.
(*Lippincott* 1961 as THE LAND AND PEOPLE OF HOLLAND) *Lutterworth* 1963. Illustrated by photographs.

Battersby, C. QUEER QUAINT HOLLAND. Aylesbury, *Fred K. Samuels Printing Works* 1909. With photographs, maps and reproductions.

Boehm, Lincoln A. HOLLAND IN PICTURES. Visual Geography series.
(*Sterling* 1963) *Oak Tree Press* 1963. Illustrated with photographs in colour. The text is directed at adult readers, but informative captions should help the young reader to enjoy an unusually varied collection of pictures.

Brown, Ingeborg. CHILDREN OF HOLLAND. Wellington, *New Zealand Department of Education* 1969. Photographs by Ans Westra.

Buckley, Peter. JAN OF HOLLAND. Around the world today. (*Franklin Watts* 1956) *Chatto and Windus* 1959. Photographs by the author.

14

HOLLANDER.

HOLLAND, formerly called the United Province and now united into a kingdom called the Netherlands, consists of seven provinces, which are exceedingly well peopled, and make a considerable figure among the commercial nations of Europe.

The Hollanders are distinguished from other nations by their peculiar cleanliness, industry, and economy.

The whole of the United Provinces was formerly a swampy, marshy tract of uninhabitable land; but by industry and perseverance, the face of the country is entirely changed, and well-built towns, intersected with canals, and populous villages, are seen in every direction. Their houses and buildings are mostly erected on piles of wood driven deep into the earth.

15

The Dutch people are peculiarly excellent skaters. In the winter season, which in Holland is particularly severe, their canals, and even the entrances of their harbours, are frozen over, and covered with people skating in all directions; some with large burdens on their heads, some with the goods which they are taking to or from market, and even women with little childen in their arms, or fastened to their backs, are seen darting forward with the rapidity of lightning.

VENETIAN.

VENICE is a beautiful and fruitful country, the fields abounding with vineyards and plantations of mulberries. Venice, the capital, is seated upon seventy islands, communicating with each other by canals, and by bridges of a particularly light and tasteful make.

Spread from A PEEP AT THE VARIOUS NATIONS OF THE WORLD (*c.* 1825), by courtesy of the General Research and Humanities Division, the New York Public Library, Astor, Lenox and Tilden Foundations.

Capek, Karel. LETTERS FROM HOLLAND. Translated by Paul Silver. *Faber* 1933.

Carew, Dorothy. THE NETHERLANDS. Nations today. (*Macmillan* 1965 U.S.A.) *Collier-Macmillan* 1966 U.K. With photographs, maps and portraits. Written in a deliberate, cool style, for readers from twelve or so, this book is notable for its description of the Randstad and the dangers of conurbation, and for its account of the Dutch colonies from the beginning.

Cohn, Angelo. THE FIRST BOOK OF THE NETHERLANDS. First Books. (*Franklin Watts* 1962) *Edmund Ward* 1963. Illustrated by photographs.

Corbridge, Sylvia L. WE GO TO HOLLAND. We go to . . . *Harrap* 1957. Illustrated by photographs.

Dark, Irene. HOLLAND. World Dolls. *Pergamon Press* 1964. Illustrated by the author.

Gale, Donald H. NETHERLANDS. All Over the World (assignment cards).
    Blond Educational 1968.

Gordon, Dorothy and Loftus, John J. KNOWING THE NETHERLANDS.
    Appleton Century-American Book Co. 1940. Illustrated by Veronica Reed.

Howard, Susan. MY HOME IN HOLLAND. My Home. Longmans, Green 1961.
    Illustrated by the author.

Irwin, Theodore. LET'S TRAVEL IN HOLLAND (Childrens Press 1964)
    Odhams Press 1965. Illustrated by photographs.

James, H. C. CHILDREN OF THE BARGES. This is our Country. Hutchinson 1959.
    Photographs in colour by Lex van der Pol.

Jenkins, Alan C. THE GOLDEN BAND: HOLLAND'S FIGHT AGAINST THE SEA.
    The World we are Making. (Methuen 1967) Coward-McCann 1968. Illustrated
    by photographs, maps and diagrams.

Jungman, Beatrice. HOLLAND. Peeps at Many Lands. First published 1904,
    A. and C. Black 1926. Paintings by Nico Jungman.

Kelk, C. J. THIS IS HOLLAND. Photograph Books of the World. Oxford,
    Bruno Cassirer 1953. Photographs by Cas Oorthuys. Excellent photographs
    arranged to give an idea of the nature of the different provinces in the
    Netherlands.

Kleberger, Ilse. SALLY AND STEVE VISIT HOLLAND. Sally and Steve Books.
    (Germany 1962) Angus and Robertson 1967. Photographs by L. and A. Orgel-
    Köhne.

Lauber, Patricia. BATTLE AGAINST THE SEA: THE CHALLENGE OF THE DUTCH
    AND THE DIKES. Challenge Books. (Coward-McCann 1956) Chatto and Windus
    1963. Illustrated by photographs.

Lindgren, Astrid. DIRK LIVES IN HOLLAND. Children Everywhere. (Stockholm
    1963) Methuen 1963. Photographs by Anna Riwkin-Brick.

Loman, Anna. LOOKING AT HOLLAND. Looking at Other Countries. (Lippincott
    1966) A. and C. Black 1966. Illustrated by photographs in colour and black and
    white.

Pilkington, Roger. SMALL BOAT THROUGH HOLLAND (Macmillan 1958)
    St Martins 1959. Illustrated by David Knight. A light-hearted but sensible
    travelogue; the author has a sharp eye for the odd and the dramatic, and can
    slip into the past without being boring. He could give readers in the 'teens a
    broad but reliable impression of Holland seen from her waterways.

Postma-Stolk, Ria. PETER GOES TO HOLLAND. Translated by Janet Telders-Paton.
    Wereldcontact 1969. Illustrated by Willem de Groot.

van Someren, Liesje. THE YOUNG TRAVELLER IN HOLLAND. Young Traveller
    series. Phoenix 1948. With photographs and a map.

van Someren, Liesje. ANN AND PETER IN HOLLAND. The Kennedys Abroad. *Harrap* 1959. Illustrated by Harry Toothill.

van Someren, Liesje. HOLLAND. Young Enthusiast Library, Young Explorer series. *Weidenfeld and Nicolson* 1962. Illustrated by Don Roberts.

van Someren, Liesje. UMPIRE TO THE NATIONS: HUGO GROTIUS. People from the Past. *Dobson* 1965. With photographs and prints. In this story-biography the author relates the life and achievements of the founder of international law regarding war and territorial matters to the status and duties of U.N.O. in our own time.

Vann, E. M. and C. R. THE DUTCH BOY. Children of Many Lands. *Taylor's Foreign Press* 1952, *Pitman* 1953 for *Valentine, Mitchell*.

Williams, L. S. ROBIN AND JEAN IN THE NETHERLANDS: A COLOURSLIDE TOUR OF HOLLAND. *Appleton-Century* 1939. Drawings by Sue Runyon, and some photographs.

Relevant novels and stories

De Jong, Meindert. THE WHEEL ON THE SCHOOL (*Harper & Row* 1954) *Lutterworth* 1957, illustrated by Maurice Sendak. FAR OUT THE LONG CANAL (*Harper & Row* 1964) *Lutterworth* 1965, illustrated by Nancy Grossman.

Dodge, Mary Mapes. HANS BRINKER or THE SILVER SKATES (*Scribner* 1915) *Dent*, Children's Illustrated Classics 1955. Illustrated by Hans Baumhauer.

Evenhuis, Gertie. LOCKED HARBOR (Holland 1962) *Collier-Macmillan* 1967. Translated by Eva Richter. A domestic tale showing the difficult adjustment between the fishermen and inhabitants of Zelle when a dyke has to be built across the water.

Frank, Anne. THE DIARY OF ANNE FRANK (Holland 1947. *Vallentine, Mitchell* 1952) *Doubleday* 1952.

Freeling, Nicolas. LOVE IN AMSTERDAM *Gollancz* 1962, BECAUSE OF THE CATS (*Gollancz* 1963) *Harper & Row* 1963, GUN BEFORE BUTTER *Gollancz* 1963, DOUBLE BARREL (*Gollancz* 1964) *Harper & Row* 1965, CRIMINAL CONVERSATIONS (*Gollancz* 1965) *Harper & Row* 1966, THE DRESDEN GREEN (*Gollancz* 1966) *Harper & Row* 1967, KING OF THE RAINY COUNTRY (*Harper & Row* 1965) *Gollancz* 1966, STRIKE OUT WHERE NOT APPLICABLE *Gollancz* 1967, TSINGBOUM (*Hamish Hamilton* 1969) *Harper & Row* 1969. These superlative detective stories give an undogmatic but authentic view of social structures and regional characteristics of Amsterdam and its suburbs, the Dutch-Belgian border, the seaside town on the North Sea, the bulb country and the northern province of Drenthe.

van der Loeff, A. Rutgers. THE SKATING RACE. Great Day stories. (*Abelard-Schuman* 1965 U.S.A.) *Abelard-Schuman* 1965 U.K. Translated by Henrietta Anthony. Illustrated by Robert Nix.

Knight, Captain Frank. UP, SEA BEGGARS! *Macdonald* 1964. A rousing tale of Holland's resistance to the power of Spain in the sixteenth century.

Perkins, Lucy Fitch. THE DUTCH TWINS. Twins series. (*Houghton Mifflin* 1911) *Cape* 1928. Illustrated by the author.

van Rhijn, A. THE TIDE IN THE ATTIC (Holland 1959. *Methuen* 1961) *Hale* 1962. Translated by A. J. Pomerans. Illustrated by Margery Gill.

Shemin, Margaretha. THE LITTLE RIDERS (*Coward-McCann* 1963) *Hamish Hamilton* Reindeer Books 1964. Illustrated by Janet Duchesne.

van Stockum, Hilda. KERSTI AND ST NICHOLAS. (*Viking* 1940) *Muller* 1949. Illustrated by the author.

de Vries, Leonard. THE LAND IS BRIGHT. *Dobson* 1964. Translated by Lawrence Wolfe.

2d | Honeybees

"They work so much more than they need – they make so much more than they can eat – they are so incessantly boring and buzzing at their one idea till Death comes upon them – that don't you think they overdo it? And are human labourers to have no holidays, because of the bees? And am I never to have a change of air, because the bees don't? Mr. Boffin, I think honey excellent at breakfast; but, regarded in the light of my conventional schoolmaster and moralist, I protest against the tyrannical humbug of your friend the bee."
Charles Dickens. OUR MUTUAL FRIEND

2d | Honeybees

AN epigraph should give some indication of the theme of the ensuing text. This section will be chiefly concerned with the anthropomorphism which colours books for the young about honeybees. Modern studies in animal behaviour have made it necessary for any writer of animal books, whether pure fiction, pure fact or a mixture of both, to reconcile a scientific attitude with expediency. This general difficulty is present whatever the subject, but it is peculiarly complicated in the case of social insects because, with the possible exception of those domestic animals closest to man, the horse, dog and cat, they most obviously invite comparison with humans. The pattern of their intricate and easily observed communities seems at time to differ from our own only in that they have achieved a consistent perfection which our human temperament prevents us from reaching. Ever since the first man realised that honey was sweet and a sting sharp, the bee has been envied and admired, in human terms. And since the bee produces a useful commodity, men have usually agreed to overlook its aggressive instincts. The busy bee is held up as a model: the ant, no more savage in defending its citadel, is a recognised symbol of tyranny.

The light-hearted remarks of Dickens' young lawyer are of course only the obverse side of the coin that shows the "little busy bee" of the Victorian versifiers. To most of us, one way or another, the bee "works" as we do. We think of it anthropomorphically. Is this wrong? If so, is it always wrong?

To a child of four or five, with a brand new vocabulary in a brand new world, animals are extensions of himself, to be teased and talked to as friends. It could be argued that to give him a picture-book showing an insect cooking or nursing a baby is to establish a scientific fallacy in his mind, but it would surely be pompous to press this point of view. Such personification seems as harmless as giving the sun a face or illustrating a dish running away with a spoon. These are all images which the child will store away. They will not be superseded by such facts as he may acquire later. They will become alternatives, remembered through fantasy, even becoming the raw material for poetry.

One of the most beautiful picture-books in recent years, Colette Portal's THE LIFE OF A QUEEN (1962)*, shows enemy ants lighting watch-fires outside a citadel while inside the defenders sit on bar-stools sipping nectar. The exquisite line and colour wash takes away any trace of silliness, and the details are strictly accurate though they are represented fancifully. The image of the queen tending her baby or the soldiers preparing for war need cause no confusion when a young reader later comes upon a factual account of life in an anthill; on the contrary, the general ideas suggested by this book should help him to accept scientific fact.

This young French artist has produced, with Franklin Russell, another distinguished picture-book, THE HONEYBEES (1967), in which the fantasy of her ant tale has been put aside in favour of a serenely poetic delineation of actual colour and shape. The information in the text is direct, simple and introductory. A child might respond better to the mood of the book if a parent used it as a conversation-with-pictures, for the artist calls on the sense of wonder in her rendering of bees flying, hatching, fanning, fighting. While she is never inaccurate, she does not set out to give children precise outlined shapes to teach them, but to create an impression of beauty for a young child who can be told additional facts or for one who already knows something about bees but may be grateful to reach a new vision of them. Cecilia Levandowska's picture-book, THE WORLD OF THE BEE (1959) similarly combines simple fact and artistic interpretation.

Certainly no fantasy can dispense with accuracy. The French cartoon transmitted on B.B.C.'s television programme as "The adventures of Joe" (from 15 August 1967, in twelve episodes) showed a small boy, diminished by magic, enjoying a prolonged

*The first English adaptation by Marcia Nardi was published by Cape in 1965. Marion Koenig's text for Blackie's 1969 edition is a direct translation of the original German book; it is less fanciful and more in tune with modern needs than that of the earlier edition.

visit to a hive. The lively scenes never transgressed basic truth, however fanciful the details might be. When Joe went with his guide to gather honey, each of them carried a wicker basket, an amusing (and often-used) extension of the bee's pollen basket, the special formation of its hind legs. The queen of the hive had the face of a caricatured beauty queen, the soldiers carried pantomime spears. But imagery and fact did not conflict.

Iliane Roels' picture-book THE BEE (1968), in a series *Animals at Home*, employs a less grotesque humanisation in picture and text. We see a young bee in a muslin-curtained bassinette, workers wearing aprons and carrying the tools of their special trade, a bee communicating her discovery of pollen by using a blackboard map, a soldier with kepi and spear, a queen crowned. The illustrations are delicately pretty, but however attractive they might be to a small child, they could be misleading if he were given the book without a word of advice. For instance, the picture of the bee with her blackboard and pointer has an accompanying sentence, "she dances, beats her wings and waggles her feelers", which describes the actual physical actions of a bee but not what the child sees going on in the picture. It is not easy to relate a factual text and fantastic pictures, and this particular book certainly needs an interpreter. We could contrast it with Beatrix Potter's description of the bee's invasion of Mrs Tittlemouse's burrow, where habitat and behaviour are true to life in text and illustration.

However often bees are humanised in books for the young, it is seldom that we find them used nowadays as a symbol. One exception, BENWIG THE BEE by M. K. Richardson (1968), belongs to a series of stories written for Roman Catholic primary schools, linking an animal and a saint with humour and humanity. Benwig, the Welsh bumble-bee, enjoys the garden which Saint Domnoc, visiting from Ireland, has made out of waste land for his friend Taffy, or Saint David. Soon honeybees are drawn by the smell of the flowers and Queen Blodenwedd, or Flowerface, comes with her swarm to set up house:

> Domnoc found an old skip lying about and set it up on a little wooden table, and Blodenwedd the Queen moved in with Bronwen and Bwlch and Bran and Bedwyr and all the other drones who did no work. And they set about making honeycombs in

the skip, and filling them with golden dripping honey. Some time after, Domnoc made them a proper wooden hive with a thatched roof because he liked seeing them all happy and buzzing about, but he didn't make a hive for Benwig the Bumble Bee because he knew that he preferred to live in his hole in the ground. But he planted some of his gayest flowers near the hole and a long row of sweet smelling mignonette beside it.

BENWIG THE BEE, no page numbers

The saint's kindness has its reward. The bees cannot let their friend go, and they swarm in his boat for the return journey to Ireland. Open piety and enjoyment of nature light up the story and its basis of fact.

Through careful humanising, small children can absorb general ideas about social insects – that they attack and defend, that they live in a group with a dominant head. Quite early in their lives they can be introduced to the idea that animal behaviour is not necessarily like human behaviour. We have to make the transition from Mrs Bee and her babies to the role of the queen bee in the hive; to show that when we compare the organisation of the hive to a human community, we do this as a convenience, as a metaphor in which the similarity has no reality in terms of the drives and physical changes that govern a hive. "How doth the little busy bee" can have a story-book validity for a child at the same time as the realisation of what "busy" means in terms of bee life. The most difficult task facing the writer for readers between seven and nine is to explain scientific fact so that it takes the child a step further from fantasy without destroying that fantasy, so that the transition is no more noticeable than the change from BEAUTY AND THE BEAST as a story to the fairy-tale as a parable of human nature. As children move from picture-books to topic books, the problem of tactful humanisation becomes greater if two attitudes – the factual and the fantastic – are mixed. At this stage, when a child is reaching out for information, a glass-fronted hive can tell him a great deal, or a neighbour who keeps bees, or simply a sharp eye kept on the garden in summer. Even so, books are needed.

Bees in a hive can be observed – but in motion. Bee-watching is a good deal less easy than bird-watching, to say the least, although simple versions of experiments with sugar-water and coloured paper can be conducted by juniors. But for the life-cycle, evolution, behaviour and structure of the bee a book is indispensable, with a mixture of text and illustration in suitable proportion. It is possible to describe to a child in words alone the process of swarming or the mating flight or the fanning with which bees ventilate the hive. Any of these processes involve concepts which he already has in mind, and although pictures can usefully emphasise a point, they are not essential. On the other hand it is extremely difficult and probably unwise to try to explain the bee dance or cell-building without illustration.

To understand the bee's structure properly, a child needs visual and verbal fact carefully allied. A book suitable for really young readers, Judy Hawes' WATCH HONEYBEES WITH ME (1964), has a full-page picture of a bee much enlarged and framed in a magnifying glass. This is offered as a demonstration model. It is not a diagram, no special points are marked, but they are referred to in the text quoted below and are easy to find:

> We look at the bees through a magnifying glass. We see that a bee has six legs. We can see the sting and the tongue. We also see the fuzz that the pollen sticks to. We can see the pollen comb and the pollen baskets. We can see the wings and long feelers. I found out that bees have five eyes, two large eyes and three small eyes. You can count them in the picture.
>
> Here is a picture my uncle showed me of the head of a bee. You can see the tongue even better. You can see the eyes and the feelers better too.
>
> WATCH HONEYBEES WITH ME, no page numbers

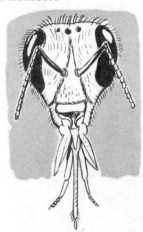

The "picture my uncle showed me of the head of a bee" shows how closely text and illustration can be allied; in this case neither would be complete or clear without the other. This is one of many drawings by Helen Stone in WATCH HONEYBEES WITH ME (A & C Black).

The last sentence of this passage raises points which need the support of a diagram: an inset picture provides this. This book has been designed with a clear idea not only of what facts are needed, but also what type of presentation will suit each fact or group of facts. Topic books often fail for lack of good designing, and one element of good design is surely flexibility. To rely on a single style of illustration can lead to wasted chances. Even the colours of this book – golden-yellow and green – have been carefully chosen to suit the subject. The American series *Let's-Read-and-Find-out-Science Books*, to which it belongs, is lively in approach and most of the examples are ingenious in the arrangement of fact. WATCH HONEY-BEES WITH ME implies a question – Where do we find find bees? – and offers an answer – on flowers. This is essentially an observation book, with a domestic note. The bee is primarily a source of honey for tea. In the first picture a small girl watches bees on flowers. She introduces herself as a "bee-watcher" and her uncle explains what she sees in easy conversation. "Honey is the best thing I know about bees" is a final sentence which young readers will endorse.

As a transition between picture-books and junior topic books, two recent collections of photographs illustrate the importance of relating text to illustration. Virgil Foster's CLOSE-UP OF A HONEY BEE (1962) and Harold Doering's A BEE IS BORN (1962) are not specifically for juniors, but they can be useful as picture-books because they bring bees, as it were, to perform for the reader. Problems of observation vanish in these two sequences of photographs: problems of anthropomorphism do not exist. Or should not. Unfortunately the texts hardly match the high standard of the photographs. Virgil Foster seems deliberately to set himself to avoid any sign of seriousness, and any adult who uses his book to help a child will be well advised to paraphrase. Harold Doering makes his simple prose restless with exclamations: his is the "wonderful" approach. But his material is excellent and his close-up photographs of the birth of a bee in all its stages are so precise and numerous that one can almost dispense with his text.

All the same, there is a text in his book, and although it is accurate and informative, it takes that jocular view of nature which adults so often mistakenly suppose is necessary in a book for the young. We may perhaps accept that such chapter-titles as "Bricklayers and construction workers" and "Guard-duty" are baits to catch readers, but "The drones – playboys of the bee world" seems excessive. The final tug between anthropomorphism and straight fact in this book may be seen in the caption for a particularly good photograph, which reads "With the vanity of a playboy, the drone poses for his picture. Notice the thick fur, as well as the large eyes. Drones are considerably larger than the female workers."

Let us consider the drones, whose fate the naturalist parson J. G. Wood saw, more than a century ago, as "an everlasting homily, presented by nature in dogmatical but most effective fashion, of the uselessness of all who labour not for their living." The names given to the various types of bees in a hive – queen, worker, drone – all carry human associations and imply value-judgment, but none more than the name of drone. Maeterlinck knew very well why the male drones did no routine work in the hive and solicited food from the workers; yet, observing bees romantically through their likeness to man, he could write like this in a chapter headed "The massacre of the males":

> If skies remain clear, the air warm, and pollen and nectar abound in the flowers, the workers, through a kind of forgetful indulgence, or over-scrupulous prudence perhaps, will for a short time longer endure the importunate, disastrous presence of the males. These comport themselves in the hive as did Penelope's suitors in the house of Ulysses. Indelicate and wasteful, sleek and corpulent, fully content with their idle existence as honorary lovers, they feast and carouse, throng the alleys, obstruct the passages, and hinder the work; jostling and jostled, fatuously pompous, swelled with foolish, good-natured contempt; harbouring never a suspicion of the deep and calculating scorn wherewith the workers regard them, of the constantly growing hatred to which they give rise, or of the destiny that awaits them.
> THE LIFE OF THE BEE, 1908 edition, pp. 285–6

Even if we can excuse some of Maeterlinck's imprecision because of his date, from the literary point of view his style is out of key with modern taste. Nor can his sensational description of the drones be dismissed as of historical interest when we can find just such a style in a book of 1947. The beekeeper John Crompton allows

himself a surprising degree of anthropomorphic comment in his
semi-autobiographical book for the general reader, THE HIVE.
Describing the functional evolution of worker, queen and drone,
he expatiates on the drone:

> The daughters were amorous. The splendour of the males
> fascinated them, and like other females they took pride and joy
> in tending their lovers. They cared for them and even fed them,
> and soon the lordly male took this as his right. It was degrading
> for such as he – he came to think – to bother to get nectar from
> flowers at all. It was a troublesome business. Let the "women"
> do it. Little did he realise that in this he paved the way for his
> own downfall.
>
> THE HIVE, p. 24

If the theory is intended to be expressed in humorous terms, it still
makes nonsense of the idea of evolution.

What harm does it do to call the drone "lazy" in books for the
young? The word is sanctioned by the dictionary in this transferred
meaning. It is unreasonable to suggest that topic books must avoid
all suggestion of humanising. But – "lazy"? The implication of the
word is obviously misleading and therefore dangerous. The writer
who calls a drone lazy without qualification on one page and offers
facts about its function as mate for the queen far later in his book
is relying too much on the young reader's power to remember two
widely separated facts and relate them to one another. An adult
can often do without every step in an argument: for a child, the
links between ideas must be present and in the right order. The
writer who says "the drone does not work" and *immediately* explains
the reason, even if he does not go into scientific detail about the
reproductive cycle of the bee, is making sure that the child will find
no barrier to understanding this later because of storing up a false
assumption.

The one fact which must not be omitted is that the drone has a
place in the reproductive cycle: yet many writers make no mention
of the fertilisation of the queen. In WATCH HONEYBEES WITH ME,
after a brief list of the duties of the worker bee, Judy Hawes explains
briefly that the queen "lays all the eggs in the hive" and then
continues:

We saw the big lazy male bees too. They are called drones. They
don't do any work at all. They don't even feed themselves. We saw
some drones being fed honey by the workers. Other drones were
sleeping and some were flying near us. Drones can't hurt you.
They have no sting.

WATCH HONEYBEES WITH ME, no page numbers

There is a floating inaccuracy here because the author has missed
the opportunity to explain the function of the drones. W. Sinclair
in THE LIFE OF THE HONEY BEE (1969), an excellent book in the
Ladybird Natural History series, explains "Drones are the true
males, a few of which will be the queen's wedding partners."* In
Mary Adrian's HONEYBEE TELLS HONEYBEE (1952), fiction is
tactfully used in a description of the mating of "the young golden
Queen" and a drone, the physical process being completely
clear.

The most lucid and sensible explanation of the function of drones
in the hive is to be found in a book likely to have as large and varied
a readership as any book on the market. THE HOW AND WHY
WONDER BOOK OF ANTS AND BEES by Ronald Rood (1962) belongs
to a soft-covered series designed to be collected into folders to
form an encyclopedia. For this reason the author has to cover
a good deal of ground in relatively few words. Reasonably informative illustrations with full captions allow extra space for detail and
specialist editing has made the book reliable for reference purposes.
In his remarks on drones the author acknowledges the current
misconception – "How strange to see this kind of bee in a bustling
hive where all the others are working!"† Then he provides the
necessary qualification:

Yet this bee has a job, too. It is one of the most important of the
bees. It is a drone, or male bee, one of a few dozen brothers
among the thousands of worker sisters. Its job will begin when
that peanut-shaped queen cell has opened and the new queen
has made her way into the world. For it must provide millions
of tiny sperm cells that the queen bee stores in a special pouch
in her body. Then, just before she places new eggs in the brood

*p. 14
†p. 8

comb, she fertilises each one with a sperm cell, so that it can develop into a new worker.

Once it was thought that the drones were lazy because they didn't help with the hive duties. But now we know that they couldn't help, no matter how much they wanted to. Their legs, heads and bodies are not shaped right for fashioning the wax into the perfect little chambers. They don't even have a sting with which they can help to drive away enemies. They just have those important little sperm cells, ready to be given to the queen in mating.

THE HOW AND WHY WONDER BOOK OF ANTS AND BEES, pp. 8–9

Perhaps the sole justification for the imputation of "laziness" in drones is to be found in the practical advice of an expert to a young aspiring beekeeper:

> There shouldn't be too many of these [drones] in a hive, for although the drones, which are the male bees, are necessary when a queen is to be mated, they are idle creatures and spend their lives loitering and eating valuable honey.
>
> THE YOUNG BEEKEEPER, p. 85

A generation ago, children were often invited to learn in a practical way by setting up their own hives. In JUDY'S AND ANDREW'S BOOK OF BEES (1954), Muriel Goaman offered good advice together with a clear, brief account of the organisation of a hive. THE YOUNG BEEKEEPER by Harry McNicol (1953) used a fictional plan in which a retired schoolmaster instructed a young grandson as they took a wild swarm in June and successfully housed it. In this book one or two of the more complex aspects of life in the hive were introduced naturally as special preoccupations of the beekeeper. The supersedure of queens, parthenogenesis, the biology of swarming, are rarely discussed in books for juniors because of the difficulty of simplifying them (and perhaps also because few authors nowadays are prepared to trust young readers to make an effort to understand them).

A fictional framework can give immediacy to a description. In A BOOK OF BEES (1950), Alexis Chesnakov dramatises himself as

Mr Chess and introduces a boy and girl from next door to the bee's life-cycle. Putting his narrative into the historic present, and using one of the children as narrator, he makes his explanations very fresh and natural. In this indirect way he explains, for example, how a young bee orientates itself when it first emerges from the hive:

> Here and there we saw one who had suddenly learnt to fly. She gently spread her wings, and in an instant she was flying in the air, with her head always pointing towards the hive. For several minutes she would continue to fly, together with hundreds of other young bees – up and down – right and left – now several feet away from the hive, now close to it, but always facing the entrance. At last she landed and ran inside, only to rush out again in a few minutes to fly once more – so full was she with the joy of having learnt to fly. Each time she flew further and further away, remembering by sight the position of the hive in relation to its surroundings – the garden walls, the trees, buildings, fields and hills.
>
> A BOOK OF BEES, pp. 10–11

It is perhaps easier for a beekeeper to avoid giving an anthropomorphic colour to a book, since his attention is firmly on the actuality of the bee's social organisation and its results for him. Writers with no particular theme seem to feel a great need for humanisation, especially when they are writing for juniors.

The title of Alice Goudey's HERE COME THE BEES! (1960) suggests a trumped-up excitement, but in fact this is a sound and sensible account, simplified for readers of seven or so but in many ways more accurate than books of more advanced content. It is notable, for instance, that Alice Goudey alone explains the chemical changes which dictate the various roles of the worker bee. Other writers are content to leave out the "how" of the phenomenon by which, as H. J. Wadey puts it:

> The Worker is the "Jill of All Work" . . . born to become at once a housemaid, she develops into a nursemaid, becomes a builder of comb, then a chemist and distiller. Later, she sallies forth and searches the fields for nectar, pollen and water. As she

advances into age she may also serve as a watcher at the gate to receive in classical manner any intruders or attackers.

INTRODUCING BEE-KEEPING, pp. 13–14

Some writers even imply that each bee has an individual duty, rather than a changing one. HERE COME THE BEES! is worth looking at more closely, for we can see here, perhaps, one good reason for humanising bees. Here, for instance, is a passage which might be, for some children, a first introduction to the idea of instinct:

> On the third day of her life Downy becomes a real worker in the hive.
> No one tells her *what* to do.
> No one tells her *how* to do it.
> No one tells her *when* to do it.
> Downy does her work without having to *learn* any of these things.
> Doing something without having to learn is called *instinct*.
> Human babies know how to suck and how to hold onto your finger, without having to learn how to do it. Bees seem to know how to do many, many surprising things without having to learn how.

HERE COME THE BEES!, pp. 31–2

An immediate, active example like this is worth more than several paragraphs of abstract exposition, at an early stage of a child's reading life; and there is nothing here to plant a false idea in a child's mind.

In HONEYBEE TELLS HONEYBEE (1952), Mary Adrian has made humanisation a convenience. Just as a research-worker colour-marks bees in order to observe individuals, so she has in effect colour-marked one worker bee by naming it and following it through its life-cycle, introducing quite naturally other workers, drones, queen, predators and so on. Although her book emphasises communication, it follows a natural time plan, starting with the queen laying her eggs after a mating flight in spring and ending as the heroine of the narrative dies and the hive is sealed for winter. The integrating of a birth-death cycle with a spring-winter one gives the book a logical shape, and its five thousand words give an

unusually succinct and satisfying outline for an alert child from
seven upwards. This is a directly educational book (in the *Life Cycle*
series). The author does not tell her reader that Honeybee "decided
to" or "thought that", but suggests that changes in the bee's duties
happen for biological reasons. "As Honeybee grew older, she had
less and less bee-milk. She did more of the other work in the hive,
and so she became a house bee." "When Honeybee came in from
flying, she had to help (to make cells) because she was old enough
for her wax glands to work."

The title of the book calls attention to one piece of behaviour in
the bee which excites the imagination perhaps more than any other.
Although at the same time it marks the difference between man
and the bee, the bee dance is perhaps most easily described for
children in human terms. To them, dancing a message should seem
natural enough. Evidently it seemed natural also to Karl von Frisch,
whose observations led to the isolating and describing of this piece
of behaviour, for his designation of "round dance" and "wagging
dance" have been generally adopted by scientists since the first
publication of his theory in 1927.

THE DANCING BEES is accessible to English readers in the
revised edition published by Methuen in 1966. The clarity and
warmth of this classic book, with its entirely respectable similes
relating bees to man, has established it as the storehouse for writers
on the bee dance, but few have succeeded in putting together a
really simple and comprehensible account of it which includes all
the important points. Let us see how Mary Adrian describes this
piece of behaviour, in an episode when her heroine, Honeybee,
discovers a field of white clover:

> The minute she got home, Honeybee began to dance. The white
> clover was too far away for her to tell the other bees with the
> Round Dance. So she danced the Wagging Dance.
>
> She wagged her body from side to side while she ran a little
> way straight up the comb, in the direction of the sun. She stopped
> and turned all the way around to the left, making a circle. Then
> she again ran straight up the comb, wagging from side to side.
> She turned to the right this time, and made another circle.
>
> She did these runs and circles over and over before she stopped.
>
> The field bees understood. Running straight up on the comb

said, "Fly with the sun straight ahead of you." The number of
circles in the dance told them how far the nectar was from the
hive.

The field bees kept smelling the perfume of the clover nectar
on Honeybee's body. When she stopped, each took a taste of
the nectar from her tongue. They rushed out to find the clover.
HONEYBEE TELLS HONEYBEE, pp. 40–41

Children reading this description might have a few questions to
ask. If Honeybee was dancing on the comb, in the darkness of the
hive, how did the bees see the direction of her dance? How would
they follow her instructions to "fly with the sun straight ahead of
you", if there was no sun? The answers to these questions are
available and could be simplified for the young. Certainly it is not
wrong to omit them in a book as simple as this one, but they are
facts which help to stress the difference between bees and man and
to show that communication in bees is not a human activity which

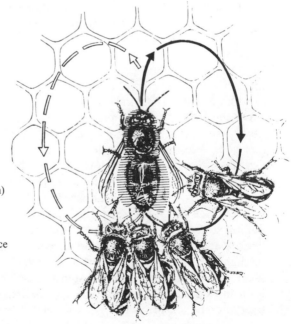

This drawing from THE
DANCING BEES (Methuen)
indicates the movement
made by the bee com-
municating information
about a newly-found source
of nectar, and also shows
how this information is
received through touch.
Compare the illustrations
in colour on p. 193.

they have been clever enough to imitate, but a unique piece of evolved behaviour.

Again, if words like "tell" and "dance" are to be used in relation to the bee's method of transmitting information, it must be only with absolutely accurate interpretation. To give an example, the loops in the figure of eight in the wagging dance are explained by Mary Adrian (and by most other writers for the young who mention it) as indicating *distance*. "The number of circles in the dance told them how far the nectar was from the hive." But "how far" is a human concept. Experiments suggest that the rhythm of the wagging dance communicates how long it will take to reach the new source of food or, better still, how much effort will be needed; in the dance, for instance, a bee includes the effect of a high wind in "distance".

There seems no reason why this point should not be made even in the earliest topic books, but I have only found it stated in John Lewellen's HONEYBEES (1959), in an exceptionally good account of the bee dance which also stresses the value of the bee's compound eye and its power to see polarised light. Nowhere in junior books can I find what is to me the most fascinating aspect of the bee dance, that it is danced with an energy proportionate to the richness of the newly-discovered honey flow, so that a suitable number of recruits is directed to the spot, thus, as one writer puts it, harmonising "supply and demand in the search for food in an almost perfect manner". But this kind of point could tempt one into the anthropomorphic comment that the bees order their society better than we do!

On the whole, junior topic books concentrate on presenting the *facts* clearly and let the *concepts* look after themselves. As far as fact goes, I know no book for the four to eight age-range which describes the bee dance more clearly than Judy Hawes' BEES AND BEELINES (1964), a volume in the *Let's-Read-and-Find-out-Science* series which was published in the same year as WATCH HONEYBEES WITH ME (see p. 110 *et seq*). Compared with the companion study, BEES AND BEELINES is specialised. The beeline – the bee's method of navigating and of communicating the results of its flight – is the sole point of the text, which makes it all the more lucid. The author moves step by step and each part of her description is illustrated with a careful diagram by the artist Aliki, whose control over line and texture is just what is needed here.

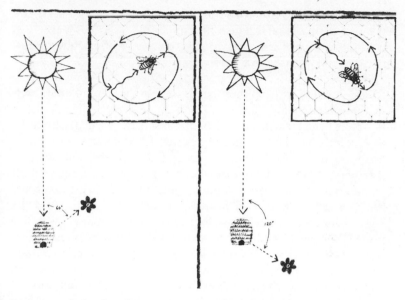

Diagrammatic drawing of the bee-dance by Aliki, from BEES AND BEELINES
(A & C Black); another method of visual explanation.

It is interesting to compare Judy Hawes' approach to this difficult
piece of bee behaviour with that of Dr Sinclair in the *Ladybird*
LIFE OF THE HONEY-BEE (1969). In the latter book, "The round
dance and the waggle dance" occupy two of its fifty-two pages;
the verbal description and the accompanying illustration both
make considerable demands on the reader. The text in particular
is very concentrated. I doubt whether a child would make much of
"The longer the dance lasts, the stronger the food source" without
some additional explanation. At the same time this book is a
remarkable piece of work. Factually, it is right up to date and, while
the author does not try to suggest how a scientist regards the life of
a bee, his outline of it is a very comprehensive one.

Need we be ashamed of admiring the bee – the busy bee? The
writer's obligation to establish correct attitudes and to offer accurate
fact does not mean he cannot enjoy his subject. Yet of all the junior
books I have read about the honeybee, only two gave me the feeling
of a personal joy in natural things. THE DANCING BEES is full of
delight in discovery, and so is a slender volume in an early series

of topic books, Evelyn Cheesman's LOOK AT INSECTS (1959).
Here one of the great English entomologists, who has never lost
her humility or her sense of wonder, pauses to offer children this
charming and precise piece of observation:

> Bees . . . make maps in their heads to help them to find their way
> without wasting any time.
>   While I was standing near a flower-bed in my garden, a bumble-
> bee, which had been collecting pollen from flowers, came near
> to hover in my face for a few seconds before she flew away to
> her nest. It was not because she hoped to know me if we met
> again, but because she was putting me into her map to help her
> find her way back to those flowers.
>   . . . There were three things in the bee's map that day. I watched
> her looking at them closely to make sure of knowing them again.
> First she looked at some dark leaves, at the tip of a branch, then
> she looked at a bright yellow leaf on another bush, then she had
> a good stare at my face. I was the last of her three landmarks.
> LOOK AT INSECTS, pp. 46–7

Why cannot we take our occasional education – that is, our topic
books – more easily? Why not more humour, more personality,
more enterprise? It is fashionable still to decry the didactic stories
and fictionalised teaching books of the last century, but the best
of these have a warmth, an intimacy, a glow of pleasure in them.
Over a hundred and forty years ago, a book on bees for the young
offered the following as its contents list for Chapter I:

> Introductory Description. Country stroll. A ladies' school setting
> out for a walk. Sudden terror of the females. One of them taken
> up and carried by the others. All return home. The Author
> discovers that they had trodden on a Bees' nest and been stung.
> Finds a book. Meets the Clergyman of the village. Gets introduced
> to the Misses R. Explains that he is studying the economy of Bees.
> Invites them to see his hives.
> Mrs C. I. Johnstone. SCENES OF INDUSTRY DISPLAYED IN
> THE BEE-HIVE AND ANT-HILL

A series of informal lectures on this "laborious and indefatigable race" ends with a moral so firm that Letitia "as she lingered by the garden-gate" promised "I will emulate the bees for their industry, and the bee-master for his patience; and I shall ever feel grateful for the sting, which brought me so much entertainment."

Writers of today, shrinking from so bald a statement of intent, do not find it easy to weave exposition so gracefully into a vignette of country life. Nor can we be as unselfconscious about humanising animals as Mrs Richardson was when, in THE STORY OF A BEE AND HER FRIENDS (1862), she told the story of Rosa the leaf-cutter bee and her search for a home. Seven other species of bee found in English gardens make their appearance before Rosa finds her long-lost husband and is entertained to a party by Mrs Brown the kindly humble-bee. As Rosa prepared for the party she muses:

> "I hope they will like my husband. I must see if I can brush his coat, and trim his wings and hair, and make him look spruce and young again. He is really a very handsome bee still, and so good-natured that I am sure he would help me if he could. It is his misfortune that he does not know how to work, and has no wish to learn. I shall be proud to shew him to my friends, and I expect to pass a very pleasant evening; and I shall tell everybody that I have built my house at last, quite to my own satisfaction.
>
> Farewell, dear little reader. I must now go and finish my nursery door, that all may be safe whilst I am away, and no harm befall my precious little unhatched family."
>
> THE STORY OF A BEE AND HER FRIENDS, p. 63

Most accomplished of the Victorian fact/fiction works on bees is perhaps A.L.O.E.'s WINGS AND STINGS (1865), in which the fortunes of two cottage families are skilfully involved with the inhabitants of a hive – Sipsyrup, Stickasting, Honeyball and others. The moral implicit in the story is clearly stated at the end when the author invites her readers to decide whether they will be classed with kind Minnie (called Wings because she flew to help little Johnny when he was marooned in a tree) or bullying Tommy, who well deserves the nickname of Stings. The purpose in the comparison appears in a simile early in the story, as the children in the village school watch bees flying in and out of the hive:

The house might itself be regarded as a hive, its rosy-cheeked scholars as a little swarm of bees, and knowledge as the honey of which they were in search, drawn, not from flowers, but from the leaves of certain dog's-eared books . . .

WINGS AND STINGS, p. 10

These busy bees, as they quarrel and strive and get into trouble, have a more direct appeal (whether they are Polly, Minnie and Tommy or the hive-bees) than Isaac Watts' toiler in the sun.

The graceful prose and sympathetic mood of A.L.O.E.'s book I can match only with a poet's fantasy, the recently translated LADIS AND THE ANT by Sanchez-Silva. John Leeming's CLAUDIUS THE BEE, a rumbustious tale of a small boy and a bumble-bee, and Dorothy Crowder's FLYING NATION with its personified store-keeper, architect and others, seem clumsy beside the mellifluous, leisurely Victorian tales.

The books I have discussed so far have had either a pictorial, a fictional or in some way a specialised approach. For children between seven and nine who want a straight survey of the life of the bee, John Lewellen's HONEYBEES (1959) a *Junior True Book*, promises "Factual information for curious young minds, designed for independent reading with 98% of the text in words from the Compiled Word List for Primary Reading." This advertisement sounds a warning note. The book, which comes from the United States, is an interesting example of misguided care for the young. First of all, the author has complied with a word-limit and the desire to include a wide range of material by an altogether excessive simplification.

Some statements have been so drastically pared down that, even with accompanying pictures, they must either bewilder or actually mislead a child. Sentences like "They carry pollen dust on their hairy bodies as they fly from flower to flower. This helps the plant make seed that will grow", or, "Men have discovered how a bee finds its way on cloudy days", or (of drones), "The eggs are the same as those that turn into females except that they are not fertilized, and the queen controls that" – sentences like these do need amplification, for they raise questions of extreme interest.

This author's care for his readers (who could be as young as seven) has one agreeable aspect. The sequence of somewhat bald

WORKERS IN THE HIVE.

The village school compared with a hive; from WINGS AND STINGS (T. Nelson & Sons).

facts, made still more monotonous because of a relentlessly childish syntax, is lightened by sprightly analogies which should aid memory. Thus the variety of jobs done by the worker bee with her built-in tools are indicated in human terms; she may be at various times, the author says, "a wax factory, a flying bottle of nectar, a purse, a policeman or a street sweeper", and he clinches a description of the bee's structure with the following comparison:

> The bee's body has "built-in" tools for the jobs to be done. It's as if a motor-car mechanic had wrenches and screw drivers for fingers, and could make oil and grease inside his body and squeeze it out through a grease gun on his chest.
> *The Junior True Book of* HONEYBEES, p. 33

On the whole, though, this book is not likely to impress a youngster of good intelligence because the author is so obviously reluctant to ask his reader to make any effort at all.

A. B. Tibbets' more robust survey, THE FIRST BOOK OF BEES (1952), has a short, simply written text arranged under headings and covering a surprising amount of ground. A calm, orderly manner of marshalling fact still allows personal feeling. There is no suggestion that bee behaviour is comparable with ours, but scientific fact is made interesting by the apt choice of words and details. Indeed, a child who did not wish to pursue the subject at a higher level of detail could achieve an adequate knowledge of the subject from this book, though he would find Mervyn Kaufman's HONEY-BEES (1966), slightly more up to date. Like Tibbets' book, Kaufman's relies considerably on illustrations which are attractive and informative; it is a book, in fact, adventurous in its manipulation of fact. For example, two pages show a horizontal row of cells, a queen laying in the first, then larvae at various stages, then cocoons, and finally two bees hatching. The sequence, more orderly and complete than it would be in the natural state, usefully impresses the order of events without being misleading.

Each of these books is accurate, reasonably well expressed, reasonably persuasive, but in substance they have not moved far from the most junior topic books. They discuss the nuptial flight of the queen without trying to explain the system by which the queen controls the sperm and regulates the proportion of workers

to drones in the hive. They describe the bee dance without discussing the bee's internal time-rhythm. They mention the workers'
relation to the queen without referring to the queen substance which
may be the clue to the pattern of life in the hive. They skirt round the
subject of instinct and avoid the mathematics of the bee cell.

Publishers, readers and critics all realise the practical difficulties
of keeping topic books up to date, particularly in scientific subjects.
Yet in many cases writers omit points which they could know and
should introduce in some form. An article written in the autumn
of 1968 (*The Times Educational Supplement*, 20.9.68) celebrated
the retirement of Mrs Rosina Clark as an educational adviser to
Surrey's Education Committee, and described her trenchant and
effective method of teaching at her apiary – teaching beekeepers,
biological students and school-children. To all of them, children
included, she introduced the latest facts; many of them were known
in time to appear in topic books of the past six years or so, but they
are not included. Mrs Clark is recorded as explaining to children,
for instance:

Bees are rather like cells in the body of a multicellular animal . . .
Each one is doing a vital job towards the function of the whole;
they are hopelessly lost without contact. Yet a bee that is chasing
you down the garden path acts very like an individual.

This is not a brand-new idea; it would have been available in the
text-books which, one supposes, writers of recent topic books would
have consulted.

Mrs Clark is obviously a teacher of remarkable calibre. But is
there any good reason why the latest facts should not be used by
writers – or, for that matter, why the charm and vivacity of the
spoken word should not be transferred to print?

Each of the subjects I have mentioned above removes the bee
from man and obliges the reader to realise bee behaviour as an
intricate process with its own rules and results. To discuss these
aspects with the young would be to discourage anthropomorphism
but to offer something better in return – an understanding of
biological principles through the examination of fascinating and
potentially comprehensible facts. Here is a discussion of queen
substance and its function, from the *Life* volume on INSECTS:

If an old queen dies, the colony can usually produce another queen simply by transferring one of the dead queen's latest eggs to a queen cell and feeding royal jelly to the larva that hatches. But what causes the workers to build a queen cell? The answer seems to revolve around a tiny gland in the mouth parts of the queen bee. This gland is the source of a substance that the queen spreads over its own body when grooming itself. Worker bees serve as courtiers. Constantly licking and grooming the queen, they receive a supply of this queen substance. Their supply passes by mouth from bee to bee throughout the hive and with it the information that the queen still exists. The queen substance inhibits the workers from constructing a queen cell.

However, if the queen dies, the substance is no longer available, and the colony's inhibition comes to an end. The workers quickly prepare the outsized queen cells and stock them with the dead queen's most recent eggs. Within two weeks a number of new queens will reach maturity. The conqueror assumes power and produces a supply of the inhibiting queen substance; thereafter, no additional queen cells are prepared.

Peter Farb. "Flowers, pollen and bees," in INSECTS, pp. 129–30

This passage was written for the general reader; the material could be modified for the young and it could satisfy that curiosity which is almost always more acute and far-reaching than we realise. It seems obvious that they should be curious also about the research experiments which have led to our knowledge of the bee's life. How did von Frisch isolate and describe the bee dance? How do we know that bees cannot see certain colours? How can a particular bee be observed over a period of time? Martin Lindauer's COMMUNICATION AMONG SOCIAL BEES (1961), though this is another book not written for the young, is direct and simple enough for them to understand, and the writer has the confidence of authority when he writes, in an almost affectionate manner, of his experiments – for example, when he analyses the record of a day in the life of an individual bee:

Another thing is striking in this day's record: the bee spent a surprisingly large part of her life loafing. During 69 hours and 53 minutes of the total 177 observation hours, she just sat around,

seeming lazy. But if anyone thinks we should now revise our old
ideas of the bee's industry, they must be reminded that among
the bees even laziness has an important social function. The
loafers in the beehive are the reserve troops, employed at critical
points in the labor market as the necessity arises. This is especially
true for temperature regulation and food gathering.

COMMUNICATION AMONG SOCIAL BEES, pp. 19–21

Although Lindauer does not press scientific terms and concepts
in this book for the popular market, he prepares the ground for
acceptance of them, and makes it easier for his readers, among
which there certainly should be some children of middle school
years, for standard works like THE DANCING BEES or Colin
Butler's definitive THE WORLD OF THE HONEYBEE. Modern
biological research seems to be passing from a particularly austere
reaction against sentimentalism towards the view that one may
recognise affinities and idiosyncrasies in animals without confusing
the drives that move them with our own thoughts and feelings.
Topic books for the young can and should foster a scientific attitude
that is natural and comfortable as well as sharply geared and
intelligent. We need more books for the young on the natural world
which are humane, lively, accurate and reasonable, with some touch
of humour and personality in them. To conclude this section I offer
a description of the bee's world written in excitement and in scientific
idiom. The pleasure of proper learning seems implicit in the passage:

It is a world of silence, as the worker bee is almost certainly
completely deaf. It is a world in which the movement, colour and
perfume of a flower are more important than its shape; in which
cornfields glowing with scarlet poppies appear as a rather dull
shade of blue, and in which many white flowers are blue-green,
and some white painted hives also appear as this colour whilst
others are white; a world in which there are no reds but plenty
of blues and greens, a world of four colours, yellow, blue-green,
blue and ultra-violet. It is a world in which the sun is useful as a
compass but almost unheeded as a clock, where time is measured
in terms perhaps of some internal metabolic rhythm, and distance
possibly by the length of time during which certain body-hairs
are bent; where scent is all important in finding food, in recog-

nising home and in distinguishing between friends and foes. It is a world dominated by one love, that of the queen – because she tastes so good; and in which . . . the light of a tiny scrap of blue sky is enough to place the position of the sun extremely accurately. Most surprising of all, it is a world in which companions exchange information by dances.

THE WORLD OF THE HONEY BEE, p. 132

Reading List

Adrian, Mary. HONEYBEE TELLS HONEYBEE. Life Cycle Books. (*Holiday* 1952) *World's Work* 1964. Illustrated by Barbara Latham.

Butler, Colin. THE WORLD OF THE HONEYBEE. New Naturalist. (*Collins* 1954, 1962 U.K.) *Macmillan* 1954 U.S.A. Photographs in colour and black and white by the author, and some diagrams.

Cheesman, Evelyn. LOOK AT INSECTS. Look at . . . *Hamish Hamilton* 1959. Illustrated by the author.

Chesnakov, Alexis. THE BOOK OF BEES. *Owl Press* 1950. Illustrated by Basil Jonzen.

Clegg, John. THE TRUE BOOK ABOUT INSECTS. True Books. *Muller* 1957. Illustrated by E. C. Mansell. Useful for general perspective rather than for details, because of the brevity of individual treatments.

Cooper, Elizabeth K. INSECTS AND PLANTS: THE AMAZING PARTNERSHIP. (*Harcourt, Brace* 1963) *Lutterworth* 1965. Illustrated by Shirley Briggs. An exceptionally interesting simple account of pollination, colour-attracting and other cognate subjects, with an outline of the life of the honeybee in general. The book should be within the scope of intelligent children from nine or ten.

Crompton, John. THE HIVE. *William Blackwood* 1947. Illustrated by A. E. Bestall.

Doering, Harold. A BEE IS BORN (*Sterling* 1962) *Oak Tree Press* 1963. Translated by D. S. Cunningham. Photographs by the author.

Farb, Peter. FLOWERS, POLLEN AND BEES in INSECTS. *Time-Life International* 1962. Illustrated with photographs and diagrams. See also THE INSECT WORLD. *Constable* 1960. Illustrated by John Howson. This simple book is dedicated to the author's children, thanking them for "their curiosity about the six-legged creatures with whom we share the globe". There is a touch of anthropomorphism in this playful introduction, but the book could be useful for beginner-readers all the same.

Foster, Virgil. CLOSE-UP OF A HONEY BEE (*William R. Scott* 1960) *Gollancz* 1962. Photographs by Martin Iger.

Free, J. B. and Butler, Colin. DUMBLEBEES. New Naturalist. (*Collins* 1959 U.K.) *Collins* 1959 U.S.A. Photographs by Colin Butler, and some diagrams. A specialist monograph for the general reader which could be tackled by older school children.

Frisch, Karl von. THE DANCING BEES: AN ACCOUNT OF THE LIFE AND SENSES OF THE HONEY BEE (Germany 1927, *Harcourt, Brace* 1965) *Methuen* 1966, from 5th German revised edition, translated by Dora Isle and Norman Walker. Illustrated by photographs and diagrams.

Goaman, Muriel. JUDY'S AND ANDREW'S BOOK OF BEES. Judy and Andrew Books. *Faber* 1954. Illustrated by Hazel Cook.

Goudey, Alice. HERE COME THE BEES! Here Come . . . (*Scribner* 1960) *Macmillan* 1962. Illustrated by Garry MacKenzie.

Hawes, Judy. WATCH HONEYBEES WITH ME (*Crowell* 1964) *A. and C. Black* 1968. Illustrated by Helen Stone. BEES AND BEELINES (*Crowell* 1964) *A. and C. Black* 1969. Illustrated by Aliki. Both in the Let's-Read-and-Find-out Science series.

Johnstone, Mrs C. I. SCENES OF INDUSTRY DISPLAYED IN THE BEE-HIVE AND ANT-HILL. London, *John Harris* 1827.

Kaufman, Mervyn. HONEYBEES (*Coward-McCann* 1966) *Angus and Robertson* 1968. Illustrated by Douglas Howland.

Levandowska, Cecilia. THE WORLD OF THE BEE (Poland 1959) *Heinemann* 1964. Illustrated by Mateusz Gawrys.

Lewellen, John. HONEYBEES. Junior True Books. (*Childrens Press* 1953) *Muller* 1959. Illustrated by Patricia Jackson.

Lindauer, Martin. COMMUNICATION AMONG SOCIAL BEES. Harvard Books in Biology. (*Harvard University Press* 1961) *Oxford University Press* 1961. Illustrated by diagrams.

Lockley, R. M. ANIMAL NAVIGATION. Pan Piper Science series. (*Pan* 1967) *Hart* 1970. Illustrated by diagrams. A capable, clear survey for the general reader which could give a broader scene of reference for older readers who have already read more selective books. Recommended for descriptions of experiments.

McNicol, Harry. THE YOUNG BEEKEEPER. *Warne* 1953. Illustrated by drawings, no named artist.

Maeterlinck, Maurice. THE LIFE OF THE BEE (First published Paris 1901) *George Allen* 1901, translated by Alfred Sutro. Pocket edition 1908. *Dodd* 1912. *Allen and Unwin* 1969.

Newman, L. Hugh. MAN AND INSECTS. Modern Knowledge series. (*Aldus Books* 1965) *Doubleday* 1965. Illustrated by photographs and prints. A general book

by a professional entomologist and butterfly breeder, recommended chiefly for a
fine range of illustrative material, including useful graphs.

Portal, Colette. THE LIFE OF A QUEEN. (Germany 1962. *Braziller* 1964) *Blackie*
1969. Translated by Marion Koenig. Illustrated by the author.

Richardson, M. K. BENWIG THE BEE. *St Paul Publications* 1968. Illustrated by
Ann Archer.

Roels, Iliane. THE BEE. Animals at Home. *W. and R. Chambers* 1968. Translated
by Marion Koenig. Illustrated by the author.

Rood, Ronald. THE HOW AND WHY WONDER BOOK OF ANTS AND BEES.
How and Why Wonder Books. (*Grosset & Dunlap* 1962) *Transworld* 1962.
Illustrated by Cynthia Iliff Kochler and Alvin Kochler.

Russell, Franklin. THE HONEYBEES. *Knopf* 1967. Illustrated by Colette Portal.

Sinclair, W. THE LIFE OF THE HONEYBEE. Ladybird Natural History series.
Wills and Hepworth 1969. Illustrated by Jill Payne.

Sullivan, Navin. ANIMAL TIMEKEEPERS (*Prentice-Hall* 1966) *Phoenix House*
1967. Illustrated by Haris Petrie. A book for the general reader giving examples
of the physiology of time in connection with migration, navigation, hibernation
and so on. Young people from twelve or so should find this a valuable
introduction to difficult concepts.

Thompson, Sir D'Arcy Wentworth. ON GROWTH AND FORM (First published
1916) (*Cambridge University Press*, U.S.A., 1952) *Cambridge University Press*,
U.K., abridged edition 1961. Illustrated by diagrams. For the mathematically
inclined, this book contains the classic description and analysis of the structure
of the bee-cell.

Tibbets, A. B. THE FIRST BOOK OF BEES. First Books. (*Franklin Watts* 1952)
Edmund Ward 1963. Illustrated by Hélène Carter.

Wadey, H. J. INTRODUCING BEE-KEEPING. Bognor Regis, *John Crowther
Educational* 1946. With photographs.

Wood, Rev. J. G. BEES: THEIR HABITS, MANAGEMENT AND TREATMENT.
Routledge 1853.

Worthy, William. ALL ABOUT A JAR OF HONEY. All About . . . *Longmans, Green*
1964. Illustrated by Donald Dosset. An attractive school pamphlet containing
a surprising amount of information in a form simple enough for beginner
readers.

——— BEES. Starters. *Macdonald* 1971. Illustrated by Tancy Boran. One of a series
of vocabulary-controlled information books for younger children, introducing
rather than explaining details of life in the hive. A list at the end of special
words is helpful.

Relevant stories

Crowder, Dorothy. FLYING NATION. *Hutchinson* 1951. Illustrated by Helen Haywood.

Kipling, Rudyard. "The mother hive" in ACTIONS AND REACTIONS. *Macmillan* 1932, Centenary edition 1965. For an ambitious reader, an intricate, witty and provocative allegory.

Leeming, John. CLAUDIUS THE BEE. *Harrap* 1936. Illustrated by Richard B. Ogle.

Richardson, Mrs. THE STORY OF A BEE AND HER FRIENDS. London, *Wertheim, Macintosh and Hunt* 1862.

Sanchez-Silva, José-Maria. LADIS AND THE ANT (Spain 1967. *Bodley Head* 1968) *McGraw-Hill* 1969. SECOND SUMMER WITH LADIS (Spain 1968) *Bodley Head* 1969. Both in the Acorn Library, translated by Michael Heron. English editions illustrated by David Knight.

Tucker, Charlotte (A.L.O.E.). WINGS AND STINGS: A TALE FOR THE YOUNG. *Nelson* 1865.

2e | Cowboys

"Ma," says she, "do cowboys eat grass?"
"No, dear," says the old lady, "they're part human."
Charles M. Russell. TRAILS PLOWED OVER

2e | Cowboys

FOR nearly thirty years I have listened to the distant sounds of cowboy games in the village. Indian howls and cowboy yells remain constant and unchanged, but I have never heard any sound that acknowledged the existence of a cattle herd. The myth of the cowboy, for adults, is linked with dreams of space and freedom: for children, only speed and violence seem to count. To them, the cowboy is concerned with crime, not with cattle. The Lone Ranger and his almost human horse were type-specimens for my children as the gentler Tom Mix and his horse Tony were for me; both heroes spent the greater part of their time chasing villains.

The cult of the Western and the cowboy has a fluctuating life in the world of fashion and a safe one on the railway bookstall. Teachers discuss the cult, sometimes earnestly in conferences on "The film as an educational medium", at other times more frivolously. An advertisement for a history course for teachers including sessions on "The Wild West" promised to examine "The legends and facts of the American expansion into the west", and announced further that "the wearing of period costume by students is encouraged but is not essential. Barbecue on Saturday night."*

The exploits of astronauts have probably caused some drop in the popularity of the cowboy among the young. However, two series of books for backward readers, published not long ago, were confidently based on cowboy clichés; titles included THE ROBBER OF RED VALLEY and PETE THE OUTLAW as well as the slightly more realistic ON THE RANCH. Television circuits offer a monotonous stream of trashy Western films and an occasional classic to

*The Times Educational Supplement, 28 February 1969, quoted under "No comment"

educate children in the cowboy myth. So far as books are concerned, the subject of the cowboy is an example of sadly wasted opportunities, of a stirring past dimmed into dullness by lack of enterprise, poor writing and stereotyped attitudes.

In any case, do children need *books* about cowboys? A seven-year-old "learns" about them through that mixture of imitative play and unconscious assimilation which also teaches him singing, games or the rules of football; alternatively, he absorbs the romanticised image of the cowboy from television series. If he does still play cowboys, he is not likely to want to read about the origin of chaps or the Stetson; it is enough that he wears these credentials. What he knows about cowboys will have little to do with mental processes.

Joan Walsh Anglund's THE BRAVE COWBOY (1959) illustrates the cowboy game shrewdly and directly. This is a recognition picture-book of the simplest kind, listing the various things which a cowboy might do, and which a child might want to imitate – riding a bucking bronco, lassoing, chasing rustlers, stopping a stampede. Each picture has a double function. Strong colours depict the small child playing at home with chairs, the cat, a washing line, and insets in fainter line show the action as it seems to the child in imagination, when house and garden have melted into ranch house and range. The book wittily illustrates the particular niche the cowboy may occupy in the life of a small child.

Right from the start a child is asked to accept "the smooth-cheeked tartan-shirted cowboy of the cinema screen" who, as R. A. Kelly has remarked, "is far removed from the sombrely dressed puncher with his walrus moustache and battered felt Stetson". Even in Jean Bethell's *Easy Reader*, THE CLUMSY COWBOY (1963), where a small boy abandons broncos for an affable cow with a broad back, the artist has carried a filmic neatness into her caricature of cowboys, bandits and pioneer spectators.

For many, the cowboy of the screen remains the dominant image throughout life. A child may graduate from picture-books to gaudy paperback reflections of films and the less literary Western adventures, cherishing to the last the idea of a tight-lipped, two-gun hero, regardless of the fact that the cowboy of the past rarely carried more than one; as "Teddy Blue" remarked in his old age, "a cowboy

A whole generation of children took its idea of cowboys from the adventures of the Lone Ranger, on television or in print. Eric Dadswell's cover for THE LONE RANGER (Adprint), one of many popular story-collections, fairly represents the stereotype of the cowboy, usually engaged in opposing crime, always moving at a speed which in reality would soon destroy his mount. By contrast, the photograph of cowboys taken in 1898, on the opposite page, is as authentic as it is unromantic. The photograph comes from COWBOYS AND CATTLE COUNTRY (American Heritage), by courtesy of the University of Texas.

with two guns is movie stuff."* Common sense is often powerless against "le cowboy" of the boutique or the latest John Wayne revival. But supposing a child has a whim to discover what cowboys were and are really like. What books are there to satisfy him?

Let us start with a child of five or six who can read a little and has worn out two or three books of idealised cowboy tales full of the usual Western clichés. Without cutting him off arbitrarily from the agreeable speed and excitement of such reading matter, how can we bring some sense into the picture; how can we suggest that cowboys were not types but, as one of them said, "Merely folks, just plain, everyday, bow-legged humans"? I have found only one book which I would trust to catch the attention of a child at the stage where he wants facts supported by colour and action. Marion Clark's BILL OF THE PONY EXPRESS (1964), in a series *Children of Other Times*, shows one of many manifestations of Buffalo Bill since the birth of the real William Cody over a century ago; here

*E. C. Abbott. WE POINTED THEM NORTH, p. 29

we have, very briefly, his exploits as a rider for the Pony Express at the age of fourteen. Not as a representative cowboy, perhaps, but one who has been so persistently romanticised that this little book may make a useful point all the same. Here, prettily coloured but with no purple patches, is a perfectly accurate, though simplified, account of what young Bill Cody actually did – his early trails, his record run of 322 miles to help a sick comrade, the way he cheated a couple of outlaws with a false mail carrier (the author has used the proper term, mochila, for this pocketed leather blanket), how he made friends with some Indians and fought others. Here are historical facts for background, like the building of the railroad; dates and routes and payments on the Pony Express; the well known advertisement of 1860 for "Young skinny wiry fellows not over eighteen . . . willing to risk death daily"; pictures of chuck-wagon and camp fire, longhorns, pistols and small wiry horses, in a style that is a subtle blend of American primitive and text-book illustrative.

This little book has everything to attract a child, with its clear colour, distinctive layout, easy prose; it carries lightly its generous allowance of fact. It would certainly have pleased Will R. James, for he knew that the truth must support the most colourful journalism. One of his stories, "Filling in the cracks", describing how he and a friend took on a film job, illustrates the more usual way of presenting the cowboy to the public:

> I played some pony express, a few close-ups by my lonesome, and others with the leading man showing where I'm delivering some important papers; then again where my horse breaks a leg in a badger hole and how I catches me a wild horse as he comes in to water, saddles him when he's down, gets on and proceeds, riding a bucking streak of greased lightning and delivers the important message at the other end.
>
> "Filling in the cracks" in THE DRIFTING COWBOY, p. 53

BILL OF THE PONY EXPRESS is both exciting and accurate. There is nothing in the book to spoil a child's dream of the West, but plenty to relate that dream to actuality. The life of a cowboy is not like any life that most children will come to in adult life. Presenting a true picture of this unusual job, to a child, need not mean reducing a fast-riding dare-devil to nothing but a routine ranch handyman. In the cowboy of today, as of yesterday, there is still something free and arresting to catch the imagination – as it caught the imagination of a small girl in New Mexico some forty years ago:

> The first rancher I can remember was a tall man riding past our home on the Upper Niobrara River. He sat his saddle so the fringe of his gauntlets barely stirred in the long easy trot, his horse a fine star-faced, well-coupled black, spirited but not shying from the small girl who ran from her grandmother's grasp to see. That rancher, I know now, was not very different from the old Texas cowmen of the 1850's, not in saddle, use of rope, or in the slant of his eye over the range – not even very different in these things from the early vaquero. Although my first glimpse of the rancher was back in the homestead period, when much of the higher Plains region was still free grass, government land, he could be riding through my home regions today, with the same saddle

and coiled rope. Even if he was in a range jeep or a light plane
his eye would still slant in the same way over the grass and the
stock.

THE CATTLEMEN, Foreword, pp. xiii–xiv

The little girl who watched the rancher pass by grew up to write one
of the most scholarly, informative and thoughtful histories of the
Western cowboy. But Mari Sandoz' THE CATTLEMEN (1958) has
more than graphic descriptions of the great blizzards of 1885, full
statistics of prices and markets, summaries of the theories on the
origin of the Bowie knife and the term "maverick". It has the *feel*
of space, of man against nature, of effort and exploration – good
basic reasons for keeping the cowboy as a symbol even while we
look beyond the film star to the bewhiskered Victorian cowhand
with his baggy pants or the pilot dropping feed for his cattle from
a helicopter.

This feeling for the essential spirit of the cowboy's life and
environment is lacking in almost all books for the young. It is
certainly missing from the pages of Carla Greene's ingenuous
I WANT TO BE A COWBOY (1960), which belongs to a classroom
series clearly designed to lure children towards books by offering
certain congenial roles for their inspection. It is to be hoped that
no lively child would accept the devitalised picture in these pages
as a substitute for his own noisy playground impersonation.
Opposite the title page, a page of small drawings headed "New
words to find in this book" offers the reader *ranch, cabin, cowboy,
corral, brand, chuck-wagon, cow-pony*. New, indeed! The child who
bypasses this insult to tribal knowledge will find a brief account of
a visit to a ranch in winter. While Dan's mother exchanges family
news in comfort indoors, Cowboy Pete takes the boy and his cousin
Ellie on to the range to dump hay for the cattle and bring the horses
to the corral. Dan learns to ride, the children go out in the chuck-
wagon and watch (from a suitable distance, in case the hard physical
facts become evident) while the calves are branded. The cowboy
offers incidental information about lassos, saddles and circle
horses and there is more inset fact from the author about rodeos,
fence-mending and the round-up.

If there is nothing inaccurate in the book, there is nothing
positive either – no hint of enjoyment from the author, no hint of

real excitement from Dan and Ellie. The illustrator, Janet La Salle, cannot even show the boy's delight in his first ride in his expression, since she has observed the convention in junior books of this kind that whatever people are doing or feeling they must wear a vapid smile on their near-caricatured faces. The daily work of a cowboy has here been reduced to parochial scale.

If the part played by young Dan in this book is minimal, at least it is a step towards the dream of being a cowboy; he does learn to ride and even handles a lasso. The small boy in Teri Martini's JUNIOR TRUE BOOK OF COWBOYS (1955) is hanger-on and waver-off to a set of filmic cowboys whose serene, handsome faces show no sign of dirt, sweat, beards or harassment, departing or returning. The book offers about a thousand words of description, the text being broken into easy-to-read blocks of monosyllabic prose, two or three simple statements to a paragraph, accompanied by blue and black pictures, some showing frozen action in or near the ranch, others depicting branding-iron, spurs, ten-gallon hat and other appurtenances.

The "cowboy today" approach is timid; the author has chosen, in the main, details of work and equipment of a traditional kind which could have been in use a century before her book was written. The nearest we get to mechanisation is a comment that "When it snows, they take tractor loads of hay out on the range"; the nearest to any mention of modern treatment of disease is the general statement that "in summer some of the cowboys ride the range to take care of the cattle". There is little here to suggest that "the cowboy of today" has anything to do with real life, little to tell the child that he will not already have discovered elsewhere. The material would serve a better purpose as a bright annotated wall-chart for a boy's bedroom. The child who whips through the book will use it simply as a reminder and will supply, or we hope he will, the necessary colour from what he has seen on the television or the cinema screen – for these are filmic cowboys and on every page the present has slid gently into the past.

A similar reminder-book, a typical Christmas present, Frank Sayers' COWBOYS (1955), with the format of a large picture-book and a simple text, is openly traditional. The author stresses that a cowboy of today, while he "knows how to handle a jeep or a truck as well as he does a horse" and is well able to inoculate calves

against infection, still calls a ranch an "outfit" or a "spread" and
carries on in the spirit of the old-timer for whom a refrain of "yi yi
yippee" was obligatory at the end of a long nostalgic ballad about
the range. The atmosphere of the book is stiffened by one or two
scraps of history about the origin of brands, the sheriff-rustler
situation, the first rodeos, and it ends with the broad statement that
"The American cowboy did more than just herd cattle. He helped
to settle the West and build America. In the great cattle drives
he brought meat to the cities and helped them grow." There is
a hint, in fact, that there might be more to find out about the
cowboy.

All the same this, too, is also essentially a play-book which does
its job no better than a picture would have done. The text is dull
and lacking in enthusiasm, the cowboys depicted are clean and
photogenic. A child may well find most interest in the front end-
papers, where the wood panels of a stable are decorated with carved
initials and ranch signs and hung with Bowie knife, pistol, spurs,
keys, horse-shoes; through a large knot-hole we discern a wide
prairie. This is an imaginative touch to an otherwise uninteresting
book.

A young reader will probably turn from play-books so un-
entertaining to something more directly factual – perhaps to the
thirty-two page octavo pamphlet by Henry Saltiel, BEEF AND GOLD
(1966), which belongs to a series on American history including
RAILROADS AND INDIANS and REB AND YANKEE. The text
occupies perhaps 800 words (with three pages at the end of things
to do, and questions). Each opening contains one full-page picture
and some fifty to seventy words of careful, simple exposition, about
the cattle range and the great drives, the cowboy's work and play,
the gold rush, outlaws and rustlers, the coming of the homesteaders
and the railroads and the end of the great cattle period.

This intelligent booklet is the first to offer the junior reader a
map (of Texas and the trail north to Abilene and Chicago) to add
to the reality in pictures of cattle in a drive (strung out in a line,
correctly, not in the usual filmic bunch) or cowboys at night by
the chuck-wagon. No doubt it is easier to make a cattle-drive
exciting than the routine of life on the home range. All the same,
this pamphlet offers a good simple exposition and clear pictures
in a form that will not be daunting to children in their early

reading years, but which is honestly and plainly instructive as well as attractive.

Another classroom series, Blackwell's *Learning Library*, with neat, bright pictures and reliable texts, includes cowboys among its congenial subjects. The scope of T. A. Thompson's COWBOYS (1966) is firmly stated in the opening pages. Cowboys on television, says the author, have more exciting lives than cowboys in reality ever had; this is a description of the life of the old-time cowboy as he was, not as the screen would have him. The chapter titles include "On the range", "Rodeos", "The cowboy's horse"; familiar enough, but there is something different here from the play-books in which the purpose of the cowboy's existence, to look after cattle, is pushed into the background by the more obviously dramatic details of his exploits with his horse. Here the locale of the cowboy's activities is defined and the author directs his readers to a map or globe; unfortunately no space has been spared for a map in the book, even when the best-known cattle trails of the last century are mentioned.

This is not the ideal book by any means. The author is not altogether happy with his generalisations, spending more space than he need on details of equipment, which could have been allowed for in illustration, and leaving certain essential points inadequately explained. For example, the sentence "The cattle they took were those to be found in Europe at that time" falls flat for want of definition, and as the Spaniards are not mentioned, the young reader may well think that "the settlers" in the earliest days of Texas and Mexico were English. Still this is a firm outline, particularly to be commended for Trevor Stubley's illustrations – of night camp, a round-up, Mexican cowboys with a herd – whose spontaneous and active style recalls those great artists of the West, Remington and Russell. Here, at least, is something of the spirit of the old-time cowboy.

So far "cowboy" has meant "American cowboy". Despite the popularity of that fine drover film, *The Overlanders*, nobody has tried to describe factually in a separate book the routine of an Australian stockman on a cattle station. Older children may turn to Reginald Ottley's reminiscences of Yamboorah or to Frank Dalby Davison's classic story of a bush cow, MAN-SHY; but for the younger reader, Australia will probably still be largely associated with

A cattle drive as it was, rather than a filmic version. Drawing from BEEF AND GOLD
(Johnston and Bacon).

sheep and wool. There is no rule, however, that a youthful interest in cowboys is to be confined to the American West; among other writers, Les Landin in ABOUT COWBOYS AROUND THE WORLD (1963) and Benjamin Brewster in THE FIRST BOOK OF COWBOYS (1950) have tried to improve the balance.

Landin's book has an easy encyclopaedic framework. Cowboys from Texas, Mexico, Canada, Hawaii, Chile, Spain, the Camargue, Central Asia and Australia are discussed in turn, each on two or four pages with an accompanying two-colour picture. Detail is well chosen, and consistently too; for example, the author describes the tools used by each man, from the pole which the cowboy in the Amazon lands uses to stand on to see over long grass to the special pole used to keep cattle moving in the Camargue. There is an unobtrusive but essential point in the book, expressed in the introduction:

> Wherever he rides, the cowboy's work is the same – to look after his herd. His tools are not always the same, however. And the climate of the country, together with the conditions under which he works, help determine the kind of clothes he wears.

The pages on the Australian cowboy contain details of railheads, air ferries and markets; those on the Camargue describe the unique landscape and the local customs and festivities which have grown round the cattle herds. In each instance the *Why* of the cowboy's life accompanies the *How*; the author expects his readers, however young they may be, to accept something more than elementary description.

THE FIRST BOOK OF COWBOYS is a good deal less broad in its scope than at first appears. Brief accounts of the work of cowboys in South America, Russia, the Camargue and Australia are pushed in at the end of a book which is in the main about the American cowboy and, disappointingly, again purports to describe "the whole vivid story of a cowboy's life today", while in reality emphasising mainly the old-timer element. The compromise between romance and realism is foreshadowed in the blurb, which promises "the whole vivid story of a cowboy's life with . . . his own language of cavvies and remudas, sugans and war bags, and his very special ways and customs." But there is no early history of cattle breeds or trails, only a playful description of round ups and rodeos which, in association with unrealistic pictures, makes everything into a game.

More than half the book is concerned with a bunch of cowboys – Shorty, Pedro the bronco-buster, Riley and Buck the line-riders. Through them the author describes routine matters like the spring round-up, branding and cutting out, which a junior reader will find pretty familiar. Occasionally a tart note of realism reminds one that the book is supposed to be about the cowboy today – for example:

> Nowadays most rustlers do not trouble to use branding irons. They simply drive off a bunch of cattle to a place where they have parked a refrigerator truck. They slaughter the cattle then and there and load the meat on to the truck. They destroy the hides which would prove whose cattle had been stolen, and they drive off to market.
> THE FIRST BOOK OF COWBOYS, no page numbers

Delivered in the same tone of monotonous told-to-the-children simplicity as the rest of the information in the book, this choice piece inevitably sounds like part of the game too. Lacking any details of the cowboy's wages, the country and the weather in which he operates, the breeds of cattle that he has to look after, the book makes little impact. It can hardly expect to be *introducing* the subject of cowboys to any child with the technical ability to tackle the text, nor has it the zip and enthusiasm needed to persuade this child that he does not yet know everything about the subject. THE FIRST BOOK OF COWBOYS, like THE JUNIOR TRUE BOOK OF COWBOYS, (a comparison of the texts suggests the two are closely related) is a scissors-and-paste compilation of the most perfunctory kind.

What eight-year-old is going to sit down to a dull catalogue of facts if he can find them incorporated in a strip-cartoon or in one of the adventures of Rex Dixon's Pocomoto? The hearty old-timer idiom and behaviour is what he is looking for, and he will hardly pause to discriminate between cliché and authentic spirit if he is given a good story.

Robert J. Hoare has made story and exposition into efficient yoke-fellows in THE OLD WEST (1969) in which he uses a piece of

fiction (it may be a brief anecdote or an extended story) to introduce
an historical outline of the Louisiana Purchase, the Pony Express,
the life of a cowboy, Wells Fargo and so on. This is no mythical
"Wild West" but the Old West as it can be discerned in reliable
accounts. The book is designed partly for classroom use at middle
school level, with book list and suggestions for project work, but
the fictional element and the lively style as a whole make it a
congenial companion for a lazy Saturday afternoon too.

It is arguable that non-fiction forms of literature are unsuited to
this particular subject. Certainly most of the attempts to add a
seasoning of Yi-yippee to topic books have been a laughable failure.
H. C. Holling's attempt more than thirty years ago in THE BOOK
OF COWBOYS (1936) was a near-miss. His "visit to the ranch"
formula is contrived and more than a little dull, but he cleverly
contrasted the dry, detached lecturing voice of Uncle Harry of the
Circle Cross with the rambling but thorough explanations of cowboy clothes and behaviour which old Alkaly Jones provided in
answer to the incessant questions of the New York visitors, Peter
and Barbara Ann:

"Ever seen the bottom of a hoof close up? Take a squint. This
middle piece, heart-shaped, is called the frog. It's soft – feel it –
like rubber or a tire. The part around the frog is softish, but it
keeps gettin' harder out toward the edge till it's like hardest
rubber. Does it hurt to nail the shoe on? Of course not. Doesn't
hurt to pare your fingernail, does it? Well, a hoss's hoof is
just one big nail. But if it's once split on the rocks, with steady
poundin' at a gallop, that split is liable to keep on goin' toward
the soft part inside, and then the hoss goes lame from the hurt.
So shoes are put on not only to save the hoof from wearin' away
on the bottom, but also as an iron hoop to keep the nail from
splittin'. Get th' idea? Most cowboys can shoe their own hosses
– they're mighty poor pickles if they can't – and I'm just finishin'
my string of broncs. But you better jog along down to the pens.
If I ain't mistaken they've begun dustin' off the bad ones. I'll
be down soon, myself!"
THE BOOK OF COWBOYS, p. 76

This is an honest attempt to get at the reasons behind the picture that the city children have in their minds of "cowboys in flapping chaps, high-heeled boots, big felt hats" and "wild horses, racing with the speed of wind, sometimes bucking riders off their backs". Old-fashioned now, the book is to be preferred to the line-shooting melodramas of Ross Salmon, whose years as a cowboy and ranch manager in South America provided endless stories of fights with a jaguar and with rustlers in the Rio Grande, a rebellion of Caribs, the breaking of a wild colt. Among the cheap picture-books bearing his name which were so popular a decade or two ago, ROSS SALMON'S COWBOY BOOK (1955) began in bracing fashion, "Any English boy can become a real-life cowboy, you know; you don't have to be born in Texas," and offered unabashed advice on how to round up cattle, how to catch wild horses and so on. "Whenever a bandit holds you up at gun point and you yourself are armed," the author remarks, sharing the dream with the child as he explains how you seem to hand over your guns but in fact prudently conceal one for future use. Out of a rattle of anecdote there emerge snatches of fact about the cowboy's life in the West, mainly as it was a century ago.

Although this farrago of charade and concrete detail, loosely woven and delivered in nonchalant style, seemingly comes from personal experience, much of it seems to belong to the scissors-and-paste school, drawing on such books for the general reader as Philip Rollins's detailed study THE COWBOY, which since its publication in 1922 has been much used as a source. It is noticeable that in his more directly informational TRUE BOOK ABOUT COWBOYS (1956), Ross Salmon continues to write of the North American cowboy as he was in the last century. Other sections in this book concern the llaneros of the Orinoco Plains, the vaqueros of central South America, the gaucho of the Argentine, Australian stockmen and English cowboys. In the last section he describes his own ranch on Dartmoor and his theories of cattle-raising in a responsible and restrained way, and the truth of what he says is beyond dispute. But though he was also drawing on personal experience in writing of certain of the South American cowboys, he selects exceptional and sensational incidents rather than giving an authoritative diary of a day's work. Some of his readers might prefer atmosphere to fact; others might wish for more of the practical details of costume and equipment and the reasons for variations between one climatic range and another which he occasionally inserts.

Most topic books are compilations, of course; the genre hardly allows for personal experience. Still, we must expect the author to work over his ground properly, for the simplest outline will be all the better if it is based on the widest possible collection of material. None of the books I have discussed so far suggests that the authors have done more than glance at the wealth of good literature about the cowboy of the past written by men who knew him at first hand, nor that they have gone much further than a dude ranch in their search for the cowboy of today.

As for the cowboy of the past, would it not interest the young to learn that when he was on the trail he did not carry fuel with him but used dried buffalo droppings, which were picked up along the route and carried in slings under the wagon? I have never found this point mentioned in a junior book. Would it not be a welcome change from the perfunctory deference to cowboy songs as essential on the trail, if children could read what "Teddy Blue" has to say from his own experience about the old chestnut, "Bury me not on the lone prairie":

> ". . . it ended up just like a lot of songs on the radio today; they sung it to death. It was a saying on the range that even the horses nickered it and the coyotes howled it; it got so they'd throw you in the creek if you sang it. I first heard it along about '81 or '82, and by '85 it was prohibited."
>
> WE POINTED THEM NORTH, p. 261

Would not the reader get some idea of the realities behind the typical Western if he were told that cowboys did not as a rule ride yelling and shooting round the herd, because cattle were only too easily stampeded; or that Indians were usually very willing to bargain for a steer or two in order to avoid a fight; or that to the accepted romantic wardrobe of the cowboy must be added a capacious oilskin, because it was not all sunshine on the trail; or as Charlie Siringo explains:

> Sometimes we had to sew up the eyelids of these old mossy-horn steers to prevent them running for the timber every chance they

got. It required about two weeks' time to rot the thread, allowing
the eyes to open. By this time the animal was "broke in".
RIATA AND SPURS, p. 24

Instead of reading the bald statement, meaningless as it stands,
that "often he (the cook) will give the cowboys cold canned tomatoes, which they all like very much", how much more interesting to
learn the reason why tinned tomatoes were popular, perhaps
through the naïve remarks of Owen Wister's visiting journalist in
THE VIRGINIAN:

> Through my dozing attention came various fragments of talk,
> and sometimes useful bits of knowledge. For instance, I learned
> the true value of tomatoes in this country. One fellow was buying
> two cans of them.
> "Meadow Creek dry already?" commented the proprietor.
> "Been dry ten days", the young cowboy informed him. And
> it appeared that along the road he was going, water would not
> be reached much before sundown, because this Meadow Creek
> had ceased to run. His tomatoes were for drink. And thus they
> have refreshed me many times since.
> op. cit., p. 44

To this might be added one of the many accounts by old-timers
about the hours that might be whiled away, not by singing or by
stopping stampedes but by reading the labels on cans and reciting
them from memory in competition!

Such details from authentic sources, far from destroying the
stereotyped image of the cowboy which most children possess,
will put new life into it; the truth, in this case, is often far stranger
than fiction.

It is hard to forgive any writer for reducing to dullness a subject
as vigorous and interesting as this, even when he is faced with a
drastic word limit. It is inexcusable in a writer who is given the scope
of a topic book for children of nine or so – children at the right age
to respond to an honest approach to detail. Quotation is rarely used
in books for these older readers. Suppose they were offered, as a
corrective to the description of an idealised cowboy, the following
picture of Ab Blocker, a Texan trail-boss of the 1870s, provided by

the wife of a relative and quoted by a modern student of the West who combines scholarship with an intuition for the past:

His boots had low heels, tops up nearly to the knee, not scalloped in front but even – like a stove pipe. Long leather ears hung down from the boot tops. He always had his breeches tucked inside the boots. He wore a white shirt fastened at the neck with an old brass collar button that had once been gold-plated. After the style changed to sewed-on collar buttons, he'd bring any new shirt he bought to me to cut the button off and make a buttonhole. He wore a white handkerchief around his neck – never a bandana, never a necktie. He wore a woolen vest, the pockets always handy, summer and winter, along with long-sleeved under-shirts and long-legged drawers – never changing from anything he was used to. In a vest pocket, he carried a big watch with a long gold chain attached by a gold bar through a buttonhole of his vest. His pocket knife, long-bladed and white-handled, was as old as his collar-button, watch and spurs. He kept it very sharp, often whetting it on a boot-leg. His heavy felt, wide-brimmed, high-peaked hat was black. Very likely he'd never had a straw hat on his head.

J. F. Dobie. COW PEOPLE, p. 35–6

There are plenty of photographs available from the '70s to support this lifelike description. Boys and girls who are interested could be offered a more general picture of the cowboy, and one nearer to the traditional figure, written by Joseph McCoy in the '70s; they could ponder the reasons why this cattle-owner, who played a major part in the establishing of Abilene as a centre for the shipping of meat and hides, should take a somewhat severe view of the men on whose work he depended for his wealth and prestige:

The life of the cowboy is one of considerable daily danger and excitement. It is hard and full of exposure, but is wild and free, and the young man who has long been a cowboy has but little taste for any other occupation. He lives hard, works hard, has but few comforts and fewer necessities. He has but little, if any, taste for reading. He enjoys a coarse practical joke or a smutty story; loves danger but abhors labor of the common kind; never tires riding; never wants to walk, no matter how short the distance he desires to go. He would rather fight with pistols than pray; loves tobacco, liquor, and women better than any other trinity . . . He enjoys his pipe; and relishes a practical joke on his comrades, or a corrupt tale wherein abounds much vulgarity and animal propensity. His clothes are coarse and substantial, few in number, and often of the gaudy pattern.

HISTORIC SKETCHES OF THE CATTLE TRADE OF THE WEST AND SOUTH WEST, p. 85

Certainly one way to help the young to understand that it is impossible, now or ever, to choose any single picture of a typical cowboy would be to quote against this picture the comments of Granville Stuart, a cattle-baron who described the cowboy as he knew him over many years of ranching in Montana after the Civil War; "they always patronized the best restaurant or eating place in the town", he says, "and ice cream or fresh oysters were never omitted from their menu";* but "few of them drank to excess, some of them gambled";† and he gives as his considered opinion that:

The noisy fellow in exaggerated costume that rode up and down the streets whooping and shooting in the air was never a cow puncher from any outfit. He was usually some "would be" bad man from the East decked out in paraphernalia from Montgomery, Ward's of Chicago."

FORTY YEARS ON THE FRONTIER, vol. 2, p. 184

It is also worth remembering that a few years ago an argument in print about whether cowboys ever really used old-timer language such as decorates the average Western was vigorously conducted by individuals whose personal experience of the West ranged from the first-hand to the snobbish-illusory; here again, no conclusion was, or could be, reached.

The reminiscences of Teddy Blue, Andy Adams and Charlie

*FORTY YEARS ON THE FRONTIER, vol. 2, pp. 183–4
†ibid., p. 183

Siringo seem to have been used in one or two books for children on the cowboy, but always as though they wrote from a common point of view; here, surely, is an opportunity to indicate to children the nature of the evidence. Surely it would be valuable for them to be told that Teddy Blue, son-in-law of a rancher, who worked with longhorns in Texas and Montana in the '70s and '80s, talked of the past to a writer skilful enough to preserve his idiom and his stories unaltered so that, apart from the legitimate exaggerations of old age, WE POINTED THEM NORTH gives one man's truthful view of the great drives.

From this simple narrative it is some way to Charles Siringo's A TEXAS COWBOY of 1885, with its polite versions A LONE STAR COWBOY (1919) and RIATA AND SPURS (1927), for Siringo, a cowboy for fifteen years and a detective for twenty, was clearly a flamboyant figure, who said his "excuse for writing . . . is money – and lots of it". Siringo's first book, a runaway best-seller with the subtitle "Fifteen years on the hurricane deck of a Spanish pony", is considered one of the earliest and most vital ancestors of the *popular* Western.

Beside this dramatic but truthful raconteur, his contemporary Andy Adams may seem a quiet writer, but his classic LOG OF A COWBOY, which first appeared in 1903, played a major part in establishing the minutiae of the trail drives; every step of the way from the Mexican border to the Blackfoot Indian agency in Montana is described with a working cowboy's attention to detail – his reaction to weather and terrain, his watchful eye for every flick of a cow's ear, his appreciation of the oddity of people as a relief to the long days on the trail. Small wonder that this superbly concrete account has been used as the basis of one of the best Western tales for young readers published in recent years, Richard Wormser's RIDE A NORTHBOUND HORSE. The experience, the attitude of these writers is varied and significant; yet, in so far as their work is used in topic books, it is used without comment on the source and so it loses part of its interest.

There is much to be said for offering to the young, instead of a book "on" the cowboy, a book of extracts from every kind of writer from frankly professional yarners like Will James to ranchers, investors, meat merchants, pioneers and their wives, lawyers, government officials. R. F. Adams' anthology, THE BEST OF THE

AMERICAN COWBOY affords a good starting point for such a
book, which would do more than twenty conscientious text-books
(though not more than twenty *good* pieces of fiction) to give children
a rich and varied picture of the past. A step in this direction has
been taken by Edith McCall in COWBOYS AND CATTLE DRIVES
(1963). The cover of this book suggests drama in the milling cattle
of the faint background and realism in the sturdy, untidy cowboy
who stands out in the foreground; but the text combines some fairly
sensational material with a great deal of accurate incidental detail.
Here are four pieces of real life experience rewritten in story form.
The method can be seen in the opening sentence of the first section,
which reads "Charlie Goodnight woke up very early on a certain
day in the autumn of 1845", and in its last paragraph:

> Charlie himself liked the West so well that he opened a big ranch
> in Colorado, becoming one of the West's biggest cattle ranchers.
> Oliver Loving was not so lucky. The Comanches came to the
> new trails, as he had expected, and one day, when Mr. Loving
> and Bill Wilson were riding alone, the Comanches wounded him.
> By the time Bill could ride for help and Charlie Goodnight
> reached his old friend, it was too late. The older man was dying.
> His name lives on in Texas and New Mexico, given to a county
> and a town, as well as to the trail up the Pecos.
> COWBOYS AND CATTLE DRIVES, pp. 59–60

Drawing by Glen Rounds from TRAIL DRIVE (Whiting and Wheaton), an edited
version of Andy Adams's LOG OF A COWBOY

Charlie Goodnight's story takes us from the trail-driver's boyhood to the period when he and his employer Oliver Loving pioneered the Pecos route to Colorado. Since the discoveries they made then about droving in dry country contributed largely to the success of later trail-drivers, the author has a right to stress this part of the journey. Her narrative is simple, with bridging talk of a somewhat unconvincing kind, and with an intelligent choice of detail to make the importance of this famous journey clear. Like Goodnight's story, the three that accompany it are historically true – namely, the story of James Cook as a boy on the Chisholm Trail, of Tom Smith standing for law and order in the Abilene of 1869 and of Will Rogers, who realised a youthful ambition to be a cowboy somewhat indirectly by winning fame as a vaudeville comedian.

In each of the sections of COWBOYS AND CATTLE DRIVES the central episode is used to carry informative detail. There is young Jim Cook's initiation into the art of making a Tucson bed – "You just push your stomach onto the ground, like this. Then you cover it up with your back"; the water-melons commandeered from old Rich Coffee on Goodnight's famous drive; the camp coffee that is too weak "if a horseshoe will sink in it"; the thirst – and cattle jostling one another to death in the Pecos river. The strong engravings, by Carol Rogers, of horses, man and scenery, with their rendering of action, should do as much as the text to catch and hold a young reader.

As the title of this book makes clear, COWBOYS AND CATTLE DRIVES deals with only a part of the whole subject of cowboys in the past. It satisfies in a modified way the appetite for fiction – that is, for a book capable of containing action, excitement, character; and many children will prefer to take their facts in this form rather than from a deliberately informative survey. They will certainly find in Edith McCall's book something of the vivacity of the *Rawhide* series (the only television series of recent years with a real regard for authenticity of detail).

There are young readers, up to thirteen or fourteen, who would prefer a sensible historical account of the cowboy's place in American history, putting him in perspective with other occupation-groups like homesteaders, prospectors, railroad-surveyors, who opened up the West, and keeping a sense of proportion about

rustlers, gunmen and "savage" Indians. As far as English publications are concerned, he will have to be content with the American-
derived REAL BOOK OF COWBOYS by Michael Gorham (1951), a
book whose material owes something at least to such authorities
as Paul Wellman and Mari Sandoz and old-timers like Will James.
The virtues of THE REAL BOOK OF COWBOYS are not immediately apparent, for the author's sober realism about the life of a
working cowboy, then and now, is only reached after three light-
hearted and occasionally facetious chapters on rodeos which make
you feel you are still playing cowboys. But in Chapter 4 the author
tightens his belt and launches into a brief, straightforward account
of the origin of the longhorn, the change from the Mexican vaquero
to the incoming American cowpuncher, the modification of the
Spanish saddle and the sensible shift from Spanish pikes for droving
to the lariat better suited to rough country. History continues with
the Civil War and its aftermath in herds of wild cattle, the coming
of the railroad and the opening up of the great trails to northern
cow towns, life on the open range and the contest between cowboys
and settlers when barbed wire began to cut up the great ranges.
The market for beef, the crossing of the longhorn with the more
docile Hereford and shorthorn, the breeding and training of horses,
leads to a discussion of modern ranches like the Trinchera in
Colorado and the King ranch in Southern Texas, with such inno-
vations as battery breeding, artificial insemination and the increased
use of private aircraft. Here the author turns from his historical
outline back to the more obviously romantic aspect of cowboy life,
with a chapter on rustlers, an account of the Rodeo Cowboys'
Association and the Madison Square Garden show, and a final
round-up of jottings on clothes, horses, films and cowboy idioms.
    Admirable though his intention is, Michael Gorham has spent
more time than he need have done in beckoning to the young
reader with cheap and lengthy effects, which leave him little enough
space for the history of the opening up of the West. Quotation is
lacking; the illustrations are extremely dull, and there is no map,
so that brief references to localities and trails are impossible for an
English reader to appreciate. But this is a sensible book and its
approach is salutary:

    A trail drive went on for several weeks or for two or three months, depending on how far from the railway it started. All along the way the cowboys slept out under the stars, often in the rain. Day after day they rode in clouds of dust from dawn to late afternoon. They got hot and sweaty and bearded and shaggy-haired – and mighty tired of one another's company.

THE REAL BOOK OF COWBOYS, p. 73

There are touches of dry humour, for instance in the following description of cowboys leaving New York after competing in an indoor rodeo:

One group dismounts at a grocery store to buy supplies. A little wearily they answer questions. They are going home to Texas. They expect to get there by January – that is three months from now. The one who is riding with his leg in a cast broke it bull-dogging a steer. In a few minutes they are off again. The young fellow with the broken leg ties his crutch to his saddle, opens a comic, and reads as his horse ambles on towards Texas.

ibid., p. 163

English children are mostly extremely ignorant of the background of American history. While they may acquire random facts from current Westerns, the average film about courageous homesteaders shooting it out with the trigger-happy hands of a greedy rancher or gold-haired and gold-hearted harlots dying for love of a handsome cowboy are not likely to put the working cowhand in perspective for them. Certain spheres of action, indeed, belong essentially to fiction. Out of the gangster feud has arisen that subtle character, the lone gunman (*Shane* is the great example) who embodies some of our deepest feelings. But a topic book can correct some of the ambiguities of screen and novel by offering the facts about Billy the Kid, Calamity Jane, Wyatt Earp and other legendary figures and making it impossible to romanticise them.

The cowboy is not a character to be grimly analysed as a cog in a social wheel. At the same time it seems logical that when a child has looked at the man's daily life, he should be invited to look a little further and see how he fits into the pattern of a national economy, and what part he played in the development of that economy. "Cowboys" can be isolated as a subject for a topic book but this is no self-contained subject, any more than the story is finished when the cattle have reached Abilene.

A recent book for America, THE COWBOY by Vincent Paul Rennert (1966), promised a wide perspective, with its series title *America in the Making*, but the subtitle of the book, "The lore and lingo of the cowboy from the days of the open range to the present", gives a more honest idea of the contents, which are descriptive rather than historical. Here for the first time are references to classic sources of information; McCoy's HISTORIC SKETCHES and Theodore Roosevelt's reminiscences are quoted among others, and there is a substantial reading list. Here, too, instead of lame approximations of life on the range, are reproductions of pictures by Russell and Remington, executed from life, and one picture in particular, of a cowboy in full dress, which will delight anyone who is tired of the slick television hero of the West.

But for illustration, for fact (brief but far-ranging), for a broad sweep of idea, let the child who is really interested stay with his games and his stories and his television serials till he is old enough (and eleven would do) to dive into a pictorial study in the American *Junior Library* series, Don Ward's COWBOYS AND CATTLE COUNTRY (1961). A foreword by J. C. Dykes not only asserts that the book hopes to correct the Hollywood view of the cowboy, but also that this will be done through the works of Andy Adams, Jim Cook, Siringo and the painting of Russell, Remington and Seltzer. This is a spacious and decorative production. Illustrations of every kind (photographs, maps, primitive paintings, drawings of scenes and of single objects, film stills, cartoons) echo and enlarge upon generalisations, details and anecdotes.

P. A. Rollins once said that the cowboy of the adventure story came in three species:

He is portrayed in these several species as being necessarily clownish, reckless, excessively joyful, noisy, and profane; or else wolfish, scheming, sullen, malevolent, prone to ambush and murder; or else dignified, thoughtful, taciturn, idealistic, with conscience and trigger-finger accurate, quick, and in unison, and also in all these species as being assuredly freighted with weapons, terse in utterance, and picturesque in apparel.

THE COWBOY, p. 40

Each of these types can be discerned in Don Ward's survey, and, in addition, the vaquero of the 1830s, the laconic cowboy of Andy Adams's day who thought nothing of "spreading his clothing on an anthill to remove the vermin" and the modern cowboy who must be expert jeep-driver, mason, electrician, carpenter, mechanic and vet. Stanley Vestal has pointed out, in SHORT GRASS COUNTRY (1941), that concentration of event in American history which English children do not find it easy to appreciate:

> White men still breathe who began as buffalo hunters, turned cowboy when the bison vanished, plowed and reaped on farms with the first settlers, freighted goods to the new towns and made fortunes as frontier merchants, drilled oil-wells, dug mines, built factories as industrialists, and ended as financiers sitting behind mahogany desks in sky-scrapers. Such men experienced every phase of human civilization in a single life-time.
> SHORT GRASS COUNTRY, p. 10

My son-in-law, on a reconnaissance trip to the United States as an agricultural specialist, visited a ranch in Montana where the owner and his wife ran a carefully selected breed of cattle on grimly barren butte country, riding the ranges themselves by day in plain and economical versions of cowboy clothes and at night doing paper work on breeding records and artificial insemination possibilities. They were helped by an old-timer in his late seventies who, when pressed, would describe life on the ranges at the turn of the century. Gun-law and lynch-law had once been taken for granted in his working life; "We strung them up" was no affectation on his lips. Now he took artificial insemination for granted as well. I am still hoping for the perfect book for the enquiring young reader which will truly balance past with present and will convince him beyond all doubt that a cowboy was and is not a myth or a folk hero but an ordinary individual leading what, for him at least, is an ordinary working life. Here is the excitement, here is the romance.

Reading List

Abbott, E. C. ("Teddy Blue"). WE POINTED THEM NORTH: RECOLLECTIONS OF A
  COW PUNCHER, with Helena Huntington Smith. *Farrar and Rinehart* 1939,
  University of Oklahoma Press 1955. Drawings by Ross Santee, and some
  photographs.
Adams, Andy. LOG OF A COWBOY (First published 1903). Edition used,
  TRAIL DRIVE: A TRUE NARRATIVE OF COWBOY LIFE FROM ANDY ADAMS'
  LOG OF A COWBOY. (*Holiday House* 1965) *Whiting and Wheaton* 1966. Edited
  and illustrated by Glen Rounds.
Adams, R. F. THE BEST OF THE AMERICAN COWBOY. *University of Oklahoma
  Press* 1957. See also THE OLD-TIME COWHAND, *Macmillan* 1961, illustrated by
  Nick Eggenhofer; THE RAMPAGING HERD, *University of Oklahoma Press* 1959;
  WESTERN WORDS, *University of Oklahoma Press* 1945, revised edition 1968.
Anglund, Joan Walsh. THE BRAVE COWBOY (*Harcourt, Brace* 1959) *Collins*
  1959. Illustrated by the author.
Bethell, Jean. THE CLUMSY COWBOY. Easy Readers. (*Grosset & Dunlap* 1963)
  Muller 1968. Illustrated by Shel and Jan Haber.
Brewster, Benjamin. THE FIRST BOOK OF COWBOYS. First Books. (*Franklin Watts*
  1950) *Edmund Ward* 1965. Illustrated by William Moyers.
Clark, Marion. BILL OF THE PONY EXPRESS. Children of Other Times.
  (*International Copyright Institute* 1964) *A. and C. Black* 1967. Adapted by
  Ellen M. Dolan, illustrated by Marie Wabbes.
Dobie, J. F. THE LONGHORNS (*Little, Brown* 1941) *Nicholson and Watson* 1943.
  Illustrated by Tom Lea. See also COW PEOPLE (*Little, Brown* 1964) *Hammond
  and Hammond* 1964. With photographs; TALES OF OLD-TIME TEXAS (First
  published in the U.S.A. 1928, *Little, Brown* 1955) *Hammond and Hammond* 1959.
  Illustrated by Barbara Latham; and many other books.
Frantz, Joe B. and Choate, J. E., Jr. THE AMERICAN COWBOY: THE MYTH AND
  THE REALITY (*University of Oklahoma Press* 1955) *Thames and Hudson* 1956,
  Bailey Bros. 1968. A book of strong opinion for the general reader, tracing the
  development of the cowboy as a folk hero and analysing many of the books and
  films that made him so.
Gard, Wayne. THE CHISHOLM TRAIL. *University of Oklahoma Press* 1954.
  Drawings by Nick Eggenhofer, and with photographs and prints. A lively,
  discursive book on the period 1867 to c. 1872, full of anecdotes and with useful
  maps and an extensive bibliography.

Gorham, Michael. THE REAL BOOK OF COWBOYS. Real Books. (*Doubleday* 1951)
Dobson 1959. Illustrated by C. L. Hartman.

Greene, Carla. I WANT TO BE A COWBOY. I want to be . . . (*Children's Press* 1960)
W. and R. Chambers 1961. Illustrated by Janet La Salle.

Hoare, Robert J. THE OLD WEST. *Muller* 1969. Illustrated by Douglas Phillips.

Holling, H. C. THE BOOK OF COWBOYS. (*Platt* 1936, revised edition 1968)
Cassell 1938. Illustrated by H. C. and Lucille Holling.

Horan, James D. and Sann, Paul. A PICTORIAL HISTORY OF THE WILD WEST
(*Crown* 1959) *Paul Hamlyn* 1965. Illustrated with photographs and prints. The
wealth of material from detective agencies, police records and private sources
makes this a fascinating quarry for illustrative matter.

Horgan, Paul. GREAT RIVER: THE RIO GRANDE IN AMERICAN HISTORY.
Rinehart and Co. 1954, 2 vols; *Holt, Rinehart and Winston*, revised edition 1960.
This extremely interesting popular history contains a composite picture of the
cowboy drawn from contemporary literature, with records of old-timer
reminiscences and many cowboy ballads.

James, Will R. "Filling in the cracks" in THE DRIFTING COWBOY. *Scribner* 1925.
Illustrated by the author. See also SMOKY (*Scribner* 1926) *Penguin* 1941.

Landin, Les. ABOUT COWBOYS AROUND THE WORLD. Junior Look, Read and
Learn. (*Melmont* 1963) *Muller* 1966. Illustrated by Harry Timmins.

McCall, Edith. COWBOYS AND CATTLE DRIVES (*Childrens Press* 1964) *Odhams
Press* 1965. Illustrated by Carol Rogers.

McCoy, Joseph. HISTORIC SKETCHES OF THE CATTLE TRADE OF THE WEST
AND SOUTHWEST. Kansas City 1874, privately printed, edited by R. P. Bieber;
California, *Arthur H. Clarke Co.* 1940. Illustrated by photographs and prints.

Martini, Teri. THE JUNIOR TRUE BOOK OF COWBOYS. Junior True Books.
(*Childrens Press* 1955) *Muller* 1959. Illustrated by Charles Heston.

Prothero, C. C. WILD WEST READERS. *Pergamon* 1969. Illustrated by Frank Bird.

Rennert, Vincent Paul. THE COWBOY. America in the Making. (*Macmillan*
1966 U.S.A.) *Collier-Macmillan* 1966 U.K. Illustrated by photographs and
prints.

Rollins, Philip A. THE COWBOY: HIS CHARACTERISTICS, HIS EQUIPMENT,
AND HIS PART IN THE DEVELOPMENT OF THE WEST. *Scribner* 1922.

Rudge, Kenneth. FAR WEST READERS. *Pergamon* 1969. Illustrated by Frank Bird.

Russell, Charles M. TRAILS PLOWED UNDER (*Doubleday* 1953) *Heinemann* 1927.
Illustrated by the author.

Salmon, Ross. ROSS SALMON'S COWBOY BOOK. *Nelson* 1955. See also TRUE
COWBOY TALES, *Muller* 1953, and JUNGLE COWBOY, *Hodder and Stoughton*
1953.

Salmon, Ross. THE TRUE BOOK ABOUT COWBOYS. True Books. *Muller* 1956. Illustrated by De Marco.

Saltiel, Henry. BEEF AND GOLD. It Really Happened. *Johnston and Bacon* 1966. Two-colour illustrations, no named artist.

Sandoz, Mari. THE CATTLEMEN (*Hastings House* 1958) *Eyre and Spottiswoode* 1961.

Sayers, Frank. COWBOYS (*Golden Key Books* 1955) *Adprint* 1958. Illustrated by Hans Helweg and Frank Bolle. The story of a lifetime spent in the saddle as cowboy and detective.

Siringo, Charles. RIATA AND SPURS *Houghton Mifflin* 1927; A TEXAS COWBOY: FIFTEEN YEARS ON THE HURRICANE DECK OF A SPANISH PONY. First published 1885. *William Sloane Associates New York* 1950, with introduction by J. F. Dobie. Illustrated by Tom Lea.

Stuart, Granville. FORTY YEARS ON THE FRONTIER. Cleveland, *Arthur H. Clarke Co.* 1925.

Thompson, T. A. COWBOYS. Learning Library. *Blackwell* 1966. Illustrated by Trevor Stubley.

Vestal, Stanley. SHORT GRASS COUNTRY. *Duell, Sloan & Pearce* 1941

Ward, Don. COWBOYS AND CATTLE COUNTRY. American Heritage Junior Library. *Harper and Row* 1961. Illustrated with paintings, prints, drawings and photographs of the period.

Wellman, Paul I. THE TRAMPLING HERD: THE STORY OF THE CATTLE RANGE IN AMERICA. *Foulsham* 1958. An extensive, very practical history, commenting on the relative value of contemporary records and writings. The end-papers contain a useful map.

Relevant novels and stories

Davison, Frank Dalby. MAN-SHY. (Australia 1931. *Penguin*, Puffin Books, 1956, *Angus and Robertson* 1962) *Tri-Ocean* 1969.

Gipson, Frank. COWHAND (*Harper and Row* 1953) *Corgi* 1957. A rousing novel based on the life of Fred Alford, reputed one of the best cowboys in West Texas, who went after life "as if it were something to be roped in a hurry before it got away". The picture of a *working* cowboy.

Humphrey, William. THE ORDWAYS (*Knopf* 1965) *Chatto and Windus* 1965. A sardonic novel satirising the romantic idea of oldtime Texas.

Ottley, Reginald. BY THE SANDHILLS OF YAMBOORAH. *Deutsch* 1965; THE ROAN COLT OF YAMBOORAH (*Deutsch* 1966) *Harcourt, Brace* 1967; RAIN COMES TO YAMBOORAH (*Deutsch* 1967) *Harcourt, Brace* 1968. Time, place and action books. Illustrated by Clyde Pearson. Stories full of zest and humour giving a picture of a boy growing up and working on a cattle station in the Australian outback in the nineteen-thirties.

Richter, Conrad. THE SEA OF GRASS (*Knopf* 1937) *Constable* 1937. A classic romance in which the Texas ranch which provides the background has an almost symbolic significance.

Wister, Owen. THE VIRGINIAN (First published 1902) *Harper and Row* 1966. *Mayflower* 1967. Quotation from *Macmillan* edition 1928.

Wormser, Richard. RIDE A NORTHBOUND HORSE (*Oxford University Press* 1964) *Morrow* 1964. Illustrated by Victor G. Ambrus.

2f | Time

This peculiar non-existent and therefore intangible non-element Time . . .
Kenneth Ullyett. BRITISH CLOCKS AND CLOCKMAKERS

2f | Time

MANY of the books on time written for the young prove to be in fact about clocks. The evasion is understandable. The writer of junior topic books faces no stiffer challenge than the need to express concepts simply. It is easier to select and arrange known facts about the development of timepieces, the calendar, international date-zones and so on, and convenient, perhaps, to assume that if scientists and philosophers cannot agree on a workable definition of time as an abstraction, children should not be expected to consider this aspect of the subject at all. But a child *should* be invited to make a leap at understanding abstract problems. The intellectual boldness of the young is underrated in almost all the books on time which I shall discuss.

The confusion that exists about time as a concept may be detected in the terms used in current topic books – for example, *discover, learn, solve, invent*. There are certain ways in which abstract ideas can be made more palatable for children – through image or analogy, for instance – but first the writer must be clear about the meaning of the terms he uses. *Invent* may be legitimately used in connection with, say, the verge-escapement, but not of time itself. In *discovering* the difference between walking and running you have not discovered time but only a manifestation of it. You can *learn* by trial and error what particular measurement of duration will be most convenient for your tribe, city or organisation, but you cannot *learn*, at any stage of civilisation, about the existence of something which has no existence as such.

Are words in fact the ideal way to communicate either ideas or facts about time to the young? From the moment when the inbuilt rhythm of a new-born baby begins to conflict with the super-imposed time-order of family life, it becomes clear that time may be defined in more than one way. Indeed, a small child already possesses the knowledge of one possible definition, that time is a biological rhythm, though she lacks the power to put into words her perception of light and darkness, hunger and thirst and other rhythms which she shares with all animals. Yet another definition, that time is a mental process, she may have within her grasp when she dreams or when she imagines scenes in the past or future. Another, that time is relative to emotion, she may suspect when she is old enough to notice the difference between waiting at the dentist's and waiting for an expected treat. In fact by the time a child can recognise the figures on a clock and learn how to read them (when she learns to "tell" the time) she has already enough experience to recognise time as a dimension. Any one of the definitions suggested above could be expressed as a concept, in a suitably practical way, if it were properly isolated from purely general remarks about the human organising of time, not because at this stage we want to teach the child but simply to confirm experience which has been unconsciously absorbed.

To help a child to externalise and recognise his own experience, picture-books can extend their usual role. Helga Renneisen's MR CLOCKMAN (1967), a picture-story book from Germany, tells how rebellious Dora, unwilling to stay in bed at night while her parents are out, is taken by Mr Clockman on a tour of the city to ask various clocks their opinion of her behaviour. Timepieces on the town hall, station and factory explain the kind of people for whom they mark the passage of time, and finally the school clock firmly sends the little girl back to bed. Each occupation has its own timing; the point is neatly made. Long before statements of fact as such can make much impression on a young child, picture-books with domestic themes can lay down the rules, customs and conventions of human society.

A rather more complicated idea is contained in an artless tale by Esphyr Slobodkina, THE CLOCK (1956). A small town in Vermont is ruled by the homely chimes of the clock on the church tower:

Very early in the morning – when the chimes ring five times – they wake up the milk-truck driver so that he can bring the milk from the farms into town in time for breakfast.

When the chimes ring eight times, they tell the grocer it is time to open his store so that the people can buy eggs and bacon and oranges, and all the other things they need.

In the afternoon the chimes tell the postman when it is time to meet the mail train, and late at night they remind the baker that it is time to start baking if he wants the townspeople to have fresh rolls in the morning.

THE CLOCK, no page numbers

But one morning the clock strikes one instead of six and seven, and all the people turn over and go to sleep again – all but one. Mrs Johnson "was deaf and never waited for the chimes. She just knew that when she woke it was time to get up." So, as the old lady goes down to the shops for her breakfast rolls and milk and wakes her astonished neighbours, the idea of biological time is amusingly offered to the child, who will find it later in more abstract terms, and will find it all the easier to accept for this simple first statement.

The first conscious step the child takes is to learn the customary divisions of time and how they are marked on the clock. Here, obviously, books are only one of many useful ways of learning, and probably not the most useful, since they are further removed from reality than a real or even a toy clock. Nils Werner has brought his picture-book, WHAT O'CLOCK? (1968), nearer to reality by adding to his verses about little Klaus and his day a clock-face which is seen through a circular hole in each page and which can be manipulated to fit each statement in the text.

Another picture-book, Frank Jupo's A DAY AROUND THE WORLD (1968), introduces the difficult subject of time zones. In New York a boy gets up to take his dog for a walk before breakfast and school; another boy helps his father in a Brazilian town and the author explains that for this boy it is 9 a.m., not 7 a.m. Moving to Senegal, London, Greece and so round the world to Fiji, he ends his cycle with a little girl fast asleep in Fiji and a boy in Mexico leaving home at six in the morning to go to market:

But now it is only six o'clock in the morning – too early for Miguel to know whether it will be a lucky day. Nor does he know, while he watches the sunrise, that it is lunchtime in Nikos'

village in Greece, and suppertime in Yuri's town in Siberia, and time to sleep on Kaliti's island in the Pacific.
A DAY AROUND THE WORLD, no page numbers

Real children, named and depicted, give warmth to the mathematical facts about time. This approach seems more likely to attract a young child than the more generalised examples in Jane Hart's LET'S THINK ABOUT TIME (1965), a book which combines a picture-book format with openly instructive sentences, enumerating the divisions of time from seconds to seasons and the year. Unlike the picture-books already mentioned, which would probably be read to a young child, LET'S THINK ABOUT TIME is designed for solo reading, with short sentences broken up by small illustrations and with coloured fancy type to emphasise important words. The book is shaped not only by the simple time-scale but also by the suggestion that time is not as simple as it may seem. The first two pages introduce the idea of psychological time:

Sometimes, when you are in bed with the measles or with a cold an Hour can seem like a whole Day. But when you're riding your bike or when you're playing tag . . . an Hour may seem like only a *minute*. It's so hard to tell how long something takes.
LET'S THINK ABOUT TIME

And the book ends firmly, "A YEAR is a long time, and TIME goes on forever."
This stretching of simple statement is absent from THE JUNIOR TRUE BOOK OF TIME by Feenie Ziner and Elizabeth Thompson (1956) which tends towards the more formal approach of a classroom topic book. Taking the accepted divisions of time for granted, the authors enumerate them in relation to a child's daily life. Statements like "It is morning at sunrise" or "It is evening when the sun sets" are illustrated with folksy little pictures in which happy folk act out the points in the text – a small boy watches the sunrise, father comes home from the factory. Each sentence is likely to do no more than remind children of what they already know and each is, as it were, end-stopped. Thus the statement "When the sun shines on the other side of our round earth, it is night time for us" stands on its own. One picture shows Japanese

children flying kites, bowing, carrying loads, and in an accompanying picture of a globe, children are seen asleep in bed. Perhaps this
is no place to introduce greater complexity about the relationship
of earth to sun, but the illustration of this same point in Leslie
Waller's TIME (1959) is more effective because it shows a globe
bisected on a double spread. First an English child is depicted with
a parasol and a Japanese boy asleep: then the position of the children is reversed. The pictures could therefore help a child to realise
that the earth has turned and light and dark have been reversed.

In both these books, while their direct, simple prose is suitable
to a child reading early in life who has adult help at hand, there is a
baldness, a lack of invitation which makes them in fact a poor substitute for contact with life at first hand; questions about time rising
naturally from the events of each separate day will be more helpful.

The purpose of the series *Our Book Corner* from W. and R.
Chambers is to supply children in their first years at school with
easily accessible facts but, far more importantly, to help them to
learn how to absorb facts through the printed word. TELLING
THE TIME (1962) by Jean Wilson belongs to this series of twelve-
pagers. Taking this little booklet more or less at random from the
classroom shelf, a child beginning to read will find simple, single
statements about natural time, shadow clocks and sundials, sand-
glass and cuckoo-clock, matched with equally simple pictures. If
there is nothing inspiring about text and illustrations there is
nothing misleading either, but in fact such books provide little
more than useful reading practice, since there is not enough space
to relate facts to a final concept.

More fully informative, TIME AND CLOCKS by R. H. C. Fice
and R. H. Simkiss (1967) must take more responsibility for its
statements, since this pamphlet seems to be intended for direct
study. Statements and questions alternate. The questions presuppose
answers, written or spoken, and in order to supply answers the
pupil will need to search his memory and experience or else to
perform a simple experiment. The questions are of a revision type,
following the information in the text:

One afternoon measure the time you are in school.
Use the school clock,
a shadow clock,

a candle clock,
a water clock.
Are all these times the same?
Write down which of these clocks:—
Can be used by day and night.
Can be used indoors and outdoors.
Can be carried about with you.
Can be used more than once.
TIME AND CLOCKS, p. 15

To use a book like this the child must be able to read fluently and
also to assimilate facts; finally, he must take the sophisticated step
of translating what he has read either into a new statement of his
own or into practice. By the time he is ready to take this step from
reading to action, intellectual or physical, he should be ready for a
less elementary text than this one, ready to accept more detail and
to execute more complex and interesting experiments than those
suggested here. The only real appeal to intelligence in the book
lies in the negative questions at the end of each definition of an
early form of time-keeping – for example, "Can you tell the time
by a sundial on a dull day?" or "Can you carry water-clocks around
with you?" These are questions already asked positively, and they
are hardly exacting enough for a child who can read; they may, of
course, suggest to him that man's time-keeping inventions have
been a matter of trial and error.

In fact, the method of expressing facts in this book seems better
suited to the child himself; this is the way he might construct a
"book" on time-keeping after he has done experiments under the
eye of a teacher or a parent. To use the book *first* might be to
misunderstand statements which are telescoped or over-simplified.
TIME AND CLOCKS, explaining the working of a pendulum, points
out with suitable diagrammatical illustration that with four pendulums of varying lengths a child can find out which is the slowest and
which the quickest:

A pendulum always swings at the same speed. A pendulum makes
the hands go round at the same speed. If you make the pendulum
shorter it will swing faster. This makes the clock go faster.
ibid., p. 21

There is a verbal ambiguity here which is due to extreme simplifying and saving of words. An adult demonstrating the point can make it clear to the child that each individual pendulum swings at the same speed on each of its swings. But this is a book designed for children who are learning to apprehend the meaning of a statement by reading, and they may not be able to supply the linking point which the author has omitted. The impressive array of diagrams and explanations about the working of pendulums in an educational pamphlet on Time prepared for the Nuffield Science Six to Thirteen project shows how experiment properly directed can lead to proper generalisation.

We should not expect a book that describes a process verbally to do its work fully with children in the middle years until they have used it to make an experiment and then to confirm their actions. This throws on the writer the onus of describing the process with absolute clarity and also of suggesting a definition or a conclusion resulting from the experiment. To extract information from the written word is a technique which has to be learned and, where children are concerned, there can be no hard and fast rule about the particular educational tool to be used at a particular time; but teacher, parent and child have a right to expect that the tool, whether book, filmstrip, picture or demonstration, should be efficient.

The dangers of simplification are greater when we are concerned with statements of abstract ideas. R. W. Purton's MAN TELLS THE TIME (1966) is not intended solely for use in school. Format, coloured pictures and layout suggest casual reading in private, mainly for an intelligent seven-year-old. The author does not only enumerate the various methods of indicating time, from shadow clocks to caesium watches; he is also concerned with the way man has divided time. This matter he approaches in an interesting way:

Do you sometimes find that time goes very quickly or very slowly? Our holidays always seem to pass quickly. If we are doing something we do not like doing, time seems to pass very slowly.

But this is only what it *seems* to do. A minute is always sixty seconds. An hour is never more than sixty minutes.

All our periods of time are decided by the movement of the earth and the moon.

MAN TELLS THE TIME, p. 5

From here he goes on logically to explain the relation between earth/
sun and earth/moon on one hand and year, month and day on the
other:

> People noticed that there were about thirty nights and thirty days
> between full moons. So thirty days and nights were a MONTH.
> . . . It was also noticed that there were about twelve full moons
> between one harvest time and the next harvest – a YEAR later. So
> twelve full moons (or months) was a year.
>
> ibid., pp. 8–9

One simple stage in the argument would have made this clearer.
What is a child to make of ". . . *were* a MONTH" or . . . "*was* a
YEAR"? Why is he not directly told that man in dividing time took
a decision, that he has in fact used his observation of light and dark,
life and death, to name and define that invisible, essential part of
his environment, time, which only exists when he recognises it?
If a child is old enough to be expected to understand the way the
Babylonians divided the periods of light and dark, he is old enough
to be told also that because of what the Babylonians and others
observed, they found it necessary to suppose a combination of
distance and duration and call it time. In using the verb "to be",
the author has obscured man's part in the matter.

The last chapter of the book similarly begs the question of time
and what it is:

> . . . how old is time really? Is it one thousand years old, or ten
> thousand years or fifty thousand?
>
> You may hear somebody say that something is as old as the
> stars.
>
> The stars are millions of years old.
>
> We cannot say how old time is. We do not know. We only
> know that we can measure time very far back.
>
> The time line at the side [a diagram of centuries] helps to show
> you how long ago some things happened. It shows part of the
> time men may have lived on earth.
>
> Suppose you could make this line fifty thousand times as long.
> The line would be about five miles long, but it would still not
> show when the earth was formed.

The earth is very old, but the sun is older still.
ibid., pp. 31–2

The author has moved from time as a concept to historical time without warning, and the child will get no clear idea which aspect he is supposed to be considering.

It is noticeable that the Nuffield Science project on time already mentioned, which is very thorough, not to say ambitious, in its suggestions for classroom activities and for ways of evoking response

On this spread from MAN MUST MEASURE (Rathbone), time is being reckoned by Egyptian, Babylonian, Roman and Chinese scribes, so that calendars can be drawn up; it is being recorded, on a Maya stele; and it is being used in husbandry. Lancelot Hogben's text is concentrated and scholarly, but he arranges facts clearly in a logical way and this is paralleled in the illustrations and their layout. The subject of the calendar becomes interesting because the kinds of signs, symbols and figures used for calculation are clearly shown, and similarly the close relation of time and husbandry is demonstrated in the Mayan scene. The Wonderful World series to which MAN MUST MEASURE belongs is notable for the intelligent integration of text and illustration in large-format books; pictures clarify and often add to the information in the text and each spread shows an appropriate design and balance. This method of illustration does much to counteract the dangers of generalisation in a broad treatment of historical subjects.

from children, still avoids defining time. The case for an extended
study of time in school is put firmly:

> Time is a theme which has many elements to delight children.
> They can follow the history of timekeeping, improvise clocks
> and take pleasure in their movement, observe the heavens, talk
> about scientists of the past and look at the fossil remains of
> plants and animals from long ago. All this they can do in a true
> spirit of inquiry which will lead them across subject barriers and

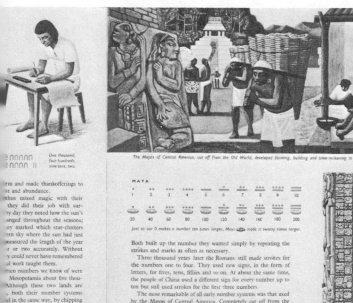

The Mayas of Central America, cut off from the Old World, developed farming, building and time-reckoning in their own way.

One thousand,
four hundreds,
nine tens, two.

rm and made thankofferings to
st and abundance.
thus mixed magic with their
they did their job with sur-
y day they noted how the sun's
anged throughout the seasons;
ey marked which star-clusters
ern sky where the sun had just
measured the length of the year
r or two accurately. Without
y could never have remembered
al work taught them.
ten numbers we know of were
Mesopotamia about five thou-
Although these two lands are
, both their number systems
ed in the same way, by chipping
ie stone to record the passing
of Egypt wrote on papyrus
those of Mesopotamia on soft
of their numbers are naturally
used simple strokes for ones
s for tens and higher numbers.

MAYA

•	••	•••	••••	▬	• ▬	•• ▬	••• ▬	•••• ▬	▬▬
1	2	3	4	5	6	7	8	9	10

⬭	• ⬭	•• ⬭	••• ⬭	⬭	• ⬭	•• ⬭	••• ⬭	•••• ⬭	⬭
20	40	60	80	100	120	140	160	180	200

Just as our 0 makes a number ten times larger, Maya ⬭ made it twenty times larger.

Both built up the number they wanted simply by repeating the
strokes and marks as often as necessary.
   Three thousand years later the Romans still made strokes for
the numbers one to four. They used new signs, in the form of
letters, for fives, tens, fifties and so on. At about the same time,
the people of China used a different sign for every number up to
ten but still used strokes for the first three numbers.
   The most remarkable of all early number systems was that used
by the Mayas of Central America. Completely cut off from the
civilisations of the Old World, these people could write any
number with the help of only three signs – a dot, a stroke and a
kind of oval. With dots and strokes only, they could build up
any number from one to nineteen (▬▬▬▬). By adding one oval
below any number, they made it twenty times larger, thus:
• 1 ⬭ 20. Adding a second oval would again multiply the
number by twenty. In time-reckoning, however, they adjusted
this system: adding a second oval, multiplied the number by
eighteen instead of twenty, so that ⬭ meant not 400 (1 × 20 × 20)
but 360 (1 × 20 × 18). If we recall the moon-calendar of 360 days,
we can understand why they used their number sign in this way.
   In time the Mayas used a sun-calendar of 365 days. For their
records of dates, carved on stone columns called steles, they
used special numerals shaped like human faces.

Maya stele.

show the unity of work and of knowledge at this stage in their lives.

p. 7

But in asserting that "Man, the most advanced of all animals, even attempts to measure this elusive phenomenon that he calls 'time'", and in enquiring "What would happen to our sense of time if the world stopped spinning", the author has not gone so far as to suggest that time is a concept of man's devising. It would seem that

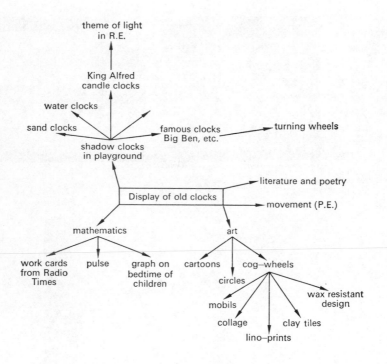

Figure 1. A variety of activities connected with time developed from the starting point of a display of old clocks.

This diagram from the Nuffield pamphlet on TIME (Macdonald Educational) emphasises in a different way the suggestions made in the text.

the child involved in a classroom exploration of time by way of modelling, mathematics, dancing and the like, is not going to get any nearer to understanding time than the child who sits down and reads a book on the subject, and at the least it should be suggested to him that there *is* something to understand.

In this context, SPACE AND TIME (1968) by the American Jeanne Bendick, in a recently launched series for beginner readers called *Science experiences*, makes a notable attempt to relate concepts to actions. After she has suggested various ways of measuring space by "how long", "how wide" and "how high", she points out that time can only be measured by "how long", and continues:

> Maybe you think that seconds and minutes and hours and days and years are different ways of measuring in time, but they are not. They are just different units for measuring "how long" in time. SPACE AND TIME, p. 49

She points out that "you can't measure time with a measuring-stick" or "pour it into a cup, or pack it into a basket"* and after mentioning such measuring techniques as a clock, a candle and a sundial, she contrasts these man-made techniques with tides and seasons, emphasising that "We can measure time by change, when things change in a regular, orderly way."† She explains further that we can measure time by "motion – by something moving through space".‡

All through this exceptionally lucid exposition the author has taken the unusual course of putting concept first and method afterwards, so that a child could become aware, just by the pattern of argument, that the idea of time preceded and overshadows objects like clocks and sundials. The relation of fact and concept has been as carefully thought out in this very junior book as in the longer THE FIRST BOOK OF TIME which I discuss later (see p. 179).

Most topic books are built round a subject rather than a theme, but it can be easier to simplify and isolate important points in a book with a thematic approach. TIME AND WEATHER by P. Hunt

---

*SPACE AND TIME, p. 51
†ibid., p. 56
‡ibid., p. 59

and E. M. Edwards (1963) has the same form as the pamphlets already discussed, with pages of brief statements broken up with questions and suggested experiments, but its scope is enlarged and simplified at the same time by an interesting connection between time and weather, with the seasons as the obvious link. The book is not limited in subject; it conveys the idea that time may be thought of in many different ways.

If the facts that a child collects from books lead to an idea that inspires him to look further, the facts will be more than pieces in a collection. They will stay in his mind because they are relevant to something that is going to grow with him. For an idea to be communicated to a child, a book must be substantial, to make personal private reading worth while, and it must have in it an enthusiasm, commitment, personality to keep the author in touch with his reader.

Of the more formally planned books on time, the most persuasive and personal is undoubtedly EXPLORING TIME by Henry Brinton and Patrick Moore (1962), The emphasis they place on astronomy usefully stresses the fact that time has been most reliably viewed by man in the way he first recognised it, in connection with the movements of earth, sun, moon and stars. The theme of the book is suggested in chapter titles like "The Earth is a time keeper" and "Time in the universe" and in the paragraph that sums up the first chapter:

We can see, then, that there are three natural time-units. The *day* depends upon the Earth's spin on its axis; the *year* upon the Earth's journey round the Sun, and the *month* upon the Moon's journey round the Earth. Once this had been discovered, the ancient peoples started to think about making proper clocks.
EXPLORING TIME, p. 11

and the paragraph with which they conclude their survey gives their point of view very clearly:

What time is it?
    Today, we have our clocks and our watches to tell us. But who knows, in the future, what man and super-man will devise, or what new and exciting turn our measurement of time will take?
ibid., p. 80.

Henry Brinton and Patrick Moore are expert simplifiers. They can conduct the young round the museum of knowledge with an eye for the beginning of fatigue or the glazed look of incomprehension. They write with a cheerful, even jocular note that just avoids the facetious, and have no hesitation in using schoolmasterly tricks of joke, exclamation or hinting to catch attention. With an ease of manner that rests on experience they offer facts in a way that should be palatable to children from seven right up the junior ladder and offer them, moreover, as one interested person to another. This is a book for a child to read for pleasure; in doing so, he can enjoy the stimulus of two lively writers who believe the young can be trusted to respond to ideas as well as to facts. The child who goes exploring time with these authors may well end with a lively curiosity about more than the physical workings of a clock.

Jeanne Bendick also uses the written word with direct personal force as a teaching instrument. THE FIRST BOOK OF TIME (1963), intended for readers from eight or so, offers not only knowledge, clear thinking and logical planning but also a lively humour and, in her illustrations, something almost amounting to wit. A pencil visibly inscribes details of months and days, a boy flees from a pack of girls to illustrate Leap Year, and children in the costume of ancient Egypt, Rome, Revolutionary France and so on illustrate the days of the week.

One of Jeanne Bendick's assets is her highly professional planning of factual subjects; the structural virtue of her book on time has more than clarity to commend it. Her sixty-eight pages are divided into clearly marked sections which develop her thesis point by point. The first of many rhetorical questions opens the book – "How do you think about Time?" – and the reader is put firmly into relation with all men of all periods:

For thousands of years, philosophers and men of religion, mathematicians, physicists, geologists, astronomers, and many other people have been thinking and arguing about time. And they are still arguing . . .

What *do* we know about time?

It doesn't start or stop. As far as we know, it has no beginning or ending. The scientific word for this condition is *continuum*. Is time a continuum? We do not yet know.

. . . we measure time by motion. We measure it by the regular motion of real things – the gears or pendulum of a clock, the flow of electricity, the ebb and flow of tides, the movements of the earth and the moon, the swing of stars across the sky.

Sir Isaac Newton remarked that we measure time by motion, and we measure motion by time.

THE FIRST BOOK OF TIME, pp. 9–11

The transition from such abstract statements to practical explanations of the seasons, the lunar and sidereal month, the names given to divisions of time, is easily managed, and from here the step to the history of various methods of time-keeping is easy too. In this book for the first time we come to the expressed definition of biological time, surely one that could be offered to children far earlier than this. Sections on "Plant and animal clocks" and "The clock in your body" confidently stress facts that children will have noticed without connecting them particularly with the idea of time. And so, naturally, the author returns to time as a concept and to relativity – this last theory being illustrated by a topical analogy. She first introduces Einstein's ideas about motion and its effect on matter, and continues:

According to the Theory of Relativity, if you were a spaceman, travelling 163,000 miles a second, time aboard your spaceship would go only half as fast as time on earth. For every half-hour that passed on board the spaceship, an hour would pass on earth. It has been thought that if your flight took a year, two years would have passed on earth, and you would come back to the earth's present, but into your future. This "paradox" is removed in other theories.

If you could fly at the speed of light, time would stand still.

At C [speed limit of universe, as we know it], space shrinks to nothing and time stands still.

ibid., p. 65

The assumption behind this book is that children can be trusted to think for themselves. It is not intended to be an exhaustive account of man's manipulation of time. Jeanne Bendick selects examples to support ideas and does not multiply them to show off her knowledge or her superior conscientiousness as a teacher. She recognises that the best way to learn is to recognise that facts are a step towards reasoning, and her book ends with an invitation to the reader to take over from her:

Do you know the word *eternity*?
For some people it means *infinite time* – all the time there ever is or was, time without beginning or end, time going on for ever.
For some people it has the meaning of *timelessness* – absolute time, time not related to space or motion, time itself, by itself.
Some people think that time is an eternity, with no beginning or end, going on for ever.
Some people think that time will last only as long as there are creatures to measure it and to place things in it; and that time by itself, like numbers with no one to count them, would mean nothing.
Some people think that time will last until everything in the universe has stopped moving – until every star and moon and planet has fallen to dust, until every atom has stopped vibrating.
What do you think?
ibid., pp. 66–7

Jeanne Bendick has chosen a prose style which will put no strain on a reader trying to understand the points she makes; a child of above-average intelligence would hardly find her book daunting in his earliest reading years. Irving Adler's TIME IN YOUR LIFE (1957) would naturally be tackled later and could satisfy a reader up to thirteen or so. Its simple arrangement, with sections of a few paragraphs only, its anecdotes and asides, examples and analogies, put it within the grasp of readers in the middle years as well, and there is a brisk, take-it-or-leave-it attitude that reveals the teacher, who offers facts, suggests experiments and uses underlining in an almost audible fashion:

You live in an *ocean* of space, but you live in a *river* of time. Space surrounds you on all sides, but time flows past you in a steady stream.
. . . Every moment is a new *now*. Your life is made up of a stream of *nows* arranged like beads on a string, and slipping past

you in a steady flow. The future becomes the present, the present becomes the past, and the past moves on behind you never to return.

TIME IN YOUR LIFE, p. 7

The book has a stimulating central theme which gives it a wider application than if it had been confined to time as such. From the first chapter with its emphasis on palaeontology and geology to the final chapter on sound and music, the idea of time as rhythm is kept in the foreground. The attempts of Hebrew, Roman and Gregorian scholars to devise an acceptable calendar are shown as attempts to match rhythms that exist outside man with the necessary rhythms of a civilised community. The natural rhythms of animal life are demonstrated through cell change, migration, hibernation, digestion and excretion and so on, the rhythm of nature through geological eras, atomic structure and carbon dating, the rhythm of space in discussion of sun cycles and light waves. There is no suggestion that the author has a magic word to open the secrets of time, but his approach is stimulating and makes of time an expanding subject.

From ten or eleven, if not before, a good many children will be choosing the books they read from personal points of view. Those with a mechanical bent may be looking for books on time which pay more attention to those mechanics of time-keeping than has been appropriate in the last two books under discussion. They will need a specialist as well as an expert disseminator of facts. The two may sometimes be found together and certainly are in Eric Bruton, whose professional knowledge of clocks, shown in many handbooks for adults, is made available for the young in THE TRUE BOOK ABOUT CLOCKS (1957). Here technical detail is varied by anecdote and by quotation from documents of many dates. The author blows the dust off Galileo and John Harrison and presents them as technicians putting curiosity to particular use. A fortuitous interest in timepieces would certainly be deepened by this kind of writing:

The history of clock making is really the history of engineering. Many wonderful inventions come from the seventeenth century horological industry that are in common use in many different kinds of apparatus today. The thermostat, for example, used to switch the refrigerator on and off and to keep the electric iron at a constant temperature, was invented by a clockmaker to control his clocks in different temperatures. The differential gear used in the back axle of all motor cars was first used in a clock mechanism; so were the jewelled bearings in your gas meter. Every machine has somewhere in its ancestry gears and levers and actions invented by clock-and-watch makers.

THE TRUE BOOK ABOUT CLOCKS, pp. 65–6

A more recent book for the ten-upwards age group, CLOCKS, FROM SHADOW TO ATOM by Kathryn Kilby Borland and Helen Ross Speicher (1970), proceeds at a brisk and businesslike pace through the subject and might better suit children who are not prepared for too much detail. This book, too, puts more emphasis on time-keeping in the present, on timing devices and alarms, and indicates what research is currently being done on the caesium atom as a regulator. Unfortunately the illustrations are crude and uninspired and the older book will give readers a better idea of what certain clocks looked like – assuming that they have already visited museums and factories to see what examples they can find in actuality.

Another topic book which relates facts consistently to ideas, Isaac Asimov's THE CLOCK WE LIVE ON (1959), argues that the whole notion of time starts "to the steady spin of our planet, Earth". Dr Asimov relates man's thinking to his mechanical inventions clearly and with confidence. There is no ambiguity in his explanation of how man *decided* to measure time, and the actual time-keepers he describes (sundials, water-clocks, zonal time) are used to illustrate this decision. For example, when he discusses sundials he also discusses the multi-divisible number twelve and how it was used for the dividing of days and hours. When dealing with time zones he starts with the Greek idea of dividing the world, and works from this point to a lucid explanation of why time must differ in various places. Brilliant in simplification, his book is direct and clear, with a careful arrangement of chapters stressing earth, sun, moon and stars as man's means of measuring time. Here is one aspect of time excellently portrayed; time as a biological rhythm, historicity, relativity are not discussed.

Among the most recent general books on time, Roger Burlingame's DICTATOR CLOCK (1966) states its approach rather ponderously in its title and in the opening lines:

> We are naturally and rightly happy that we live in a free world and in a democracy in which there is no Mao or Franco to oppress us with absolute rule. But are we truly without a dictator? Are we completely free to do whatever we want *when* we want to do it?
>
> The fact is that there is a despot – a benevolent one to be sure – who regiments our lives as rigidly as any king or emperor or president who ever lived. Even in the free United States this dictator controls the behavior of men, women and children. He never lets us alone. He keeps after us day and night, saying: "Do this now! This very minute!" Yet none of us, truly, would want to get along without him. Without him in this modern world, we should be lost – indeed, we should lose what freedom we have and the whole structure of our civilization would collapse.
>
> That despot is the automatic machine we use for the measurement of time. We call it "clock", "watch" or "chronometer"! Can you imagine a world without it; a world in which the question "What time is it?" would remain forever unanswered; a world in which no single person is able to give a reply to that simple question?
>
> DICTATOR CLOCK, p. I

This is not a scientist's book. Accurate and thorough though it is, it is the work of a man of affairs whose chief concern is to demonstrate to the young the stages by which man has been able to free himself from the prison of "worry and boredom" by giving himself the freedom and machinery to plan his life. The paradox is an interesting one and serves as continuity for chapters which follow the pattern of most other books on time, enumerating the course of man's invention of the calendar, the pendulum, the atomic clock.

This is in the main a descriptive book, with the appropriate subtitle "5,000 years of telling time"; it is perhaps more valuable than any other in its clear explanation of how certain mechanical processes are designed and operated. It is less satisfactory in the region of abstract thought, and its humour is a trifle condescending. For a discriminating young reader Lawrence Wright's CLOCK-

WORK MAN (1968) might be more congenial; the pervasive flippancy (aimed at adult readers) has an invigorating saltiness that does not conceal a considerable talent in arranging facts about time zones and almanacs and in emphasising man's *organising* of duration in matters such as betting, working hours, meal-times, photography and the like.

In many scientific and near-scientific subjects, it is almost impossible to keep up to date with facts, under the present systems of publishing. Most general books on time leave in the air or omit altogether questions that are still under investigation, although these are just the matters which the schoolboy or girl should want to pursue. Patrick Moore's suggestion that our attitude to time depends on the exploration of space is one which could certainly be taken further by a writer of today. The recent experiments by speleologists on our inbuilt time-sense should also find a place in any book on time for older readers. Millicent Selsam in HOW ANIMALS TELL THE TIME (1967) discusses the experiments of Michel Siffre and of a group of young people living under control conditions in Spitzbergen, as well as giving a few facts about the rhythms of disease. Navin Sullivan's ANIMAL TIMEKEEPERS (1966) ranges widely over the subject of biological time from the point of view of the physiology of bees, migratory birds and so on. In both these books the theme is rhythm and an abstract concept of time would be out of place; the material, though, is seldom to be found in general surveys. There is material in plenty to be given to the young about carbon dating and other techniques and about the development over the centuries of a sense of history, a rewarding way of looking at the nature of time which G. J. Whitrow has posed as a subject in THE NATURAL PHILOSOPHY OF TIME (1961):

Our actual perception of time is a complex process. Beneath the level of consciousness beat the innumerable clocks of cellular and physiological activity, culminating in the alpha rhythm of the cerebral cortex. But our conscious awareness of temporal phenomena involves psychological factors as well; it is dominated by the *tempo* of our attention and is acquired by learning. The primary function of mental activity is to face the future and anticipate the event which is about to happen. Our recognition of the past is probably a relatively late product of human

slow, fast, and regular watches

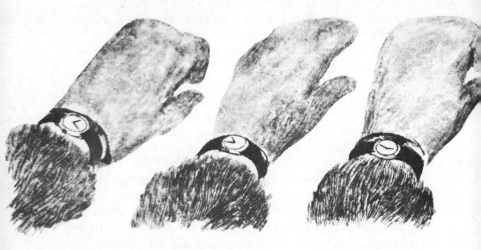

The point made verbally about variations in time is hindered rather than helped by this curiously unspecific illustration, a drawing by John Kaufmann from HOW ANIMALS TELL THE TIME (World's Work).

> evolution, for coherent memory is not just a simple re-excitation of mental traces but depends on an imaginative reconstruction of events and may originally have been intimately associated with the invention of language.
>
> THE NATURAL PHILOSOPHY OF TIME, p. 311

Young people should have their due of broad, up-to-date treatments of a subject which leads in so many directions. We have such a book in RIVER OF TIME by Timothy Johnson (1967), the first of a series, *Yardsticks of Science*, whose aim is described by the general editor, David Fishlock, in these terms:

> The *Yardsticks of Science* introduce you to some of the principal properties of matter which the scientist – whether chemist or engineer, materials scientist or plant pathologist – wants to measure. These properties are common to all science, so the authors have drawn their examples without regard to the modern, highly artificial division into "pure" and "applied" science. Each

book extends across the entire spectrum of its chosen property, from the smallest to largest, from coldest to hottest, and so on. RIVER OF TIME, p. 12

This book is divided into four sections. "How long ago" discusses methods of dating and, to some extent, the history of History. "Calendars and clocks" supplies a selective and fascinating account of the way man has arranged time to suit himself. In "Nature's

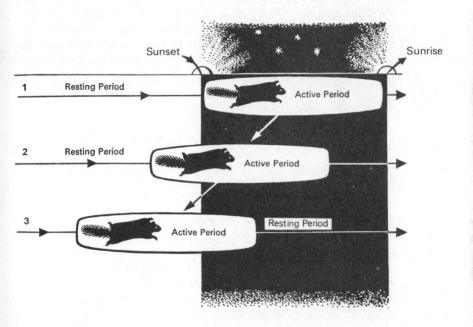

FIG 13

1 Normally flying squirrels are active only at night.

2 If they are put in complete darkness, they have to rely on their internal clock to tell the time. This clock is often a little fast, so the squirrels wake up a few minutes earlier each evening.

3 After being kept in complete darkness for a week or so they are active when it is broad daylight outside.

By contrast, this diagram from RIVER OF TIME (Deutsch) clarifies diagrammatically the information given in caption and text.

clocks" the question of internal rhythms in man, mammals, birds is discussed. Finally, "Less than a second" brings us up to date with formal methods of measuring time and raises the question of relativity and its relation to modern science. The author has not tried to cover any one aspect of his subject exhaustively, but he suggests very clearly how much is known and how much still remains to be discovered, learned, suggested, about the nature of time. Thirty-five years ago it was possible for an author to write that "we are never deceived by the silent courses of the stars, undisturbed and unchangeable"; today our children know better than we do how uncertain we are even of the course and character of those stars. The adventure of learning can hardly be better illustrated than in the subject of time, which has so often been diluted, muffled and bedevilled for the benefit of the young who are far more ready than most writers realise to engage in this particular area of thought actively and intelligently.

Reading List

Adler, Irving. TIME IN YOUR LIFE (*Dobson* 1957) *John Day* 1958. Illustrated by Ruth Adler.

Asimov, Isaac. THE CLOCK WE LIVE ON (*Abelard-Schuman* 1959, revised edition 1966) *Hale* 1965. Diagrams by John Bradford. For the 'teens and the general reader, a lively exploration of man's manipulations of time.

Bendick, Jeanne. THE FIRST BOOK OF TIME. First Books. (*Franklin Watts* 1963) *Edmund Ward* 1964. Illustrated by the author.

Bendick, Jeanne. SPACE AND TIME (*Franklin Watts* 1968) *Watts* 1970. Illustrated by the author.

Borland, Kathryn Kilby and Speicher, Helen Ross. CLOCKS, FROM SHADOW TO ATOM. *World's Work* 1970. Illustrated by Robert Addison.

Brinton, Henry and Moore, Patrick. EXPLORING TIME. Exploring . . . *Odhams Press* 1962. Illustrated by Cyril Deakins. See also NAVIGATION. Outlines. *Methuen* 1961. Illustrated by David Hardy and Christine Mellor, and some photographs.

Bruton, Eric. THE TRUE BOOK ABOUT CLOCKS. True Books. *Muller* 1957. Illustrated by Peter Shrives.

Burlingame, Roger. DICTATOR CLOCK (*Collier-Macmillan* 1966 U.K.)
Macmillan 1966 U.S.A. Illustrated by photographs and diagrams.

Cipolla, C. M. CLOCKS AND CULTURE (*Collins* 1967) *Walker* 1967. A fascinating
survey of the social and economic effect of the development of mechanical
timepieces, within the capacity of the middle 'teens.

Cordin, P. W. MEASURING TIME. Mathematics and measuring. *Macmillan* 1968.
Illustrated by Peter Chadwick. A pamphlet for the primary classroom which
shows by carefully designed experiments that by measuring movement we can
measure time; incidental history shows how man contrived methods of
measuring.

Fice, R. H. C. and Simkiss, R. H. TIME AND CLOCKS. We Discover . . . *E. J.
Arnold* 1967. Illustrated by A. E. Harris.

Fraser, J. T. (editor). THE VOICES OF TIME (*Braziller* 1965) *Allen Lane, The
Penguin Press* 1967. A series of deeply-considered essays on time in relation to
history, music, philosophy, religion, linguistics, neurology and other sciences
and disciplines.

Hart, Jane. LET'S THINK ABOUT TIME (*Hart* 1965) *Odhams Press* 1966.
Illustrated by Judy Varga.

Hogben, Lancelot. MAN MUST MEASURE: THE WONDERFUL WORLD OF
MATHEMATICS. *Rathbone Books* 1955. Artwork by André, Charles Keeping and
Kenneth Symonds. Maps by Marjorie Saynor. A broad view of mathematics
including measuring time. An exciting text is complemented by numerous
informative and lively coloured pictures.

Hunt, P. and Edwards, E. M. TIME AND WEATHER. *Macmillan* 1963. Illustrated
by Cedric Chater.

Hutchinson, W. M. TIME. Outlook series. (*Follett* 1959) *Oliver and Boyd* 1963.
Illustrated by photographs. A short, copiously illustrated book for the nine to
eleven ages, containing a great deal of information. Unusually interesting on the
Maya investigations of astronomy and the nature of time.

Irwin, Keith G. THE 365 DAYS: THE STORY OF OUR CALENDAR (*T. Y. Crowell*
1963) *Harrap* 1965. Illustrated by Guy Fleming. A rather chatty book for the
general reader, useful in co-ordinating many streams of fact. Suitable for the
middle 'teens.

Johnson, Timothy. RIVER OF TIME. Yardsticks of Science. (*Deutsch* 1967)
Coward-McCann 1968. Illustrated by diagrams.

Jupo, Frank. A DAY AROUND THE WORLD (*Abelard-Schuman* 1968 U.S.A.)
Abelard-Schuman 1969 U.K. Illustrated by the author.

Kerry, F. G. FINDING OUT ABOUT TIME AND CLOCKS. Finding out About . . .
Wheaton 1963. Illustrated by Dorothy H. Ralphs. A typical example of a first

school pamphlet, with explanations keyed to observations and experiment, and with suggestions for further independent work.

Naylor, A. H. TIME AND CLOCKS. Study Books. *Bodley Head* 1959. Illustrated by Heather Copley. A practical survey for the nine-up reader, notable for an intelligent use of technical terms which are clarified by context.

Priestley, J.B. MAN AND TIME (*Aldus Books/W. H. Allen* 1964) *Doubleday* 1964. Illustrated by photographs and prints. A personal and idiosyncratic interpretation of time, including notes on his own experiences and those of others relevant to his interpretation of relativity.

Purton, R. W. MAN TELLS THE TIME. Star Books. *Hamish Hamilton* 1966. Illustrated by Elsie Walker.

Quill, Humphrey. JOHN HARRISON: THE MAN WHO FOUND LONGITUDE (*John Baker* 1966) *Humanities* 1966. Illustrated by photographs. A full and authoritative biography by an authority on horology.

Renneisen, Helga. MR CLOCKMAN. *Chatto and Windus* 1967. Illustrated by Eberhard Binder.

Richards, Roy (with others). TIME: BACKGROUND INFORMATION. Science Six to Thirteen. *Macdonald Educational* 1969, sponsored by the Schools Council, the Nuffield Foundation and the Scottish Education Dept.

Russell, Bertrand. THE A.B.C. OF RELATIVITY (First published 1925. *Allen and Unwin* 1958, revised edition 1969, revised by Felix Pirani) *Oxford University Press,* revised edition 1958, U.S.A.

Selsam, Millicent. HOW ANIMALS TELL THE TIME (*Morrow* 1966) *World's Work* 1970. Illustrated by John Kaufmann.

Slobodkina, Esphyr. THE CLOCK. *Abelard-Schuman* 1956. Illustrated by the author.

Smith, Thyra. THE STORY OF MEASUREMENT. Story Books of How and Why. *Blackwell* 1959. Illustrated by Leslie Green.

Sullivan, Navin. ANIMAL TIMEKEEPERS. See page 185.

Toulmin, Stephen and Goodfield, June. THE DISCOVERY OF TIME (*Hutchinson* 1965. *Penguin* 1967) *Harper & Row* 1965. Part of an extensive study of man in the universe, considering the development of a sense of history. Stiff reading even for Sixth Forms, but important for its bold speculations and scholarly detail.

Waller, Leslie. TIME. Open Gate Library. (*Holt, Rinehart* 1959) *Oliver and Boyd* 1964. Illustrated by Elizabeth Dauber.

Ward, F. A. B. TIME KEEPERS. Science Museum illustrated booklets. *Her Majesty's Stationery Office* 1963. Illustrated by photographs. Frequently revised; an excellent guide to historic timepieces.

Werner, Nils. WHAT O'CLOCK? (Germany 1968) *Macdonald* 1968. Illustrated by Gertrud Zucker.

Whitrow, G. J. THE NATURAL PHILOSOPHY OF TIME. *Nelson* 1961. A stretching book for the general reader, taking up many aspects of the subject, including relativity, migration and natural rhythms and the problems of cosmic time.

Wilson, Jean. TELLING THE TIME. Our Book Corner. Things Men have Learned. *W. and R. Chambers* 1962. Illustrated by Sally Michael.

Wright, Lawrence. THE CLOCKWORK MAN. *Elek* 1968.

Ziner, Feenie and Thompson, Elizabeth. THE JUNIOR TRUE BOOK OF TIME. Junior True Books. (*Childrens Press* 1956) *Muller* 1959. Illustrated by Katherine Evans.

Colour plates

1 A page from THE BEE (Chambers),illustrated by Iliane Roels. This picture is discussed on page 108 as an example of a fanciful version of the bee dance which could create confusion in a child's mind. The text associated with this picture specifically states that the bee "dances, beats her wings and waggles her feelers" to tell her fellow workers where to find the nectar-source she has located; but in the picture the bee communicates information by Chalk-and-Talk. The two pictures below may be compared with the drawing from THE DANCING BEES on page 119, which shows clearly how by touch and feel the hive-bees receive the information contained in the "dance".

2 Picture by Jill Payne from LIFE OF THE HONEY-BEE (Wills and Hepworth). The use of colour, attractive though it is, has made the action of the bees less clear than in the drawing on p. 119; and as the relevant piece of text is particularly compressed, it would have been a help if the picture could have added to and clarified the verbal explanation of the bee-dance.

3 Part of an illustration by Colette Portal from THE HONEYBEES (Knopf). Here the same piece of behaviour is illustrated, but this time the picture is intended to be primarily decorative; the book is designed for younger children and the artist aims to encourage a sense of wonder rather than to communicate precise fact.

A bee has come back from looking for nectar.   She dances, beats her wings and waggles her feelers.   She is using bee language to tell the others exactly where to find the flowers that hold the nectar.

1

2

3

4　Frederic Remington's superb paintings reflect what he himself saw in the West. "Suspended by Lightning" comes from COWBOY AND CATTLE COUNTRY.

5　(below) Spread from GUMDROP GOES TO LONDON (Brockhampton) by Val Biro, a fantastic but topographically

the Grenadier Guards, skidded round the Victoria Memorial and roared up Constitution Hill.

Gumdrop was stopped by Drummer Thumpit. "I'll make mincemeat of them for this!" he cried and jumped in. "After them!" And Gumdrop did just that.

It was half past one when they reached Buckingham Palace. The bandits drove their car recklessly through the band of

5

6

For washing-up there is a bowl,
mop and brush, powder and liquid soap,
sink basket and drying-up cloth.

6 Robert Nix's impression of a winter scene, from THE SKATING RACE, a story in the Great Day series (Abelard-Schuman). The Great Day in Holland described here is the Eleven Towns Race held regularly in Friesland.

7 Spread from BEN IN THE KITCHEN (Methuen) by Pat Albeck, one of a series of small books for small children, designed to help them to identify familiar objects. The sturdy, positive style is in line with the reaction against softer and more consciously pretty fashions in illustration for the very young.

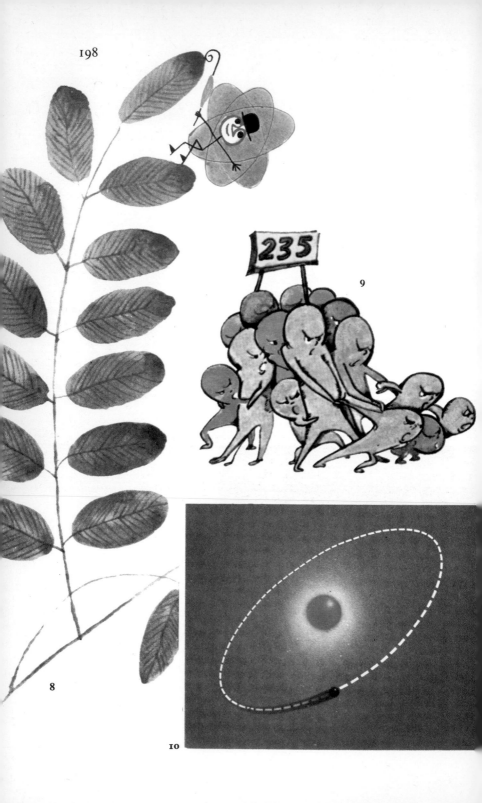

8 Illustration by Adam Wurtz from THE ADVENTURES OF A CARBON ATOM (Sadler)   9 Illustration by Nadine Forster from THE ATOM (Harrap). Humanisation is used to introduce scientific concepts; see text, p. 269.   10 Ric Wylam in ATOMS (Longmans) uses dotted lines to show atoms have only an apparent outline; compare illustrations on pp. 273 and 277.   11 Illustration by Lynd Ward from AMERICA'S ABRAHAM LINCOLN (Houghton Mifflin); see text, p. 384.

12

Two unusually imaginative jacket designs which clearly state the subject of the book and suggest a lively approach. **12** Design by Gerald Wilkinson for HERE COMES THE POST! (University of London Press). Its effect is due partly to the hint of texture, partly to the unexpected and apparently accidental position of title and author's name. **13** Design by Negus/Sharland for KNOW ABOUT NEWSPAPERS (Blackie). The gaiety of the colour contrasts amusingly with the studious faces of the passengers, and lures the reader inside to the text.

13

3 | The Multiple Subject

3 | *The Multiple Subject*

INFORMATION books provide one of many ways in which knowledge can be sorted and arranged for the young. So far I have discussed mainly specific problems raised by certain subjects which, for good or ill, a writer can treat individually. All of them could be included in a larger subject – for instance, under the umbrella term Communications. I shall now be considering mainly those problems of selection which arise when it is desirable to break down a wide area of knowledge – a multiple subject – into its component parts.

One method of "selection by collection" can be discerned in the new kinds of encyclopedias published over the last decade. The main difference between the ENCYCLOPAEDIA BRITANNICA and the OXFORD JUNIOR ENCYCLOPEDIA, for instance (setting aside the matter of readership), is that instead of the simple alphabetical system for arranging knowledge used by the BRITANNICA, the OXFORD JUNIOR uses arrangement by subject, with volumes bearing titles like "Law and order", "Industry and commerce", "Natural history" and (boldly) "Mankind". However, this is still essentially a reference book rather than one to read through for information. The alphabet arrangement is kept within each volume, so that there is no continuity of text other than that indicated by the subject titles. Each multiple subject is broken down into compact columns or half-columns of fact, arranged so that the reader can find the particular information he needs.

An encyclopedia may be said to become an information book when there is a planned continuity of text. The MACDONALD ILLUSTRATED LIBRARY, for example, uses much the same headings as those of the OXFORD JUNIOR – among them "Communication and language". "Man the artist", "Growth of ideas" and the still more general "Nature". The series follows a pattern that has become standardised over the last few years. The text consists of a continuous piece of exposition, usually on a broadly chronological plan, coming to a temporary halt in a description of the state of play in our own time. Efficient indexing means that volumes like this can be used for reference, but they are most often used by the young as browsing books. The varied illustrations that appear on every page are an essential factor. Although these have sometimes provoked from critics the derogatory phrase "coffee-table", they are chosen with discrimination to reinforce, to expand and to illuminate the text. A boy or girl with a grasshopper mind can ignore the pattern of exposition in the text, but it is available for more serious readers.

A compendium of this kind will carry within it the germ, even the outline, of scores of smaller, more specialised books. It may also have a perceptible relevance to the reader himself. Another series, of *Wonderful World* books, has titles that suggest a straight description of environment (THE WONDERFUL WORLD OF THE SEA) or of human activity (THE STORY OF THEATRE), but the theme of the series as a whole is the effect of man on the actual world and the world of ideas. The multiple subject is fragmented under a number of headings. For instance in MAN MUST MEASURE, Lancelot Hogben adopts a firm classification for facts about numeracy, the measurement of time, the development of geometry and so on; the basic concept of man using intellectual power to order his world holds all the facts together and gives them point.

A particularly clear example of a multiple subject with an overriding theme may be seen in three linked books with the general title INTERDEPENDENCE IN NATURE (1969). These three books have the format of the illustrated encyclopedia and could have been simple descriptive reference books – MAN'S IMPACT ON NATURE being apparently the story of the rise of industry, Joyce Joffe's CONSERVATION a description of sociology and NATURE'S NETWORK by Keith Reid a summary of ecological studies. In fact these are continuous linked essays with a theme of the utmost importance to young people today; the multiple subject of mankind has been interpreted in a cogent and broad-based argument about man's responsibility to society and to his environment. These books, too, could be used for reference, but they are not reference books; they will be more properly used as books of persuasion carrying a challenge to the intelligence and reasoning of those who read them.

It is useless to try to set any particular readership for this type of compendium. It may be equally congenial to a child who just likes to look at pictures and an adult who wants to come to terms with the future. When facts and ideas relating to many aspects of one large subject are assembled within the covers of a single book, people will use such books for various reasons and in various ways.

A child may sometimes want to amass a few facts about a number of associated subjects, and at other times he may feel happier coming to terms with a limited subject in some depth. A multiple subject can be treated piecemeal in one book or it may be dispersed in books on various subdivisions. Two problems of selection arise here. The writer must decide first what particular aspects of a multiple subject can be treated separately and then at what age a child can be introduced to a particular aspect of it. Local history may provide an example here. Originally this subject seemed to be a branch of history as a whole. Somewhere along the line it acquired the more dignified and more appropriate title of environmental studies. This subject has always been closely, almost exclusively, associated with school; or, rather, it has emerged as a way of looking at home under direction from school. Environmental studies are in fact no longer formal history but an amalgam of theoretical and applied history with archaeology, mass media, domestic economy, natural history and a host of other subjects which may help a child to look at his environment intelligently.

Children have always satisfied their curiosity about people and places with their own lives as the point of departure. When this curiosity was turned into a curriculum subject the provision of books quickly followed, and from the start these seem to have been written on the assumption that *all* aspects of the subject could be appreciated by all ages. Simple picture-books might show small children exploring the village pond or the city street: equally simple books like Marie Neurath's FRIENDS AND ENEMIES (1966) could also suggest the problem of aggression in the societies of man and other animals. At one end of the scale a pioneer book, H. J. Deverson's THE MAP THAT CAME TO LIFE (1948), helps young children in a friendly way towards the technique of map-reading, and suggests to them some of the interesting things they could look for on a walk: at the other end of the scale Professor W. G. Hoskins, in FIELD WORK IN LOCAL HISTORY (1968), offers a broad and authoritative interpretation of the word "local". Again, the interaction of economic interests may be demonstrated to children as young as eight or nine in cheerful books like R. P. A. Edwards's THE TOWER BLOCK and THE BY-PASS (both 1969), where the expansion of a typical village and the rehousing of tenants from a typical town centre are illustrated in terms of individual places and people. Books like this are rehearsals, as it were, for specialist studies of environmental change which could take the form of national and local government documents, the autobiography of a social worker, the systematic study of one particular place or a world-wide survey like John Hill's study of the world distribution of wealth, THE DISINHERITED (1970).

In breaking up the multiple subject of environmental studies, writers have not as a rule reserved any of its parts for any particular age-group. At first sight it may seem that the broad subject of religion has followed the same trend. Beside the simple stories for beginner-readers which domesticate Old and New Testaments, we have an occasional book like Napoli's GOD'S WORD FOR US (1970), which introduces some of the basic concepts of Christian belief. Beside picture-books which treat the books of the Old Testament as adventure stories, we have books like Ivan Southall's THE SWORD OF ESAU and THE CURSE OF CAIN (both 1968), which set out to explain such stories to readers as young as eight or nine in terms of modern psychological theory and universal aspects of social man. Children may read the Bible in the many simple versions which offer no interpretation or they may use the notable paraphrases published under the editorship of a Dutch minister, Jessie Klink, in which each piece of narrative has an accompanying explanation of allegory or theological meaning.

In these subdivisions of the main subject a child of any reading age may find a suitable book, but all of them deal with the Christian religion. It is not until we reach the early 'teens that we find a book like Katharine Savage's THE HISTORY OF WORLD RELIGIONS (1966) to introduce children to differing and sometimes conflicting beliefs. There are obvious reasons why this wide treatment has not been used for younger readers, but it may be time for a change of attitude, and Maud Kennedy's interesting book, A CHILD'S

QUESTIONS ANSWERED (1969), may point to a new direction, for she discusses Buddhism and other Eastern faiths in terms comprehensible to children in the middle years.

The decision to align a book towards a particular age-group can only be made on the basis of an average child, and the overlap in the capacities of children at any age gives the writer of information books an essential flexibility in the way he selects his material and the techniques he uses to present it to the best advantage. In any group of books concerned with one major subject there will be stereotypes and works of strong originality, books that are pedantic and books that establish a bond straight away between the enthusiastic writer and the receptive reader. The two multiple subjects which I shall discuss in the following pages, London and Atoms, have been treated in books tremendously varied in style, format and outlook.

Reading List

Deverson, H. J. THE MAP THAT CAME TO LIFE. *Oxford University Press* 1948, revised edition 1967. Illustrated by Ronald Lampitt.

Edwards, R. P. A. THE TOWER BLOCK. THE BY-PASS. Both *Burke* 1969. THE NEW TOWN. THE BRANCH LINE. Both *Burke* 1970. Illustrated by Gareth Floyd.

Fisher, James. THE WONDERFUL WORLD OF THE SEA (*Macdonald* 1970) *Doubleday* revised edition 1970. Originally published by *Rathbone Books* 1956 as ADVENTURE OF THE SEA. Variously illustrated.

Hill, John. THE DISINHERITED: SOCIAL AND ECONOMIC PROBLEMS IN THE UNDERDEVELOPED COUNTRIES. *Benn* 1970. With photographs.

Hogben, Lancelot. MAN MUST MEASURE. See pages 174–5 and 189.

Hoskins, Professor W. G. FIELD WORK IN LOCAL HISTORY (*Humanities* 1967) *Faber* 1968. With photographs.

Joffe, Joyce. CONSERVATION. Interdependence in Nature. (*Aldus Books* 1969) *Doubleday* 1970. Variously illustrated.

Kennedy, Maud. A CHILD'S QUESTIONS ANSWERED. *Regency Press* 1969. Illustrated by Richard Kennedy.

Klink, Jessie L. THE BIBLE FOR CHILDREN, VOLUME I: OLD TESTAMENT (*Holland* 1959. *Burke* 1967) *Westminster* 1968. VOLUME 2: NEW TESTAMENT (*Burke* 1969) *Westminster* 1969. Translated by Patricia Crampton. Illustrated by Piet Klaase.

Lauwerys, J. A. MAN'S IMPACT ON NATURE. Interdependence in Nature. (*Aldus Books* 1969) *Doubleday* 1970. Variously illustrated.

Napoli. GOD'S WORD FOR US. *Macdonald* 1970. Illustrated by the author.

Neurath, Marie. FRIENDS AND ENEMIES. *Parrish* 1966. Illustrated by Evelyn Warboys.

Priestley, J. B. THE STORY OF THEATRE. *Rathbone Books* 1959. Variously illustrated. Revised as THE WONDERFUL WORLD OF THE THEATRE *Macdonald* 1969.

Reid, Keith. NATURE'S NETWORK. Interdependence in Nature. (*Aldus Books* 1969) *Doubleday* 1970. Variously illustrated.

Savage, Katharine. THE HISTORY OF WORLD RELIGIONS (*Bodley Head* 1966) *Walck* 1967. Maps by Richard Natkiel.

Southall, Ivan. THE SWORD OF ESAU. THE CURSE OF CAIN (Both *Angus and Robertson* 1968) Both *St Martin* 1968. Illustrated by Joan Kiddell-Monroe.

—— THE OXFORD JUNIOR ENCYCLOPEDIA. *Oxford University Press* 1948. 12 volumes. General editors Laura E. Salt and Geoffrey Boumphrey. Illustrations editor Helen Mary Petter.

—— THE MACDONALD ILLUSTRATED LIBRARY. Networks of Thought and Action. *Macdonald/Aldus Books* 1970. 9 volumes.

3a | London

We make our London, as we make our world, out of what attracts and interests ourselves.
Anon. review of J. T. Smith. AN ANTIQUARIAN RAMBLE IN THE STREETS OF LONDON, in *Blackwood's*, Dec. 1946, p. 673

A man may go from Bond Street to Blackwall, and unless he has the luck to witness an accident, or get a knock from a porter's burthen, may be conscious, when he has returned, of nothing but the names of those two places, and of the mud through which he has passed.
Leigh Hunt. THE TOWN, 1848, pp. 1–2

3a | London

ANYONE who has watched a bus load of primary school-children on the portico of Bloomsbury's British Museum will agree that the "diaries" written up in the classroom later would probably be something like this:

> I saw a mummy of an Egyptian's pet cat. I couldn't eat all my picnic so I gave some to the pigeons. I nearly touched one. Mary's plastic bottle split and all her orange juice went on the stone.

How can we help children to get the best out of a school trip to London, or to any place of historical interest, without turning them into little prigs? How can we convince them that history has a bearing on their lives? Ideally, the history of a city should include geography and art, sociology and architecture, biography and politics; it should examine both national and local events and should give the broadest possible interpretation to the general term social history. In the past few years, studies of Birmingham, Chester, Gloucester, Edinburgh and other cities have been published in which carefully presented details give an impression of the *character* of a place. The very names of these towns mean something to most of us; they provide a mental picture which, though not literally true, yet has some truth in it. But . . . London? Size: noise: greyness: crowds: "sights".

What methods have writers used to come to terms with this multiple subject? Books on London for the young fall into three categories – the obvious, the recondite and the specialised. A history of London is not quite the same as a history of England. As a rule, writers assume that their readers hope to visit London

at some time, they want to help them to decide where to go, what
to see and how to appreciate it. Instead of following an orthodox
historical sequence, they are most likely to choose and arrange
events so that they can introduce the key buildings of London –
St Paul's and Westminster Abbey, the Guildhall and the Houses of
Parliament, the Thames and its bridges – or such repositories of
history as the museums and art galleries.

Whether you regard London as a city of courtiers, merchants or
dockers, it is obvious that a great many particular events important
in history have taken place there. In theory at least a history of
London could be a history of England – that is, London could be
used as a focal point for an historical outline. But a book planned
like this will be in danger of false emphasis. Either there will be
great leaps from one significant event to another or, to fill the gaps,
the route of the national march will have to be diverted in the
direction of the city.

This is occasionally noticeable in Dorothy Margaret Stuart's
LONDON THROUGH THE AGES (1956). To keep London in the
forefront of her chronicle she has to resort now and then to a kind
of contrivance, as seen in this passage about Richard I and his
connection with London:

> England paid dearly for the privilege of having a Crusader King;
> and when on his homeward way from that luckless enterprise he
> was captured and held for ransom by the German Emperor, the
> good folk of London were compelled to contribute towards that
> ransom a sum equal to two million pounds in modern currency.
> His reign was none the less memorable in the history of the City,
> for it was in 1193 that in any document still existing the chief
> citizen was first called the "Mayor": "Lord Mayor" he would
> not be called until the very end of the Plantagenet period. It was
> under the name of "Mayor" that he was appointed one of the
> official treasurers of the royal ransom-money.
> LONDON THROUGH THE AGES, pp. 34–5

A child with only a limited knowledge of history might wonder,
with some reason, just why this particular connection between
Richard's imprisonment and the initiation of the term Mayor
should be considered important.

Again, there is an uncertainty of emphasis in the linking of
Elizabeth I and London:

> The story of the struggle against Spain is part of the story of
> England, but London bore her part in it – and so did London's
> Queen. Like the great City Companies, Elizabeth invested money
> in these expeditions, and like them she collected her profits in
> due course, though keeping carefully in the background all the
> while. Once, however, she did come boldly forward as the
> patroness of the greatest pirate of the whole far-journeying
> brotherhood. This was in April, 1579 when the Londoners
> beheld with their own eyes the *Golden Hind* in which Francis
> Drake had sailed all round the globe – the first Englishman to
> perform that feat.
>
> ibid., pp. 122–3

It seems that the author is trying to do two things here – to pinpoint
events important at this period of England's history and at the
same time to emphasise the special relationship of the Queen to
her city. In a book for the young, an historian must say what he
means; he cannot expect his readers to fill gaps in his argument or
to pick up hints based on specialist knowledge.

The same manipulation of fact can be seen in THE YOUNG
LONDONER THROUGH THE AGES (1962), by the same author.
There are many children in this book whom we can recognise as
true Londoners – John Stow, Lamb and Dickens among them.
There are others who were the centre of important scenes in London,
like the young Victoria or the young Prince Henry who escorted
Catherine of Aragon, as the betrothed of his brother Arthur,
through the city on a state visit to the Lord Mayor. But as for
the anonymous faces in the crowd – chimney-sweeps and boy
actors, schoolboys studying Claudius Hollyband's Anglo-French
dialogues at St Paul's and school-children visiting the Great Exhibition at the desire of Prince Albert – these could belong to any
other city, though they serve usefully here as a peg to hang history
on.

LONDON THROUGH THE AGES is the book of an historian, and a
very relaxed and approachable one. Many important moments in
the past are enlivened by a telling visual detail. In a chapter des-

cribing the state of Britain after the departure of the Legions, the author makes her point by direct description:

> Meanwhile there had been a hasty strengthening of the wall which had already for more than two hundred years surrounded the city. It was done, says one historian, "at panic speed", as some of the existing fragments show. Even broken pieces of tombstones were wedged into the gaps, telling a silent story of desperation and dismay.
>
> ibid., p. 11

and the London of the thirteenth century is brought before our eyes in this word-picture:

> In the ground-floor chamber of these two-storeyed wooden dwellings merchants displayed their wares and craftsmen plied their craft. In the room above (there was seldom more than one) the owner of the house lived with his family. Among the thatched roofs silver blossom peeped out in May and golden apples in September. Upper storeys had to leave a space of nine feet to enable a horseman to ride by without bumping his head.
>
> ibid., pp. 44-5

A writer who has in mind a continuous history gives himself a difficult task. To begin his book with an Ancient Briton peering through the rushes on the banks of the Thames and to end with workmen on the scaffolding of a Barbican building is not necessarily to tell the story of London in the best way, nor does a collection of the events that happened in London result in the "character" of the city. To show London past through London present it is necessary to choose those events which contributed to the *growth* of the city. By this I do not only mean events that promoted demonstrable growth – as for instance the building of the first stone bridge over the Thames in the twelfth century or the reconstruction of the City after the Great Fire – but also the shifts of population and their causes and the effect on certain localities when refugees, at various times, repaid London's hospitality by bringing their trades with them.

Above all, a writer must be prepared to select – to leave gaps in time, if need be, to abandon the conventional framework of "dates and reigns". It is better for children to be offered a great deal about one subject than a little about a great many. In a book that is truly a "history of London" the events chosen and the buildings described may be of national importance (like the Tower, the Gunpowder Plot, Wat Tyler's entry into the City) or they may be local and parochial, like the Plague and Fire of 1665–6, or the plan of the great crescent from Regent's Park to Piccadilly. Whatever is chosen, the material must above all reflect *London* specifically.

Selection is not, of course, the whole story. By selecting romantic, startling or amusing events, the buildings that are beautiful and interesting, an author may capture attention; but without a scheme of arrangement his book is likely to become a handbook rather than a book for concentrated reading.

The growth of London can be described as an expanding circle. As the years pass, the old London Wall ceases to be a boundary; the built-up areas of the City and Westminster gradually merge and boundaries are pushed further and further out. The map on page 95 of Eric de Maré's LONDON'S RIVER (1964) shows this in visual form; surprisingly few writers make use of this type of diagram to enforce what can be a useful arrangement of facts. This arrangement could be historical – that is, period and date could provide headings – or it could be geographical, with places as focal points. The logical conclusion of the latter method is the "visit" or "tour", which imposes a natural order.

Books are often built, however, round a random collection of famous streets or buildings. The direct conversational manner of Kenneth Allen's STORY OF LONDON TOWN (1967) is persuasive but his chapters on the Thames, St Paul's, the Strand and so on are arranged in no detectable order and with no particular centre other than "London". It is noticeable, also, that almost all the anecdotes in this book are of an easily isolated and somewhat sensational kind – Blood's raid on the Tower, the Danes pulling down London Bridge, the apprentice rescuing his master's daughter from the Thames. It is not surprising, perhaps, that the book ends with a chapter entitled "Did you know that . . .?" consisting of snippets of London lore about the Haymarket, Covent Garden, Pall Mall, Scotland Yard and so on. In a charitable mood I would describe this as a dip-into book   more critically I would call it a so-what one.

The sensible brief survey by John Lewesdon in THE LADYBIRD BOOK OF LONDON (1961) does not pretend to do more than describe "briefly some of the sights of London most likely to appeal to children"; it matters less that there is no continuity of subject because the ultra-simple format and style make it impossible for a child to lose his way in its pages.

Children need not, of course, study on their feet; given enough mental energy and the right books, they could see London in a library. Brian Rees's LONDON, now thirteen years old, attempts "to inspire rather than appease curiosity about the history of London". This extended essay covers a surprising amount of ground in a friendly fashion, fitting architecture and event neatly together and offering easy generalisations based on sound fact, like the following description of medieval London:

> Between the signing of Magna Carta in 1215 and the Battle of Bosworth 1485, which brought the Tudor kings to the throne, London grew to be one of the greatest cities in Europe. Streets were built outside the walls since safety was no longer such a problem. No foreign invader has landed in England since the reign of King John. The walls, however, were rebuilt, and as the city was cramped as a result, space was found by making the streets narrow. Knights off on crusade, priests in processions, pilgrims and carters were all forced to drive their horses and mules through narrow alleys infested with garbage.
>
> LONDON, p. 18

This book is chiefly notable, however, for its imaginative suggestions for "Things to do"; they include:

> Many City churches were damaged during the war. Perhaps you can find one that is in need of funds to restore the buildings. Learn about its history, and try to help it to raise the money it needs.
>
> ibid., p. 47, q. 14

and

> If you live in one of the London suburbs mentioned on page 36,

picture what you imagine the ground on which your street lies
looked like in the 15th century. (Chelsea, Chiswick, Limehouse,
Croydon, etc.)
ibid., p. 48, q. 20

This is one of the few books that looks beyond a single visit to
London to that special apprenticeship to history which can come
from environmental study. Brian Rees provides the historical
framework into which personal investigation can be fitted, and by
his lively way of writing he provides the incentive for study as
well.

Another book now somewhat old-fashioned, L. G. Bullock's
THE CHILDREN'S BOOK OF LONDON (1948), shows an interesting
compromise between history in event and history through place.
For the benefit of readers at junior level, the author divides the city
into sections, choosing in each case a locality important at a particular date and starting, as most writers do, with the site and
conjectured plan of Roman London. Each section is preceded by
a map in bright colours, very much simplified, showing one or other
of the great roads *into* London – the Watling Street, the Dover
Road, the highways from Brighton, Bath, and so on. London
emerges not as an isolated phenomenon but as a part of England's
map and, incidentally, as a city whose suburbs are investigated as
well as its centre. You feel you are reading about a real place and
not about a museum piece. Most praiseworthy of all, the general
outline of the book is not obscured by detail; no child need suffer
from mental indigestion through this interesting survey of people
and places.

One of the chief problems in local history is to marry the particular
to the general. Barbara Whelpton in LONDON MAJESTIC (1963)
has chosen particular buildings or developments associated with
certain periods – for instance, the Wren churches after the Great
Fire and the larger parks in their association with particular
monarchs – so that all her material is, in theory at least, pertinent
to the history of London. In practice there is a certain lack of
direction in some of her descriptions.

She begins a definition of Tudor London, for instance, with an
admirably concrete statement that refers *directly* to London as a
port and as a growing city:

Brick became a popular building material in London, and bricks
were often brought across the Channel as ballast on the return
voyage by ships which had transported wool from England to
the Continent.

LONDON MAJESTIC, p. 60

But in the next sentence she veers from the particular to the general,
telling us that the bricks were used "to build imposing palaces,
small half-timbered houses or beautiful manors" and the rest of
the paragraph consists of a picturesque description of coats of
arms and "elaborate, tall twisted chimneys" and linen-fold
panelling, whose architectural features could be found in many
places besides London. Here there is an opening for a description
of an individual building but, instead, the actual appearance of
London is blurred in a generalised background.

On the whole a chronological arrangement of material seems
better than a spatial one. To approach the history of London period
by period is to sharpen the advantages of selection. A writer can
draw attention to a succession of details and direct them towards
a general conclusion about architecture and its economic basis,
about manners and their origin, about the pattern of change and
the shift of population.

One attractive variation on the arrangement by periods shows
that affinity of fact and fiction which makes separation so often
meaningless – for where does the historical *novel* end and the
incidental narrative element in a book of information begin?
C. Bunt's LONDON, published sixteen years ago, is subtitled
"Journeys through our early history", but the journey is in fact a
single one, in time and place. A clerk describes how he left
Wigraceastre in 954 A.D., with Bishop Dunstan, to make the
hundred-mile journey to London, travelling by the Watling Street
through St Albans and Hampstead to the West Gate and so into
the City. A map of the city boundaries in the tenth century helps
the reader to follow the conversation as priests of St Mary's Church
in Milk Street talk to their guests about the great city and its
changes. With one of the priests as guide, the narrator is taken to
see the surviving parts of the Roman Wall, the Walbrook, the
fish wharves at Billings Gate and other markets, the London Stone
in Candlewick Street (even then a "sight" for tourists), London

Bridge and Holborn. Each day he returns to their centre near St Paul's and the great building looms over the book, its history explained and its structure described in detail (so that, incidentally, children today can imagine the Gothic edifice that Londoners knew before the Great Fire).

Although nowadays we are self-conscious about the mock-conversation technique of information books, the formula by which an enthusiastic Londoner pilots country cousins is successfully used here. Esgar the priest has the preoccupations of his calling and thus the pattern of medieval life, with religion as a stabiliser, is imperceptibly drawn. The practical details of daily life are not neglected, though, and the book as a whole gives a fair idea of how people lived, dwelling lightly on dirt, disease and violence, but taking a practical attitude to such essentials as food supply and transport. Allowing for a rather naïve style which dates it a little, we can see in this book a marked vitality and a certain confidence in summarising:

> Within the next few days, during which we made further excursions under Esgar's guidance, we came to a very momentous decision. It is no less than a determination to settle here in London for at least some time. After all our wanderings we feel the benefit of living under the "King's Peace", with law and order and a variety of good food and other things to be had without trouble. Fish and meat and fresh vegetables can be had in the markets; good wine, ale or fresh water to drink, clothes to be purchased and many churches besides the Cathedral to serve our spiritual needs. We find the Londoners are industrious and hard working and, though we do not mix with them a great deal, we learn that they are friendly and good companions.
> LONDON, pp. 45–6

Clearly orientated towards the classroom, Juliet Dymoke's LONDON IN THE EIGHTEENTH CENTURY (1958), in Longman's *Then and There* series, is unusual in that it emphasises people rather than localities. We do begin by beating the bounds of the city with a walk during which we recognise some historic buildings or note the absence of others, but very soon we have opened a street door and stepped into the house of the Burneys, noting clothes and furniture, sharing food and drink, hearing about schools and church and about such visitors to the house as Johnson, Reynolds, Sheridan and Burke. In the humbler household of Robert Gibbon, a draper, we can see how some of the middle classes live and can find out what it is like to be an apprentice in London two hundred years ago. National history impinges when the author shows us London in a panic as news comes of Prince Charles Edward's march southwards in '45; the Lord Mayor and London's chief citizens review available defences and the king appears briefly as a lonely figure. The hint of a travel in time means that there is a forward movement in the book that makes an easy transition between one subject and another and an easy mixture of political and social history.

The ideal reader for such a book is a child of eleven or older who has at least a rudimentary sense of period and an interest in people and how they lived in the past. However, when the imaginary visit is over, appendices shift our view from people to places, for if we cannot meet the men and women of the eighteenth century face to face, we can look at some of the streets and buildings they knew. Having excited curiosity through words, the author offers practical advice on what the reader can actually do himself – what places he can visit, where he might find old prints or commemorative plaques on house fronts. Her advice is given in active terms:

> Go to your school or public library and find a good book about Old London – there are plenty of these . . . Look up a street that is well known, such as the Strand, or Fleet Street, or Cheapside, and find out all you can about it. Then go to this street and walk up and down it using your eyes. You will find an old building here, an ancient church there, a narrow alley or a quiet square, that were much the same in the eighteenth century. London is full of surprises, and the busiest street is often the place where we can find many signs of the past.
> LONDON IN THE EIGHTEENTH CENTURY, p. 85

One can hardly resent such friendly advice (which could apply to the study of any town) nor object to rhetorical questions in a book that gives such a comprehensive yet totally clear picture of London at a certain period. G. Fry's drawings, which are based entirely on contemporary sources, give yet another medium through which imagination can work.

To enlist the help of a Holbein, a Canaletto or a Hogarth in surveying bygone London seems an obvious course. Indeed, the history of a city can hardly dispense with illustration, though the proportion of pictures and maps in some books is surprisingly meagre. Certainly there seems to be some point in adapting picture collections like Stella Margetson's FIFTY YEARS OF VICTORIAN LONDON (1969), which covers the years from the Great Exhibition to the Queen's death. The compiler of this fascinating book has the particular advantage of being able to use contemporary photographs – in fact, there is here an incidental history of the camera as well as of London and Londoners. Here are John Thomson's studies of working-class streets and the remarkable studies which Paul Martin made in the 1900s with a concealed camera focussed on certain streets; here are portraits of royalty and high society by the Downeys and superb architectural studies by Roger Fenton (as well as grimmer pictures by him of Britain at war). Here is Lily Langtry in her drawing-room, thoughtful and intelligent; here is the Queen relaxed but formidable, writing a letter; here are muffin men, a group of servants, Mikado's three little maids on the stage, Fleet Street crammed with horse-drawn traffic. The effect of the book is exciting, startling, often astonishing, and if young readers find the introduction too concentrated, they can go a long way with the pictures and their excellent captions.

If they do not know London well enough to make their own comparisons between past and present, David Whitehead's LONDON THEN LONDON NOW (1969) will help them to do this. Few books for children give enough consideration to present-day demolition and building, road-making and the movements of people. The comparative views in this book of St Paul's and the Elephant effectively show the changes in London which war and population pressures have made necessary.

What you see you remember. But in the context of history, visual material is of little use without some verbal accompaniment. A picture or a map can enhance a piece of written history, but a child will usually need some advice on how to look at an illustration. The view of London in Ralph Agas's map of 1570 is valuable for historians, but a child would find it hard to identify the figures in

it without a guide-line such as Eric de Maré supplies in LONDON'S
RIVER when he writes:

> It shows such lively details as a man bringing two horses down
> to the river to fill the barrels on their backs with water; some
> housewives are laying out their washing, and up at Moorgate,
> just outside the City wall on the north, some young men are
> practising with bows and arrows.
> LONDON'S RIVER, pp. 50–51

An historian may rely on illustration to do some of his work
for him, or again he may supply his own illustration by writing
pictorially. It may not be misleading to illustrate this from a book
for adults, ELIZABETHAN LONDON by Martin Holmes (1969),
which may be confidently recommended for boys and girls in the
'teens. The author's urbane style and confident generalisation
depends on a great deal of background scholarship. London as a
"market-planned town" is described vividly and as vividly explained, general statements being clinched by particular examples.
The change from Tudor to Stuart architecture, an important stage
in London's growth as a whole, is discussed in general terms and
clinched by a particular example:

> The Italian classical style, practised so intensively by Inigo Jones
> after Elizabeth's death, has been brought by the later architect
> [Wren] to such a pitch of excellence and appropriateness in this
> building, that it takes a conscious effort to remember that the
> Elizabethan "Paul's" was a very different structure, but one with
> an impressiveness of its own. Look up Ludgate Hill and imagine
> it surmounted by something like Salisbury Cathedral, with
> Gothic buttresses and a thin spire apparently reaching as high
> as Heaven. The substitution does much to alter, in a moment,
> the whole character of London, revealing it as essentially a
> medieval city – which, as we have seen, it was.
> ELIZABETHAN LONDON, p. 111

This may be an obvious example but it is also a pertinent one;
moreover, it is a practical choice, since a school or private visit to
London will nearly always include St Paul's in the itinerary and

the author's point about architectural style and impression can be
checked by referring to a picture.

I have suggested that illustrations do need interpretation. Martin
Holmes uses the map by Braun and Hogenberg included in
CIVITATES ORBIS TERRARUM of 1575 partly as a guide to the
extent and appearance of London beside the Thames in Elizabeth's
reign and partly as a way of introducing a discussion of the typical
Londoner of that date. He prepares for an important historical
generalisation by describing the group of four figures standing in
the foreground of the map. He points to aspects of their costume –
the merchant's robe, the neatness and lack of ostentation in his
wife's gown, the workmanlike appearance of the attendant apprentice and maid-servant. Then he remarks "These are the people whom
we must consider as Elizabethan Londoners, and whom Franciscus
Hogenberg wished his readers to consider as such when he engraved
the plate." He explains that the Tudor court "had no habitual
residence in London itself" and lists the various palaces and
mansions the Queen chose to stay in and the "form of elaborate
country-house society" that obtained as the court moved with her
from one or another of the royal estates. He concludes:

> "Londoners know no King but their Mayor" had been the proud
> contention of the London merchants of an earlier day, and at
> this time it was still flat cap and furred gown, not short Spanish
> cloak and cartwheel ruff, that betokened the Londoner of
> quality.
> ibid., p. 5

"At this time" refers, as he is careful to indicate, to the heyday
of Elizabeth's reign. As she grew old "her excursions about the
country were not so many, or so wide-ranging, as they had been,
and her court was gradually establishing its headquarters at Whitehall." House-building, the conversion of monastic property and the
use of empty sites, naturally followed; the last ten years of Elizabeth's life saw changes which the author can summarise now that
he has suggested reasons for these changes:

> The old bridge-head market-town had developed in its own way
> into a great commercial city; now it was acquiring two new

features – a leisured population and a purely residential quarter. This period saw the birth of the West End.

ibid., p. 86

The Hogenberg map and others like it are quaint and fascinating, but they are not likely to be given more than a passing glance unless they are properly interpreted. Too often in books for the young a map or a print will be left to explain itself or will even be used with only a superficial relevance to the text. A proper consideration of the relationship between pictures and text can help a young reader who has long been a collector of random facts, historical facts among others, to join up some of these random facts by adding questions of How and Why to the easier ones of When and Where.

Current books on London for children show such variation of method that it would be hard to put them in an order of merit – and perhaps not really very useful. However, I have not so far found any book I would rank higher than Eric de Maré's LONDON'S RIVER. A bright child of ten could follow its arguments: many adult readers enjoy its suave style and apposite detail.

LONDON'S RIVER is not as specialised as its title suggests. It is subtitled "The story of a city" and without deserting his theme or straining topography, the author has found no difficulty in fulfilling the promise of both title and subtitle. The few passages that seem about to deviate from the Thames-side route turn out to be contingent. For example, a passage on the social structure of eighteenth-century London in general grows out of an account of the imported foodstuffs and textiles coming to the docks and how they were distributed. A general description of living conditions a century before this, when London was wreathed in the smoke of sea-coal and suffering from congested streets, has its climax in a sentence on the sewage which "often found its way into the streams and wells from which people drew their water" and which were supplied by or flowed into the Thames: and a horrific description of conditions in the hot summer of 1858 (known as the Great Stink) leads to an account of the building of the Embankments and the "new sewage-disposal scheme" in which pipes on both sides of the river ran down to outfalls where the "sewage was treated, loaded on to ships and carried out to sea, where it could be dumped." The author adds ruefully that the river is still far from pure today.

The Thames is kept in the forefront of a narrative which moves steadily forward like a film camera recording the stages of London's history. Like a film camera, too, the book picks up small details that have the charm and memorability of the unexpected. Here, for instance, is the river at the end of the seventeenth century:

> The river was still full of fish and fairly clean and clear, except after a storm. Then the water became so thick with mud washed down from the banks and along the streams, that fish could not see where they were swimming. At such times, fat haddock could be lifted straight out of the river below the Bridge by anyone who cared to dip a hand into the water.
>
> LONDON'S RIVER, p. 73

This is a book about the Thames, its function in successive centuries, the bridges over its tidal waters and the buildings on its banks. It is also a book about the people who travelled on it, lived beside it and, pretty often, drowned in it. Some of the books offered to children almost give the impression that London grew through an invisible agency, or as though the city were "a massive parking problem, or an overwhelming sea of bricks and mortar, or a scene of pageantry," instead of "a city of people". In a score of descriptions of Nonesuch House, glory of old London Bridge, the point that seems most to interest writers is the fact that wooden pegs were used in its construction and not a single nail. Only Eric de Maré actually treats Nonesuch House as a dwelling. "There a number of lords lived in grand style", he says, "for the Bridge had become very fashionable."

In his pages we are always aware of people – Roman engineers inspecting possible sites for a bridge, a foreign visitor to Elizabethan London watching a bull-baiting, Evelyn enjoying the Frost Fair of 1683, Sir Marc Brunel marching in a procession to celebrate the public opening of the Thames Tunnel in 1843, and a score of anonymous figures claiming London and the river as their birthright.

To vary his technique in displaying London at various periods, he uses with conspicuous success a dramatic as opposed to an expository approach, imagining "a young sailor on his first visit to London from the Continent in the year 1400, when Henry IV had been on the throne for a year." What did the whole riverside and the City look like then, the author asks, and proceeds to steer his traveller round the Isle of Dogs to the Tower, past a fleet of "long, elegant galleys" from Venice "manned by 180 oarsmen and protected by a company of archers", up to the great Bridge, where sixpence must be paid for the raising of the drawbridge, till he leaps ashore at odorous Billingsgate to explore the city and, later, hires a boatman to row him to Westminster.

The imaginary tour is varied by an occasional brief summary of historical fact or an explanation of an architectural feature; sometimes the author makes a point of social history as an afterthought to the description of a street; sometimes he lets a piece of description make its own impact:

The splendid Nonesuch House, built with a timber framework about 1577 to replace the old Drawbridge Gate on London Bridge.

Drawing from LONDON'S RIVER (Bodley Head), illustrated by Heather Copley and Christopher Chamberlain

A wealthy merchant passes by with slow dignity, dressed in a
velvet robe of purple lined with fur, with sleeves trailing to the
ground, and wearing a coloured turban on his head and long
pointed shoes on his feet.

ibid., p. 39

At the end of this sustained piece of tourism, he draws a forceful
conclusion which would have been confusing without the preceding
piece of fictional history:

Now we can begin to see how the bones of modern London,
inside its ever-swelling mound of flesh, were formed. There was
the Bridge which made the city – the merchant's City itself
behind its old defensive wall – the busy port on the river – the
Tower on the south-east corner of the City, first built as a royal
threat and conveniently linked by the river with the Royal Palace
at Westminster – Southwark facing the City across the river
around the south gateway of the Bridge – Westminster two miles
up river, centre of the country's laws and government, where
the King often lived with his court, and which was often at odds
with its rival, the City – and, running between the City and
Westminster, the Strand with its riverside row of noble palaces
and gardens.

ibid., pp. 44–5

It is not enough for an historical writer to know his facts. He
must interpret them and he must arrange them to the best advantage.
LONDON'S RIVER has the advantage of a good, lively prose style
and it is coloured by a very evident enthusiasm. Above all, it is a
well-organised book. The variety of approach prevents dullness,
but every page is part of a consistent plan. This is emphasised by the
penultimate paragraph, which follows some account of proposals
for a Thames Barrage and other revolutionary changes and a
heartfelt plea for the proper use of the Thames as London's
principal amenity. In this penultimate paragraph the author harks
back to earlier chapters and brings his book to a close that is
artistically pleasing and wholly logical:

We could learn from old London, and use the best ideas of

every age. For example, we could build bridges with houses along both sides, like Old London Bridge. We could make parts of the City as intricate with passages, twists, turns and surprises, as mediaeval London was, but without the poverty, dirt and squalor. We could have calm squares of terrace houses surrounding gardens, like the seventeenth and eighteenth centuries built. We might have new ideas of our own, made possible by the new skills and materials of building – tall, elegant, revolving towers, a quarter of a mile high, and gigantic transparent domes, thin as eggshells, covering winter play-grounds half a mile across. ibid., p. 121

London as Eric de Maré sees it is a "riverside port", and a recent portfolio in the *Jackdaw* series, on THE PORT OF LONDON,

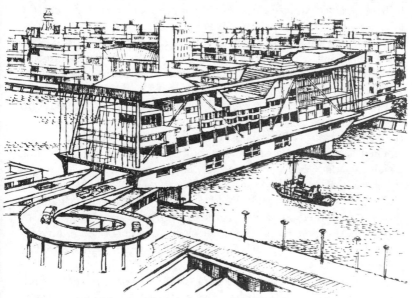

A project for a new bridge having buildings on it like Old London Bridge. Called Crystal Span and designed by a group of well-known architects and engineers for the glass-making firm of Pilkingtons, it would contain an art gallery, an hotel, a theatre, a skating rink and shops.

Drawing from LONDON'S RIVER (Bodley Head), illustrated by Heather Copley and Christopher Chamberlain brings this aspect into prominence. A series of pamphlets for use in schools, the *People in Britain* series, includes THE PORT OF LONDON (1962), in which Robert Clayton follows a modern cargo ship bringing butter and cheese from New Zealand as it is navigated from the mouth of the river up to the Royal Docks. Within this framework there is space for some account of the work of a river pilot, the organisation of the Port of London Authority, the integration of unloading and reloading with a fresh cargo. We are introduced to a lighterman, Peter Harvey, and his son David who is learning the business; we see them carrying part of the cargo up river by barge to a warehouse, and a section about hours and conditions of work and the planning of the simplest job allows also for a light-hearted description of the traditional sculling race for lightermen.

Anyone who writes books on history has to accept in his readers (old as well as young) a certain resistance to history too near the present. At some date – it may be as early as 1485 or as late as 1815 – history, for many, ceases to be colourful and exciting and takes on the greyish hues of everyday. It is easier to make an interesting paragraph out of the building of Morice's water-wheel under London Bridge than out of the working of London's water-supply in the 1960s. It does not seem to occur to writers for the young to discuss, for instance, the distribution of milk through London over the last century or to explain exactly how a large multiple store is stocked. We have to go back to 1909 to find a book for the young which explains consistently and in plain terms *how London works*. F. W. G. Foat's LONDON READER FOR YOUNG CITIZENS is dry and poorly illustrated and would rouse little interest in a child of today accustomed to livelier formats, but here are discussions of money matters, elections, public services, schools, borough government; the author is not thinking of an architectural model but of an inhabited city.

A recent pamphlet in Longman's *Colour Geography* series tends in this direction. The author of the LONDON volume (1955), T. Herdman, explains, in connection with a discussion of the kinds of buildings west of the docks:

Though the bargain between buyer and seller may be quickly fixed, each deal involves much work for other people. Months

before, brokers had arranged for the hire of a ship or part of its
cargo space to carry the goods. It was someone's job to fix the
time of its arrival, its loading abroad, the unloading and storage
of its cargo in London, and finally the despatch of the goods
to the buyer. Insurance against loss of the goods and the ship
must also be arranged. All this involves the writing of many
letters, the completing of many documents and the keeping of
many records. These are the reasons for the blocks of offices
and the crowds of clerks, the network of telephones and the
numerous post-office vans seen in the district. The payments to
be made and collected explain why there seems to be a bank at
every corner.

LONDON, pp. 13–14

In this book, short chapters describe London from the point of
view of a sailor, a business-man, a railwayman, a labourer, and
there are brief discussions of government, the organising of food
supplies and so on. Some of the types chosen stand clearly for a
particular part of London – the sailor for the docks, for instance,
and the business-man for the City.

This suggests another way in which the multiplicity of material
on London can be organised – in a consideration of some of the
"villages" that make up the whole. This is different from a division
by "walks" and in a way it might allow more room for personal
feeling than any other, for it is essentially a method that calls for
inside knowledge, not to say affection.

Stevie Smith's reminiscences of Palmers Green in the second
ALLSORTS collection must have made many children think about
the special character of their locality. A London anthology with
contributions by A. P. Herbert, Clemence Dane, and others might
be equally stimulating.

The village character of London is emphasised in an interesting
study by Michael Foxell in a series, *Portraits of Cities*, which seems
to belong on the borders between "young adult" and adult reading.
With much detail capably organised and compressed, the author
succeeds in communicating an impression and in making you feel
what London is actually like. While this is a very personal book,
it is neither vague nor sentimental. There is good historical sense
in its generalisations. Michael Foxell offers explanations for the

character of the East End by enumerating the foreigners who have settled there, from the Huguenot weavers in Spitalfields to the Chinese in Limehouse, and he stresses also the cottage-industries ("Clothing in Stepney and Hackney, furniture-making in Shoreditch and Bethnal Green") which meant that in Dickens's day the East End was "composed of tight-knit communities, brought together by their trade, their nationality, their religion and by the topography of their area." Slum clearances have not altogether destroyed this particular local flavour, nor will anyone acquainted with London deny the truth of this passage on Kensington and Chelsea:

> What both these places have in common is that they are London's principal lodging districts, consequently they have a constantly shifting population of young people. Though many of the smaller houses are private homes, most of the larger ones, of which there are a great many, are divided into flats and bed-sitters. Rank upon rank of milk bottles stand on the door-steps. Rows of bell-buttons line the door-jambs. Parties start up without warning and break up at dawn. The population is always on the move. There's a restlessness in the air of lonely people in search of companionship, and there's also a liveliness that does not exist in the business areas or in the dormitories of London.
> LONDON, pp. 56–7

Many of us would be prepared to try to define the character of some particular area of London, but how many of us would do the same for "a Londoner"? The best description I have come across so far is the wry comment of Maurice Gorham in a consciously entertaining book for light adult reading called simply LONDONERS (1951). "One of the favourite London amusements," he says, "is to stand outside something waiting to see somebody."* Any definition would have to change from place to place and from year to year. Lady Nicholson's list in THE LONDONER (1944) of "Archbishops, bookies, policemen, newsmen, busmen, dustmen, all the professions (and some are very queer), business men, chairmen, directors, stockbrokers, typists, and heaven knows how many

*LONDONERS, p. 105

charladies", which ends with club "idlers", is barely recognisable thirty years after it was written.* We have to catch the Londoner unaware, as Michael Foxell does in a picturesque description of a street market and the "stout old women and hoarse young men who practise, with a mixture of abuse and salesmanship, the amusing technique of the Dutch auction":

> Here is all the variety of human life, stripped to shirt sleeves in summer, working under bare electric bulbs strung like fairy lights along the stalls in winter, probing for a bargain, laughing, gossiping and complaining. Here are the young and the old, Jew and Christian, coloured and white, rich and poor, forming a community that makes up the total population of this vast, ancient, dirty, much-loved city.
>
> LONDON, p. 96

But if a Londoner as such defies definition, much may be done, and often is done, when a celebrity born in or visiting or associated with London, a character recognisable for what he was or what he did, is used as the central point for a "story". This approach can be less superficial than it sounds. It is the link between a personage and a building, for instance, that gives a special sharpness to LONDON'S PRIDE (1951) by A. Parish and I. Goddard. Although this is introduced as the study of "some buildings of special interest", the connection of Inigo Jones with the Queen's House at Greenwich, Robert Adam with Kenwood, George Moore with Ebury Street, Swinburne with Putney Hill, makes us look more attentively at the superb pictures. This book for the general reader must be classified as "recondite"; many of its subjects are out of the range of the average child (Tecton's Health Centre at Finsbury, for instance). In a book for children the choice is likely to be more obvious.

An early example of the anecdotal type of history, THE CHILDREN'S LONDON PAGEANT (1935) by Stanley Snaith announces that "These stories are not about history, though history enters into some of them . . . They deal with events exciting in themselves, and most of them are records of fine human courage." There are, none the less, such familiar historical figures as Wat Tyler, Guy

*THE LONDONER, pp. 7–8

Fawkes and Lord Nithsdale; but, besides, we have the less pre-
dictable stories of Lunardi and his balloon and of the young pilot
who shot down the Zeppelin S.L.II in 1916, and a rousing account
of the siege of Sidney Street.

This book has considerably more dignity than the chatty collection by Kathleen Fidler called TALES OF LONDON (1953), in which
invented dialogue is mixed with exposition and stiffened by a very
occasional quotation. Boadicea's attack on London, the young
Victoria hearing she is Queen and Wat Tyler appealing for justice
are given the same sensational treatment in the same popular style
as less august folk – like Master Faryner the King's baker stumbling
drunk to bed in Pudding Lane, leaving smouldering brushwood in
his bakehouse, or a cat staying by her kittens in the blitzed church
of St Augustine's. It is easy to laugh at this very casual technique,
but it is dangerous when, as here, the anecdotes are offered out of
chronological order and with little period detail. Each one begins
dramatically, often giving a false impression. For example, in one
"tale" Wat Tyler starts up on impulse as leader of the people
gathered to march on London; only later does the author explain
something of the slow maturing of plans for the rising and Wat
Tyler's part in them.

The anecdotal method is an uneasy one but when it is handled
well it becomes something more – more even than the "historical
episode" which is how Barbara Leonie Picard describes the chapters
of THE TOWER AND THE TRAITORS (1961). There is nothing
pedantic about her treatment of history. Indeed, she allows a certain
flexibility in her treatment of sources, for where contemporary
versions vary, she has chosen "that version which seems to me to
be nearest to the truth", but "where it is merely the details which
differ, I have chosen those details which, all other things being
equal, seem to me the most interesting." We may trust her choice
and her manipulation of dialogue which is "either authentic or else
accepted by tradition", and we may excuse her occasional change
of reported speech to direct speech, because her particular blend
of exposition and narrative would be dull indeed without the sound
of voices and the feel of tension between individuals.

In THE TOWER AND THE TRAITORS nine historical personages
are seen at the particular crossroads in their life which led them
to the Tower. In each case the author has pitched her voice suitably.

Gravity is needed in telling of More and Raleigh, feeling (even romantic feeling) in describing the downfall of Anne Boleyn and Catherine Howard; a certain hardness of temper is perceptible in the chapter on James Scott, Duke of Monmouth and George, Baron Jeffreys, and a strong suspense in the stories of Nithsdale's escape and Thomas Blood's attempt to steal the Crown Jewels; while in the chapter on that Jacobean *cause célèbre*, the Overbury murder, it is with the skill of a detective story writer that the author marshals all the facts of the case and examines the credentials and attitudes of the many witnesses.

The dignity of history is never sacrificed to the exigencies of a story in this book, as it is often in Kathleen Fidler's TALES OF LONDON, yet Barbara Leonie Picard is far from dull. Her account of the Nithsdale escape seems a great deal more vivacious, in fact, than Kathleen Fidler's. It is more scholarly to quote the two letters to Lady Traquair that survive (one from Lady Nithsdale describing her two-hundred-mile journey on horseback in the snow, the other from Lady Traquair's brother about his impending execution) than to make up conversations in more or less modern idiom. Not only this, but the actual letters speak so eloquently of their writers that they transcend anything that descriptive detail could ever do. Both these authors aim to make history palatable and interesting to the young: one underestimates her readers and the other pays them the respect they deserve.

The dust-jacket of LONDON'S WONDERFUL BRIDGE (1959) by Philip Rush hardly does the book justice with its announcement that "thrilling" and fascinating episodes "from the lives of Wat Tyler, Henry VIII, Samuel Pepys and others are related in these pages". Certainly the proportion of dramatised incident is high and the author does not always show exactly where invention ends and historical explanation begins. An eye-witness style can bring the past nearer to a child, but it lends itself to a certain coy cosiness. The following paragraph about the building of Peter Colechurch's revolutionary bridge has an attractive pictorial quality, but the "told to the children" note is unattractive:

These loungers on the wooden bridge would begin to take a fatherly interest in the work. Most would be workmen or house-wives or foreign sailors from Billingsgate or Queenhithe Ports.

But many a knight dressed in a long belted gown, with a mantle thrown over his shoulders, would glance at the strange proceedings in the river as he rode over the bridge on his horse, followed by his squire, who might envy the workmen their comparative freedom. They did not have to live with one master all their lives! Certainly many an abbot and lady in their horse-litters would draw aside the curtains to take a peep, anxious to be able to tell the people at home of the odd goings-on in London. LONDON'S WONDERFUL BRIDGE, pp. 13-14

Compared with the rather similar description quoted from Eric de Maré's LONDON'S RIVER on page 226, Philip Rush's passage shows an underlying diminution of facts for the benefit of readers who need no such thing.

All the same, children would not be in any doubt about the technical aspect of this ambitious work. The author supplies them with all the details they could want about the dimensions and materials of the bridge, the way the workmen dealt with the problem of sinking piers in water and the disasters that accompanied the revolutionary methods of construction, the revenue derived from tolls on the bridge, the kinds of buildings that stood there and the dangerous current produced by the starlings on which each pier stood. A book published in the '60s would probably carry more illustrations than this one, but to some extent Philip Rush's particularly concrete and visual way of writing makes up for this.

Moreover, he enlivens his book with the kind of anecdotes most likely to intrigue the young. He tells us of the Tudor baker at the Bridge House on the Southwark side who was often reported for using mouldy flour; he describes the fire of 1633 which was caused when a maidservant in the house of Mr John Briggs, a needle-maker, "placed a container full of hot ashes under the stairs before going to bed"; he makes the most of the daring rescue as a result of which Edward Osborne, apprentice to the wealthy clothmaker William Hewett, later won his daughter's hand in marriage, and he enlarges vigorously on the Frost Fair of 1684.

The later history of Peter Colechurch's great bridge is less productive of incident and is told briefly, with an equally brief mention of the opening of the new bridge in 1831; this book dates before the time when this "bridge we still use, a mere youngster of little more than a century and a quarter" became an old bridge destined to leave London and make way for yet another in the succession. On this nineteenth-century bridge, then, a City gentleman, described a little facetiously, stands as "a polished example of modern civilization". "What can he have in common," the author asks, "with those jostling mobs we have seen cross the Old Bridge for six hundred years, men who were ready at an instant's notice to fight for their lives or their money, or even their principles?" His reply leads up to a statement of the theme of the book:

> Those people on the Old Bridge lived only for the present as they knew it. They cared nothing for the past or the future, and our City gentleman is just the same. He too regards himself as completely up-to-date and modern and existing only by his own efforts.
>
> Yet in a few years our well-nourished City friend will seem as hopelessly out-of-date as an Elizabethan merchant would to him. Time passes – and passes quicker as the world gets older.
>
> So that, as we inevitably lose the polite race with this gentleman to secure the last seat on the 5.9, we can tell ourselves that by watching those people on Old London Bridge we have learned something he has forgotten or never troubled his head about. Those people on the Bridge have taught us that the present wells up out of the past like a river from an underground spring.
> ibid., pp. 133–4

LONDON'S WONDERFUL BRIDGE is an interesting example of a *specialised* treatment by which the various and intractable material relating to London can be brought within the range of a young reader. Books like this built round a single aspect of London are more often found in the adult library than on junior shelves, oddly enough. Studies of a particular locality – a street, a borough, an area – are surprisingly rare. The best I have come across might tempt other writers to do something like it for their own habitats. Jessie Waller, author of THE STORY OF FINSBURY RETOLD FOR CHILDREN (1965), is a member of the staff of the Finsbury Central Library and her book reflects an active as well as a scholarly interest in Norman Clerkenwell, the open space at Moorfields dear to medieval Londoners, the conduits erected by Sir Hugh Myddleton

early in the seventeenth century, the medicinal springs known as
Sadler's Wells, the amalgamation of Finsbury with Islington in our
own day.

The book is frankly didactic in purpose. Each chapter ends with
suggestions that involve further reading. "Draw a picture of Dame
Alice Owen and the milkmaid" the reader is urged, or "Find out
why Cromwell's Puritans closed the theatres." But the tone of the
book, if it is didactic, is also friendly, personal and *enthusiastic*.
The author clearly wants to create an active interest in the past, to
relate past to present and to set children hunting for historical
evidence.

The book opens like this:

Fairy tales very often start off with a Door in a Wall. The door is
usually fast shut; behind it there lies a secret which only those
having the right key can find. There are doors like that in real
life, too, so let us start our Story of Finsbury with a door. Find
numbers 14 to 16 Farringdon Road, near Clerkenwell Green.
Between two warehouses look for a door in a wall. Secretly
hidden behind it, there lies something over 800 years old, going
back to the time when Finsbury was a quiet country place. When
we open the door what do we find? Eight steps leading down to
an underground cellar below the street. Lifting up a large wooden
hatch we discover a well, filled with clear water. Now, when
Norman kings were still on the Throne of England, this Well was
famous. Not hidden away then, it stood beside a grassy slope
leading down to a river, surrounded by green fields across which
could be seen the walls of the City of London.
THE STORY OF FINSBURY, p. 5–6

Here is the well that gave Clerkenwell its name. The author explains
how it got the name and how the locality has changed.

She is always aware that children want to know "Why". She
tells them why Sir Robert Falconer had a causeway built over
Moorfields in 1415 and why this invaluable open space was covered
with small houses after the plague of 1665 had subsided. Out-of-
the-way facts can be fascinating and even funny:

Mount Pleasant Post Office replaces the old Middlesex House

of Correction, which closed in 1885; this is the largest post office in the world. The name Mount Pleasant is a humorous reference to the fact that the area was once a huge dung-heap, then called a "laystall", and far from "pleasant"; a little further along Rosebery Avenue, towards Holborn, there is still a Laystall Street.
ibid., p. 60

A compact, persuasive book like this can give children a useful outlet for their energies and their curiosity.

A particular event can also make a useful subject for a single book. The Great Fire of 1666 stands so obviously as a dividing line between old and new London that we shall expect this event to occupy a good deal of space in any history of the city – though it is surprising that few writers have made a point of the parallel with the Blitz of 1940–1. Certainly there is room now for a separate treatment of London's Blitz for the young readers who can see it as history; documentation is as rich for events many of us can remember as it is for the earlier fire which Pepys and Evelyn, the Rev. Thomas Vincent and the apothecary William Boghurst, Westminster schoolboy William Taswell and journalist Daniel Defoe, among others, described in such forthright and concrete terms.

Although all the current information books about the Plague and Fire have an element of the eye-witness account in them, they vary in their approach and in the degree to which they relate these sensational events to the history of London and her inhabitants. The shortest and easiest book for children to read is THE PLAGUE AND THE FIRE OF LONDON (1966) by Michael and Mollie Hardwick. This compilation does not lack historical ballast, but its main purpose is to tell a story and to bring *events* as close to the reader as possible. From the opening sentence – "Somewhere, in the fetid dark, a rat died" to the dramatic account of the confession and death of Robert Hubert – scapegoat for the Fire, the book abounds in scenes described with an immediacy that almost demands the historic present:

A sleepy baker named Farynor groped his way through the darkness downstairs to his bakehouse in Pudding Lane, in the

City of London. He was hoping to find a light for a candle, but he had drawn the oven two hours earlier and no glowing timbers remained.

THE PLAGUE AND THE FIRE OF LONDON, p. 50

The emphasis on the actual is such that even when the authors are explaining rather than narrating, the effect is still that of an eye-witness description:

Amongst the firefighters were seamen from the dockyards at Deptford and Woolwich; tough, tireless men who could pull down a building and clear its timber from the path of the flames far quicker than landsmen could. But they were not called in early enough, and then only in small numbers.

ibid., p. 74

They support their narrative technique by quoting often, and effectively, from contemporary diaries, sermons and so on. It is not in their brief to relate plague or fire very closely either to seventeenth-century politics nor to the history of architecture and town planning. Their book belongs to a series entitled *Famous Events* and it fulfils the intention of the series admirably.

Faber's *Men and Events* series is more directly historical in aim, and Sutherland Ross's book on THE PLAGUE AND THE FIRE OF LONDON (1965) is an excellent example. As I see it, this type of book can through the medium of a striking event suggest to children (from ten or so) an historical attitude to the past. One of the virtues of this thorough and fascinating account is the author's scepticism. He does not accept the standard view (the "ancient lie" as he calls it) that plague epidemics were halted because so much of London burned in 1666; he points out that "The parishes destroyed were not those in which the disease raged most fiercely", and emphasises that London was still a "filthy place" in 1703 when "plague as a cause of death was removed from the Bills of Mortality because it had vanished completely, with not a single case being reported for the previous twenty-four years." His suggested reasons for the epidemic of 1665 are exceptionally full and cogent (exceptional for children's books, that is). He finds it impossible to believe that the figure of six dead after the Fire can be correct, and his account certainly shows that mistakes could easily have been made in assessing these facts.

His sense of period should communicate itself to readers whose historical knowledge is small. There is nothing of the quaint or the picturesque in his account. He warns young people:

> From the houses of this period which have survived until now, from the prints and pictures of the time, from the fine workmanship our ancestors have left to us, we are in danger of imaginging that things were better than they were. It is only the fine essence of the past that takes our admiration today, the things that other generations have thought worth preserving; their rubbish has perished and we are not surrounded by it as we are surrounded by our own.
>
> THE PLAGUE AND THE FIRE OF LONDON, p. 22

and by discussing William Boghurst's painstaking records of plague symptoms, seventeenth-century scientific theory and research and the disciplined action of the Dukes of York and Albemarle in these years of crisis, he forestalls the complacency with which writers occasionally view the efforts of doctors and fire-fighters three centuries ago. When he compares the Great Fire with the air-raid on London in 1940, it is in firm historical terms, and his analogy is entirely comprehensible:

> Suppose that some future outbreak of fire, neglected at the beginning, spread so far and so fiercely as to overwhelm all our fire brigades until, when it ended, it had destroyed everything between Hammersmith and the Tower and between Hampstead and Wimbledon. We should then have to clear an area of some sixty square miles before even beginning to think of rebuilding and, in the meanwhile, we should need to shelter and maintain a million or so homeless people. Our plight would then resemble that of the men of 1666.
>
> ibid., p. 121

The concluding paragraph of the book shows the sound foundation on which it is built:

> St Paul's Cathedral justifies them, as Coventry may justify us.

The chances they missed can be set against the opportunities we
have lost. If, in spite of all, we live on a higher level than they did,
it is only because they built a lower one soundly. There are
people who say that there is no purpose in studying history, that
it is dead and done with, that it repeats itself and that nobody
ever learns from it. If this is true, there are even greater catas-
trophes ahead. If it is wrong, however, if men are at last ready
to read and to learn, the towering of human effort may one day
reach the stars.

ibid., p. 133

Within the framework of a proper thesis, Sutherland Ross
marshals quotation and description to bring events to life. His
book combines the stimulus of historical generalisation with the
stir of particular detail. His opening paragraph brings London
before our eyes:

The year was nearly spent. As the last hours of 1664 dwindled
towards midnight in darkness and bitter cold, lights were bobbing
on the Thames to mark the passage of watermen, ferrying
revellers homeward to the northern shore. Torches flared in the
narrow streets as shivering linkboys ran to light the way of
citizens bound for bed. From smoky taverns came the sound
of drunken singing, but the houses of respectable Londoners
were already shuttered and silent, their occupants confidently
asleep, with the old year behind them and the new one ahead.
ibid., p. 11

On the eve of 1665 Pepys sat in "the gracious parlour of his brick-
built residence in Seething Lane and congratulated himself on the
work of twelve months gone." His familiar voice sounds in and
out of the story as he walks through the plague-ridden streets,
advises royalty about the fire, takes his valuables to a friend in
Bethnal Green and, later, smuggles them back, in terror of looters.
Sutherland Ross spares the time to suggest, from the abundant
evidence, the very man in action:

As he went along Tower Street he saw houses blazing on both
sides of the narrow way, which was littered with abandoned

goods of all kinds. His neighbour, Sir William Penn, the father of the founder of Pennsylvania, was digging a pit in his garden to harbour his expensive wines. Pepys was always ready to seize a good idea so he hastened home and brought back some documents for Penn to bury. Later on he dug a pit in his own garden in which he hid both some wine and some Parmesan cheese.

ibid., p. 108-9

Nor does he confine himself to the evidence of Pepys. The schoolboy William Taswell, whose curiosity carried him safely through some horrifying sights of plague and fire, is a material witness, and the most mundane contemporary records have yielded details that add to the strong impression of reality in the narrative – for instance, the fact that the postal service greatly suffered because of the general belief that the plague could be transmitted by materials such as paper, or the comment that the "gale of heated air" caused by the combination of heat and wind at the height of the Fire was so strong that "smoke darkened the sky above Oxford and littered the lawns of Windsor with fragments of charred paper" (page 105).

From Harrison Ainsworth onwards there have been plenty of fictional treatments of this crucial event in London's history, but a book like Sutherland Ross's can prove, if proof be necessary, that fiction is not the only medium that can bring the past to life, and, indeed, that it is idle to look for an over-strict separation of fact and fiction as pertaining to history.

The Hardwicks and Sutherland Ross round off their books with some account of the official investigations into the causes of the Fire and the rebuilding of the City, but they are concerned mainly with the dramatic aspect of the story and especially with the Fire itself as a striking single event in London's history. Edward Fox's LONDON IN PERIL 1665-66 (1966) belongs to Lutterworth's *When and Why* books, a series which aims "to take a familiar event in history and examine the cause and effect so that it no longer stands isolated from its background." The "no longer" is begging the question, of course, as blurbs so often do when they imply comparison with rival books. In fact, neither of the books I have already described isolates plague and fire from events or

city before or after. All the same, the balance in LONDON IN PERIL
is unusual. The description of the actual fire is relatively short and
lacks the colour of most others, but the account of London before
the fire is exceptionally long and careful and the summary of
subsequent events is as thorough as a limited word allowance will
allow.

The book might seem a useful introduction for children of ten
or so who were not prepared to tackle a concentrated study. But
brevity does not necessarily mean easy reading. Sutherland Ross
and the Hardwicks use far more words, speaking numerically, but
they are more interesting and often more concrete words; their
prose is racy, crisp and figurative where Edward Fox's tends to be
heavy and abstract. Moreover, the insipid drawings in his book
are a poor alternative to the numerous prints and portraits of the
late seventeenth century which, with reason, are more usually
offered.

The Fire of London is a superlatively exciting subject and one
can hardly blame writers for treating it as such. All the same, there
is room for a closer attention to practical detail and, in particular,
for a more thorough treatment of the aftermath, if only because the
rebuilt London relates so closely to London today. John Bedford's
general study, LONDON'S BURNING (1966), introduces facts which
might be of interest and concern to the young. He tells us where
builders found the brick and stone specified by Parliament for the
new houses and how legislation was passed to prevent City
authorities from employing only their own work-people and
excluding labourers from outside. He quotes building costs and
current prices of raw materials; he corrects the impression that
London rose again as rapidly as the Phoenix by giving dates at
which many important buildings or streets were completed. He
tells us that in spite of the apparent urgency of the rebuilding, a
great many houses were left empty because people preferred the
greater freedom of living outside City jurisdiction, and explains
that ultimately the City was forced to relax some of its regulations
to tempt tenants to return.

Points like these help to show that if the Fire was a tragic accident,
it was not an isolated happening but one which crucially affected
the future of London and its citizens. Children's books have not
given enough time to aspects of the subject like these which invite

the reader to ponder and conclude as well as to exclaim and wonder.

The search for variety in the techniques of history-writing for the young has brought a few writers to specialisation by theme – and not necessarily in fictional form, though this seems to be the chief medium at present. There is interest, for example, in the provision of water for a city, and enough documentary evidence about London to make an information book encompassing history, chemistry and technology, a book that could help children to see London as a planned entity and not the spontaneous growth it might sometimes seem to be. But London's water supply has so far occupied only a corner in general studies of London and it has been left to novelists to fill the gap, and then only to a small degree. Agnes Ashton's WATER FOR LONDON combines fact and fiction in an easy and lively way, but her tale of Sir Hugh Myddleton and the New River of 1609 is chiefly concerned with people. Peripheral to the struggle against landowners and personal rivals, in which, as usual, a lad plays a significant part, there are scenes showing Raleigh in the Tower, Robin Carr the King's favourite riding through the City, a case of plague in which the French doctor at Court is concerned, London Bridge and its houses.

In fact, this is a panorama of London at a certain date; when the author comes to the actual digging of the channel and the diverting of the River Lea or the setting up of conduits in London streets, she gives very little technical detail. In this respect a later story, THE WATER WHEEL by Brian Read, is more effective. In this short book a Southwark lad working as messenger for the Warden of the Bridge in 1580 is involved with Peter Morice's plan for a paddle-wheel to raise water for Fish Street and Cheapside. There is technical detail here and a shrewd side-glance at the hostility of the water-carriers who believed their livelihood was threatened by the invention. This is first and foremost a story, not a history, but the narrative is properly supported by accurate and interesting fact.

To chronicle the changes in London over the centuries, a thematic plan might seem ideal. A book on London's parks, for instance, would not only have to contain selected historical facts about planning and personages but could suggest investigations which boys and girls could pursue through books or by collecting certain facts on the spot. T. H. Girtin's study of THE LORD MAYOR OF

A gruesome but realistic view of Old London Bridge in a drawing by Graham Oakley
from THE WATER WHEEL (World's Work)

LONDON was published twenty-three years ago in one of those
gently informative series for the adult reader which seem now to
have given place to more sophisticated coffee-table books. Its
straightforward narrative is perfectly within a secondary school
child's capacity, and with a new format and new illustrations it
could stimulate interest, indirectly, in the administration of the City.
The street names of London – another obvious way of approaching
the history of any settlement – are touched upon in a recent series
of project books for the classroom; a book combining etymology,
topography and history could go further in encouraging private
enterprise.

Some such encouragement is intended, presumably, in F. R.
Elwell's MR COLLINS AND TONY IN LONDON (1960), in which a
boy sets out with a knowledgeable companion to study the natural
history of the city. A visit to Trafalgar Square gives Mr Collins a
chance to discuss the evolution of the domestic pigeon from the

rock-dove, while St James's Park offers a lesson in identifying water-fowl. In a chapter on London's river, the tides and the investigation of silting by means of radioactive dust combine with details of sparrow roosts and an anecdote about the sighting of a porpoise a long way up river. A train journey to Greenford via North Acton takes the couple to an embankment quartered by kestrels and to fields where fieldfares and lesser black-backed gulls are flying. Finally, Tony learns about extinct animals pleasantly during a visit to the Natural History Museum. The gentle expository style of the book shows the question-and-answer formula at its most spontaneous.

There is another formula there, too – the fictional tour, through which a reader may imagine himself seeing the sights of a city. We may be wary of the "We go" formula, and certainly a book like Thomas Burke's BILLY AND BERYL IN OLD LONDON shows its age – thirty-six – in jocular talks with George the taxi-driver and in the artificially induced sentences in which the learned Mr Sprang discusses the history of Pye Corner and the Temple or describes the various versions of Gog and Magog.

Another coy and long-winded story, MICHAEL'S LONDON (1936) by Elizabeth Montizambert, has an interesting framework for its motley collection of facts. A lonely boy nicknamed Mr Why finds his life more interesting when his governess takes him about London and sets him playing the Discovery Game. In the course of this and other games he collects lions (stone, plaster, paint – there is plenty of scope) or lists the birds, the regiments or just the oddities to be found in London. Activity is paramount, for the book aims to help children "to see in any town a place full of discoveries and adventures in which they can play many parts."

Continuous history is, obviously, for older readers, but exploration can start at almost any age and if a little incidental history is thrown in, so much the better. Dale Maxey has recognised this in SEEING LONDON (1966) by working out five particular excursions in which children as young as seven could join, plotting them in simple words and illustrating them with pictures of some elegance whose shades of grey are diversified by the scarlet of a girl's blazer, a boat on the river and recurrent red elephants representing that old favourite the London omnibus.

Instead of imagining an ideal boy or girl infinitely receptive and untiring, the author has set his sights on ordinary children of ordinary capacity. He can and does introduce historical fact in paragraphs often as packed as this:

> Trafalgar Square was not always the polite and well-behaved place it is today. Originally, it was a rather dangerous and very untidy mass of old buildings, houses and tiny streets, until 1829, that is, when the site was cleared and the new Square was designed by Sir Charles Barry to commemorate Nelson's victory and tragic death at Trafalgar.
>
> The Square covers several acres altogether, and its most famous landmark – the Devonshire granite column supporting the 17 foot statue of Lord Nelson – is 184 feet 10 inches high. The huge capital on which Nelson stands is made from bronze melted down from the guns of the *Royal George*, while the bronze reliefs at the case of the column are in metal taken from French cannons captured in Nelson's many sea-battles. The column was finally completed in 1867, when the four twenty-foot Landseer lions were placed in position.
> SEEING LONDON, p. 6

But he is careful to choose accessible and obvious sights, and he intersperses his more informative passages with more openly persuasive words which sound very much as though he is standing in Trafalgar Square (the point of departure for each excursion) with a group of children about to set out for a walk:

> You'll visit a famous art gallery built out of sugar cubes, find a big cathedral tucked away in a tiny back street, make a trip to the Royal Mews. You'll see the Palace – and the pelicans that can trace their ancestry right back to the days of Nell Gwynn.
> ibid., p. 9

If exclamation marks are scattered pretty thickly on the pages of this engaging book, a generous amount of interesting fact is scattered too in the course of tours to Westminster, Kensington, Regent's Park, Bloomsbury or the City. Children who consult Dale Maxey's book before they visit London will have some idea of what they might see and, with the effective pictorial maps on which the places are clearly indicated with labels and red asterisks, they will know how to get there. The author's attitude is made clear in a prefatory note; he wants to help children to get about, but also "to experience the pomp and pageantry, the magic and the ever changing moods of this breathtakingly beautiful city for yourself." Londoners may find the American's admiration somewhat supercharged, but they will not deny his devotion and enthusiasm.

Younger readers might catch fire too from Miroslav Sasek's THIS IS LONDON (1959) – not only from the breezy satirical text, but also from the open humour and stimulating colour of pictures that start with a page of uniform soupy green indicating London in fog, career blithely past all the most obvious buildings and end with the sight of a street-cleaner ("At the end of all things comes the broom") and a boy posting a letter, holding an umbrella ("And at the end of your picture of London there should come a mention for that familiar friend, your umbrella! Because this is London").

The many tour-books of a more sedate type could be divided into those which are best read before a visit to London, or simply as a substitute for one, and those which could be best described as field-guides. LET'S LOOK AT LONDON (1965) by Guy Williams, belongs to a series *Junior Travel*, but in spite of its title, it does not use a geographical framework consistently. The author sorts his material under headings like Monarchy, God, Fairs and Market Places more often than the more viable Soho or Piccadilly. A sentimental and exclamatory style mars this book. Indeed it is noticeable that most authors who imagine themselves walking alongside a group of boys and girls find it difficult to strike a happy medium between a tediously instructive or playfully avuncular tone of voice. M. M. Pearson's LONDON ADVENTURE (1951), described as "a guide and story book for children of all ages", has an interesting scheme, with sections on London's Lion and Unicorn, London's Tower, London's Whitehall, but although the information at first sight appears to be well arranged, the facts are given no special emphasis, so that the book seems dull and rambling and occasionally indulges in non-sequiturs ("Sir Christopher Wren was married twice. The first time he married Faith Coghill, who spelt her name 'ffaith'.")

Anthony Weymouth's book in a series called *Excursions*,

GOING TO LONDON (1953), is packed with interesting information and arranged in a series of walks, with an occasional bus-ride, starting in the City and ending with the Kensington museums. Events and people predominate and are discussed so allusively that you need some knowledge of history to tackle the book at all. At the same time, facts delivered with a compression fit only for the 'teens and a correspondingly advanced reading list are couched in a style that would insult much younger children:

> I have kept a visit to Westminster Hall to the last because I think it is in many ways the most interesting part of the Houses of Parliament, and I believe you will agree with me when you hear its history and have seen it for yourself. I am fascinated by the idea that I am standing in a hall built by William Rufus between the years 1097 and 1099. I can almost picture this square-set King with his ruddy complexion and yellowish hair, his shifty blood shot eye watching the masons and carpenters as they toil and carry the stones and heavy oak . . . When Richard II became King he set about restoring it . . . And who do you think was the Clerk of Works when Richard reconstructed this hall? His name was Geoffrey Chaucer, whose Canterbury Tales tell us with humour and in graceful language how the twenty-nine pilgrims assembled at the Tabard Inn at Southwark and journeyed to Canterbury.
>
> GOING TO LONDON, pp. 44–5

Malcolm Saville's businesslike approach in COME TO LONDON (1967) is far more likely to persuade children to do just that. Addressing the reader directly, he assumes that he is interested in seeing the sights, that he is willing to take some trouble in preparing for his visit and that he will appreciate really practical directions. Here is an extract from the chapter on Hampstead and Highgate:

> On the opposite side of the High Street at the corner of North Hill with its slabs of modern flats is Highgate School for boys founded by Sir Roger Cholmeley in the sixteenth century. On the other side of the road is a tavern called The Gatehouse where once there stood a toll gate and here you turn into Hampstead Lane. It is possible to get a single-decker bus along here to

Hampstead if you've had enough walking, but Kenwood House, which you must see, is less than a mile away and the walk is easy and pleasant enough. After about ten minutes you will see an unassuming entrance gate on the left of the road which leads you into Ken Wood itself. At once you are in the country again with London below you and the Post Office Tower dominating the sky-line. Look back and you will see the spire of Highgate church above the trees. Almost due south is Parliament Hill, and below to the south-east you may see the gleam of Highgate Ponds. COME TO LONDON, p. 85

This is an entirely personal book. The author says roundly that he finds the Tower too bloodthirsty and that he dislikes Poets' Corner. He accepts the fact that London has grown and will grow and has discriminating views on the Barbican plan, the new Piccadilly and the engineering of the Post Office Tower. He mingles description and history expertly, not trying to move far from the beaten track but writing in a way that can make the hundreds of previous directions "not to miss" St Paul's or Covent Garden or the Albert Memorial take on fresh meaning. In short, this is a book that could persuade a blasé young student to go and see for himself. It is also a book that could be *used*.

This, too, is the chief value of an interesting pamphlet by Margaret Kirby with the lively title MEET ME IN TRAFALGAR SQUARE (1968). Her "walks" have been tried by several groups of schoolgirls in their middle 'teens. Routes and distance are attested and carefully worked out. The aim of the pamphlet is to help young visitors to London to "lose the main thoroughfares and well-known sites". In Walk A, for instance, they are advised to look out for a variety of buildings from South Africa House to the All-night Post Office, from the Westminster Friends' Meeting House to Pollock's Toy Museum; in Walk J they could go past Aldwych on to the Old Curiosity Shop, could look at Lincolns Inn Fields and visit the Sir John Sloane museum. But intending visitors are advised not to feel obliged to follow the sensible suggestions, but to spend plenty of time on things that interest them; and the author suggests that as an alternative to a specific route they could decide to make a study of lamp standards, birds, foreign agencies or, simply, traffic. This is in fact a project book, meant to be used in the same

way as a more obvious guide like Leslie Daiken's LONDON
PLEASURES FOR YOUNG PEOPLE (1957) or the entertaining
EXPLORING LONDON (1965), in which Isobel Barnett and Ronald
Searle act as convenient and lively guides for young tourists.

Guides of this practical kind do not pretend to deal with history
except incidentally, nor do we expect their authors to make
generalisations or follow chronological patterns. These diagrammatic books provide yet another way of simplifying the available
material in such a way that children might in the long run be
guided to more detailed study. Any such simplification would seem
better designed for the young than a composite book with a very
general theme. There is one series, however, which embraces almost
every aspect of London's history, touching also topography and
architecture and offering an efficient gazetteer as well. This is
Macdonald's *Discovering London* paperbacks, which developed
from the television series with the same title, and which map
London from Roman times to the end of Victoria's reign.

A certain allusiveness and breadth of generalisation puts these
books out of the range of most children under fifteen or so. Their
pattern and choice of material might well be noted, however, by
anyone who has written or intends to write a junior book about
London. Each has a general introduction giving the necessary
background of events, and provides discussions on general points
(entertainments, public services, literature, dress and fashion,
architecture) together with other subjects of special relevance to
one or other of the periods – for instance, sanitation in the volumes
on Regency and Victorian London, coffee houses in the Georgian
period, pilgrimage in the Middle Ages. This gives a sense of period
which should contribute to the pleasure of anyone who follows up
the many suggestions of places to visit. Moreover, these suggestions
range from the inevitably familiar to the unusual; we are directed
to the Burlington Arcade for an example of Regency architecture,
to the statue of Captain John Smith in a Holborn churchyard, to
Roman survivals in the little known Cuming museum. The series
as a whole suggests an important point. The presentation of material,
allowing for an allusive manner of writing, is not essentially
different from the presentation we might find in junior books;
but the choice of subjects is very often different – more personal,
more idiosyncratic, less hackneyed.

The basic misconception that spoils so many information books for the young is that they must be different from those designed for adults. A little simpler, certainly; a little more direct in exposition; but surely not essentially different. We need writers who will approach a subject they want to write about and refuse to let considerations of age or capacity interfere with what *they* want to say. If a writer is bored by what he is doing, children will be bored too; and why should we expect them to submit to boredom any more than we expect to submit to it ourselves?

The name of the series from Macdonald is *Discovering London*. Anyone using these books as a guide will in fact be accepting someone else's discoveries, and indeed it is hardly likely that a visitor to London will discover anything hitherto unknown. But *personal* discovery – this, surely, is what we want for the young. We want them to read about London and go and see it with wits sharpened by what they have read so that they make what they see truly their own. And whether or not they do go to London, what we should finally want for them is that they should think of that collection of villages that we call London as a place where people have lived and continue to live. For London is a city, not a museum.

Ronald Searle's cartoon, from EXPLORING LONDON (Ebury Press) aptly illustrates a familiar aspect of the city.

Reading List

Allen, Kenneth. THE STORY OF LONDON TOWN. *Odhams Press* 1967. Illustrated by Janet Duchesne.

Atkinson, Alex. THE BIG CITY or THE NEW MAYHEW. *Perpetua Books* 1958. Illustrated by Ronald Searle. Night-clubs and street boys, a journalist, a parson, American soldiers, street traders – here is a procession of London's poor in a sardonic imitation of Mayhew; the comment is worldly and sharp, the illustrations superb.

Barnett, Isobel. EXPLORING LONDON. Shell Junior Guides. *Ebury Press/ George Rainbird* 1965. Illustrated by Ronald Searle.

Barton, N. J. THE LOST RIVERS OF LONDON (*Phoenix* 1962) *Verry* 1962. With photographs and maps. A scholarly book offering details of many streams that flowed through London and how and why they were used. A good quarry to ensure more varied books for the young.

Bedford, John. LONDON'S BURNING. *Abelard-Schuman* 1966. With photographs and prints.

Biro, Val. THE TOWER OF LONDON: A BIRD'S-EYE VIEW. *Benn* 1970. A poster-size annotated map, ideal for classroom or home walls.

Brooke, Brian. ART IN LONDON: A GUIDE. *Methuen* 1966. Photographs by Frank Herrmann. For adults or older school parties, a survey of museums and galleries, many of them little known to the average visitor. As well as paintings, the author discusses statuary, ceramics and glass, textiles, musical instruments, tapestries and so on.

Bullock, L. G. THE CHILDREN'S BOOK OF LONDON (*Warne* 1948, revised edition 1960) *Warne* revised edition 1960 U.S.A. Drawings by Cyril Deakins. Colour maps and plates by the author.

Bunt, C. LONDON: JOURNEYS THROUGH OUR EARLY HISTORY. *Bruce Publishing Co.* 1955. Illustrated by photographs.

Burke, Thomas. BILLY AND BERYL IN OLD LONDON. *Harrap* 1936. Author also of BILLY AND BERYL IN CHINATOWN (1935) and BILLY AND BERYL IN SOHO (1936).

Carrier, Robert and Dick, O. L. THE VANISHED CITY. *Hutchinson* 1957. Illustrated by photographs and prints. A useful source book for its extremely varied collection of illustrative material.

Church, Richard and Hofbauer, Imre. LONDON, FLOWER OF CITIES ALL. *Heinemann* 1966–67. An intensely personal book in which author and artist plan a wheel-spokes' journey and discover unfamiliar aspects of familiar places;

the scene is largely Dulwich and its environs. A book for a mature reader who welcomes an unusual view of the city.

Clayton, Robert. THE PORT OF LONDON. People in Britain. *Oxford University Press* 1962. Illustrated by photographs.

Cowie, Leonard W. PLAGUE AND FIRE: LONDON 1665–66. Wayland Documentary History series. *Wayland Publications* 1970. Illustrated with photographs and prints. A useful source book; a collection of quotations from the year of the Great Fire onwards, lightly linked.

Daiken, Leslie. LONDON PLEASURES FOR YOUNG PEOPLE. *Thames and Hudson* 1957. Illustrated by maps and photographs.

Dane, Clemence. LONDON HAS A GARDEN. *Michael Joseph* 1964. With photographs and plans. A pleasant description of Covent Garden, its history and its atmosphere today, by someone who lived round the corner for many years.

Deighton, Len. LONDON DOSSIER. *Penguin* 1967. This sophisticated collection of essays looks at Sport, Jazz, the River and other aspects of the city not usually covered by school or childhood visits, and one piece entitled "Mood" by A. J. Marshall goes a long way towards defining the essence of London.

Dobbing, Douglas S. and Roger. THE HOW AND WHY WONDER BOOK OF THE TOWER OF LONDON. How and Why Wonder Books. (*Grosset and Dunlop* 1970) *Transworld* 1970. Illustrated by John Page. An inexpensive paper-covered book in popular style, packed with interesting and entertaining detail; a useful preliminary to school visits.

Dymoke, Juliet. LONDON IN THE EIGHTEENTH CENTURY. Then and There. *Longman* 1958. Drawings by G. Fry from contemporary sources.

Elwell, F. R. MR COLLINS AND TONY IN LONDON. *Heinemann* 1960. Illustrated by Nan Fullarton.

Fidler, Kathleen. TALES OF LONDON. Heritage series. *Lutterworth* 1953. Illustrated by Douglas Relf.

Fletcher, Geoffrey. THE LONDON NOBODY KNOWS. *Hutchinson* 1962. Also CHANGING LONDON (*Collins* 1969 U.K.) *Collins* 1970 U.S.A. Illustrated by the author. The text of these books is probably too mature for most young readers; the drawings in the latter book were made to accompany remarks about the demolition of fine buildings in "Peterborough's" column in the *Daily Telegraph*. The two books give a unique view of a London that is rapidly disappearing. As well as whole buildings, the artist has depicted lamp standards and public lavatories of unusual design.

Foat, F. W. G. A LONDON READER FOR YOUNG CITIZENS. *Methuen* 1909.

Fox, Edward. LONDON IN PERIL 1665–66. When and Why. *Lutterworth* 1966. Illustrated by Peter Sharrocks.

Foxell, Michael. LONDON. Portraits of cities. *Lutterworth* 1965. Illustrated by photographs.

Girtin, T. H. THE LORD MAYOR OF LONDON. Chameleon Books. *Oxford University Press* 1948. Illustrated by J. Bevan.

Gorham, Maurice. LONDONERS. *P. Marshall* 1951. Illustrated by Edward Ardizzone.

Hardwick, Michael and Mollie. THE PLAGUE AND THE FIRE OF LONDON. Famous Events. *Parrish* 1966. Illustrated by Zena Flax.

Hartley, Rachel. A LITERARY GUIDE TO THE CITY. *Queen Anne Press* 1966. A pamphlet published in association with the Corporation of London, in dictionary format. Useful for planning projects or walks.

Hayes, John. LONDON: A PICTORIAL HISTORY (*Batsford* 1967) *Arco* 1969. Illustrated by photographs and prints. The Assistant Keeper at the London Museum uses illustration to show how London has changed and grown through the centuries; he gives proper attention to modern building.

Herdman, T. LONDON. Colour Geography series. *Longman* 1955, revised editions 1957 and 1966. Illustrated by photographs and maps.

Hibbert, Christopher. LONDON: THE BIOGRAPHY OF A CITY (*Longman* 1969) *Morrow* 1970. Illustrated by photographs and prints. A massive, civilised book, valuable as a quarry for illustrations and notable for the balance of its treatment of the subject in different periods.

Holmes, Martin. ELIZABETHAN LONDON (*Cassell* 1969) *Praeger* 1969. Illustrated by photographs and prints.

Howgego, J. L. THE CITY OF LONDON THROUGH ARTISTS' EYES (*Collins* 1969) *Walker* 1969. Introduction by Nikolaus Pevsner. This varied collection of reproductions includes works by Nevinson, John Piper, Canaletto and a superb painting of St Paul's in the snow by David Thomas exhibiting the beauty of strict realism; another useful source book.

Jefferies, Greg. THE PORT OF LONDON. Jackdaw series. (*Cape* 1970) *Grossman* 1970.

Johnson, David. THE TOWER OF LONDON. Jackdaw series. (*Cape* 1969) *Grossman* 1969.

Kirby, Margaret. MEET ME IN TRAFALGAR SQUARE: TEN WALKS AROUND WESTMINSTER FOR YOUNG PEOPLE. *Schoolmaster Publishing Co.* 1968. Maps by K. J. Wass.

Langdon-Davies, John. THE PLAGUE AND FIRE OF LONDON. Jackdaw series. (*Cape* 1963) *Grossman* 1963.

Lewesdon, John. THE LADYBIRD BOOK OF LONDON. Ladybird Books. *Wills and Hepworth* 1961. Illustrated by John Berry.

Manley, Deborah; Royds, Pamela; Tuft, Nancy. USING LONDON. *Penguin* 1971, *Deutsch* 1971. A guide not for tourists but for denizens; lively, splendidly well-documented and useful for all ages.

Maré, Eric de. LONDON'S RIVER: THE STORY OF A CITY (*Bodley Head* 1964) *McGraw-Hill* 1965. Drawings by Heather Copley and Christopher Chamberlain.

Margetson, Stella. FIFTY YEARS OF VICTORIAN LONDON FROM THE GREAT EXHIBITION TO THE QUEEN'S DEATH. *Macdonald* 1969. Illustrated by photographs; based on Macdonald's Discovering London series, q.v.

Maxey, Dale. SEEING LONDON (*Collins* 1966) *Vanguard* 1967. Illustrated by the author.

Mitchell, R. J. and Leys, M. D. R. A HISTORY OF LONDON LIFE. *Longman* 1958, *Penguin* 1963. Illustrated by photographs. London seen from the starting point of particular people associated with the city – More, Chaucer, Fielding, Dickens and so on. Among unusual visitors, a governess walked 538¾ miles during her visit and, as well as seeing the obvious sights, watched a balloon ascent and attended Byron's funeral. Children's introductions to London through books could be as lively as this.

Montizambert, Elizabeth. MICHAEL'S LONDON: A BOOK FOR CHILDREN IN ANY CITY. *Hamish Hamilton* 1936. With photographs and drawings.

Nairn, Ian. MODERN BUILDING IN LONDON. *London Transport Board* 1964. With photographs. A guide-book that usefully corrects the predominant antiquarian slant. See also NAIRN'S LONDON (*Penguin* 1966).

Nicholson, Lady. THE LONDONER. Britain in pictures. *Collins* 1944. Illustrated by photographs and prints.

O'Malley, Raymond (editor). LONDON STREET LIFE: SELECTIONS FROM THE WRITINGS OF HENRY MAYHEW. *Chatto and Windus* 1956. A convenient selection from the unique reportage of Dickens's associate on London's street life.

Osmond, Laurie. THE THAMES FLOWS DOWN. *Oxford University Press* 1957. Illustrated by Edward Osmond. A substantial, pleasantly written historical/geographical survey, illustrated with pictorial maps, especially recommended for its attention to all reaches of the river and to multifarious activities from commerce to sport.

Parish, A. and Goddard, I. LONDON'S PRIDE: SOME BUILDINGS OF SPECIAL INTEREST. *Ward Lock* 1951. With photographs.

Pearson, M. M. LONDON ADVENTURE: A GUIDE AND STORY BOOK FOR CHILDREN OF ALL AGES. *Harrap* 1951. Illustrated by the author.

Pevsner, Nikolaus. LONDON, EXCEPTING THE CITIES OF LONDON AND WESTMINSTER. *Penguin* 1952. Also THE CITIES OF LONDON AND WEST-

MINSTER. *Penguin* 1957. Illustrated by photographs. Definitive architectural reference books.

Picard, Barbara Leonie. THE TOWER AND THE TRAITORS. Living in History. *Batsford* 1961. Illustrated by William Stobbs.

Piper, David. THE COMPANION GUIDE TO LONDON (*Harper & Row* 1965) *Collins* 1966. Illustrated by photographs. A witty and comprehensive guide intended for adults and full of personal delights and prejudices. For young people to dip into for its good style and for the way the author develops his idea of "a network of villages about the twin cities of London and Westminster".

Priestley, Harold. LONDON: THE YEARS OF CHANGE. *Muller* 1966. With photographs. A good example of how to make specialised history palatable to the intelligent general reader. The author traces the attempts of the Crown to stop the growth of London from the Tudor period to 1700; he is especially good on the rebuilding after the Great Fire.

Pritchett, V. S. LONDON PERCEIVED (*Chatto and Windus/Heinemann* 1962) *Harcourt, Brace* 1962. Photographs by Evelyn Hofer. A brilliantly perverse interpretation of a city "which smokes gratuitously and pensively in your face", really communicating the feel of the place.

Rance, Peter. TEACHING BY TOPICS. *Ward Lock Educational* 1968. The thoroughly varied "blackboard outline for a Grade 4 Topic – top juniors 9+–11+" on the subject of London, offered here as an example of technique, includes many familiar places and some less obvious sidelines.

Rees, Brian. LONDON. *Blackwell* 1958.

Ross, Sutherland. THE PLAGUE AND THE FIRE OF LONDON. Men and Events. *Faber* 1965. With photographs and prints.

Rush, Philip. LONDON'S WONDERFUL BRIDGE. *Harrap* 1959. Illustrated by Nancy Sayer.

Sasek, Miroslav. THIS IS LONDON (*W. H. Allen* 1959) *Macmillan* 1959. Illustrated by the author.

Saville, Malcolm. COME TO LONDON: A PERSONAL INTRODUCTION TO THE WORLD'S GREATEST CITY. *Heinemann* 1967. Illustrated by photographs.

Smith, Stevie. "The same place" in ALLSORTS 2, edited by Ann Thwaite. *Macmillan* 1969.

Snaith, Stanley. THE CHILDREN'S LONDON PAGEANT: STORIES OF THE GREAT CITY. *Obros Press* 1935.

Sorrell, Alan. ROMAN LONDON (*Batsford* 1969) *Arco* 1969. Illustrated by the author. A lucid discussion of sites and people, with authoritative and beautiful reconstructions in line.

Stuart, Dorothy Margaret. LONDON THROUGH THE AGES: THE STORY OF A CITY

AND ITS CITIZENS, 54B C.–A.D. 1944. *Methuen* 1956. Illustrated from original sources by Sheila Maguire.

Stuart, Dorothy Margaret. THE YOUNG LONDONER THROUGH THE AGES. *Harrap* 1962. Illustrated by photographs and prints.

Thompson, Godfrey. LONDON FOR EVERYMAN. *Dent* 1969. A revision of William Kent's classic guide; a useful reference book.

Tomlinson, H. M. LONDON RIVER. *Cassell* 1921, revised edition 1951. Photographs by Charles Tomlinson. Personal reminiscence, chiefly of the docks below the Tower. A heightened style lightened by character sketches of seamen and landsmen.

Waller, Jessie. THE STORY OF FINSBURY RETOLD FOR CHILDREN. *Finsbury Central Library* 1965. Illustrated by J. Jarvis.

Warwick, Alan R. A NOISE OF MUSIC (*Queen Anne Press* 1968) *Crescendo* 1970. A survey of pageants and spectacles through the ages, including details of military bands, bells and peals, and discussing the Barbican plan for the arts.

Weymouth, Anthony. GOING TO LONDON. Excursions series. *Phoenix* 1953. Revised edition 1959, revised by Christopher Trent.

Whelpton, Barbara. LONDON MAJESTIC. *Burke* 1963. Illustrated by the author.

Whitehead, David. LONDON THEN, LONDON NOW. *Dalton Watson* 1969. Illustrated by photographs.

Williams, Guy. LET'S LOOK AT LONDON. Junior Travel series. *Museum Press* 1965. Drawings by the author, and some photographs.

Yee, Chiang. THE SILENT TRAVELLER IN LONDON. *Country Life* 1951. Illustrated by the author. This "Chop Suey of London", as the author describes it, is a book of seasonal atmospheres, distinguished for its fragile, misty coloured pictures, which give a new look to old sights.

—— DISCOVERING LONDON. *Macdonald.* The series is as follows: ROMAN LONDON by Grace Derwent, THE CONQUEROR'S LONDON by Derek Brechin, MEDIEVAL LONDON by Kenneth Derwent, TUDOR LONDON by A. R. Robertson. All published in 1968, and all illustrated by David Newton, and with photographs and prints. Also STUART LONDON by Malpas Pearse, GEORGIAN LONDON by Derek Brechin, REGENCY LONDON by Douglas Hill, VICTORIAN LONDON by Graham Norton. All published 1969, and all with photographs and prints.

Relevant stories

Ashton, Agnes. WATER FOR LONDON. *Epworth Press* 1956. Illustrated by Monica Walker.

Coates, Ann. DINOSAURS DON'T DIE. *Longman Young Books* 1970. Illustrated by John Vernon Lord. A small boy escorts his friend the Iguanodon, a stone figure come to life, from the Crystal Palace Park to the South Kensington Museum; an enchanting and amusing tale.

Meynell, Laurence. BRIDGE UNDER THE WATER: A STORY OF THE AGE OF STEAM. Pageant of History series. *Phoenix* 1954. Illustrated by J. S. Goodall. An exciting tale of the Brunels and the building of the first tunnel under the Thames.

Read, Brian. THE WATER WHEEL. *World's Work* 1970. Illustrated by Graham Oakley.

Wilson, Barbara Ker. ANN AND PETER IN LONDON. The Kennedys Abroad. *Muller* 1965. Illustrated by Harry and Ilse Toothill. An agreeable mixture of thriller and guide, in which two children help a young musician from Eastern Europe seeking asylum.

3b | *Atoms*

[The Rutherford Bohr period of research] ... will probably not be recorded very completely as history. As history, its re-creation would call for an art as high as the story of Oedipus or the story of Cromwell, yet in a realm of action so remote from our common experience that it is unlikely to be known to any poet or any historian. J. Oppenheimer. SCIENCE AND THE COMMON UNDERSTANDING, (1953)

3b | *Atoms*

IN the various spheres of science, information books are looking to an earlier readership now than they were twenty years ago. In the last generation children would be most likely to meet the subject of the atom formally when they were ten or older: today they may encounter atoms in a picture-book before they go to school, and they would be quite likely to find a simple introduction included in the book corner of the junior classroom. Because the subject of the atom can be artificially isolated, they may even meet the principles of physics and chemistry for the first time from this special point of view. Every statement in a simple book on atoms is of extreme importance, but most of all because it may establish an idea in the child's mind upon which he will build later on or, more probably, may introduce a visual image which he will later have to translate into abstract terms.

The multiple subject of The Atom falls naturally into three parts – atomic structure and the scientific facts behind nuclear fission, the history of atomic research, and the peaceful and military uses of atomic energy, with consequent moral and social judgment. This material is necessarily interlocked and one line can hardly be pursued to the exclusion of the others. All the same, at present the emphasis in most books for the young seems to depend on the relative age of the reader. In a book for younger children, most attention will be given to description, the explanation of scientific terms and so on. The biographical and historical element is usually slender until we come to books for the reader of ten upwards, and any extensive discussion of the moral and social problems of the Atomic Age seem to be reserved for the 'teens, almost as though conscience had in each of us a specific birthday. The reason for this situation may lie at least in part in the difficulties of simplification. It must often seem easier to simplify a set of facts than a set of ideas.

In writing an introductory book a writer may in fact go no further than stating the existence of his subject. George Stephenson's sixteen-pager ATOMS (1964), designed for the reference shelves of the primary school, makes a series of simple statements, each of which is a subject in itself. He explains:

> This atom is made of two parts. The centre part is called the *nucleus*. The tiny part moving round it is called an *electron*.
> The electron is always moving round the nucleus, rather like the way the planet Earth moves round the Sun. The whole atom is held together by electricity.
> ATOMS, pp. 3–4

and again:

> Just as a torch sends out a ray of light, so some atoms send out rays of tiny particles. These atoms are called *radio-active* atoms. The rays are used a lot in hospitals and often help to cure people who are ill.
> ibid., p. 8

In making statements as general as this, the author can only hope that the beginning of an idea will sink into a child's mind and act as a magnet for other pieces of information as and when they come his way. The extreme simplicity of such statements need not be misleading, especially if they are supported by carefully devised pictures. The passage I have quoted above on the structure of the atom is clarified by an image placed immediately above it (see plate 10, p. 198).

When there is no room to modify very simple statements a picture can be misleading, especially since visual images will usually be taken literally by young children. Stephenson names the atoms making up a molecule of water and ends his explanation:

> All the water you drink is made of molecules like this. There are millions in every drop of water.
> ibid., p. 6

The accompanying picture shows a molecule, but because it is shaped like a water drop, it is not immediately obvious that this picture supports the statement that "there are millions in every drop of water". Children will be more likely to accept the image as that of the water drop itself. It could be argued that this is a book to be used in school and that the teacher will be able to resolve doubts of this kind – as, indeed, similar books with a distribution outside as well as inside schools could depend on adult explanation. For that matter, children may not necessarily meet atoms for the first time in a book. But if a book is the medium of information, it should be as complete as possible within its defined limits. The writer should not rely on any outside agency to make his point clear; it is his duty to use his medium as fully and as expertly as he can.

He is faced with the problem of writing about something which has identity and at the same time does not exist. The physical identity of atoms is established by consent, as it were, and the terms of this identity may change where the existence of a hand or a table may be demonstrated in actuality. It is not easy to interpret to the young the relation between theory, experiment and description, and even in books for readers at secondary school level it is rare to find a writer who as well as treating atoms as actualities can at least suggest the possibility of a different approach (as J. A. Harrison does, for instance, when he writes that "Rutherford's concept of a central positive nucleus with electrons circling round it still remains valid today.").* Very reasonably, first junior books – that is, books for children up to eight or so – are mainly concerned to translate atoms into physical terms and to describe their size, shape and structure. They may do this by using analogy or visual symbol or even by personalising.

George Stephenson's pamphlet is unusual in that the author avoids whimsicality completely and manages to offer his information in an almost wholly direct way, but he cannot avoid using analogy in at least one instance. A child must somehow be given an idea of the size of an atom. This means relative size, and so Stephenson writes:

Atoms cannot be seen even with the most powerful microscope.

*J. A. Harrison. THE STORY OF THE ATOM (1959), p. 44

If a hundred million atoms could be put in a straight line it would
be only about an inch long!
ibid., p. 2

The exclamation mark suggests that the writer realises he is only
offering an approximation, as others do in different ways. Like
Stephenson, the Adlers in ATOMS AND MOLECULES (1966) use
distance to give an idea of the size of molecules:

One hundred million oranges arranged side by side would make
a line that is five thousand miles long. But the same number of
water molecules would make a line that is only one inch long.
ATOMS AND MOLECULES, p. 10

Another book offers an interesting relation between time and size:

Listen carefully: if you could count a million molecules of sugar
a second, it would take you about 20,000 years to reach the number
in that one small lump of sugar that you so unthinkingly put in
your tea this morning.
G. de Maere and H. H. Harnacq. THE ATOM (1969), p. 5

By far the most usual analogy is one of mass. Felicia Elwell writes
in ATOMS AND ENERGY (1958):

If you could imagine a magnifying glass of such intense power
that it could enlarge a single carbon atom to the size of a small
mouse, then a real mouse, looked at through the same glass,
would be magnified to the size of the whole Earth.
ATOMS AND ENERGY, p. 8

In a somewhat exclamatory way Jerry Korn in his book ATOMS
(1959) makes a determined effort to relate molecules to atoms, and
both to objects that children can readily recognise:

In order to imagine the size of an atom, look at a grain of sugar.
From a few feet away you can't even see it. Yet it contains
trillions of molecules, and each of its molecules contains 45
atoms!

Suppose there were a microscope so powerful that, if you could see your little grain of sugar all at once, it would appear to be as big as the entire earth. You would then be able to see the molecules which make up the grain of sugar, and each of them might appear to be the size of a large house. You would also be able to see the 45 atoms in each molecule, each atom being about the size of a room in the house. But there is something smaller than the atom. It is called the nucleus, and is found in the center of each atom; it would be barely visible as a speck of dust in the middle of the room. And if *that's* hard to believe, think of this: each nucleus is composed of still tinier objects, called protons and neutrons!

ATOMS, pp. 7–8

Perhaps writers are excessively preoccupied with finding ingenious ways of indicating size – ways which remind one of the hoary joke "How long is a piece of string?" Analogies of this kind probably produce only a vague impression on a young reader, and it hardly seems reasonable to look for more. If the idea of relative size is pressed too hard it may conflict with the more important information about shape and structure. This is especially likely if a visual image is used to give the idea of the size of an atom. It is not easy for a child to move from a panorama to one of the numerous illustrations showing the atom as a round ball on its own. He is likely to think of the round ball as being as big as the ball he plays with, and so perhaps it is best to keep the explanation of size and structure rather widely apart.

Let us assume that the child has accepted the idea that the atom is very small indeed, and virtually invisible. Confusion can be avoided or at least lessened if writers make it absolutely clear that in using analogy, visual or verbal, they are not actually representing atoms. This clear statement of intention is not often found in books for the youngest reader, who obviously needs it most. He needs a simpler version of the caveat that Felicia Elwell wisely includes in her book for the middle years:

There are, in fact, two ways of regarding atoms. One is to think of them in terms of mathematical formulae which seem to explain their behaviour; this method is far too difficult for a book of this

kind, and many scientists are not very happy about it, either. The other way is to picture little models of the atoms, and this is what we shall do; remember, however, that our models may not be complete ones.
op. cit., p. 11

Some such statement is needed in any book in which similes and symbols are used for concepts of the shape and structure of atoms. Seeking to make abstractions palatable to children, writers have ranged far and wide for images that will be recognisable and entertaining. The attitude of a writer in this respect may be detected in his terminology. Many verbs used in describing the behaviour of atoms have a personalising and flippant effect; atoms do not "whizz", "rush" or "bounce", but they are often said to do so. George Sommerhoff, for example, in ELECTRICITY FOR BOYS (1957),* uses an elaborate analogy to help his readers to understand the process of heating iron to a liquid state. He describes atoms lined up like an army on parade; when the iron is in a liquid state they have been "ordered to dismiss" and when a gas is formed they are rushing apart to scout separately. It is doubtful whether such a figure really clarifies the point.

There are of course verbs which have attracted to themselves a specialised sense in addition to their more general one. Sommerhoff writes:

Protons and electrons behave in a strange and special way. Each attracts the other and they try to move closer together. They hate their own company however. Thus protons will attract electrons, but a proton meeting another proton will try to push it away or repel it. Electrons repel each other in the same way. Neutrons have no such force.
ELECTRICITY FOR BOYS, p. 6

Here the writer is using the word "repel" in both a whimsical and a scientific-popular sense. Herman Schneider, an experienced writer of science information books for the young, is emphatic on the subject of terminology:

*pp. 2–4

... I would not accept an anthropomorphic explanation such as the following: "When the water vapour reaches cool air, the tiny drops of which they are made come closer together; they huddle together to keep warm." An author who needs to endow water drops with human desires is usually shaky about his facts or his ability to explain them.

Learning about science. A pamphlet on the science policy and programme of Brockhampton Press, published in 1962, p. 5

But to the layman a verb like "repel", when it is used in a precise sense, will still carry overtones of a broader meaning; even without images of armies or crowds at a football match or roundabouts at a fair, the non-scientific reader will probably quite unconsciously think of the atom to some extent in human terms.

Scientific terminology can never separate itself entirely from the general language. Most of the technical terms applied to atoms are derived from concrete images. The word "atom" itself, which means "that which cannot be cut", has proved to be inaccurate as a description. Avogadro's term "molecule", which may be translated as "a little bundle", was chosen to refer to an important fact when it was first isolated and described. Every child has to learn by experiment and usage the ambiguities and associations in simple words. The writer must be scrupulous in drawing attention to shades of meaning instead of obscuring them. If he wants his atoms to whizz or bounce or huddle together, he must indicate how and why he is using such terms; but he may do better to avoid word-wasteful and potentially distracting figures of speech.

If this applies to verbs indicating behaviour, it applies as much to nouns of description. Atoms have been compared with spinning tops, balls, beads or building bricks, and indeed the idea of a circle is traditional in popular science. Because by convention the atom is presented as circular, a layman may find it hard to move from the idea that it is symmetrically and constantly circular. Besides, the circular shape lends itself naturally to personalisation. In a recent picture-book from Hungary, THE ADVENTURES OF A CARBON ATOM (1969), the illustrator has converted the concept of nucleus and electron into a jaunty, bowler-hatted pin-man whose appearance does not contradict that concept (see plate 8, page 198). However, the basic accuracy of the carbon atom-man's appearance (in suggesting the physical relationship of nucleus and electron) could not be appreciated by a child unless he had a good deal of basic information to start with, for the book does not set out to describe what an atom is but rather to make points about its "life" and mutability.

One editor of children's information books has poured scorn on "the scientist who thinks that all he has to do is leave out the hard stuff, sugar coat what is left, and come up with something like 'The story of Tommy Tooth', 'Little Ronny Raindrop', or 'Soap and your skin'."* István Volly's book certainly belongs to the Ronny Raindrop class. Should we therefore condemn it out of hand?

THE ADVENTURES OF A CARBON ATOM is possibly to be accepted as a picture-book but its text presents a trickier problem. A child of four who sits on his mother's knee and looks at pictures of a carbon atom clinging to a leaf (in its position within a sugar molecule) or (in the starch molecule of a wheat-grain) thrown out of a wheat ear, need not necessarily start along the wrong track towards science. The author has been less successful in the relation of text to pictures. The playfully descriptive illustrations trace the journey of a carbon atom from a fern in prehistoric times by way of coal, carbon dioxide gas, sugar, starch, to a moment which the child can relate more directly to his own life – for it ends in a loaf of bread. The journey is clear, but no concept is likely to remain with a four-year-old except perhaps a very general notion of change and movement.

It is worth mentioning that the arrangement of facts in this book makes it perfectly clear by examples that atoms go to make up something – a plant, a piece of coal, a wheat-grain and so on. In many books for the very young, this point is taken for granted, and after a general sentence pointing out that everything is made of atoms, the atom is thereafter treated as a separate static unit. It is good for a child to be reminded that an atom like the one which he sees depicted on the page as a red or green circle could be an infinitesimal part of the bird he sees out of the window or the cover of the book he is looking at. In science books for the young, nothing is so obvious that it does not need stating, and often. The plan of

*Thomas G. Aylesworth. LOOKING AT PUBLISHING: SCIENCE BOOKS FOR YOUNG READERS: SELECTING AN AUTHOR. Children's Book Circle Inc., Calendar, vol. xxx, no. 1, Jan./April 1971

István Volly's book does emphasise this point. However, he also brings up a number of extraneous points involving geology, palaeontology, chemistry, industry and natural history. The text is far in advance of the pictures, and the child who is ready to follow any of the paths indicated in words is likely to find the pictures tiresomely juvenile.

Another very elementary book using image in a playful way is open to such criticism, but the method used by Guy de Maere and H. H. Harnacq in THE ATOM (1969) may be justified by its results. Volly's book is a passive book. Whether a child looks at the pictures while the content is paraphrased for him or whether he reads it himself, he is not called upon to do more than receive information. In the Belgian book, THE ATOM, the reader is stopped every few pages by a brief questionnaire – "What do you know so far?" – or an exhortation – "Now remember". Moreover, the pictures are devised with tremendous gaiety and charm to involve the reader. This is perhaps the chief justification for the use of tadpole-manikins who demonstrate facts and principles to a small boy in a figurative way. The small boy is visibly interested, dubious, bored, apprehensive and excited by turns and so, probably, the reader will be also.

Many of the points are made by simple domestic analogy in which text and illustrations work closely together. For instance the authors begin a discussion of the role of electrons in an atom by pointing out that "Playing all alone in a corner is not at all the same thing as playing with a lot of other people", and they go on to say:

When one single electron circles a nucleus, shall we call it "hydrogen"? When two electrons circle a nucleus, that atom is "playing a game" which we might call "helium". (Helium is a gas which is used to blow up air balloons . . .)
THE ATOM, p. 11

The comparison between games and the behaviour of an electron seems far-fetched when it is so briefly stated, but the accompanying illustration clarifies it.

At times the pictures in this book are a good deal clearer than the text. The complicated matter of the orbit of electrons is opened with a general analogy – "Around each nucleus there are several orbits or circular routes along which the electrons move. Each

electron has to stay on one of these orbits just as you have to stand
in line at school."* This is not easy to understand in these words,
nor does the ensuing list of "vacant places" and "rules" make the
matter any clearer. Far more detail is needed on this point. But a
picture of concentric circles, each with a carefully counted number
of coloured chairs on the line, should dispel at least some clouds of
doubt, and if the comical illustration of nuclear fission in terms of
crowds and intruders does not really explain the point, at least it
might reassure the child that the matter is explicable and interesting.

Artist and authors are on an identical wavelength in this book.
They are dealing with the same concepts at the same level and their
enthusiasm is contagious. Perhaps they undertake too much.
Sometimes the need for compression in words leads to confusion.
The statement that "an atom of a particular element is made up
of the same ingredients as that element"† needs more explanation.
The authors are trying to express two concepts that are not very
closely related – first, that an element is composed of only one kind
of atom, whereas compounds contain at least two different kinds
of atom, and secondly that one atom differs from another in the
number of protons, neutrons and hence electrons which it contains.
To squeeze both concepts into one sentence the authors have had
to give the word "ingredients", which is inappropriate and inaccurate in any case, meanings which the reader is not in a position
to appreciate.

In one instance at least the desire to put a great deal of fact in a
little space has led to inaccuracy. When the authors state ". . . if
the nucleus was the same size as a nut, an electron would be as
enormous as a twenty-storey block of flats" and (in the summary
of this section) that "the nucleus is very tiny and the electrons very
large",‡ they presumably refer to the orbit of the electron and not
to the electrons themselves. Then, too, the book needs to be clearer
on its use of figurative explanation, though perhaps its very
sophistication suggests that it is aimed at readers who will accept
and understand the figurative basis of the various explanations.

Four recent books presenting atoms through fantasy come from

*ibid., p. 12
†ibid., p. 7
‡ibid., pp. 8–9

Australia, where Noel Wilson, an educationist and Raymond Smith, a graphic designer, devised four books about the "Atom Family" in order to "enlarge the child's ideas" about scientific words which may come his way when he is too young to understand them, "to help to clarify their meanings, and in so doing improve his comprehension of the physical world around him."*

The four books are conceived in a spirit of gay fancy. A small boy imagines he is an atom or an electron and announces what would happen to him if this intriguing situation came about. As illustrator, Raymond Smith has given the small hero a visual image (large head, tiny limbs and torso) near enough to the spherical shape of the atoms to ensure that he can be picked out on every page without seeming at all incongruous. The first object of these dual-purpose books – reading and looking – is made extremely pleasing by the simple sentences of the text and the brilliant graphics which at once illustrate fantasy situations and scientific truth.

In the first two books of the group, IF I WERE AN ATOM and IF I WERE AN ELECTRON, the numerous analogies are readily understood by context and through the lively illustrations; children in assembly, a moth circling a light, a bee in a bottle, clearly illustrate the given facts about atomic structure. The second two, IF I MET A MOLECULE and IF I WERE RADIO-ACTIVE, go further in introducing basic concepts of chemical change and nuclear reaction, and the inherent complexity makes the analogies often more of an interruption than a help. A cumulative image of "Killer Dan the radio-active man" doing desperate deeds in a Western saloon does not really clarify the explanation of the changes of electron, nucleus and neutron in a chain-reaction. The first two books could be comfortably enjoyed and at least partially understood by a child on his own (in an age-group broadly conceived as six to eight with "interest up to eleven and twelve year old in the case of remedial readers"); the last two books need classroom interpretation.

In fact all four books are primarily intended to be used in school. Author and artist have devised a leaflet explaining the second part of their intention. They suggest games to be played in class which rise naturally out of the images used; children can mimic the various

*Headstart Science series; teachers' guide. *Hutchinson of Australia* 1970. First page of leaflet.

actions attributed to the little hero and his atom friends in order to demonstrate melting and boiling, gases and liquids, orbiting electrons, controlled and chain reactions; they can cling together, jostle, separate, in certain precise and ordered ways. The leaflet ends in a surge of *bonhomie*, with a suggested additional activity using mousetraps:

> This demonstration is too fascinating not to attempt. An enclosed space is packed with mousetraps, each loaded with two table tennis balls. A ball is then thrown into the middle of the mousetraps. A chain reaction occurs, to the immense joy of all.
>
> HEADSTART SCIENCE leaflet, back page

There is tremendous zest in the glowing illustrations and exuberant text of these books. Atoms are thoroughly personalised – they jostle and bubble and dance and play – but each personalisation is matched with a straight factual statement:

> Oxygen atoms in the air move around in twos.
> Shaking and spinning and tumbling,
> Joined together like two boys wrestling, or two girls dancing.
> This is called an oxygen molecule.
> A molecule of oxygen is just two oxygen atoms joined together.
> IF I MET A MOLECULE, no page numbers.

There is a certain ambiguity in the last two books of the group, in that examples from the world as we know it (for instance, about the peaceful medical uses of radio-active substances) are juxtaposed with fanciful images of policemen or rustlers. All the same, the four books taken as a whole do offer young children a way to that easy familiarity with certain scientific terms which they can also achieve, more superficially, by watching television or listening to the conversation of their elders. If they follow the fantasy adventures of the atom-lad carefully they will have a sound basic idea of what the words imply; the books are not designed to teach science so much as to help them towards an intelligent and accurate use of words.

To see really successful simplification we may turn first to Marie Neurath's INSIDE THE ATOM (1956). The author makes her intention clear all through her book. A minute spot of diamond dust, she says, according to scientists "would seem to be made of balls arranged in regular patterns. These balls are called atoms";* and when she goes on to discuss the structure of an atom, she indicates her method:

> We have given the different kinds of particles different tints, to distinguish them. But it would be wrong to think they are really tinted in this way, or that they are arranged so regularly.
> INSIDE THE ATOM, p. 8

The scheme of this book is based on the closest possible relation of text and illustration. The Isotype Institute has devised many ingenious ways of communicating fact simply; for instance, the use of pin-men and strip-cartoons in some of the history books published thirty years ago has not yet been improved upon as a medium for very small children. For INSIDE THE ATOM a system of colour-identification has been devised which is used consistently all through the book. The author explains many of her points by using colours and terms of colour – green particle, red particle and so on – and gives the correct technical terms at the end, when the child should be more ready to receive them "In the future," she says, "we shall be able to read what scientists have discovered about these things; to understand them we should know the names they give to the flying particles and waves",† and she gives a table showing "a green particle" with its true name, "an electron", and ending by translating "the heart of the atom" into the correct term, "the nucleus".

The extreme neatness and clarity of the symbols used in this book, and their absolute consistency, mean that the author can make plain statements that either expand the pictures or are expanded by them. Inconsistencies in the use of colour in symbols can cause confusion. For example, in Jerry Korn's ATOMS, colours are sometimes used purposefully (as in a diagram of helium and lithium atoms, in which black is used for protons and red for neutrons) but elsewhere the circular symbols for the component parts of atoms are shown in various colours which seem to have no significance. The illustrations in books about atoms are of great

*ibid., p. 7
†ibid., p. 36

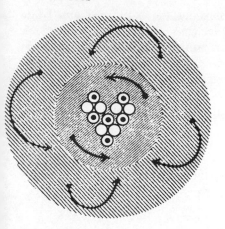

This drawing from INSIDE THE ATOM (Parrish) shows the diagrammatic method devised at the Isotype Institute, and illustrates the points about atomic structure made by Marie Neurath in the text. Although the idea of the movement of electrons is suggested by the use of arrows, the circular shape inevitably suggests that the atom has a fixed outline. Compare the drawing on p. 276 and the coloured diagram on p. 193.

importance; they can make, as it were, a second statement of certain facts which have to be firmly established and properly understood. Because a book cannot make use of the wealth of movable visual aids available for television and films, colour is relied on a good deal as a medium. A colour code can only be useful, however, if it is completely consistent. Used merely for decoration, it can distract the reader's attention from the very point which the illustration is designed to make.

Some children find that an element of fantasy helps in their thinking, and they move as easily from it later as they move from the Initial Teaching Alphabet to orthodox type and spelling. But sooner or later the facts will be put before them in a straight way. It is possible that Marie Neurath's book and the Belgian THE ATOM might be picked up by the same child, around eight or nine. We can contrast their methods by comparing their definitions of protons and neutrons. The Belgian book states simply that the nucleus is made of "two kinds of very tiny balls: protons and neutrons"* and demonstrates this by means of red and green marbles which the small boy is instructed to pick up in certain combinations – one of each colour to make "a model of a hydrogen nucleus"* and two of each to make a helium nucleus. Marie Neurath's plain, factual text explains clearly what is known about the properties of protons

*op. cit., p. 16

and neutrons (called, at this stage of the book, red and white particles) and their relation to electrons. Where the Belgian book deals only with the nucleus at this point, the text and illustration in INSIDE THE ATOM bring protons, electrons and neutrons together and on a single page demonstrate step by step the way an atom of hydrogen can become an atom of helium. The demonstration ends with a simple diagram and an equally simple, non-figurative sentence:

> This strongly-bound group of two red, two white and two green particles is an atom of helium, the light gas with which airships are filled.
> ibid., p. 11

The text of INSIDE THE ATOM is so logically planned that the author is able to introduce a variety of subjects, including electricity, carbon dating and nuclear fission, in a way that shows how one thing depends on another, whereas in other books the various aspects of the atom sometimes appear to be self-contained. The plan of the book is helped by running titles ("How the atoms can hold together to make something new", for example, and "The flowing streams of many millions of particles we call an electric current") which define the subject of each spread and mark its position in a continuous piece of exposition. Most important of all, the author stimulates the child's natural desire to find out, as she links it with the curiosity and open-mindedness of the scientist. "In this wonderful world of the atom," she writes, "there are still many things we do not understand."* Where research is continuing, no subject should be closed at the end of a book.

Writers avoid the misleading impression of finality in various ways. In BIOGRAPHY OF AN ATOM (1965), Jacob Bronowski and Millicent Selsam take a cosmic view. In their circular argument the narrative of the "life" of a carbon atom starts in a "young star" – "a mass of hydrogen nuclei" – and ends with the collision of other stars. This is not fanciful narrative like Volly's ADVENTURES OF A CARBON ATOM, but a straight piece of exposition which first suggests that the carbon atom which we see precipitated from

*ibid., p. 36

space to earth may become part of a diamond – "a pure crystal of carbon" – or it may join with two atoms of oxygen to form carbon dioxide and to form part of a plant, as sugar. From this point the authors locate this second atom in coal, in a plant, in a cow, in "your forefather" in whom the carbon atom became "part of one of the chromosomes which was passed on to your parents, and then to you"*, in the air and again in space. There is hard fact but no solemnity in this progression. Indeed, at one moment a romantic note is struck as the authors point out how many trillions of atoms are contained in the air in a man's lungs at any one moment, and comment that "sooner or later everyone of us breathes an atom that has been breathed by someone who has lived before us – perhaps Michelangelo or George Washington or Moses."†

Although this book is intended for an older readership than the books so far discussed, the very lucid text could be approached by some children as young as nine if they were prepared to stretch their minds a little; besides, some previous knowledge of technical terms is desirable. However, the authors do give readers a helping hand; before the particular "biography" begins, they offer a careful description of the general shape and structure of an atom and examples of particular cases.

In one respect this preliminary part of the book is clearer than most others. The use of the circular symbol to represent an atom must give a child the impression, unless he is told otherwise, that the atom is wholly a solid structure. It is hard to dispel the effect of a visual image. A child with some previous knowledge may realise that formalised pictures of atoms like those in Marie Neurath's INSIDE THE ATOM are meant to indicate that while the nucleus has a positive outline as we think of outline, the "outline" of the electrons is an apparent one produced by movement. Moreover, she explains in her text:

Even the atoms are not solid, in fact they are mostly empty space! But round their surface, and round other levels inside, there seem to move tinier particles still, at tremendous speeds.
ibid. p. 8.

*BIOGRAPHY OF AN ATOM, p. 38
†ibid., p. 39

But because of the formalised pictures, in which arrows indicating movement are superimposed on a shaded background forming a symmetrical circle, it is going to need one more direct statement here, explaining that the apparent outline is not one as we understand it, if children are going to be completely clear on the point.

To this extent the isotype symbols in INSIDE THE ATOM are misleading and young children will more safely take into their mind's eye the image used in George Stephenson's elementary pamphlet (see plate 10, p. 198), though here the text, which uses the popular image of planets circling the sun, does not give adequate direction for understanding the image. Raymond Smith, artist for the four fantasy-science books from Australia (see p. 270-1), uses circular symbols in his striking pictures but in IF I WERE AN ATOM he chooses a pointillist style to support the sentence, "If I were even bigger, I might look round, like a ball, like a moving ball." Here the lack of outline is at least suggested, and the second book, IF I WERE AN ELECTRON, goes further, as the text shows:

> Whooshing around and around the nucleus of the atom.
> Zooming around and around the nucleus of the atom like a moth around a bright light.
> IF I WERE AN ELECTRON, no page numbers

To illustrate this passage the artist uses the geometric figure of dotted lines familiar in senior science books but by no means common in first introductions. There is room here, however, for a more specific statement about the structure of the atom.

The illustrator of BIOGRAPHY OF AN ATOM has used images of many kinds, including closed circles, but in any part of the text explaining the structure of the atom we have a symbol suggesting movement, and the text (properly sited on the same page) makes one more essential point:

> The heavy particles, the protons and the neutrons, are tightly bound together in the center of the atom, called the *nucleus*. Far away from this center are the light electrons. They are in constant movement, circling the nucleus much as planets circle

the sun. But because their orbits are less exact, they form a kind of spinning cloud or shell.

BIOGRAPHY OF AN ATOM, p. 15

Even this passage is not really specific enough for young readers. J. A. Harrison's book for older children, THE STORY OF THE ATOM (1959), suggests the kind of instruction that is needed if children are not to misunderstand their first visual description:

> At first sight it is difficult to understand how hard matter, such as your house or table, can be made up of particles which consist of so much empty space. The reason for this is the enormous speed at which the electrons travel round their orbits. When an aeroplane propeller is rotating at speed, its path appears and acts as though it were solid. Now the speed of the tip of an aeroplane propeller is much less than the speed of electrons in their orbits round the nucleus, and this is why the atom appears so solid.
> THE STORY OF THE ATOM, p. 43

Armed with a simple explanation like this, children will be able to understand what they are told of the experimental background of our present knowledge of the atom; and this is the next step they will need to take. If they come upon an account of Rutherford's

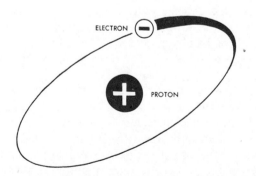

ATOM OF HYDROGEN

ELECTRON

PROTON

This drawing by Weimer Pursell from BIOGRAPHY OF AN ATOM (Harper and Row) suggests a "spinning cloud or shell", as the authors put it.

experiments, for example, with the image of a solid ping-pong ball in their minds, they will find it hard to understand how the bombardment of the nucleus by particles could possibly succeed. One analogy is particularly popular with writers as a way of explaining these experiments. As one writer puts it:

Imagine a room full of furniture, and a few gaps in the walls all round; imagine, too, that the only way in which you can find out anything about the furniture and the material of which it is made is by firing revolver bullets into the room and picking up the chips of wood and metal that may emerge through the holes in the walls . . .
John Rowland. ATOMS WORK LIKE THIS (1955), p. 22

Without a simple statement as a guide, a child is likely to be perplexed even by such a lively metaphor.

In any information book, but perhaps most of all in books about scientific subjects, accuracy is not enough. A sequence of impeccably correct facts is useless if the reader cannot understand them. Science books come from authors of vastly differing kinds. Harry Stubbs, reviewing new science books in the *Horn Book*, comments that as a result of the Apollo 8 expedition many new books would appear:

Some will be written by competent scientists who are also good at explaining, some by scientists who should have had editorial help, some by good writers with shaky scientific backgrounds, and some by people with no particular qualifications who are riding a promising bandwagon.
"Views on Science books", in *The Horn Book*, April 1969, p. 190

The quotation may be used in contexts other than that of the exploration of the moon. Publishers often prefer laymen expert in writing for children to specialists, although he would be bold indeed who undertook to write of atoms without a proper basic knowledge and a strong disposition to the subject. Even so, the combination of intelligent layman and specialist consultant must always have its dangers, and perhaps most of all in the simplest books.

The layman will be better able to decide how much children can

be expected to understand at any one age than to decide which are
the essential facts that he must understand. A book for the middle
years, ATOMS AND MOLECULES (1966) by Irving and Ruth Adler,
shows that experienced popularisers can sometimes mistake the

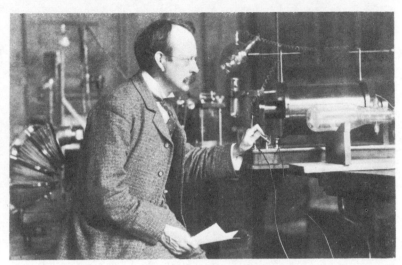

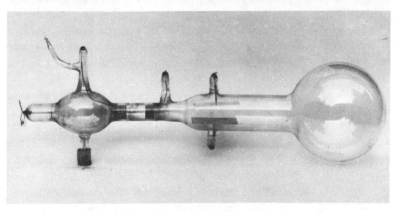

Thomson at work in his laboratory, from THE STORY OF THE ATOM (Hulton
Educational); and (below) a discharge tube used in his experiments, both by
courtesy of the Cavendish Laboratory, Cambridge. Photographs like these have an
immediacy which helps children to understand something of the process of
experiment in science.

real meaning of simplification. A look at the first two pages of their book shows a basic weakness in design. To introduce the nature of the atom the authors use four analogies in their text, comparing atoms with bricks in a wall, stitches in a piece of knitting, rooms in a block of flats and letters in a word. Each of these analogies is represented visually in the margin (and in the margin also there is an inexplicable fragment of type which may be meaningful or just a printer's error). At the bottom of the page a strip of diagrams and captions uses statements which are stylistically simple to suggest complex ideas. "Most atoms of hydrogen," we read, "are made of one proton and one electron. Some atoms of hydrogen are made of one proton, one neutron and one electron."* In trying to avoid too many technical terms, the authors, here and elsewhere, have left the reader with many unanswered questions.

Visually, the design of this first double-spread is bad because it does not convey a single idea adequately but forces the reader to make several intellectual moves to discover that idea. There is no harm in asking a child to make an effort, but in this instance he is going to waste time which he could spend better in moving confidently from one idea to another. So far as the text goes, the technique of simplification is no better. As I have suggested, the words used are simple enough, but they are used in a telescoped and even an allusive way. The authors do not spend long enough on any one point; in sentence after sentence a new point is introduced. A child may feel he is learning a great deal as he reads, but he is unlikely to retain a clear sequence of facts in his mind.

The pseudo-simplicity of this book is largely due to the fact that the authors are combining physics and chemistry in a short space, where it would have been better to cover the atom in two books. The Adlers have, in fact, produced a book of definitions. Their method, which in theory could be very useful, is to print technical terms in italics, so that they will be marked and, supposedly, understood. Some of the terms defined are not used again and therefore call for an effort of memory that is not rewarded. Again, in order to fill their book as full as they can, the authors have included a table of chemical elements with their atomic weights which is preceded by brief comment but with no suggestion of how

*ATOMS AND MOLECULES, pp. 7–8

these weights were determined. The inherent value of the knowledge in this book has been obscured by the compressed and difficult way it is arranged.

Children must be given a sound, comprehensible introduction to the nature of the atom. In junior books this is usually done without historical detail; an author will summarise what is known about the atom at the moment when he writes. Unless his reader is told otherwise, he may imagine that "the atom" can be described as an immutable and perfect concept, and that this concept was arrived at in a moment of time. It is an inherent defect of all science books that, with the present system of book publishing, they can never be perfectly up to date. To give one example, over a period of fifteen years or so the numbers of elements known are variously given as 92, "about 100" and 103; no writer has yet caught up with the 120 or so elements that can now be named.

It is at least possible for authors to make it clear that research is still changing our concept of atoms and that such ideas as can be outlined at any given time were reached gradually in the past and by many people. In the most elementary books we should look for something more explicit than George Stephenson's opening paragraph:

This man is an atomic scientist. He works in a laboratory, and tries to find out all he can about atoms.
ATOMS, p. 11

Children need something more than a non-committal "Scientists have found out", and for this reason Jerry Korn's ATOMS must be welcomed, for although he covers the ground very rapidly and requires of his middle-year readers a good deal of concentration, he does offer a chronological outline of experiments. This spreads out scientific facts and concepts and gives children more time to understand them, and also of course more help – for if you know how somebody discovered something, you will probably find it easier to understand what it was that he discovered. The concept of the atom is attached, in Korn's book, to particular names from Democritus and Aristotle onwards; experiments in identifying elements begin with a summary of the work of Boyle and Dalton; in the same way, the steps by which the various parts of the atom were isolated and named are described with due attention to the scientists concerned.

This method of assembling material produces a book well suited to readers from ten upwards, for it has a varied texture, offering not only scientific fact but also biography and history leading directly to a topical discussion of the uses of atomic energy. There is a more interesting spread of fact here than in the selective books for younger children; a different kind of selectiveness is called for to satisfy children with more experience of learning to bring to bear on the subject.

Though the plan of Korn's book is clear and appealing, it rests on a limited attitude. In general, information books for children tend to be too self-contained. Obviously the easiest way to simplify a subject is to keep it within its own bounds rather than letting it merge into other disciplines. But the effect, in books about science, is to imply that the subject under discussion is all-important. Korn's book, like many others, is likely to give readers the impression that atomic research was, during the centuries before our own, the only aspect of "science" worth considering – even, that it was its be-all and end-all, a path already existing along which one man after another found his way. The falseness of this attitude can be seen in the following passage in Korn's book, especially in the last sentence:

> Aristotle believed that everything was made of four "elements" – fire, water, earth, and air – a theory which was not much different from the theories of Thales and other early philosophers. Because Aristotle was a wise and learned man, people accepted his idea of the four elements so completely that all real progress in the study of matter simply came to an end for many centuries. During this time there were no *chemists* who spent their time investigating the secrets of matter; instead, there were *al*chemists, experimenters who spent their time trying to turn various cheap materials such as lead into gold, so that they or their masters could become rich. Aristotle suggested that this might be possible since all metals were supposedly made of the same four elements.
>
> Finally, slowly and laboriously, chemistry began to get back on the right track.
>
> ATOMS, p. 10

The misleading idea of a "right track" is probably the result of the author's decision to simplify in a certain way and to exclude even the barest reference to any subject other than one particular aspect of chemistry and physics.

Further, his scornful allusion to "alchemists" rises from an unhistorical statement that "all real progress in the study of matter simply came to an end for many centuries." This statement reflects the widespread assumption that modern science owes more to the pure logic of the Greeks than to the empirical approach of the craftsmen-engineers of the Middle Ages. To invent windmills, pumps or heavy cannon, as they did, they had to study matter and reach some working knowledge of acceleration, inertia, momentum and kinetic energy. Korn ignores the experiments of men like Grosseteste and Roger Bacon, for instance, he makes no reference to the applied mathematics of the Arabs or to the syntheses made by Galileo in the course of tackling problems in ballistics and so on. The history of science, as Korn offers it in his book, can hardly be trusted.

A rather fuller and more advanced book, THE ATOM (1969) in the *Marshall Cavendish Learning System*, has a more flexible plan and terms of reference altogether broader than those of Korn's book. Relativity, carbon dating, lasers, electro-magnetic waves and other subjects are included and the contributors use terms of mathematics, physics, chemistry or philosophy with equal freedom. Biographical material appears as and when it is needed, and with the wide interpretation of the subject the reader should gather that scientific research is a normal human activity rather than a self-perpetuating mystery. This book is not for every child, and even to the child of scientific bent it is not primarily a book of instruction, in spite of the unusual amount of up-to-date detail in it. In a sense it is a miniature version of more familiar encyclopedia series like Macdonald's *Wonderful World* books or the American Heritage series. Illustration (especially of experiments) forms an excellent and integral part of the book, which I would regard as a starter, a book to excite readers perhaps by one small point, perhaps on a whole area of speculative knowledge, but in any case to rouse a desire to look for more detailed and probably more specialised books.

As a whole the Marshall Cavendish book offers a broad and

humane view of the scientist and his work, and a more international one than usual. Today no single country, with the exception of the U.S.A. and Russia, can afford to build the machines necessary for deeper research – for instance, into the structure of the nucleus – and scientists will inevitably become less and less satisfied by a purely nationalistic attitude. Many books for children, however, still take a limited view. Donald Barr's ATOMIC ENERGY (1964), in the widely advertised series of *How and Why Wonder Books*, comes from America ostensibly "specially re-edited for publication in Great Britain", but it retains an almost exclusively American slant. A super-dramatic section attributes the first experiments in nuclear fission to John Dunning, Otto Frisch being named only in a list, surrounding a map, of "some of the scientists who have contributed to our understanding and development of the Atomic Age". The steps of research are rarely confined to a single laboratory; two men may, and often do, reach the same conclusions at more or less the same time. This book, with others, shows the danger of writing too devotedly for a national readership.

It is, besides, crude and distasteful in its treatment of the first experiment with the atomic bomb in New Mexico in 1945 and its use at Hiroshima. It is reasonable enough to aim a series at average readers, but there is no evidence that average readers would rather find facts dressed up in melodrama or facetious humour than delivered simply but in a straightforward way. The remarkably ugly and often vulgar pictures do nothing to correct the uneasy impression given by the style of the text. This is all the more unfortunate because the author is on the whole in command of his scientific facts. In particular, he distinguishes carefully between the different kinds of energy in a way that sheds light on the whole of his subject. He arranges his material in a careful progression under headings consisting of the kind of questions children are likely to ask – "What is the difference between matter and energy?" for example, and "Why do the electrons keep flying around the nucleus?" It is a pity that a book of this kind, which is likely to circulate widely among fairly uncritical readers, is so much open to criticism for its general tone and its historical bias.

We can hardly expect the young to understand a science as a whole unless they can come closer to individual scientists and their work. This is most often made possible for them through explanatory

A tasteless and facetious way of illustrating the relation between energy and mass
from ATOMIC ENERGY (Transworld)

narrative, but in the first part of DISCOVERING THE ATOM (1963)
Donald Hutchings uses the story formula typical of this series with
some success. An oddly detached story of the dropping of the first
atom bomb begins, "A Super-Fortress was flying through the
night"; in the second chapter a dramatic account of Becquerel's
discovery of radio-activity (punctuated with Gallic exclamations)
leads to the "story" of Marie Curie; in the same style we read of
the work of Hahn, Frisch, Lise Meitner and others in splitting the
atom, and of the voyage of the *Nautilus* under the North Pole in 1958.

With these pieces to whet the appetite, a child of twelve or so may
be led on to the reference section which discusses briefly the structure
of the atom, repeats the information already given on the history
of research in a tighter form, and discusses the peaceful and military
uses of atomic energy. The book is sound, if a little dry in tone, and
the material in it is reinforced by numerous diagrams and by
appendices among which is a useful glossary of technical terms,
brief biographical notes on the important atomic scientists and
briefer advice on careers in atomic science. This last item is typical
of the book as a whole. The author seems to be trying to involve

his readers in the subject, especially by his strong comments on the political aspects of atomic research. It is customary – I would say obligatory – for authors to make some acknowledgement of the moral implications of scientific discoveries, but Donald Hutchings is unusually emphatic on this point. He introduces a section on the hydrogen bomb like this:

> Since the end of the war, the Great Powers of the world have engaged in an armaments race and have striven to build bigger and better bombs. Wise and good men have pointed out the folly and wickedness of this policy and there have been many attempts to outlaw atomic warfare and to put atomic research under international control. In spite of these efforts, the nations have not yet been able to trust each other, and the race for more and more powerful means of destruction continues.
>
> DISCOVERING THE ATOM, p. 83

It is to his credit that he has been so emphatic; if he had respected his readers enough to give them specific facts about the attempts to "put atomic research under international control", the naïveté of his writing would be less noticeable.

The full documentation and dry style of DISCOVERING THE ATOM may deter less able readers once they have got past the narrative part of the book; besides, its manner and content require some previous knowledge of chemistry and physics. Though this is also true of ATOMS WORK LIKE THIS, John Rowland's almost conversational approach makes more concessions to readers who will probably be around ten to thirteen. ATOMS WORK LIKE THIS is not detailed enough to be used as a reference book. The analysis of an atom and the history of research, isotopes and the atomic pile, X-rays and bombs, atomic power in industry – these and other aspects are briefly introduced. If the brevity be accepted, the book is seen to have some value as an introduction, especially for young people who have not previously seen any simple junior book on the subject.

Rowland's material is greatly expanded in a biographical book, THE ATOM (1965), in which he builds an historical account of research round five important figures – Marie Curie, J. J. Thomson, Ernest Rutherford, James Chadwick and John Cockcroft. There are advantages and disadvantages in a plan as formal as this. While it is particularly easy to follow, it forces the author to attach certain aspects of research rather artificially to one individual. It is reasonable to describe Madame Curie as "The woman who conquered radio-activity" or J. J. Thomson as "The man who found the electron", and in the course of each section the author does mention other scientists associated with a particular line of research; but the book is hardly long enough to dispel entirely the feeling that England – and indeed, Cambridge – was the sole scene of discovery, and the omission of Otto Frisch, to give one example, shows the limitation of Rowland's scheme.

All the same, that nebulous figure "The Scientist" emerges from the mists of superstition and misunderstanding to take part in a procession of individuals. Here we read an anecdote of a visitor dining at Trinity enquiring "who was the red-faced farmer sitting at the high table, and roaring with laughter at the jokes that were made";* he had not seen Lord Rutherford before. Here are descriptions of the Curies at home and, by contrast, of the busy social life of the Thomsons in Cambridge.

It is not enough, of course, to establish that scientists are human, though in the present state of science books for the young it is much to do this. The emphasis in Rowland's book is on experiment – the process as well as the result. There are no false dramatics here. The author makes his attitude clear when he points out that Sir James Chadwick did not guess, when he first established the existence of neutrons, what effect this would have on the world we live in:

He was, like the others with whom this book is concerned, only trying to do what he could to increase man's knowledge of the way the world works. The practical results of a scientist's experiments are, as a rule, not known to the man who carries these experiments out. It may be months or years before anyone comes to realize how valuable those experiments, and the theories that are built on them, may turn out to be."

THE ATOM, p. 83

When he discusses Rutherford's experiments on the nucleus, he

*THE ATOM, p. 66

compares his methods with those of the Curies and J. J. Thomson, quoting Rutherford's words that "the scientists who spent all their time doing calculations on pieces of paper were not really scientists at all."* Rutherford did the practical work first, Rowland explains, and continues:

> Then he sat down to see if he was able to work out a theory which would explain the results that he had obtained from his experiments. And the theory of the way in which an atom was built up took a tremendous amount of working out.
> ibid., p. 60

In all his descriptions of experiments, Rowland offers information of a concrete kind. He describes the kind of apparatus used and how it was made, and outlines the move from "The old J. J. Thomson era of what was called string and sealing wax" to the Rutherford "era of gadgetry".† The picture he gives is one of creative work depending on intuition as much as on experimental skill and reasoning. Without making any one attempt to define the "scientific attitude", as laymen like to call it, he implies throughout his book an attitude which is not narrowly scientific but is universally a creative one. Perhaps the one sentence which should be italicised for the young is the sentence already quoted defining Chadwick's aim to "increase man's knowledge of the way the world works".

Young people who read Rowland's THE ATOM may suspect that the fundamental division so widely accepted between Art and Science is one they need not necessarily accept. Linking Rutherford's research with that of his master J. J. Thomson, Rowland summarises Rutherford's initial position:

> He was asking himself how an atom was made up. Was it a solid thing, like a house built of bricks? Were the electrons the bricks? Or was it a moving thing, like the solar system of the suns and planets, with the electrons playing the part of planets? If so, what played the part of the sun?
> ibid., p. 52

*ibid., p. 60
†ibid., p. 95

From this point he traces the steps by which Rutherford and Niels Bohr worked towards a picture of the nucleus, by experiment and by reasoning, question and answer. The process he describes is seen to be similar to the process of an historian or a philosopher.

The value of THE ATOM lies partly in the relaxed style and the simplicity of arrangement that depends obviously on a good deal of knowledge not directly used. THE STORY OF THE ATOM (1959) by J. A. Harrison has a clear pattern also, but here biographical details are firmly subordinated to a cool, concentrated and fully documented analysis of scientific fact. The ladder of experiment is mounted rung by rung, the details being so compressed that the book belongs properly to a scientific classroom. For a beginner in the sciences, or for a reader generally rather than specifically interested, the book would be hard going in spite of the clarity of its individual statements. It is valuable for its wide range. Where most other books relegate the present day to a few final pages, Harrison gives full attention to atomic power in its various uses, with a particularly careful discussion of radio isotopes.

This is a very impersonal book. Most authors find it hard to reconcile an enthusiastic description of research on atomic fission with an account of its demonstration in the atomic bomb. Harrison ends a chapter on "The neutron in action" with a paragraph that opens technically, "One of the primary problems in making an atomic bomb was therefore how to separate the vital Uranium 235 from Uranium 238 in natural uranium", and ends:

> Eventually scientists and engineers working under the "Manhattan Project" devised satisfactory methods of producing the isotope Uranium 235 in a pure form, and the necessary large-scale plant was constructed. This resulted in the atomic bomb which destroyed Hiroshima in Japan on August 6th 1945, helping to bring World War II to an end.
>
> THE STORY OF THE ATOM, p. 73

If the author intended to leave his readers to react in their own way to the research he describes, he need not have used the last sentence for an implied comment of his own which, in context, seems singularly inhuman. It is a weakness of this and other books that they do not join in the running battle on the subject of responsibility in which any intelligent reader is bound to be involved. The young must surely notice the lack of balance between eulogies of advances in medicine and sentences condemning war. At the present time, when books of information for the 'teens are becoming more and more committed, books on science will not, and should not, find it easy to avoid emotion and to stand aloof on fact. Not that one would wish them merely to extend condemnation into long emotional and tautological paragraphs.

What is needed, surely, is specific fact – facts about the attitude of the United Nations assembly at various dates, summit talks and party political opinions, the development of bombs in various countries and demonstrations against the whole use of atomic power for war. For anyone growing up today the bomb throws a black shadow, and authors would do a service to the young if they opened the question as a necessary part of any discussion of the bomb, with feeling but not with vague emotion, and above all with hard fact. While events move as speedily as we accept that they do, we can all benefit from historical résumés on this and on other subjects which concern our way of life.

Scientific work is a responsible and a creative activity. The book I would most confidently recommend to older readers is Professor Otto Frisch's WORKING WITH ATOMS (1965). Perhaps it is inevitable that books for British and American markets should emphasise the work of scientists in those countries, but this does not make it any more correct that the name of Otto Frisch rarely appears in a prominent position in such books in spite of his major contribution to atomic fission. On this subject his book is authoritative in a different way from the books of scientific popularisers. He was there.

WORKING WITH ATOMS is a personal book. Within its necessary general background lies the central description of the work of Frisch and his aunt Lise Meitner. Though its authenticity is of great value, in the context of books for the young the writer's approach seems still more important. This is a book about what it is like to be a scientist. It bears witness to a scientist's dedication, his acceptance of routine and his attentiveness to the moments of leaping imagination. Discussing the painstaking experiments of the Curies, Frisch writes:

What does a scientist do if something doesn't fit? If a tailor

makes a dress or a suit and it doesn't fit, he will try to alter it;
he will be a bit ashamed and try to do better next time. But to a
scientist there is nothing more exciting than a result that doesn't
fit. It tells him that there is something new, that there may be
an important discovery round the corner.
WORKING WITH ATOMS, p. 24

but in commenting on a particular experiment, he warns his young
readers that "Chemists have made thousands of such measurements,
cross-checking the answers."*

Professor Frisch sees no reason to nurse the young along with
analogies when he is explaining the structure of the atom and the
stages by which it was described. Instead, he shows how some of
the experiments were made and with what kinds of instruments. He
explains some of the methods for determining the size of atoms –
by beating gold extremely thin, by experimenting with molecules or
studying gases – and points out that there are other far more
complicated ways "but they all give the same answers: About
one-hundred-millionth of an inch";† he satisfies the youthful desire
for concrete fact:

> The so-called "electron microscopes" do a lot better, but still
> don't show single atoms; and they were invented only recently,
> when the size of atoms was already known. But still more recently,
> atoms have been clearly seen with the "field ion microscope".
> ibid., pp. 11–12

and a photograph of this instrument is included in the book. When
he was working in Blackett's laboratory, he tells his readers, he
went to Woolworth's and bought pencil caps which he used as the
basis for his own home-made Geiger counter, for in those days
young researchers were not offered expensive equipment for their
exclusive use.

Writers of science books for the young may take up attitudes
matey or reserved, facetious or strictly efficient. I know no book
that is as friendly and lucid as WORKING WITH ATOMS; I know

*ibid., p. 10
†ibid., p. 13

no other book in this sphere that displays at once the authority and the humility of a great man. The boy or girl who discovers Frisch's book may find other descriptions of atomic fission very flat and less easy to understand. In Harrison's STORY OF THE ATOM, Frisch is only mentioned by name in a table of dates and his work is alluded to in a severely concentrated paragraph:

> In the examples of atom splitting which we have considered so far, atomic bullets had done no more than chip a piece off the nucleus. But the Uranium 235 nucleus turned out to be unique. A bombarding neutron splits the Uranium 235 nucleus into two roughly equal halves; electrons collect round each half and two new atoms such as barium and krypton are formed. Gradually a picture was built up of what happened when the neutron struck the nucleus – a picture of the uranium nucleus stretching, forming a waist and finally breaking in two. This resembled the way that living cells divide, and biologists call it fission. The splitting of the uranium nucleus was therefore called nuclear or atomic "fission". The two new atoms produced, such as barium or krypton, are called "fission" products.
>
> THE STORY OF THE ATOM, p. 63

This method of explanation is necessary for the particular plan of Harrison's book, which gives a far more detailed survey of the work of other scientists than Frisch sets out to do. What *he* tells us is exactly how his particular contribution began – and how he felt. He describes how he went to discuss the problem with his aunt Lise Meitner, in a Danish village:

> I remember how we walked up and down in the snow (I was wearing skis, but Lise Meitner wasn't), trying to think of some explanation. Could it be that the nucleus got cleaved right across, as with a chisel? It seemed impossible that a neutron could act like a chisel, and anyhow, the idea of a nucleus as a solid object that could be cleaved was all wrong; a nucleus was much more like a liquid drop.
>
> Here we stopped and looked at each other. Was that the way to a solution? One might imagine a drop getting pulled out into an oval shape, then into a shape with a waist in the middle; when

that waist was thin enough the drop might be torn in two with little effort. Could such a thing possibly have happened to Hahn's nuclei?

At first we thought it couldn't. A liquid drop is held together and kept round by what we call surface tension; the drop behaves as if it were enclosed in an elastic skin, like a rubber balloon, which resists stretching. In the same way a nucleus has surface tension, and pretty strong it is. But then I remembered something I had learned. When a drop gets electrically charged its surface tension becomes less. A uranium nucleus has a high electric charge, due to its 92 protons. Well . . .?

At that point we sat down on a fallen tree, found pencils and bits of paper and began to calculate. How many protons would be needed to destroy the surface tension of a uranium nucleus? . . .
WORKING WITH ATOMS, pp. 66–7

Although this book is directly concerned with the work of one man, there is no suggestion that his work was unique or that it could be isolated from that of others. Frisch comments, "You may well ask why such an excellent chemist as Otto Hahn had not spotted this earlier. The reason is that there were no grounds to expect such light elements to be formed, and so they had not been looked for,"* and he continues:

And yet it could have been foreseen if only one had been clever enough. When I came back to Copenhagen after that Christmas with my aunt I went at once to my boss, Niels Bohr. I had hardly begun to tell him about Hahn's experiments and the conclusions Lise Meitner and I had come to when he struck his forehead with his hand and exclaimed, "Oh, what idiots we have been! This is just as it must be! We could have foreseen it all!" And yet even he, perhaps the greatest physicist of his time, had not foreseen it.
ibid., pp. 68–9

It was a conversation with an American biologist, not long afterwards, which gave Frisch and his colleagues the words "nuclear

*ibid., p. 68

fission"; and the reader can feel that he had taken part in all the exchanges that led to this tremendous step forward.

There is no suggestion in Frisch's book, however, that scientific discoveries come solely from single moments of enlightenment. Before he was ready to communicate his theory, it had to be verified by experiment:

> I worked until three in the morning. Many checks had to be carried out. From time to time I removed my neutron source to make sure the counter stopped clicking; it might have merely been counting some electric disturbances, like those atmospherics that make the radio crackle. Once I took the uranium out of the chamber, and again the counter was silent, as I had expected. Could my batteries have run down? I put the uranium back, and the counter clicked again, once or twice a minute. It was slow and tedious work, but I assure you I was not bored! When I went to bed I was dead tired, but very happy; I had obtained clear physical evidence for the fission of the uranium nucleus.
> ibid., pp. 71–2

So he has put on record his knowledge of the past and the present. He ends his book, after introducing the synchrotron, with a statement of faith in the future:

> Here is a whole new field for research, and I, for one, find it fascinating. We don't know what those particles mean; we are only beginning to understand the laws by which they are born and die, and the forces by which they act on each other. I have no idea if they will ever be of practical use. But until we understand them properly, I am sure we won't understand the nature of matter. And that is what my work, and the work of my students, and the work of my colleagues all over the world is about – the nature of matter.
> ibid., p. 94

In the last century the scientist was conceived as working within a Divine Pattern which he might ultimately be able to understand completely. Perhaps this was the only way in which religious belief and scientific theory could be reconciled – and, on the whole, scientists as well as laymen desired that they should be reconciled. The idea of a predetermined end to research has changed in the present century. The picture of a scientist seeking a distant set of "natural laws" is being discarded, and so is the customary antithesis between the cold, remote scientist and the warm, human poet. Frisch's book (not alone but more than any other in the field) shows how far a lifetime of scientific research is a personal matter, a matter of intellectual activity directed towards one more picture of man in his world to add to the pictures that philosophers, artists and scientists have given us over the centuries. It is not enough for us to look for errors of fact, misleading arguments or confused design in science books for the young. We must be suspicious of any writer who seems to be trying to separate and to associate differing values with the multifarious activities of the mind of man.

Reading List

Adler, Irving and Ruth. ATOMS AND MOLECULES. The Reason Why. (*John Day* 1966) *Dobson* 1969. Illustrated by the authors.

Asimov, Isaac. INSIDE THE ATOM (*Abelard-Schuman* 1956 U.K. Third revised edition 1966) *Abelard-Schuman* revised edition 1961 U.S.A. Illustrated by John Bradford. See also THE NEUTRINO. *Dobson* 1966. For top school pupils and the general reader, expert popularisation including a great deal of up-to-date detail of research.

Barr, Donald. THE HOW AND WHY WONDER BOOK OF ATOMIC ENERGY. How and Why Wonder Books. (*Grosset and Dunlap* 1964) *Transworld* 1969. Illustrated by George J. Zaffo.

Bronowski, Jacob and Selsam, Millicent E. BIOGRAPHY OF AN ATOM. *Harper & Row* 1965. Illustrated by Weimer Pursell and with photographs. Based on an article in *New York Times* 1963.

Elwell, Felicia R. ATOMS AND ENERGY. Outlines. *Methuen* 1958. With drawings, diagrams and photographs. This survey for the twelve-up reader begins by outlining the explosion theory of the origin of matter and tackling the question of energy and matter, before explaining atomic structure and giving a broad account of the uses of atomic power today.

Frisch, Professor Otto R. WORKING WITH ATOMS. World of Science. (*Brockhampton* 1965) *Basic* 1966. With photographs, diagrams and a map.

Gaines, Matthew J. ATOMIC ENERGY. Hamlyn all-colour paperbacks. (*Paul Hamlyn* 1969) *Grasset & Dunlop* 1970. Illustrated by Design Bureau. For the adult reader, within the range of older school pupils, "concerned only with the peaceful uses of atomic energy" and "demanding very little prior knowledge of science".

Gamow, George. MR TOMPKINS EXPLORES THE ATOM (*Cambridge University Press* 1945 U.K.) *Cambridge University Press* 1945 U.S.A. Also in MR TOMPKINS IN PAPERBACK (*C.U.P.* 1965 U.K.) *C.U.P* 1967 U.S.A. with MR TOMPKINS IN WONDERLAND, *C.U.P.* 1939 U.S.A. Witty scientific fantasies originally published in *Discovery* to help the ordinary reader to understand the quantum theory, relativity, atomic fission, and other subjects. Mr Tompkins, a bank clerk interested in science today, has various Carrollian adventures that might appeal to young eggheads.

Grey, Vivian. SECRET OF THE MYSTERIOUS RAYS: THE DISCOVERY OF NUCLEAR ENERGY (*Basic* 1966) *Constable* 1967. Illustrated by Ed Malsberg. A somewhat over-dramatic but sensible survey of research from Roentgen to the breaking of the atom, within the reading range of children from about twelve.

Harrison, J. A. THE STORY OF THE ATOM (*Hulton Educational Publications* 1959) *Dufour* 1963. With photographs and diagrams.

Hatcher, Charles. THE ATOM. Quantum Books. (*Macmillan* 1963) *St Martin* 1963. Drawings by the author. A book for readers in the middle 'teens, with many helpful diagrams and a particularly clear analysis of the experiments leading to atomic fission.

Hutchings, D. W. DISCOVERING THE ATOM. Discovery Reference Books. *University of London Press* 1963. Illustrated by Malcolm Carder and Terence Freeman, and with some photographs.

Korn, Jerry. ATOMS: THE SMALLEST PARTICLES AND THE ENERGY THEY CONTAIN. *Golden Press* 1959. Illustrated by Norbert van Houten.

Maere, Guy de and Harnacq, H. H. THE ATOM (Belgium 1969) *Harrap* 1970. Translated by Eve Barwell. Illustrated by Nadine Forster.

Makepeace-Lott, S. ALAN WORKS WITH ATOMS. Career novels. *Chatto and Windus* 1962. A secondary schoolboy on a school visit to an atomic energy plant is fired with enthusiasm and enters upon an apprenticeship that leads to research in fuel elements. The book skirts technicalities in fulfilling its brief as a career guide in story form.

May, Julian. THERE'S ADVENTURE IN ATOMIC ENERGY. *Bailey and Swinfen* 1957. Though research has by now outstripped the material in this book, it is an interesting example of the resuscitation of an old formula. American schoolboy brothers question their father, a science writer, and many other people, and receive fully informative answers.

Neurath, Marie. INSIDE THE ATOM. Colour Books, *Parrish* 1956. Illustrated by the Isotype Institute.

Oppenheimer, J. SCIENCE AND THE COMMON UNDERSTANDING *University Press* 1954. B.B.C. Reith Lectures 1953. A valuable mind-stretcher.

Rowland, John. ATOMS WORK LIKE THIS: A BOOK FOR YOUNG PEOPLE. (*Phoenix* 1955, revised edition 1965). Illustrated by Charles Green.

Rowland, John. THE ATOM. The conquerors. *Parrish* 1965. With photographs.

Sommerhoff, George. ELECTRICITY FOR BOYS. *Blackwell* 1957.

Stephenson, George. ATOMS. Read About Science. *Longman Educational* 1964. Illustrated by Ric Wylam.

Tudge, Colin. LASERS. Now Books. *Macdonald* 1969. Illustrated by K. I. Ramsay. One of a series of paper-covered technical books, fully documented and with good diagrams, explaining some of the most recent developments in the use of atomic power.

Volly, István. THE ADVENTURES OF A CARBON ATOM. Wise Owl Books. (Hungary 1969) *Richard Sadler* 1970. Edited by David Fishlock. Illustrated by Adam Würtz.

Wilson, Noel *and* Smith, Raymond. IF I MET A MOLECULE; IF I WERE AN ATOM; IF I WERE AN ELECTRON; IF I WERE RADIOACTIVE. *Hutchinson of Australia* 1970.

—— THE ATOM. The Marshall Cavendish Learning System: Physical Science. *Marshall Cavendish Books* 1969. Illustrated by photographs in black and white and colour, and with prints and diagrams.

4 | *Biography*

All biographies should have the sub-title: Myth versus reality.
George Sims. SLEEP NO MORE (1966)

4 | *Biography*

FEW terms of literary criticism need definition more than biography. THE SHORTER OXFORD DICTIONARY provides a broad definition: "The history of the lives of individual men, as a branch of literature. A written record of the life of an individual." In the sphere of children's books, such a definition could be made to cover many kinds of book, from the Briggs picture-books about Shackleton (1969) and Richthofen (1968) or Georges Onclincx's NEFROU THE SCRIBE (1969) to historical studies like C. V. Wedgwood's MONTROSE (1952) or Sir John Summerson's SIR CHRISTOPHER WREN (1965), which could as well satisfy an adult reader as the students for which they were written. The bibliography compiled by Keith Golland for the London Borough of Havering (edited in its fourth edition (1967) by R. W. Thompson) includes compendiums like Josephine Kamm's MEN WHO SERVED AFRICA (1957) and Norman Wymer's SOLDIERS AND SAILORS (1960) under the biography heading; the dominant adjective in the bibliography is "Great".

Very few lives written for children are biographies, in fact, as we normally use the term. Some other word is needed – but what? "Junior biography" is convenient but grammatically ambiguous. "Story biography" is a true description, but only of studies which take a narrative form. "Lives" can be a useful term if it is qualified by some series title of intention. But a "Life" for children is more often an account of deeds than an interpretation of character, and this latter element is surely essential to true biography. It seems inevitable that we shall continue to use the term "biography" loosely, but that it can never be relied upon to define a book which could be a picture-story book, a selected episode, a dramatised study, a monograph or an historical novel in disguise.

Deciding upon terms is only part of the problem. The excellent
Story Biography series from Methuen is defined like this:

> This series gives clear and accurate accounts of great characters:
> what they were like as children, their background of home and
> neighbours, town or village, their early beginnings in their chosen
> work, and finally their achievements.
> Catalogue of Books for Children. Methuen, 1970

A biographer must be prepared to be simple and confident in his
statements in order to bring a personality within the comprehension
of a young reader. In a review of new biographies for adults, Dennis
Potter sharply indicated the basic problem of the biographer:

> As soon as they pick up their pens to pin another person on to
> the page biographers take a licence which is so enormous that it
> far transcends the humble virtues of mere impertinence. It helps
> to make sense out of your subject (hero or victim) when you can
> dare to assume that the child is father to the man, that thought
> is prior to the deed, that what we do is what we are, and a score
> of other such familiar little tags designed to diminish the irre-
> ducible mysteries of the human personality into prosaic order.
> "The art of trespass", in *The Times Saturday Review*, 29 Nov-
> ember 1969

To explore that "tangle of contradictory motives, warring
emotions, habit ridden responses, fearful apprehensions and
improbable longings" beneath a man's "outer front" (as Dennis
Potter puts it in his review) the biographer needs the imagination
of a novelist; even when he uses imagination to go behind fact and
interpret character, he is faced, in the end, with mystery. How can
a biographer, with all the resources of contemporary record, yet
put into a true relation Abraham Lincoln's innate melancholy and
his particular kind of rustic ribaldry? Yet these seemingly contradictory sides of his nature are crucial to any proper account of his life.
Myth and reality are constantly at war in the biographer's enterprise.
And even if he could have been present at any of the scenes he
describes at second hand, he would be little nearer to understanding
his subject. Boswell's life of Johnson is in some way the most

immediate biography ever written; but this is Boswell's Johnson. No biographer can leave himself behind when he goes to meet his subject.

A recent new series for the young, Harrap's *As They Saw Them*, is designed to draw on eye-witness accounts, diaries and other contemporary documents to show how a man fits his century and how he was then regarded. This would seem to give the biographer the chance to withdraw and let other people speak for him – as, for example, two Sellonite nurses offer a sharply personal view of the Lady with a Lamp in the Crimea, as it were on behalf of Alan Delgado, author of FLORENCE NIGHTINGALE (1970). This method of writing a "Life" is a logical extension of the quotation which any biographer has at his command, but even here the author himself decides, from his personal prejudices and pre-occupations, the particular aspect of the subject that will be presented. The volume on CHARLES DICKENS (1970) by Michael and Mollie Hardwick in this same series abounds in vignettes, caustic comments, sentimental reminiscence from a host of contemporaries of Dickens, eminent or obscure. Yet in the long run the authors have really directed us to a conclusion, to the interpretation which shows us a sociable man tormented by the need to be private. This disparate method of constructing "biography", so-called, is nearer to suggesting diversity of personality than more regular studies, but this is not necessarily the method that will best suit children if they are meeting a man or woman for the first time; and at all events it is a method which exposes a writer to the same difficulty of reconciling myth with reality.

Biography is an illusion, a fiction in the guise of fact. In Desmond McCarthy's phrase, the biographer is "an artist upon oath". He is working with facts and calling upon imagination – his own and the reader's – to warm those facts, as Paul Murray Kendall suggests in picturesque terms:

At best, fact is harsh, recalcitrant matter, as tangible as the hunk of rusty iron one trips over and yet as shapeless as a paper hat in the rain. Fact is a cold stone, an inarticulate thing, dumb until something happens to it; and there is no use the biographer waiting for spontaneous combustion or miraculous alchemy. Fact must be rubbed up in the mind, placed in magnetic juxtaposition with other facts, until it begins to glow, to give off that radiance we call meaning. Fact is a biographer's only friend, and worst enemy.

THE ART OF BIOGRAPHY, p. 17

Here is a clue to the paramount duty of the biographer who writes for the young. If he cannot guarantee to show a man as he really was, he can try to draw from his readers the admission "This is a living human being". If the man or woman he writes about does not live in his pages, the child would do better to turn to an historical treatise or to fiction. Biography can, and occasionally does, give him the best of both worlds in a form he can understand. A story biography like Elfrida Vipont's WEAVER OF DREAMS (1966) could wake an interest in Charlotte Brontë because the writer has fused facts and invention in the fire of her own enthusiasm. Elizabeth Grey in WINGED VICTORY (1966), another biography that takes narrative form, shows the perception of a novelist in her discussion of Amy Johnson's restricted girlhood and the skill of an historian in the way she illuminates events with accurate technical detail and by feeling herself into the social pressures and ideas of the 'twenties.

Social detail – an important tool of the biographer – plays a dominant part in lives for children. Many such lives are in fact social histories in which facts are grouped round a central figure. The title of Josephine Kamm's story biography, JOSEPH PAXTON AND THE CRYSTAL PALACE (1967), suggests the way her material has been organised; the man comes to life but in particular circumstances. A very lively book, INVINCIBLE MISS (1968) by Jean Hughes, provides a panorama of Africa in the last century through a study of Mary Kingsley's scientific work and her attitude to science, and to the native tribesmen who helped her researches. Betty Schecter's book on THE DREYFUS AFFAIR (1965) employs the resources of history to explain the tragic dilemma of an individual. The purpose of books like these is as much to help a young reader to develop a sense of period as it is to give him a view of a particular man or woman. Details of personality which would be out of place in a direct study of a period or an event can be accommodated in a story biography about a man or woman who played a significant part in that period.

I do not believe that authors of books like these consider themselves biographers in the strict sense. They have written about real people through the means of a story, establishing them by means of techniques used in fiction. One obvious indication of this is the use of deduced or invented conversation to enliven an episode. In a true biography this kind of licence would, or should, be out of place. The orthodox view is outlined by André Maurois in "The ethics of biography":

> Under no account has the biographer a right to invent a single fact. He is writing history, not fiction, and witnessing under oath. He cannot even say that the weather, on such and such a day, was good or bad, if he has no evidence for it. He should not put into his hero's mouth, nor attribute to any character, sentences they have not spoken. In *Ariel*, I took the liberty, not to attribute to Shelley things he had never said, but to turn into dialogue conversations that we possessed, in indirect form, in his letters. I have never done it since, nor do I approve of that method. It undermines the confidence of the reader, and also there is always a risk, even with the best of good will, of mutilating or deforming a thought. If you have a letter, quote it, or part of it; if a conversation has been preserved by a reliable witness, make use of it. But never indulge in imagination. Once you cross the line between biography and fiction, you will never be able to retrace your steps.
>
> André Maurois, quoted in James L. Clifford. BIOGRAPHY AS AN ART, p. 168

Such austerity would be difficult to achieve when writing for children whose historical knowledge and experience of life were limited. To draw a line too sharply between known fact and reasonable deduction would be to deny them a great deal of persuasive detail. Story biography must claim a degree of flexibility if it is to remain a viable and necessary alternative to historical fiction.

The distinction between the two literary forms is not a purely artificial one. It is not merely a technical difference that the writer of a story biography will sometimes introduce a dramatised scene by a piece of direct explanation of historical background or will add to such a scene an appropriate comment or summary of a general kind, whereas a novelist interrupts his narrative with a change of style at his peril. A biography is overtly didactic in a way that a novel is not. In a story biography a judicious mixture of narrative and exposition helps the writer to make the points round which his interpretation of character is built. Equally, the invented episode can often clarify as well as invigorate a general idea. The writer of a life of Dickens might choose to describe in direct terms the kind of people and places that lie behind his novels. He might, on the other hand, take certain liberties with his material to make fact more interesting for the young. In THE BOY WHO ASKED FOR MORE (1966), Elisabeth Kyle presents certain events in Dickens's life in a form so dramatic and active that a child could readily guess how an ostler might have suggested the character of Sam Weller, how Bowes Academy was translated into Dotheboys Hall, how evenings with Maria Beadnell and her harp helped to shape his conception of domestic felicity. This is "how it might have been" based on recorded fact of a general kind. This is, I believe, a necessary licence, but one which, as I shall try to show later in more detail, is highly susceptible to abuse.

When a writer attributes certain words or actions to a person when he cannot be sure of their authenticity, he is certainly departing from the strict truth – if such a thing exists at all in relation to a man's life. But truth can be dealt more serious blows than this. Biography for children is basically didactic. It sets out to instruct them in certain sets of facts and, very often, to convey a certain message as well. The subject of a biography is usually chosen as an example – in most cases of a virtue though, as the OXFORD JUNIOR ENCYCLOPEDIA puts it, "Occasionally ... a man is included because, like Adolf HITLER, his evil character and ill-doing have convulsed the world and changed history."

This purposive attitude to biography is by no means confined to children's books. Until very recently most biographers would have accepted two of the ends promised by Thomas Fuller for his WORTHIES – "to preserve the memories of the dead" and "to present examples to the living", as readily as they would agree with the aim of "entertaining the reader with delight" or of procuring "some honest profit". Down the centuries the argument has gone back and forth – how should an example be given? To many it has seemed that a hero must remain a hero in every respect; the

attitude is only too familiar in the compendiums that find their way
into school libraries, whose titles, GREAT MEN, FAMOUS MEN
AND WOMEN, and so on, are a warning of the pomposity and
stiffness so often to be found within. As Edmund Gosse pointed
out, the effort to preserve "the dignity of the subject" can lead to
presenting a man "as though he spent his whole life standing,
pressed in a tight frockcoat, with a glass of water at his hand and
one elbow on a desk, in the act of preparing to say: "Ladies and
Gentlemen!"'* Dryden's view, that domestic detail could add
rather than detract from a man's stature, would find support among
the young. In defending "a descent into minute circumstances,
and trivial passages of life," he suggests:

> You may behold a Scipio and a Lelius gathering cockle-shells
> on the shore, Augustus playing at bounding-stones with boys;
> and Agesilaus riding on a hobby-horse among his children.
> The pageantry of life is taken away; you see the poor reason-
> able animal, as naked as ever nature made him; are made
> acquainted with his passions and his follies, and find the Demy-
> God a man.
> From Dryden's Preface to PLUTARCH'S LIVES, 1863–6, quoted
> in Clifford, op. cit., pp. 18–19

You may behold a human being. But, if you are a child, you may
behold this human being most often in his active moments –
Shackleton on the *Endurance* expedition rather than frustrated in
England, Churchill in Parliament rather than in committee,
generals on the field of battle rather than retired in Cheltenham.
Children respond to action, and most biographies written for them
emphasise deeds rather than words and thoughts. The biographer
who selects the events of a man's life to emphasise his achievement
may be guilty of *suppressio veri* though not of *suggestio falsi*. But
selection can give a child a false idea. How carefully Lady Hamilton
must be dealt with, in a life of Nelson for the young; how tactfully
the vicissitudes of Dickens's domestic life must be treated. Geoffrey
Trease's sane and forthright life of Byron (1969), Elfrida Vipont's

---

*Edmund Gosse. "The ethics of biography", in *Cosmopolitan*, July 1903, quoted
in Clifford, op. cit., p. 115

life of George Eliot, FROM A HIGH ATTIC (1970), might not have
found the acceptance fifteen years ago which they have found in
the past two years.

Hero-worship is natural to young people: so is cynicism. The
biographer faces a fact inherent in most types of non-fiction. It
seems to be generally assumed that if a subject is treated at all, it
must be treated from the lowest level upwards; if a life of Shackleton
or Churchill or Drake is to be offered to a reader of fifteen, there
must also be one available for a reader of ten, of eight, even of six.
In the case of biography this is tiresome and hampering. Formulas
can be found for offering great figures to very young readers – of
these, the Briggs picture-books are perhaps the best up to now, with
a simple selective text and strong pictures based on a single period
of a man's life. In the case of most "great men", though, too much
of the man has to go if the relative experience of young and very
young be considered. Certain subjects seem unsuited to biography
for all but older boys and girls, who may be expected to make
reasonable judgments of their own on irregular or unusual or
puzzling behaviour.

Few biographies have yet caught up with the changes in a school-
child's attitude to public figures of present or past. In the family
and the classroom, discussion has become freer and more open
between the generations, but books are still too often mealy-mouthed
and evasive. Nearly forty years ago, John Drinkwater voiced a
prevalent attitude when he wrote:

. . . documents can be made to support anything if you have
enough of them to choose from. Nelson possibly was a coward,
and someone may have evidence up his sleeve to prove it. But
the important thing is not the assurance that sooner or later
truth will out, but that there comes a time when certain convictions
are so firmly established that they become proof against any
spectacular revelations, become, that is, the potent truth itself.
If a select committee of the High Courts of the world were to
decide on an impartial examination of the evidence that Nelson
was a coward, we should laugh in their faces.
THE WORLD'S LINCOLN, pp. 7–8

No such easy excuse should be available to the biographer today;

his choice in the matter should be free. Yet only recently Mary Eakin could write critically:

> It is true that histories change from time to time, but the changes are, more often than not, instituted for the purpose of justifying a present action or attitude of the government rather than to stimulate a young mind to seek out more accurate information about events of the past. Even when new information is available regarding events and famous figures of the past, such information is usually made available to children only in so far as it enhances those events or figures; seldom is it included when it reveals a weakness or error of judgement. No country has ever had a history of perfection; always there has been good balanced against evil; failure against success; yet, in all too many books for children the evil and failures are selected out, leaving only a dull and wholly unbelievable account of continuous success and well-being.
>
> "The changing world of science and the social sciences"

It is not enough to present selected facts correctly; an honest attitude to all available facts is just as important – probably more important when one is addressing young people whose power to check an author's use of his material is limited.

Biography, above all, provides a pattern for the young, and its subjects will necessarily be drawn from the ranks of those who are universally known for some contribution to the history of mankind. In this section I shall look at the types of biographical material available for young people, and written specifically for them. The age-range concerned will be a wide one. It may begin at the picture-book stage with books suitable for six-year-old listeners; it may be prolonged into the late 'teens, to overlap with some adult biography. I have chosen three people for particular attention. Lives of Johann Sebastian Bach for the young illustrate the various ways in which an artist and his work can be related. Lives of Helen Keller illustrate the difficulties of avoiding sentiment in dealing with a life of service. In Abraham Lincoln we have the problem of explaining political complexities to the young and of reconciling prejudice and partiality in regard to a man who has to some extent been deified over the years. Children should know something about these and other famous people. How well can books help them?

Reading List

Brown, Michael. SHACKLETON'S EPIC VOYAGE. Briggs Books. (*Hamish Hamilton* 1969) *Coward McCann* 1969. Illustrated by Raymond Briggs.

Clifford, James L. BIOGRAPHY AS AN ART: SELECTED CRITICISM 1560–1960 (*Oxford University Press* 1962 U.K.) *Oxford University Press* 1962 U.S.A.

Delgado, Alan. FLORENCE NIGHTINGALE: THE NURSES WITH FLORENCE NIGHTINGALE TELL THEIR STORIES. As They Saw Her. *Harrap* 1970. Illustrated by photographs and prints.

Eakin, Mary K. THE CHANGING WORLD OF SCIENCE AND THE SOCIAL SCIENCES. A paper delivered at the 12th Biennial Congress of the International Board on Books for Young People, held in Bologna, Italy on 4 April 1970.

Fisk, Nicholas. RICHTHOFEN THE RED BARON. Briggs Books. (*Hamish Hamilton* 1968) *Coward McCann* 1968. Illustrated by Raymond Briggs.

Golland, K. S. (compiler). BIOGRAPHIES FOR CHILDREN. 4th edition, revised by R. W. Thompson, Central Library, Romford, Essex, 1970.

Grey, Elizabeth. WINGED VICTORY: THE STORY OF AMY JOHNSON (*Constable* 1966) *Houghton Mifflin* 1966.

Hardwick, Michael and Mollie. CHARLES DICKENS: THE GREAT NOVELIST AS SEEN THROUGH THE EYES OF HIS FAMILY, FRIENDS, AND CONTEMPORARIES. As They Saw Him. *Harrap* 1970. With photographs and prints.

Hughes, Jean Gordon. INVINCIBLE MISS. *Macmillan* 1968. Illustrated by Hilary Abrahams.

Kamm, Josephine. MEN WHO SERVED AFRICA. *Harrap* 1957. Illustrated by G. S. Ronalds.

Kamm, Josephine. JOSEPH PAXTON AND THE CRYSTAL PALACE. Story Biographies. *Methuen* 1967. Illustrated by Faith Jaques.

Kendall, Paul Murray. THE ART OF BIOGRAPHY (*Allen and Unwin* 1965) *Norton* 1965.

Kyle, Elisabeth. THE BOY WHO ASKED FOR MORE: THE EARLY LIFE OF CHARLES DICKENS. *Evans* 1966. Illustrated by photographs and prints.

Onclincx, Georges. NEFROU THE SCRIBE. Children of Other Times. (*International Copyright Institute* 1967) *A. and C. Black* 1969. Adapted by Ellen M. Dolan. Illustrated by Marie Wabbes.

Schecter, Betty. THE DREYFUS AFFAIR: A NATIONAL SCANDAL (*Houghton Mifflin* 1965) *Gollancz* 1967. Illustrated by photographs.

Styles, Showell. FIRST UP EVEREST. Briggs Books. (*Hamish Hamilton* 1969) *Coward McCann* 1969. Illustrated by Raymond Briggs.

Summerson, Sir John. SIR CHRISTOPHER WREN. Makers of History. (*Collins* 1965) *Shoe String* 1965. Illustrated by photographs, diagrams and prints.

Trease, Geoffrey. BYRON: A POET DANGEROUS TO KNOW (*Macmillan* 1969) *Holt, Rinehart* 1970.

Vipont, Elfrida. WEAVER OF DREAMS: THE GIRLHOOD OF CHARLOTTE BRONTË (*Hamish Hamilton* 1966) *Walck* 1966. With photographs and prints.

Vipont, Elfrida. FROM A HIGH ATTIC: THE EARLY LIFE OF GEORGE ELIOT. *Hamish Hamilton* 1970.

Wedgwood, C. V. MONTROSE. Makers of History. (*Collins* 1952) *Shoe String* 1966.

Wymer, Norman. SOLDIERS AND SAILORS. *Oxford University Press* 1960.

4a | Johann Sebastian Bach

... (I) am rejoiced to find that you are likely to regard his works with me as a musical Bible unrivaled and inimitable.
John Wesley in a letter to Benjamin Jacob, 1808

4a | *Johann Sebastian Bach*

NOBODY would have written a biography of an industrious, irritable, devout paterfamilias if he had not also been the greatest of all great musicians. Any man or woman who is the subject of a biography is chosen for some particular achievement, whether it is a noble body of work or membership of an important social group. But many biographers have an additional decision to make. Do they intend to write a true biography – an interpretation of personality – or a life-and-works? The distinction is often a narrow one, but it does exist. Obviously some people are easily seen as individuals in their "works" (compositions, achievements, structures or whatever they may be): others remain half hidden by them. We can see the prejudices, talents and personal reactions of Ernest Shackleton in every recorded action or saying of his during the *Endurance* expedition; we cannot so clearly see Johann Sebastian Bach behind improvisations and compositions belonging to a strong tradition. But the biographer must help us to do this if we are to be drawn to his music. Percy Young's wise words are relevant here:

> In reading this biographical sketch . . . it must be recognised that knowledge of the music . . . is the ultimate objective, both for its own sake and because it is also a true record of the composer's developing thought and convictions. In short his music is Bach's autobiography, written in a language that has no frontiers. That it is so much greater than the man is one of the mysteries that must remain; but in that mystery is an abiding symbol of faith in human values. And Bach, above all, was a man of faith. So in this case are united life and works.
>
> JOHANN SEBASTIAN BACH (1960), Preface

A special difficulty attaches to the life of a composer. A poet's words may be quoted and will be intelligible to the reader, to some degree at least. Reproductions of whole paintings or details from them can reinforce verbal descriptions, and words are capable of communicating without visual help something of the colour and composition of a picture or a statue. But words do not easily suggest sounds except in the most general sense; they can help us to understand the substance and plan of a piece of music, its origin and purpose, its technique, but this will not allow us to hear it. If we know a work beforehand, what the writer tells us will be of special interest: if we do not, we have heard less than half the story. Musical quotation, however brief, seems to me essential in any book about a musician, and yet such quotation presupposes that the reader can recognise it and can convert signs into sounds. This is an acquired ability in a way that reading a poem or looking at a picture is not.

Junior biographies begin with two assumptions. Either a child wants to collect facts about as many famous people as possible, gathering a very general impression of what they did, or he has a leaning towards a certain subject or type of person which leads him consciously to choose a particular biography. In the case of a musician, the value of general knowledge acquired in casual reading is likely to be limited. In other words, children who read books about Bach probably do so in the main because they want to. There is a substantial advantage in this. It is possible (though hardly wise) for a writer with no immediate personal interest to embark on the biography of a social reformer, a general, an explorer – simply as an assignment. In the case of a musician, none but a specialist and an enthusiast is likely to apply. The standard of lives of musicians is therefore likely to be set high.

Of all the composers whose lives children should have at their disposal, Bach's is probably the most lightly documented. We know what jobs he had and can date a great many of his works; we know where he lived, how many children he had, what caused his death. We cannot really observe the minutiae of his daily life; there is no diary to draw on, very few letters, a scarcity of contemporary comment. In itself this is no bad thing. Instead of aiming at the impertinent intimacy that often taints biographies of the great, the wise writer will let us see, through the eyes of Bach's contemporaries, the picture of a working man. He will show us Bach the teacher demonstrating how useful the thumb could be in playing the clavier, Bach the organist trying out what he called the lungs of a new organ or diagnosing the faults of an old one, Bach the conductor directing an orchestra, "singing with one voice and playing his own parts" at the same time and, as Gesner says, "full of rhythm in every part of his body".

This kind of documentation gives us the man in the musician. This kind of evidence, if it handled in a lively and sympathetic way, can be just as interesting as the more personal anecdotes which are the staple of every junior biography. We can enjoy the story of the penniless sixteen-year-old, trudging wearily on the thirty-mile journey home from Hamburg, sitting under the window of an inn and being startled by the descent of two herring heads, each containing a ducat. Anecdotes like this add to our knowledge of an individual. Unfortunately, few biographers can resist the temptation to embroider them or to offer as fact what is merely legend or supposition. Any reader of biography to some extent makes his own picture by taking from it what appeals to him, but there must be a stable foundation for all to share.

Embroidery is almost irresistible in the case of a story biography of Bach, particularly if it is designed for young readers. SEBASTIAN BACH, THE BOY FROM THURINGIA (1939), by Opal Wheeler and S. Deucher, was published over thirty years ago in a series which also included Beethoven and Mozart. A picture-book format, drawings artistically unattractive and sentimental, large print, a style occasionally coy in its domesticity – these characteristics suggest that the book was intended for readers of not much more than eight and readers, besides, who might be able to play on the piano the simple extracts from easy Bach pieces or at least to get someone in the family to play them. A book of this kind, mainly for middle-class home consumption, would be unlikely to find a market today. Children of primary or early secondary age would be more likely to meet Bach first (and far more happily) by listening to a tape or a recording, helped by comments from a parent or, more probably, from a teacher.

What is the aim behind this artless tale of the boy from Thuringia? Apparently, to give a picture of Bach's childhood which can be easily appreciated and can lead to a glimpse of the man he became.

In the first chapter the young reader is invited to watch, as it were, the Bach family collecting at Eisenach for one of their annual festivals, almost to join in as companion to the small Johann Sebastian: in the final chapter Bach stands in the doorway of his house at Leipzig saying goodnight to friends who have been visiting him for a musical evening. The book marks only the sunny hours. There is no reference to Bach's difficulties with the Leipzig Council, with his eyes, with his pupils, in the latter part of the book. Its point – a valid one – is to show a boy growing up with music. This aim has been partly frustrated, however, by a lack of balance.

A sentimental view of Bach in old age; drawing by Mary Greenwalt from SEBASTIAN BACH: THE BOY FROM THURINGIA (Faber).

In striving for a real, homely picture the authors have given far too little space to definite facts about Bach's work. His journey to Cöthen with his family to a new job is described with relentlessly trivial detail:

Bach lifted the younger children carefully into the high carriage and, when Maria Barbara was comfortably seated, he climbed to his place beside the driver.

It was a bright sunny day for the ride. Bach laughed and sang with the children as the horses galloped along the road to Anhalt-Cöthen

SEBASTIAN BACH, THE BOY FROM THURINGIA, pp. 96–7

It is not very clear why the family is moving, and nothing is said about Bach's professional reasons for accepting the new job. A simple explanation would surely bring him nearer to the reader's experience.

Again, the affair of the contest planned between Bach and the French performer Marchand has been blown up into a dramatic encounter, with invented talk and invented detail. This relatively unimportant event in Bach's life has been allowed several pages, some of which could have been used to give more practical background to the move to Weimar – reasons for the move being suppressed in the domestic and truncated version which is all we are given:

When the music was ended he [the Duke of Weimar] sent for Sebastian.

"My dear Bach, indeed you must be the same young man who played in my orchestra only a few years ago. And your own compositions – they have delighted me. I should like to have you come here to live and be my court organist."

To think of being the chief organist at the royal court of Weimar! . . .

"I thank you for this honour, Sire. I shall tell the people of Mühlhausen of your kind offer and they will surely allow me to leave. Then I shall make arrangements to come to Weimar as soon as possible."

ibid., pp. 78–9

Contrived scenes of this kind are distasteful because they are deduced and not directly authenticated, and because in seeking to domesticate the subject of the biography they usually diminish him. It is reasonable for a biographer to recast contemporary descriptions of place or to dramatise general, unspecific domestic history. A

Bach in the last year of his life, from BACH (Faber), by courtesy of Bärenreiter-Verlag

good example may be found in Jo Manton's PORTRAIT OF BACH
(1957), in which she transfers visual details from an old print of
the Golden Crown at Arnstadt into words in a paragraph which
helps us to imagine Bach at home but does not pry in at the windows:

> Arnstadt was a lovely hillside town, ringed with old walls and
> turrets and interlaced with running water. Sebastian's rooms at
> the Golden Crown looked on to a crooked square from which
> the little streets curled away like the fingers on a hand. Below his
> window a fountain plashed unceasingly. By day he saw the cart-
> horses stop to drink there, and at night he lay listening to the
> chuckle of the water as it flowed over the cobble-stones.
>
> PORTRAIT OF BACH, p. 44

The biographer is justified also in expanding authentic episodes, but he must do so with tact. Thus, in THE BOY FROM
THURINGIA, the episode of the herrings (which Bach is known to
have told often and with enjoyment in the family circle) is presented
as a scene of action, pleasantly and briefly. The boy's raid on the
forbidden music in his older brother's cabinet is another matter.
It is a fact that Sebastian was caught playing some of the music
he had secretly copied at night by the light of the moon: it is not
known exactly why Christoph confiscated his copies or what he
said or felt. All but one of the biographers for the young assume
that Christoph was angry, even "furious". Imogen Holst, in her
scholarly book, admits we do not know what he really felt, but she
does offer a guess. This is a scene which can be made appealingly
real to a young reader in terms of nursery crime and punishment,
and so it has been, with this kind of result:

> Johann Sebastian was very excited, for tonight was his last night.
> Hastily he took the book down and went over to the window
> through which the moon was shining brightly.
> "Well, young man, and what do you think you are doing?"
> boomed a loud voice from the door. It was his brother, Johann
> Christoph! Johann Sebastian hung his head. Angrily his brother
> seized the book and the music copy Johann Sebastian had made
> with such care. The book he replaced in the cupboard, carrying
> the music copy away with him as he drove the boy back to bed.

"This will teach you to obey, my fine young fellow!"
W. S. Freeman and R. H. Whittaker. GREAT COMPOSERS
(1959), p. 8

The cheap effect, echoed in a cheap illustration, has been gained
at the expense of authenticity and good taste.

A biographer can only too easily give a false impression by adding
to fact or by over-simplifying it. Perhaps this is sometimes unavoidable if he is aiming at a "story". Events must be drawn together,
telescoped to make a single effective piece of narrative. Decisions
which were presumably only taken after long discussion and
thought are made to seem instantaneous; for example the "quarrel"
with Christoph over the music, leads, in THE BOY FROM THUR-
INGIA, to the following account of Sebastian's move to St Michael's
school at Lüneburg:

> Sebastian knew now that he must find a way to go on with his
> music.
>   He hurried to find the Director of the Lyceum to ask his help.
>   "There is the fine choir school of St Michael's in Lüneburg,
> Sebastian, where you could study music. With your fine voice
> perhaps you could sing in the church. And your good friend,
> Erdmann – he is eager to study as well. Why not go there together,
> my boy?" said the Director.
> THE BOY FROM THURINGIA, p. 29

We know that in fact arrangements were made between the Director
of the Ohrdruf school and Johann Christoph Bach after suitable
talk. There is no warrant for implying, as the authors seem to imply
here, that Sebastian was forced out of his brother's home by ill-
feeling.

The fault is more serious when scenes are invented that are
directly concerned with Bach as a musician. A great deal is known
about the particular occasions for which he composed certain works
or gave certain performances on the organ. A great deal is known,
too, about the types of music which preceded his own and on which
he built, and nothing is gained by suggesting that he was a phenomenon, owing nothing to any musical ancestor. We have to remember that THE BOY FROM THURINGIA is a short introduction that

does not pretend to much detail, but we should expect one extra
sentence to counteract the simplification in this passage:

> Sebastian seated himself at the fine new instrument and a great
> chorale sounded through the church.
>   This young man had rare power! The people could hardly
> believe that such beautiful music could be composed while they
> listened.
> ibid., p. 69

The passage ignores the heritage of chorale music that Bach drew
on, and indeed suggests that he was here "composing" a chorale
instead of embellishing an already familiar tune. The facts could
be given simply and briefly – as they are, for instance, by Jo Manton
in a passage which also helps us to see Bach as a small boy:

> The soprano voices soared up to the snowy roof-tops and beyond,
> as though their singing would reach to the stars. All his life
> Sebastian Bach remembered the chorales he had sung as a
> chorister, and set them repeatedly in his own music to rich and
> tender harmonies.
> PORTRAIT OF BACH, p. 25

The most praiseworthy aspect of THE BOY FROM THURINGIA
is its wealth of musical example. Some of this is somewhat am-
biguously introduced. When we read "He hummed a jolly marching
tune to help pass away the hours" as he walked to Hamburg to
hear the aged Reinken play, we cannot be sure that the authors
do not mean to imagine a specific moment of inspiration, and in at
least one case they make an unwarranted assumption when they
introduce one of the chorales from the *Christmas Oratorio*, "Beside
thy cradle", with the words "Often there was a fretful child to care
for and Bach left his work to rock the little one and softly hummed
this lovely chorale." Again, no doubt he did, but we do not know,
and the categorical statement cannot be accepted. But it is to the
credit of the authors that they provide the young reader with
examples, and I can remember that my eldest son, who read the
book when he was a small boy learning the piano, very much
enjoyed picking the examples out for himself. The pleasure could

be achieved, and will mostly be achieved nowadays, without the benefit of a trivial and anecdotal narrative framework.

If most children are likely to wait till they are ten or older before they are attracted to story biography, this need not restrict the few who might enjoy a relatively simple book about a great man or woman at an earlier age. Reba Mirsky's JOHANN SEBASTIAN BACH (1965) has the suggested age ten to fourteen, but though its style is full and demanding, the book has a straightforward narrative plan which should put it within the reach of some competent readers before they reach the 'teens. The author is skilful in slipping important background information into what is in effect a "story" of Bach – though a story that does not accentuate the domestic aspect but rather uses it as a framework for more valuable details of musical history. By putting essential fact into a domestic context the author loses none of her authority, but makes these facts more palatable. Sometimes she offers what amounts to a close-up, paraphrasing a contemporary description or transferring details from an existing picture:

> Candles were lit in the Great Hall, the long wall mirrors reflecting their glow. On a dais in the Great Hall was a velvet chair for the young Prince. Before the concert began, Bach, in a curled white wig, a dark velvet coat with rows of gold buttons, and a white shirt of pleated lawn, bowed to the Prince and the ladies; then, sitting at the harpsichord, he signaled the eighteen musicians to begin the concert. The string players, bassoonists, horn players, trumpeters, and drummer, also in powdered wigs and court livery, were arranged round Bach. Sometimes hunting horns were added when travelling musicians came in pairs and applied for temporary work.
>
> JOHANN SEBASTIAN BACH, pp. 81–2

It is noticeable that the author does not give chapter and verse for this kind of passage. Perhaps a junior book should not be overloaded with references but Jo Manton manages to identify the source of a similar description, indicating in a brief footnote that "a portrait of him in court dress aged 38 is now in a private collection in America".

The combination of narrative and exposition in Reba Mirsky's book is on the whole successful, though now and then the lack of musical quotation is evident. When the author writes of Bach's use of earlier musical tradition in the following terms, some notation is really needed:

> He would transform another's musical theme by treating it with the utmost freedom. If he thought the basses of the original were inexpressive, he substituted others for them, or he added new or more interesting middle parts, transforming the upper voices completely. He might go his own way immediately after the first few bars, then follow the original again, branch off, omit something here, insert something there.
>
> ibid., p. 71

There seems little point in using technical material like this without suitable illustration.

Mindful of her readers, the author has kept a balance between too much and too little fact. Bach is seen, boy and man, in selected domestic situations, all warranted by fact and most of them based on known detail (though, surprisingly, the author uses very little those letters of Elias Bach which give such a human and humorous picture of the Leipzig household in Bach's later years). Passages like the following show the closeness of detail which has enabled the author to pack a great deal into a short book:

> It was the first time that Sebastian had ever been away from home, and he was full of curiosity about Ohrdruf. So slow was their conveyance that it took them all day to arrive there, but as night fell, Sebastian saw a pretty walled town with cobbled streets and gabled houses. A mountain stream flowed through the marketplace not far from Johann Christoph's small cottage.
>
> As Sebastian and Jakob entered Christoph's house, they were greeted by his wife, Dorothea. Sebastian knew his brother's wife was expecting a baby, and he worried a little about the room he and Jakob would take up in so small a house, and about the expense of extra food for him and his brother. Christoph had only a small salary, with a few extra payments in corn, wood, and brushwood. Sebastian hoped his voice would be considered

A cheerfully idealised view of the composer; drawing by Steele Savage from
JOHANN SEBASTIAN BACH (Follett).

good enough to get him into the choir so that he might earn a
little toward his keep.
ibid., pp. 26–7

Compared with the equally domestic passage from Wheeler and
Deucher quoted on page 316, this one contains practical evidence
of the period which makes it more than a pretty piece of stage
scenery.

Most of the set pieces in Reba Mirsky's book are of this quality,
tactfully done and keeping invention to the minimum; but to
paraphrase or to imagine is not always desirable. When the author

describes how Frederick of Prussia received Bach at Potsdam, the effortful phrases throw a veil of sentiment over a well-known and important scene:

> One evening, just as he had got his flute ready and his musicians assembled, a list of the visitors to Potsdam was brought to him by one of his guards. As soon as Frederick saw the name "Johann Sebastian Bach" on the list, he grew excited and said, "Bring Herr Bach here from his lodgings at once. He is the greatest living organist in Germany and the father of one of my musicians." For a long time, he had been urging Philipp Emanuel to have his father come to the court for a visit.
>
> Bach was taken immediately to the young King, who was full of boundless enthusiasm for music and a deep respect for musical talent. The King received Bach with great deference and introduced him to the court musicians, announcing, "Gentlemen, old Bach has come!"
>
> ibid., p. 122

This is a moment in Bach's carrer when humanity is warm and the reader should be taken as close as possible to the event. What better account of the scene could anyone ask for but that of Bach's first biographer, Forkel, who had it from an onlooker at the scene:

> At this time the King used to have every evening a private concert, in which he himself generally performed some concertos on the flute. One evening, just as he was getting his flute ready and his musicians were assembled, an officer brought him the written list of the strangers who had arrived. With his flute in his hand, he ran over the list, but immediately turned to the assembled musicians and said, with a kind of agitation; "Gentlemen, old Bach is come." The flute was now laid aside; and old Bach, who had alighted at his son's lodgings, was immediately summoned to the Palace. William Friedmann, who accompanied his father, told me this story, and I must say that I still think with pleasure on the manner in which he related it.
>
> Johann Nikolaus Forkel. J. S. BACH, HIS LIFE, ART AND WORK, in Hans T. David and Arthur Mendel. THE BACH READER, p. 305

It is all the more necessary to comment on an occasional lack of tact and discrimination because Reba Mirsky has in general been careful to avoid too obvious a disparity with the tone of the past. Occasionally she turns recorded opinion into speech. Using Bach's own communicated notes on his family history, she puts into Uncle Heinrich's mouth the familiar details of old Veit Bach the miller and his zither, and she has found a place in her book for authenticated remarks such as Bach's comparison of counterpoint with good conversation or of organ playing being a matter of "hitting the right notes at the right moment".

From this book you might, as it were, recognise old Bach if you met him in the street: after reading Jo Manton's PORTRAIT OF BACH you would feel you knew the man pretty well. There is a warmth and an involvement here that takes any hint of dryness from passages explaining Bach's achievements or his position in the world of music. Truly this is a portrait; the title gives a better indication of the book than the series definition of *Story Biography*. This is not in fact a story but an account, but it is all the same the most human of all the junior books of Bach available at the present time.

If this is due to the author's choice of fact, anecdote and domestic detail, it is also partly due to her attractive prose style and the literary skill with which she varies the way she introduces information. She never allows generalisation to halt the flow of her narrative but, rather, to frame it. Here, for example, is part of her account of Bach's schoolboy years at Lüneburg:

Yet Sebastian Bach's whole later life makes it clear that, in spite of cold and hunger, the hours he spent in church were precious to him. The lofty nave of St. Michael's, the clustered pillars, the altarpiece of glowing gold and the music, worthy of this exquisite setting, held all that his life knew of beauty. His strong and simple nature eagerly accepted the stern teaching of the Lutheran Church, that God is our just judge, that man of himself is nothing and can be saved by faith alone. Still more, this lonely boy, making his own way in the world without a home or the love of parents, opened his heart to the love of God. There was nothing weak or sentimental about Sebastian's faith; into it he poured all the force of his vigorous character and his creative power. He

read his Bible constantly and with care, collecting commentaries
and religious writings as a hobby, until, when he died, his book-
shelves were full of them. His set of Luther's works in eight
huge volumes was thumbed and annotated with the reading of a
lifetime.

PORTRAIT OF BACH, pp. 38–9

This passage holds very easily the important comment on Bach's
sincere love of God, an integral part of his music which must be
stressed and which, with the chronological sweep the author has
here allowed herself, is stressed in relation to its early growth and
its continued existence at one and the same time. Stylistically the
passage is cleverly placed between two passages of *particular* fact.
It is preceded by an explanation of the daily routine of the choir at
St Michael's and it is followed, in easy transition, through a paragraph on the religious aspect of Bach's compositions and his habit
of heading them "Jesus juva", to more personal details of the boy's
voice breaking, with a snatch of dialogue to give immediacy. The
conspicuous variety of this book is the result of very careful sifting
and arrangement of material; in its manipulation of light and shade
it is a fine portrait.

Passages like the one quoted above supply the element of interpretation in this book. The known facts of Bach's temperament do
not encourage "interpretation" in the sense of personal opinion;
there is little room for argument about what he was or was not like,
and even the suppressing of any strong comment on his temper in
later years hardly constitutes a personal judgment so much as a
deference to young readers. Using descriptions of Bach from early
writings, in quotation or, more often, in paraphrase, Jo Manton
lets these speak for themselves or adds the briefest of comments,
suggesting that "every disappointment in his professional work
created a crisis in their lives" as she describes the part Anna Magdalena played in his life, or commenting that a portrait painted in
the 1740s "shows a man of formidable power and stubbornness.
His heavy jaw is set, his brow frowning. His face is lined by the
disappointments and bitter fights of his life as Cantor."

Where other writers too often rush to "put in the expression",
like bad pianists playing Bach, Jo Manton keeps her opinion till
it is essential. Her restraint is all the more striking when it is

contrasted with personal interpretation as uninhibited as the following:

> And what a physique! He was bigger and huskier than any other organist in Germany. And a merry and companionable fellow for all that. Ready to hold his own with anybody over a mug of beer. None of your temperamental and weazened and aloof little old musicians, but a man of the people – hale and hearty and tough-muscled, like a blacksmith presiding over the bellows of a forge rather than the pipes of an organ. Looked as if he would be more at home fanning a flame instead of pumping a current of air.
>
> H. and D. L. Thomas. LIVING BIOGRAPHIES OF GREAT COMPOSERS (1940), pp. 5–6

The only possible reaction to such a description is to suppose the authors must have mixed up their subjects.

Jo Manton has her own idea of what Bach was like, but she keeps it for the rare moments when she needs to stand at a distance from her portrait and check the light and shade:

> Sebastian's fame, though widespread, was curiously limited. It was as a virtuoso performer on clavier and organ that his contemporaries knew him, and all the stories about him touch on this side of his genius. His glorious compositions, the great range of his musical thought, his passionate feelings and poetic imagination, passed almost unnoticed. Of the hundreds of Cantatas, so faithfully copied round the family dining-table by Magdalena and the boys, only one saw print, and that was an early production of his Mühlhausen years. Sebastian never showed the slightest personal resentment at this neglect. He had created, and in creating found peace of heart, deeper than all his daily struggles. He was content to leave his works behind him and look forward serenely to approaching death.
>
> PORTRAIT OF BACH, p. 129.

From a literary point of view this kind of passage provides a necessary contrast to sequences of fact or essential background detail. This is particularly noticeable when the author marks the stages of Bach's life between Mühlhausen and Weimar with a neat generalisation:

> Sebastian never moved far from his birthplace. In all his life he never saw the sea, or heard a language that was not his native German. Most of his journeys were not more than a day's travel from one small walled city to another. Yet the strongest natures cannot be bound by time and space, and within the narrow circle he kept his spirit free.
>
> ibid., p. 56

Such information as we have about Bach's life consists largely of a catalogue of journeys from one place of employment to another. Each biographer must decide how he will avoid monotony in mentioning the regular moves of the Bach family. You can reconstruct a coach journey once; to do it more often is to reveal a poverty of ideas. Jo Manton's various transitions, far from being too difficult for young readers, make her book conspicuously easy and interesting to read. Certainly she is not afraid to present Bach in a homely setting when the occasion warrants. She knows her sources and uses them well, whatever they may be – music, letters, reports of contemporaries, genealogies, history – quoting, para-phrasing, rendering reported speech into direct talk, choosing an appropriate method in each case. Thus a letter from Bach to Gesner is quoted and then turned into a vivid picture of the Bach household which his son Philipp Emanuel said was "like a beehive, and just as full of life".

Words seldom fail Jo Manton. The moments when they do are worth mentioning. Perhaps it was not her own decision to omit musical quotation. Her aim is obviously not to discuss Bach's music in any detail but to provide a background to that music, to show the young something of the traditions and the circumstances in which Bach worked. On the rare occasions when she does mention a particular work she makes words do what she wants them to – as when she describes the varying moods and types of composition in the *St Matthew Passion* in order to show Bach's genius. We might wish that when she wrote that he taught his pupils "when playing hymns not to treat the melody as if it alone were important, but to interpret the words through the melody", she had continued her brief mention of the church cantatas with some examples of Bach's use of musical symbol. Certainly we are justified in wishing that her description of the cantata "God is my king" had been accompanied by an illustration:

> For the inauguration of a new burgomaster he wrote a cantata, *God is my king*, which was performed with splendid ceremony in the Marienkirche. He took endless pains with the score, which can still be seen, corrected and re-corrected in his vigorous hand-writing. Sudden scratches and blots show where the quill-feather could not keep pace with his flying thoughts, and sharp scorings-out where he impatiently dismissed the second-best.
> ibid., p. 54

Words alone will not do here. But the drawings in this book, by Faith Jaques, are domestic in character – Bach walking with his sons at Potsdam, the school at Eisenach, a street fair in Leipzig –

Drawing by Faith Jaques from A PORTRAIT OF BACH (Methuen); compare the quotation on p. 318.

and they contribute to the total impression of PORTRAIT OF BACH as the most persuasive of all the studies of musician as man.

THE BOY FROM THURINGIA and Reba Mirsky's book present their subject in wholly domestic context. Jo Manton shows us the man as musician and as head of a family. Imogen Holst's BACH (1965) in Faber's *Great Composers* series is a book about music, and every detail earns its place for this reason alone. This is an account (not in any sense a story) of a craftsman working in a tradition and enriching it. It is also a book directly aimed at a musical reader, one who is learning to play an instrument and is ready to make the acquaintance of Bach's music in a serious spirit. There is room here for direct advice to performers, conveyed in the precise analysis of given examples. Lines from one of the canons exchanged between Bach and Walther at Weimar are clarified like this:

> If Ex. 12a. is written out in full it can be played on four recorders; descant, treble, tenor and bass, with the treble playing an octave higher. After the repeat, the four instruments go back to the beginning, ending with a pause on the last note shown in Ex. 12a.
> BACH, p. 43

and a detached paragraph at the end of the book shows the author's aim very clearly:

> A book about Bach should allow his music to have the last word. In the following pages the final chorus from his *St. Matthew Passion* has been arranged so that it can be played on the piano by a solitary reader.
> ibid., no page number

This book is not a biography so much as an introduction to a particular body of music, provided for young readers by a professional musician. Enthusiasm is tempered by the precision of a teacher and by a scrupulous scholarship. Nothing is invented. There are no contrived domestic scenes or assumed dialogues. Such anecdotes as are used – and these are all directly concerned with music – are given with their provenance. The incident of Sebastian copying his brother's music is given as "a story, often quoted by biographers". The author supposes that Johann Christoph was not "a very unsympathetic brother" but rather "a very conscientious teacher", and she gives an example from an allemande by Pachelbel to show the unfamiliar and difficult keys which Christoph may have felt were too much for his young brother. After telling the familiar story of the sight-reading test set by Walther, which Bach failed, she adds:

> This story is one of the many anecdotes that found their way into the earliest of Bach's biographies. Not all of them are to be believed, but it seems likely that this particular anecdote is true, for it is typical of Bach, that he should choose to repeat a story against himself. Like other really great artists, he had a clear idea of what he could achieve, and he was utterly incapable of being pompous or of showing off.
>
> ibid., p. 45

We are nearer to Bach's music in Imogen Holst's book than in any other. Alone among biographers for the young she gives the professional as well as the temperamental reasons for the difficulties Bach encountered in his relations with the Council and his pupils in Leipzig. Describing those stormy relations, she uses Bach's memorandum on his minimum requirements for cantata choir and orchestra, and explains in detail how far below the minimum was his actual allowance of singers and players. She is particularly careful to relate Bach to his musical past and to show what he had to draw on as well as what he himself added. Describing his journey to Lübeck as a boy to hear Buxtehude, she describes the kind of dramatic music he heard, "with passionate dialogues between singers representing Good and Evil, and with thrilling instrumental contrasts between Heaven and Hell", and later in her book, discussing the composing of the *St John Passion*, she writes:

> He had probably been hoping for an occasion to set the story of the Passion to music ever since his visit to Lübeck, nearly twenty years before this ... In the *St. John Passion* the drama is overwhelming: the angry crowds mutter or shout with a cruel edge to their voices, and the Narrator declaims his story with a poignancy that is unforgettable. The Leipzig congregation had

never dreamed that such music could be performed in a church:
an old lady sitting in the front pew was heard to say "Good
gracious! One might just as well be at the opera!"
ibid., p. 60

The many musical quotations offered in Imogen Holst's book
are always apt and always accompanied by lucid analysis. If the
book is aimed at the musical child, it is not a prodigy but a
beginner with enough sense to realise that the more he knows about
a piece of music the better he will be able to understand and perform
it. One of her most helpful pieces of analysis concerns an extract
from one of Bach's suites for unaccompanied strings – music all
too seldom played to children. Quoting from the "'Cello Gigue",
as she says, a "single melodic line", she goes on:

But the listener never feels the need for any additional accompaniment, because the notes of the tune have grown out of the
silently-heard chords that Bach had in his mind when he was
writing the music. And these silently-heard chords can make
themselves felt, as soon as one gets to know the tune really well.
(The tune in Ex. 17 is so completely satisfying that it is even able
to carry on an imaginary conversation with itself: the brief
comments marked *piano* might almost be part of a dialogue.)
ibid., p. 53

Without realising how it happens, a reader gathers an impression
of Bach the man as he is helped to follow some of his music.
It would be a pity to tie this excellent book to any particular age-
group; it would be more logical to suggest that the child who can
read simple music, whether with piano, voice or recorder, should
have it for a browsing book, a companion in moments when he
wants to be active with music. It is a book to serve as a bridge
between a child's first introduction to Bach and the specialist classic
biographies and studies of Spitta, Schweitzer, Terry and others,
which are for the interested amateur with some background
knowledge. This child may graduate through another book too.
Frederic Westcott's BACH (1967) makes a good pair with Imogen
Holst's book. It is written for the series *Composers and Their Times*,
whose aim is firmly stated by the general editor:

The young person has been well provided in post-war years with guides to a variety of subjects. Music has not been overlooked. Many books about the great composers attempt, however, to deal with their music as well. Each book in this series restricts itself, wisely I think, to the story of a composer's life, filling in the background in greater detail than usual. There is no technical discussion of the music; that task falls to some of the books listed in the bibliography. Here the composer is shown, not as an isolated artistic phenomenon, but as a human being, living in a particular society and period of time. He is seen not only in relation to his art, but to his fellow men and the times in which he lived.

Felix Aprahamian, in Frederic Westcott's BACH, Introduction

Without some discussion of Bach's music, it would seem impossible to offer an interpretation of the man, and this book no more strikes one as true biography than Imogen Holst's does. Westcott writes as a musical historian and fulfils the promise of the general advertisement by "filling in the background in greater detail than usual". This account for children from eleven upwards is written in a measured prose which can relax in an anecdote but which is in the main calmly expository. If particular pieces of music are rarely mentioned, there is a great deal of practical information about Bach's various duties and the occasion for his works is discussed with authority. At Weimar, we read:

As chamber musician Bach was to lead the small group of instrumentalists who performed regularly in the Duke's apartments. As court organist he was to play the organ, in its gallery high above the altar, in the strange, lofty Court Chapel known as *Himmelsburg* ("City of Heaven"), for the services which all Wilhelm Ernst's court had to attend.

ibid., p. 48

Westcott describes the creation of the post of *Concertmeister* for Bach by Duke Wilhelm, and the duty that followed of producing a new cantata every month. The particular services and compositions required by each of the churches at Leipzig are enumerated, and the amount of teaching Bach had to do there. The idea behind this

careful amassing of fact about Bach's work is made clear when the
author discusses the role of the composer in Bach's day:

> Music in those days was always written for a definite purpose,
> and often for a particular occasion. The idea of the inspired,
> unworldly composer, writing masterpieces for future generations,
> had not yet been born. Even later in the eighteenth century,
> when Haydn was asked why he had written no quintets, he replied
> simply, "No one has ever asked me to." Bach's attitude was no
> different in this from that of his contemporaries. Just as at
> Weimar he wrote organ music for himself to play while court
> organist, and cantatas for the "Himmelsburg" Services while
> *Concertmeister*, so at Cöthen he wrote suites, concertos and
> sonatas for the *Kapelle*, and keyboard music for teaching his
> family and pupils.
> ibid., p. 64

Indeed, the theme of this book may be found in the opening
pages, where the musical opportunities in Germany in the seventeenth century are discussed in relation to the proliferating Bach
family. Biography should partake of history not only in describing
outward details of costume, architecture or manners but also in
providing broad generalisations of the kind which stay in the
memory because of their impact, and attract to themselves more
facts and ideas as we read more about a particular subject. With
Westcott's BACH we have a book in which we are not invited to feel
or to listen so much as to think.

Each of the books I have discussed performs a different task.
Reba Mirsky's will provide the easiest way in for a beginner: Jo
Manton's portrait is perhaps for the occasional concert-goer,
receptive but not too well equipped: Imogen Holst's is for the
budding young musician and Frederic Westcott's for the aspiring
student. Any child who becomes a Bach obsessive early in life
could do worse than read all four books at different times. And if
he has a real appetite for the past he may also amuse himself by
tracking down anecdotes and facts in that admirable compendium
THE BACH READER (1967) by David and Mendel and finding some
of those contemporary pieces so often paraphrased for the young.
To enjoy Marpurg's phrase on Bach's fugues, that he "shook all

sorts of paper intricacies out of his sleeve": to see Bach conducting through the eyes of his friend Gesner: to meet in a version almost first-hand the often retold story of the clergyman who was shocked when the elders of Hamburg engaged as organist a man of lesser capacities but greater wealth than Bach:

> ... he was firmly convinced that even if one of the angels of Bethlehem should come down from Heaven, one who played divinely and wished to become organist of St. Jacobi, but had no money, he might just as well fly away again.
> THE BACH READER, pp. 81–2

... this is to get very close to the world in which Bach lived and worked.

Every biography of a musician, whether it contains musical quotation or not, depends on the goodwill of its reader. Performance or listening should ideally follow reading. It is possible that a boy or girl reading casually a life of Mozart or Chopin or Schumann could be satisfied with the drama of events and never feel impelled to look further. Mercifully Bach's life contains neither secret romances nor dramatic interludes. It is a life of hard work, good sense and natural behaviour which must impress by its very plainness, a life so completely made for and by music that the move from a book to a record, a piano or a concert seems inevitable. Not every biography calls for action, but the biography of a musician may be, for a receptive child, a glorious invitation to participate.

Reading List

David, Hans T. and Mendel, Arthur. THE BACH READER (*Norton* revised edition 1966) *Dent* 1967. With photographs and prints.

Dickinson, A. E. F. THE ART OF J. S. BACH. *Duckworth* 1936. 2nd revised edition, London, *Hinrichsen* 1950–51. For those who know some of Bach's music, a persuasive analysis, in moderately simple terms, of the images and techniques of the various works.

Forkel, Johann Nikolaus. J. S. BACH: HIS LIFE, ART AND WORK (*Constable* 1920) *Plenum* 1920. Translated by C. S. Terry. Also in THE BACH READER, q.v. Forkel's short biography includes material from C.P.E. and Johann Friedmann

Bach. For its lively anecdotes and open regard it is unique and should not be
missed by any enthusiast.

Freeman, W. S. and Whittaker, R. H. GREAT COMPOSERS. *Abelard-Schuman*
1959. With drawings.

Geiringer, Karl, in collaboration with Irene Geiringer. THE BACH FAMILY:
SEVEN GENERATIONS OF CREATIVE GENIUS (*Allen and Unwin* 1954) *Oxford
University Press* 1954 U.S.A. Illustrated by photographs and prints. A valuable
source of information and illustration.

Gough, Catherine. BACH. Volume 2 of BOYHOODS OF GREAT COMPOSERS
(*Oxford University Press* 1960) *Walck* 1960. Illustrated by Edward Ardizzone.
A simple domestic account for readers from eight or nine, with relatively little
comment on Bach's music.

Grew, E. M. and S. BACH. Master Musicians. (*Dent* 1947) *Farrar, Strauss* 1949
Illustrated by photographs and prints. An authoritative book suggesting many
aspects of Bach's work which could be more extensively considered.

Harrison, Sidney. THE MUSIC MAKERS. *Michael Joseph* 1962. A rapid survey of
the history of music, with useful and easily understood comments on technical
points, within the capacity of children from about ten.

Holst, Imogen. BACH. Great composers. (*Faber* 1965) *Crowell* 1965. Illustrated
by photographs and prints.

Loon, Hendrik Willem van. THE LIFE AND TIMES OF JOHANN SEBASTIAN BACH.
Harrap 1942. A warm personal tribute.

Manton, Jo. PORTRAIT OF BACH. Story Biographies. (*Methuen* 1957) *Abelard-
Schuman* 1957. Illustrated by Faith Jaques.

Meynell, Esther. TIME'S DOOR. *Chapman and Hall* 1942. A romantic novel about a
young Italian musician who, after reading letters from an ancestor who was
taught by Bach, goes back in time to look at the household. The author uses the
few letters surviving of the Bach family with tact and affection.

Meynell, Esther (as E. M. Moorhouse). THE LITTLE CHRONICLE OF MAGDALENA
BACH (*Chapman and Hall* 1925) *Schirmer* 1925. A story-biography, not written
for children, but most approachable and with great charm.

Mirsky, Reba Paeff. JOHANN SEBASTIAN BACH. *Follett* 1965. Illustrated by
Steele Savage.

Pirro, André, J. S. BACH (*Crown* 1957) *Calder* 1958. Illustrated by photographs
and prints. An analysis in fairly advanced terms, but also a useful quarry for
illustrative material.

Scholes, Percy A. THE BOOKS OF THE GREAT MUSICIANS: A COURSE IN
APPRECIATION FOR YOUNG READERS (*Oxford University Press* 1920 U.K.)
Oxford University Press 1949 U.S.A. The manner of the book is too jocular for

today's children, but the author makes many interesting points about particular works. See also his OXFORD JUNIOR COMPANION TO MUSIC (*Oxford University Press* 1954 U.K.) *Oxford University Press* 1954 U.S.A. for reference.

Schweitzer, Albert. BACH (*Breitkopf and Härtel* 1911) *Macmillan* 1962. Translated by Ernest Newman. Modern Bach scholars consider Scweitzer's detecting of symbolic phrases in Bach's works goes too far, but this pioneer book of biography and interpretation should not be overlooked.

Spitta, Philipp. J. S. BACH (Leipzig 1873. *Dover* 1899) *Novello* 1951. A standard source book.

Terry, C. S. THE MUSIC OF BACH: AN INTRODUCTION (*Oxford University Press* 1933) *Dover* 1933; BACH'S ORCHESTRA (*Oxford University Press* 1932 U.K.) *Oxford University Press* 1932 U.S.A. and BACH: A BIOGRAPHY (*Oxford University Press* 1928, revised edition 1933 U.K.) *Oxford University Press* revised edition 1933 U.S.A. Standard works for anyone who wants to study Bach's work in some depth.

Thomas, H. and D. L. LIVING BIOGRAPHIES OF GREAT COMPOSERS (*Doubleday* 1959) *W. H. Allen* 1959. Illustrated by Gordon Toss.

Westcott, Frederic. BACH. Composers and their times. (*Garnet Miller* 1967) *Walck* 1967. Illustrated by Charles Keeping.

Wheeler, Opal and Deucher, S. SEBASTIAN BACH: THE BOY FROM THURINGIA (*Dutton* 1937) *Faber* 1939. Illustrated by Mary Greenwalt.

Young, Percy M. JOHANN SEBASTIAN BACH: THE STORY OF HIS LIFE AND WORK. Great Masters. *Boosey and Hawkes* 1960. With photographs and prints.

Young, Percy M. GREAT IDEAS IN MUSIC. Great Ideas series. (*Robert Maxwell* 1967) *D. White* 1970. Illustrated by diagrams. A useful books for readers in the 'teens, with a particularly good chapter on Bach's Preludes and Fugues.

4b | *Helen Keller*

The utmost bound to which my thought will go with clearness is the horizon of my mind. From this horizon I imagine the one which the eye marks.
Helen Keller. THE WORLD I LIVE IN, pp. 74–5

4b | *Helen Keller*

HELEN KELLER has been called a citizen of the world, and in the climate of today this seems the most promising aspect of her remarkable life to use as the theme of a junior biography. The actual definable means by which the blind-deaf child was taught to communicate seem as remarkable now as they did eighty and more years ago, though less surprising in the light of modern medical and psychological research. But if the heart of biography is the interpretation of character, we should be ready to help a young reader to look deeper, to look behind the long effortful training to the person who had the temperament to work for her freedom and the inclination to use it in the service of others. We should help them to see Helen Keller as a person, not as the prodigy Anne Sullivan vowed she should never be nor the saint Helen Keller herself has never wished to be called. Pity it is that almost all the junior biographies of this strong-minded and generous-hearted woman belong to hagiography. Momentarily vivid in their accounts of her childhood – as they might be in describing a young St Joan, a young St Teresa – they surround her adult life with mists of adulation so that the individual is lost to view.

Here is one of those "patterns of living" which in theory can be an inspiration to the young but which in practice are only too apt to attract didactic, emotionally cold writing: purpose kills the person. There is a special problem also in the case of Helen Keller. The story of someone triumphing over a disability is bound to awake sentimentality, which in this case means that an author will cease to be interested in the individual because he is obsessed by the condition. At the least this constitutes a lack of tact when the subject is a dignified, reticent woman who always wanted above all to be treated like an ordinary person; nor is it honest to present

Photograph of Helen Keller from THE THREE LIVES OF HELEN KELLER (Hodder
& Stoughton), by courtesy of The New York Times

so interesting a person to the young as a monument to the virtues
that Helen Keller undoubtedly possessed.

Perhaps this is unavoidable when she is inevitably included in
juvenile collections with titles like 100 GREAT MODERN LIVES or
FAMOUS WOMEN, but passages like the following offer a good
reason for not reading the book in question:

> The first duty of you younger people for whom this book is
> written is to make the most of your education, not only to fit

you to earn your living but also to enable you to form your own opinions so that you can decide which of the modern organisations or movements you wish to support. Meanwhile it may help you to read about the public-spirited people who did so much to make improvements; how they set about the task, overcame difficulties and were determined to succeed despite opposition and disappointments.

I. O. Evans. BENEFACTORS OF THE WORLD (1968), Introduction, viii

This kind of thing is no substitute for proper biography.

One symptom of the sentimental approach is the admiring hyperbole, when instead of allowing the facts to speak for themselves, as they very clearly do in the case of Helen Keller, an author indulges in tasteless and unnecessary exclamations. Anyone tempted in this direction could learn from the sturdy common sense of Anne Sullivan. When people marvelled at nine-year-old Helen's letters or her reading, her teacher would always insist that this was no genius but a child of lively intelligence who, after years of darkness and silence, was making good use of her knowledge to catch up her contemporaries as quickly as possible.

The corrective to a sentimental, exaggerated account of Helen Keller's life is more detail and, above all, more careful reading and quotation from the authoritative sources – Teacher's reports and Helen's own books. Given the facts, a child should have no difficulty in appreciating the achievement of Helen and her teacher for what it was – no miracle, no occasion for facile exclamation, but an example of the "union of patience, determination and affection, with the foundation of an uncommon brain".*

If the author of a "life" of Helen Keller can add to the summation of events (the description of Teacher's methods and their results) a perceptive analysis of the characters of the two women and the changes in the pattern of their relationship, this will certainly justify the title "junior biography". It is obvious that a study of Helen Keller is also a study of Anne Sullivan, and vice versa, but it is a fact that while most authors tackle the parallel stories easily

*Arthur Gilman. MISS HELEN ADAMS KELLER'S FIRST YEAR ON COLLEGE PREPARATORY WORK (1898), p. 12

enough, they are not so ready to discuss those differences between the two which kept their life together invigorating and fruitful.

This two-lives-for-one approach need only be an extension of the more usual study of a single person in which his or her relations with other people are studied in depth. The junior or story biography tends to give event precedence over feeling, since it is easier for the writer to present to the young. Events form the basis of the most obviously junior of these lives, Norman Wymer's THE YOUNG HELEN KELLER (1965). The formula of *The Young* series means that events outside childhood are summarised at the end of a narrative which invites the reader to identify with the subject all through. The formula is dangerously simple. Few writers succeed in successfully hiding the join between the full story of youth and the brief summary of maturity. The adult seldom seems to be truly the product of the child. The writer of this type of story biography is writing out of his own knowledge and expects to be reviewed, chosen and often used by adults who may be presumed to have some of the same knowledge. At least when they read of the child Helen they will have some idea of the woman she became. It is not always remembered that few children who read stories of famous childhoods have this background of knowledge and reference.

In Norman Wymer's book they would find an interesting story, almost a junior novel moving from one scene and episode to another, a novel in which almost all essential facts were conveyed through conversation. It is conversation in our own idiom, moreover. The author has used the licence of a "story" to invent talk or to adapt it from first-hand reported speech or narrative. We are led into the domestic atmosphere of Tuscumbia like this:

Arthur Keller beamed with pride at the new baby as she lay gurgling in her cot.

"She's a fine child, Katie – a strong, healthy looking baby," he said.

His wife leant over the cot and gave the baby a playful tickle. "She's rather cute, isn't she? Look at her lovely bright eyes. Do you think she's going to be pretty, Arthur?"

Captain Keller laughed. "Oh, I'm sure she will be. She'll have my good looks!" he teased.

THE YOUNG HELEN KELLER, p. 9

Apart from the clumsy dramatic irony, this is hardly the way a Southern gentleman would talk to his wife in 1880; and a scene so suburbanised, so coyly explicit, will give the reader no sense of period. Yet it is the duty of a biographer to place his subject in the correct historical setting. There can be no justification for reducing Helen and her parents to this trivial level when one of the most important points about Helen's background is the cultural basis for the speech she so laboriously learned. Since she always used finger talk and writing more than oral speech, it is to her books above all that we must go to hear her characteristic mode of utterance, except where crucial sentences that she spoke ("I am not dumb now" being the first) are available to be quoted. As for Anne Sullivan, enough of her forceful sentences have been recorded to make it clear that she used no such commonplace phrases as are credited to her in this book.

The sheer intrusiveness of invented speech is most obvious in Norman Wymer's version of the well-known scene when Helen Keller realised that "everything has a name":

Annie was almost in tears, so great was her joy.
"Oh, Percy, Percy, she *understands!*" Annie cried. "How wonderful – wonderful!"
Helen bobbed down, picked up a handful of earth, and made signs to Annie to tell her the name of that. Then she gave Annie another tap to enquire who she was.
Annie took Helen's hand and spelt T-E-A-C-H-E-R.
"I am your teacher," she said, repeating the letters. She gave a happy little laugh. "Oh, and a very proud teacher, too!"
ibid., pp. 101–102

This particular moment in Helen's life is even more important, in literary terms, in a "Young" presentation than in a full-scale life, for it must be central in the study of her childhood.

The scene has been described, briefly, with feeling and without sentiment, by each of the people concerned. Here is Anne Sullivan, writing to her foster-mother and friend Mrs Hopkins on the very day of the event:

This morning while she was washing she wanted to know the

name for "water" . . . I spelled it, and thought no more about it, until after breakfast. Then it occurred to me that with the help of this new word I might straighten out the "mug–milk" difficulty. We went out to the pump house and I made Helen hold her hand under the spout while I pumped. I spelled "w-a-t-e-r" into her free hand . . . The word coming so close upon the sensation of cold water rushing over her hand seemed to startle her. She dropped the mug and stood transfixed. A new light came into her face. She spelled "water" several times. Then she dropped to the ground and asked its name. She pointed to the pump and the trellis, and then suddenly turning around she asked my name. I spelled "teacher".

Quoted in Helen E. Waite. VALIANT COMPANIONS (1961), p. 49

This description makes Anne Sullivan's methods far clearer than Norman Wymer's paraphrase does and if it seems too much of a teacher report (though the feeling in it is open enough), there is Helen's own account, written in THE STORY OF MY LIFE (1903), that girlish, sincere first book of her 'teens:

> As the cool stream gushed over one hand she spelled into the other the word *water*, first slowly, then rapidly. I stood still, my whole attention fixed upon the motions of her fingers. Suddenly I felt a misty consciousness as of something forgotten – a thrill of returning thought; and somehow the mystery of language was revealed to me. I knew then that "w-a-t-e-r" meant the wonderful cool something that was flowing over my hand. That living word awakened my soul, gave it light, hope, joy, set it free! There were barriers still, it is true, but barriers that could in time be swept away.
>
> THE STORY OF MY LIFE, 1931 edition, p. 27

Is there any need for a writer to guess or to invent what Anne Sullivan *said* on this occasion? If any other criterion is needed than one of good taste, there is the application of common sense. This moment by the well-house was one in which communication between two people was established through hand gestures leading to a coming together of ideas. It was a moment when hands did

the speaking rather than lips. If the scene is to be properly understood, the spoken word must give way here to the hand movements,
and the descriptions of these, which the actors in the scene have
given us.

An extreme instance of this kind of inaccuracy may be found in
Lorena Hickok's THE STORY OF HELEN KELLER (1958), a sentimental anecdotal book which "tells the story" very obviously for
the young. Anne Sullivan had been at the Kellers' home for a very
short time and Helen was still entirely ignorant of words when they
were driven from the big house to the garden house where Anne
had suggested they should stay alone for a time. Describing the
journey, the author rashly interprets and verbalises Helen's
"thoughts":

> The following afternoon Helen was taken for a drive, which she
> loved. But this time she did not return home. Instead, she found
> herself in an unfamiliar place, alone with The Stranger.
>   She accepted it quietly at first. "They'll come and get me," she
> told herself. They always had before.

and again:

> "No! No! No!" she cried fiercely inside herself. "I won't have
> you close to me! I won't! I won't! I hate you! Go away!"
> THE STORY OF HELEN KELLER, p. 29

What the reader needs to realise is that the child Helen had literally
no way of forming her thoughts; since she had no words, she could
react only in physical, instinctive movements and expressions.
Through slipshod thinking the inner point of the incident has been
lost.

In principle it must be accepted that children respond easily to a
fictionalised medium for information and that the story-type
biography is likely to make the best introduction to a person for a
child as young as nine – the age for which the books by Norman
Wymer and Lorena Hickok seem suitable. But should children
as young as this be introduced to remarkable people through books
at all? It might be preferable if a teacher or a parent were to tell
young children about Helen Keller out of her own knowledge and

enthusiasm. Biography, as a considered interpretation of fact and character, may be best left for children of thirteen upwards who could bring a small amount of basic knowledge, and an interest directly fostered, to one of the more advanced and better balanced junior biographies of Helen Keller.

The word "junior" suggests concessions. Many books and papers have been written about Helen Keller by people who met her at various periods of her long life. She herself wrote eight books and Anne Sullivan's reports on her education are extant. This varied material has to be simplified for the young, but not distorted. To choose what to leave out and what to keep means, first of all, a clear sense of the kind of reader (rather than the age) for which a book is intended.

Phyllis Garlick's CONQUEROR OF DARKNESS (1958) may serve as an example. The choice of episodes and the general approach suggests an age-range of ten or eleven. Less obviously a "story" than Norman Wymer's THE YOUNG HELEN KELLER, this one still takes a narrative form, with mainly invented conversation and with a deliberate filling-out of key episodes. Though the book ends in Helen Keller's late middle age, most of the chapters are concerned with her childhood, school and college days. Yet in spite of the apparent simplicity of the book, the author's nondescript, heavy prose leaves passages of action flat and remote and adds an abstract, theoretical quality to any generalisations about Helen Keller's character or her aims in life. Readers who find the book within their range of intellectual understanding are not likely to find it rouses their enthusiasm or does much to broaden their outlook on the world.

This is a very over-anxious book. The writer is so much concerned to make herself clear that she adds comment where none is needed. The most flagrant example of this occurs in the last two paragraphs of the book. Helen Keller and Polly Thomson have received the gift of a Japanese stone lantern for the garden of the rebuilt Arcan Ridge, where Helen Keller must build her life again after Teacher's death. Helen decides that the lamp must be kept always alight:

It was so like her to be lighting lamps by which people could find their way in the dark. Polly Thompson (sic) said to a friend:

"I think that that lighted lamp in the garden is a wonderful picture of the unquenchable spirit of Helen Keller."

She was right. That unquenchable spirit is an inspiration to us all. For by the grace of God Helen Keller has triumphed over some of the greatest human handicaps. She has learned to conquer the darkness of the blind and deaf, not only for herself but for other sufferers throughout the world. And that is the kind of light that can never be put out.

CONQUEROR OF DARKNESS, p. 95

The conclusion which the writer has so forcibly and sententiously rammed home is implicit in Helen Keller's actions throughout the book. If she had respected the intelligence of her readers she would have let Polly Thomson have the last, entirely adequate word.

The title of Phyllis Garlick's book – CONQUEROR OF DARK-NESS – is significant. This is the story of a miracle rather than the portrait of an individual. The author represents almost as a prig a woman with a sense of humour and a zest for life – qualities far more congenial to the young and far more likely to impress on them the unique nature of this life. When Phyllis Garlick describes the visit Helen Keller paid to Niagara Falls in 1893, when she was thirteen, she paraphrases the girl's own description of her sensations as she stood near the eddies and whirlpools and walked across the suspension bridge over the water. She ends with an addition of her own:

As she stood there in the presence of so much grandeur Helen little knew that an English traveller was to remark before long: "The United States possesses two of the world's wonders – Helen Keller and the Falls of Niagara."

ibid., p. 44

The remark may be apt but it does nothing to show us the child at Niagara. Helen felt awe and amazement at the scene, but she was a mischievous girl, after all. As she stood on Canadian soil she exclaimed "God save the Queen", and when Anne Sullivan exclaimed "You little traitor!" she defended what seemed to her a properly tactful tribute to the British monarchy.

It is this note of individuality that Phyllis Garlick misses so often in her anxiety to press the moral of her book. She seems unwilling to allow any lighter moments. She quotes from MIDSTREAM (1929) the deaf-blind woman's expressive reply to the people who asked her absurd questions:

> "I tell them that blind people are like other people in the dark, that fire burns them, and cold chills them, and they like food when they are hungry, and drink when they are thirsty, and some of them like one lump of sugar in their tea, and others more!" ibid., p. 76

But in quoting this passage as direct speech, Phyllis Garlick omits the phrase that begins it – "Putting on my Job-like expression" – and so she loses that tone of mildly impatient humour so typical of Helen Keller.

The subject has slipped away from the young readers as she did at Niagara or in this rapid summary of her writing:

> When the stage interlude was over they lived at home again and Helen worked at her voice practice and settled down to write two books which she had promised her publishers. One was the second story of her life which she called *Midstream*. It was a good description for she was now well launched on her voyage of discovery on behalf of those who like herself had to live in the dark.
> ibid., p. 81

Here was a chance to illustrate graphically the extraordinary difficulties Helen Keller met as a writer, and the combination of tenacity and respect for literature which helped her through draft after draft of her later books. Nella Braddy Hennan's introduction to MIDSTREAM describes a method of collating notes, composing, transcribing, reading over in Braille, rearranging, redrafting, which could not but clarify in a *practical* way just what Helen Keller accomplished – not as a miracle but as an exceptional woman.

No junior biography so far written really makes full use of Helen Keller's own books, although all the authors concerned seem to have studied or at least read THE STORY OF MY LIFE and MIDSTREAM.

These two books have been used as quarries for *fact* from which accurate calendars of the events of her life could be put together. Only J. W. and Anne Tibble in their book for the young, HELEN KELLER (1957), seem to have realised the importance of her own writings as a key to her personality. Yet it must be obvious that a woman who employed oral speech only with difficulty and who could communicate on her fingers only with certain people, must, if she writes at all, use the written word as an especially personal medium. While we only hear Helen Keller speak directly through reports of her friends, and then only briefly, in her books we can discover her humour, her sincere belief in God, her energy, her enjoyment of people and her occasional impatience with them, the whole of her womanliness. Even if the writer of a junior biography decides to keep quotation to the minimum, at least such *examples* as Helen Keller gives for various of her states of mind, opinions, circumstances, could be used in some form or another in building up a portrait of her.

Instead of the usual generalised description of the effect of blindness and deafness on her life, biographers could have used one of the many illustrations she has given herself, especially in that fascinating collection of essays, THE WORLD I LIVE IN (1908). We are told that Dr Howe bandaged his eyes to try to experience something of the world of the blind before he began to teach the blind-deaf Laura Bridgman. Few young readers would be prepared to go so far to understand what Helen Keller's world was like; nor will they find much in her books about its limitations, for it was her nature to find compensations and ways in which she could approximate to an ordinary life. So she always defended her use of the word "see" because she knew that imagination could make pictures for her and that they could be, and were, enriched by the inspired help of her friends. As she put it, "Since my education began I have always had things described to me with their colours and sounds by one with keen senses and a fine feeling for the significant."

If the young cannot approach her deprivation very closely, they can appreciate the positive side of it if biographers will allow them to do so. They can read what she says of her hands, of the freedom she enjoyed in dreams, of her response to vibrations:

One day, in the dining-room of an hotel, a tactual dissonance arrested my attention. I sat still and listened with my feet. I found that two waiters were walking back and forth, but not with the same gait. A band was playing, and I could feel the music-waves along the floor. One of the waiters walked in time to the band, graceful and light, while the other disregarded the music and rushed from table to table to the beat of some discord in his own mind. Their steps reminded me of a spirited war-steed harnessed with a cart-horse.

THE WORLD I LIVE IN, 1933 edition, pp. 31-2

This was no resigned, withdrawn spirit, but a vital woman, equipped to use what she had been told, enjoying the feel of life going on round her – the woman who found the world of vaudeville amusing and "liked to feel the warm tide of human life pulsing round and round me". Over and over again Helen Keller provided apt details like this, for which her biographers have substituted heavy generalisations of their own.

Similarly the clues to the relationship between Helen Keller and her Teacher have been ignored, or discarded, partly because this aspect of Helen Keller might seem beyond the experience of the young. There is a noticeable drop in the temperature of junior biographies once they have seen her through college, as though her adult life, with its widely-spaced events and its steady tempo of service, could not be brought to life. It may be less easy to describe in terms persuasive to the young a tour round the hospitals after the war than to invite them to understand the feelings of a blind girl alone in a tree during a storm. One way is open, however – to see the two women together and to trace, in simple terms deriving from Helen Keller's own words, how the love between them survived changes; to see how Teacher gradually pushed her pupil towards independence until, as Helen Keller wrote, "As I grew more mature, she let loose upon me all her varied moods and because of this I was not taken unawares by the storms of destiny"; to see how, as Anne Sullivan's health declined, Helen Keller planned for the future, showing herself as strong a character as her teacher.

The differences between the outward-looking, spontaneous, energetic girl and the emotional, inherently pessimistic Irishwoman were, as we guess from Helen Keller's TEACHER (1956), among the most important links between them. All through the years of travelling, lecturing for the blind, demonstrating the teaching of the blind-deaf, the relationship was changing, until when Helen Keller was fifty and Anne Sullivan sixty-four, the last barrier came down. Anne Sullivan talked to her pupil for the first time about the bitter years of her childhood at Tewksbury poorhouse and Helen, as she says, "was conscious of a courage of a new quality flowing into me from the fact of Teacher's crossing that awful desert of neglect to an oasis of education . . ." Children of eleven or so who take up a book about Helen Keller deserve something of this emotional history rather than a mere catalogue of what happened to her during her long life, and they deserve writers who can see the implications and possibilities of writing the life of two people closely linked so that both emerge as real people and not as models for the young.

In Helen Keller's books we can see the compensations she found in her life through imagination, through the sensitiveness of touch, through the felt pattern of nature, through the intuitive help of parents and friends, and, finally, through the power of language. In VALIANT COMPANIONS Helen Waite makes the following important point:

> Helen herself was unconscious that she was accomplishing anything extraordinary. She responded to words the same way another child would to colour or to music. She loved words. Laura Bridgman, overwhelmed by the thought of thousands of words to master, had once cried out, "It makes my head ache to think of so many words!" But to nine-year-old Helen Keller every new word was like a new door into the world that fascinated her.
>
> VALIANT COMPANIONS, p. 94

This innate love of words and an excellent verbal memory were nourished by Anne Sullivan more thoroughly than would have been possible in the pace of a normal life. The result was that Helen Keller's characteristic style in writing, and probably also in her style of speech, was conspicuously literary – which, apart from anything else, makes the invented sentences so often put into her mouth in junior biographies unsuitable as well as banal. Van Wyck Brooks wrote that she "naturally uses archaic and poetic expressions of the sort that children pick up in their reading, words that are seldom heard in the ordinary talk that she rarely hears."*

Her frequent use of Biblical phrases and idioms, her feeling towards a philosophy of life based on books – these are facets of her character almost wholly neglected by her biographers. They might have quoted, for instance, from that most revealing poem, "The song of the stone wall", in which Helen Keller, with help and encouragement from Anne Sullivan, put so much of her acquired feeling for tradition and so much of her personal response to nature. How much could be sensed by a young reader in the following piece:

> The wall is an Iliad of granite: it chants to me
> Of pilgrims of the perilous deep,
> Of fearless journeyings and old forgotten things.
> The blood of grim ancestors warms the fingers
> That trace the letters of their story;
> My pulses beat in unison with pulses that are stilled;
> The fire of their zeal inspires me
> In my struggle with darkness and pain.
> These embossed books, unobliterated by the tears and laughter
>   of Time,
> Are signed with the vital hands of undaunted men.
> I love these monoliths, so crudely imprinted
> With their stalwart, cleanly, frugal lives.
> "The song of the stone wall", published as "The chant of the stone
> wall" (1910), p. 14

This poem is mentioned only in the Tibbles' HELEN KELLER, and then only briefly.

Biographers who fear to exaggerate or falsify their portrait of Helen Keller have only to look at her writings as a corrective, yet they seldom seem to look. Two women so much in the public eye must necessarily become somewhat unreal to their public, but they must not become unreal to their biographers. The exaggeration of fact has produced some errors and false emphasis in Eileen Bigland's THE TRUE BOOK ABOUT HELEN KELLER (1957). This

*HELEN KELLER: SKETCH FOR A PORTRAIT (1956), p. 155

competent survey, which would in most respects serve as a good introduction for young readers, suffers from the author's desire to emphasise the extraordinary nature of Helen Keller's journey into light. She is seldom content to let facts make their own impact. Over and again she offers comments of this kind:

> Her determination to learn everything she possibly could was so fierce that we are tempted to believe that somehow she knew how important her own battle with life was to be to untold thousands of other blind and deaf people all over the world.
> THE TRUE BOOK ABOUT HELEN KELLER, p. 13

She quotes a letter which Helen wrote to the poet Whittier when she was nine, and remarks:

> Such a letter would be remarkable were it written by a normal girl of nine years old. When one remembers it was penned by a blind, deaf and dumb child who had no knowledge of the meaning of words two years previously, it is almost miraculous.
> ibid., p. 85

But if she had chosen to comment on Anne Sullivan's choice of books for the child or her passionate love of poetry and poetic prose, then for the child Helen, for whom education was a delightful adventure in freedom, to write "When I walk out in my garden I cannot see the beautiful flowers but I know that they are all around me; for is not the air sweet with their fragrance?" would seem perfectly natural.

Again, Eileen Bigland quotes another letter written when Helen was nearly nineteen, while she was on holiday in New England:

> I do wish . . . that you could see the beautiful view from our piazza, the islands looking like little emerald peaks in the golden sunlight, and the canoes flitting here and there, like autumn leaves in the gentle breeze, and breathe in the peculiarly delicious fragrance of the woods, which comes like a murmur from an unknown clime.

and adds her reflection:

It is almost incredible that such a descriptive passage should come from one both blind and deaf. Assuredly Helen Keller had walked a long, long way along the road to happiness and freedom.

ibid., pp. 120–21

Helen Keller's response to the world around her does not become less remarkable if we can see how it was born, if we can read of the friends who talked colours to her and of the way Anne Sullivan fed all senses through their finger talk, so that it was possible for Helen to see as well as to round out the picture from the historical and literary background of a place. The letter quoted, so far from being "almost incredible", is a natural, spontaneous and moving example of her communication with Teacher; the quotation would have more value for the reader if it had been left without annotation.

Calling something a miracle does not necessarily convince anyone that it was one. Far better if a writer describes Anne Sullivan's teaching of the child for what it was, a superb piece of intuitive communication between a spirited but deprived child and a young woman who knew what it was to be so deprived (literally so, for Anne Sullivan's eyes, neglected in childhood, were often almost useless to her). The intimacy between Teacher and her pupil is not properly explained until we allow that the two of them – the child of seven and the young woman of twenty-one – began straight away learning *together*.

Anne Sullivan's passion for the best – in books, in natural scenes, in human relations – was as strong as her natural recognition of what was the best. But she was well aware of the deficiencies in the education she had had to fight for, and once she had succeeded in communicating with Helen she had to work hard, sometimes painfully hard, to be able to give the girl the intellectual and emotional food she needed. It is one of the most important factors of their relationship that Helen came to realise this and to recognise it as yet another point of greatness in Teacher.

In her portrait of her she has much to say of the way Anne Sullivan taught her through nature; how she used the fossils sent by an uncle as the basis of lessons, how she made contour maps in mud on the banks of the Tennessee river, how she let a cageful of pigeons out in a room so that the child should "feel the air from their wings and know about the flight of birds and conceive the glory of wings". So much many teachers might have done, just for their pupils; but Anne Sullivan was working all the time to make herself worthy of her task. Helen Keller knew this; she wrote:

> . . . it was not simply knowledge she wanted, but choice English for herself and Helen and the thousand little graces and amenities which betoken true culture and refinement. In a sense she and Helen were children growing up together, but Annie blushed over the gaps in her education while Helen danced her way through her lessons and poured herself out in play.
>
> TEACHER, p. 51

In the face of such an honest and loving picture of Anne Sullivan as a teacher, exaggeration seems impossible. Yet it was possible for the authors of a junior biography of her, THE SILENT STORM (1963), to foist upon unsuspecting readers a sensational picture with the kind of crude vigour that only too easily makes its false impression. Taking up the hint that Anne Sullivan was apt to drop into brogue in moments of stress, they have reconstructed certain scenes in which the girl first outfaces Arthur Keller on the question of discipline and then wards off a tender proposal from her own former teacher, Michael Anagnos, in each case in sentences of some vulgarity.

Since THE SILENT STORM is a story-version of Anne Sullivan's life, up to Helen's graduation day, invented or deduced conversation is perhaps to be expected, but some degree of tact might also be expected. Besides, the authors have taken liberties with fact in order to make a good story. For example, anticipating Anne Sullivan's teaching methods, which in fact were very gradually worked out, they describe a situation in which she builds a snow-lady, just before leaving the Perkins Institute where she has been educated, and Mrs Anagnos remarks to Mrs Hopkins that she should go to art school:

> "Oh no!" Annie breathed aloud. She stood perfectly still in the moonlight, no longer hearing the sounds about her, only the voice within herself: "I would not fashion forms. I would not shape the snow. 'Tis more than this I want." Putting the rest of

the thought into words frightened her. "Might . . . just *might* I
sculp a soul?"
Marion Marsh Brown and Ruth Crone. THE SILENT STORM,
p. 18

Nella Braddy, in her definitive life of Anne Sullivan, records as an
incident that Anne made a snowman to amuse the children during
her days at Perkins, but the date of the incident has been arranged
to give the opportunity for presumptuous and unwarranted statements about its significance.

In another contrived scene Anne Sullivan talks to Mrs Hopkins
about training as a teacher:

> "I doubt that I could teach in the routine way – the way that's
> expected of teachers. I'd always be wanting to let the poor
> little children up out of their seats. I'd . . . Oh, it's such a false
> situation, a schoolroom. If I could teach from life . . ."
> ibid., p. 81

It is a matter of recorded fact that Anne Sullivan's free interpretation of "lessons" did not occur to her at this stage but only when
she had had time to see the problem that Helen Keller's condition
had set. Indeed, few biographers give enough weight to Anne
Sullivan's uncertainty about her future or to her concentrated study
of Dr Howe's notes on Laura Bridgman. We cannot admire her
methods properly unless we know the facts of her apprenticeship
to teaching and realise that her career did not begin, as it were, on
the doorstep of the Kellers' house at Tuscumbia. This kind of
distortion means that we are looking at the portrait of a person
who does not really exist.

THE SILENT STORM was published in 1963. More recently,
Mickie Davidson has covered the same ground in HELEN
KELLER'S TEACHER (1965). She evidently went for her material
to Nella Braddy's ANNE SULLIVAN MACY (1933) and she has
certainly been influenced by the dignity of that biography. With
Helen making her entrance only halfway through the book, Mickie
Davidson chooses from Anne Sullivan's early life such incidents as
will suggest reasons for her outstanding gifts as a teacher – the
fairy-tales her father told her in early days, old Maggie Carroll

reading aloud at the poorhouse, her friendship with Laura Bridgman. Her close attention to Dr Howe's methods with Laura is
given full weight; and only in this book, perhaps, will a reader
realise that the tremendous burst of intelligence when the young
Helen connected "water" and the word spelled in her hand
was almost exactly echoed thirty years before, when Dr Howe
put a key in Laura's hands and saw "a light flash across" her
face.

On the whole, when Mickie Davidson invents conversation she
does it for a purpose, and to emphasise the importance of this
realisation for a deaf-blind child she constructs dialogue between
Helen's mother and Teacher on that first day at Tuscumbia, when
Teacher made the letters d-o-l-l in Helen's hand:

> "It's just mimicry – excellent monkey work. Helen can make the
> symbols of the word "doll" now, but she doesn't have the
> remotest idea that those particular finger movements stand for
> all the dolls in the world. I've got to get that across to her. I'll
> have to repeat and repeat and repeat, over and over again, word,
> object – word, object. And one day she'll connect them for
> herself."
> HELEN KELLER'S TEACHER, pp. 110–11

There is no Irish brogue in this simple, straightforward book,
and the author is restrained in guessing Anne Sullivan's thoughts.
Occasionally sentimental (for instance, when she pictures the girl
musing before her graduation and after), she can also be very much
to the point. After one of Helen's tantrums, Anne Sullivan retires
to her room to think about her pupil:

> Suddenly her mind was flooded with pictures of another little
> girl. A girl who destroyed things: loaves of bread, her father's
> shaving mirror, and one Christmas the most beautiful doll in the
> world.
> "If only somebody had cared enough to tell me when I was
> wrong, and to show me there was another way," Annie thought
> now. "If only I'd had somebody to be really firm with me when I
> struck out. *If only I'd had somebody who really cared.*"
> ibid., p. 154

In a book for youngish readers, such moments need to be clearly defined. For the same reason it is natural that such a book should end, virtually, with Helen's first visit to the Perkins Institute when she was still a child. The last chapter, taking the story up to Teacher's death, is only a summary. Simple, at times over-dramatic, with a clipped, short-paragraphed form possibly reflecting a serialised origin, and more than a little "told to the children" in its general effect, still HELEN KELLER'S TEACHER is an acceptable alternative to THE SILENT STORM. But there is still no book that gives to the young the kind of authentic, honest picture which Nella Braddy's ANNE SULLIVAN MACY could give to an intelligent reader in the 'teens. Unfortunately this book has long been out of print and is not easy to find. It has the supreme value of authenticity. Nella Braddy worked as amanuensis with both Teacher and Helen Keller and became their friend; her material came either from them, from Polly Thomson (Helen Keller's companion after Teacher's death) or from close friends. The author never invents conversation; she never intrudes into private thoughts or deduces what she has not been told. When she quotes, you hear the real voice ringing through – as when she passes on Anne Sullivan's remark to her, "The truth of a matter is not what I tell you about it, but what you divine in regard to it."

In spite of its title, ANNE SULLIVAN MACY is a dual biography, though it is the only reliable source for the facts of Anne Sullivan's early life. This early life, if discussed with decent reticence and due proportion, can make the best introduction to the story of Helen Keller; without knowing something of the background of her teacher, no reader can properly understand her development. In a prefatory note to VALIANT COMPANIONS, Helen Waite records that she has consulted sources and individuals and has taken pains not to invent talk but to deduce it, where necessary, from written record or report. Keeping a balance between the joint subjects of her book, she uses the form of a story and neatly cuts in explanatory details where they are needed. She opens with a pleasantly homely description of Anne Sullivan being dressed by Mrs Hopkins for the Perkins Commencement and then switches our attention to Tuscumbia and the child Helen; the two characters are then very naturally brought together.

Anne Sullivan speaks with her own voice. Helen Waite quotes

from her letter (see page 344) instead of describing the episode by
the pump in her own words, and in other passages too she takes us
nearer to the actual event. Here, for instance, is a fragment of talk
known to be authentic, turned into part narrative, part direct
speech. Anne Sullivan is reluctantly writing a report on her pupil
for Anagnos, in 1887:

> Annie surrendered reluctantly, but the report gave her a hard
> time, and Helen was puzzled by the many sheets of torn and
> crumpled paper scattered around Teacher's chair that day!
> "When I sit down to write, my thoughts freeze, and when I get
> them down on paper they look like wooden soldiers all in a row,"
> Annie complained ruefully, "and if a live one happens along, I
> put *him* into a strait-jacket!"
> VALIANT COMPANIONS, p. 75

VALIANT COMPANIONS is a broad, honest book. It gives little
of the personality of Helen Keller, rather more of Anne Sullivan's;
taking a strict literary definition, it is hardly a biography but rather
the story of two friends, allies, fighters for freedom. It is sometimes
over-exclamatory, sometimes impeded by small details, but there
are few false notes and a great deal that is drawn directly from Helen
Keller's own writings. It could be judged the best of those junior
books which take a narrative form.

The emphasis on service in VALIANT COMPANIONS is even more
noticeable in THE HELEN KELLER STORY by Catherine Owens
Peare. In this book the author has extended the scope of story
biography by relating the education available for the deaf, blind
and deaf-blind in Helen Keller's time to the situation in the present
which owes so much to her. A foreword by the administrative
vice-president of the Industrial Home for the Blind in New York
points the direction of the book, which includes advice on how to
behave to people disadvantaged in this way and drawings demonstrating the one-hand alphabet. Some of Catherine Peare's
interpolations about this specialised education seem to drop
heavily into her narrative but elsewhere her timing is judicious; for
example, an unusually full account of Helen Keller's advisory visit
to Japan provides a natural opportunity for a discussion of the provision of deaf-blind education in the United States then and now as a

preliminary to clear facts about the results of that inspiring visit. The thesis of this book has influenced the author's choice of episodes and details very strongly. She does not discuss Helen Keller's character in any depth. It is all the more tantalising to come upon occasional passages which suggest that she could have written a biography considerably franker and more shrewd than most others currently available. When she discusses Anne Sullivan's failing health she points out the strain of a pupil who was dependent on her and yet was "filled with tremendous energy and drive and the will to accomplish as much as possible in every day". Everyone who is interested in character must regret that a perceptive comment like this was not taken further, for it suggests a real understanding of a relationship which has so often been written of in tones of vague reverence.

Again, writing of Helen Keller's relief at leaving the United States for a holiday in England after a time of exacting work, Catherine Peare adds:

> Helen Keller did not quite realize that her whole life was in a way idyllic, surrounded by those who loved her. The friends that she enjoyed were nearly all extraordinary people who were filled with exceptional generosity and thought for others. She had never really worked in an average group, where good and bad, honest and dishonest, selfish and generous are mingled together. She studied human misery and worked to end it, but she had never really lived in slum conditions or poverty herself. As a result, some of the things she has written do seem rather over-sweet, but they are a true representation of her thoughts. A trace of Little Lord Fauntleroy can be found in all of her thinking.
> THE HELEN KELLER STORY, pp. 143–4

Earlier in the book a page or two about Helen Keller's exploration of socialist theories promises to be equally candid but the author did not choose to explore the relevant essays and letters written by Helen Keller and the socialism that so much agitated her friends is dismissed almost as an aberration, rather than being considered fairly in the context of a particular period of her life. THE HELEN KELLER STORY is an uneven book but it deserves to be read for one reason. The author has described Helen Keller as a woman working for a cause, and she has discussed this work not in idealistic terms but with proper documentation and bracing good sense.

Those who prefer a broader account of Helen Keller's life, without either dramatised scenes or selective treatment, may find what they want in the short, sober study by J. W. and Anne Tibble, HELEN KELLER. In this narrative there is no invented talk and only a moderate degree of dramatising of event. Indeed, the account of the scene in the pump-house is almost too restrained. The authors seem primarily interested in the way Helen Keller was taught. They analyse Anne Sullivan's methods in some detail, using her reports and Helen Keller's own books as their sole source so as to avoid being influenced by other people's ideas. Their sense of proportion throughout show Anne Sullivan's success and Helen Keller's determination in their true light:

> Those who were closest to Helen knew well enough that she was simply a clever, bright, and attractive child, not at all shy – and certainly not at all saintly.
> HELEN KELLER, p. 44

This sensible statement is related to their comment that Mr Anagnos "compared her to Wisdom springing full grown from the head of Zeus". They stress Anne Sullivan's determination that Helen should develop in her own way:

> A tall, strong child – her movements were free, graceful, and full of mimicry. Already she was known in many parts of the world. She was as generous-minded as she was fond of company. Yet at the same time she was independent and often liked to be alone. Anne had never tried to alter her, even if that would have been possible. Anne had such faith in the young that she believed they should chiefly be helped to unfold their powers.
> ibid., p. 51

They stress, too, how good literature provided Helen Keller with a special kind of freedom. Although their book does not give a full portrait of the two women – in particular we feel little of their very individual senses of humour – this is a fine description of the power of imagination working in teacher and pupil; as such, it is a book

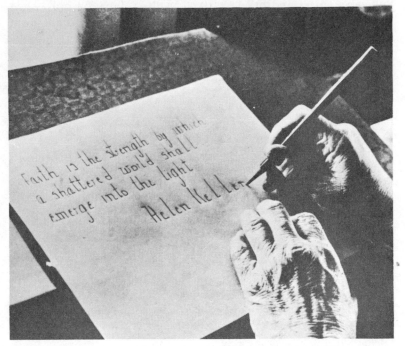

Faith is the strength by which
a shattered world shall
emerge into the light

Helen Keller

Photograph from THE THREE LIVES OF HELEN KELLER (Hodder & Stoughton), by courtesy of the General Research and Humanities Division, The New York Public Library, Astor, Lenox and Tilden Foundations

for a thoughtful child, as it analyses the forward movement by which the child called Phantom by her older self grew into a woman with a unique contribution to make to a crowded world. It is a book to provoke thought all the more because the authors, while obviously writing from admiration, keep themselves out of the way and let the story tell itself, the reader find out for himself.

In the end, though, perhaps all of us are more likely to find Helen Keller in her own words – in that touching portrait of Phantom or in the words about Teacher which say so much about herself. Unfortunately very little original contemporary material is accessible to the young. Alongside a good junior biography they would be well served by a selection from Helen Keller's writings, Anne

Sullivan's letters and other material, with explanation only when necessary. I would trust them to draw their own conclusions from such material.

Reading List

Bigland, Eileen. THE TRUE BOOK ABOUT HELEN KELLER. True Books.
 (*Muller* 1957) *S. G. Phillips* 1967. Illustrated by Janet Pullan.

Braddy, Nella. ANNE SULLIVAN MACY: THE STORY BEHIND HELEN KELLER.
 Doubleday 1933.

Brooks, Van Wyck. HELEN KELLER: SKETCH FOR A PORTRAIT (*Dutton* 1955)
 Dent 1956.

Brown, Marion Marsh and Crone, Ruth. THE SILENT STORM: A STORY OF
 ANNIE SULLIVAN AND HELEN KELLER (*Hale* 1963) *World's Work* 1964.
 Illustrated by Fritz Kredel.

Davidson, Mickie. HELEN KELLER'S TEACHER (*Scholastic Book Services* 1966)
 Macdonald 1969. Illustrated by Sally Stiff.

Evans, I. O. BENEFACTORS OF THE WORLD (*Warne* 1968 U.K.) *Warne* 1968 U.S.A.
 Illustrated by George Craig.

Fuller, Sarah. HOW HELEN KELLER WAS TAUGHT SPEECH. Washington, *Gibson
 Bros.* 1905. The authority for a vital aspect of Helen Keller's education as a
 young woman, this book consists of a report by Sarah Fuller, who taught her,
 and letters from Helen Keller to her, written some years later.

Garlick, Phyllis. CONQUEROR OF DARKNESS. Stories of Faith and Fame.
 Lutterworth 1958.

Gilman, Arthur. MISS HELEN ADAMS KELLER'S FIRST YEAR OF COLLEGE
 PREPARATORY WORK. Washington, *Gibson Bros.* 1898.

Harrity, Richard and Martin, Ralph G. THE THREE LIVES OF HELEN KELLER
 (*Doubleday* 1962) *Hodder and Stoughton* 1964. Illustrated with photographs.
 A unique source book; a chronological series of photographs of Helen Keller,
 Anne Sullivan Macy and Polly Thomson, with explanatory captions.

Hickok, Lorena. THE STORY OF HELEN KELLER. Signature Biographies.
 (*Grosset and Dunlap* 1958) *Sampson Low* 1958. Illustrated by Jo Polseno.

Hunter, Edith Fisher. CHILD OF THE SILENT NIGHT (*Houghton Mifflin* 1963)
 Macdonald 1966. Illustrated by Bea Holmes. A fictional account of the life and
 education of Laura Bridgman.

Keller, Helen. THE STORY OF MY LIFE (*Doubleday* 1903) *Hodder and Stoughton*
1903. THE WORLD I LIVE IN (*Hodder and Stoughton* 1908). THE SONG OF THE
STONE WALL as THE CHANT OF THE STONE WALL (*Hodder and Stoughton*
1910). MY RELIGION (*Hodder and Stoughton* 1927). MIDSTREAM: MY LATER
LIFE (*Doubleday* 1929). TEACHER: ANNE SULLIVAN MACY (*Doubleday* 1955)
Gollancz 1956.

Leblanc, Georgette (Mme Maurice Maeterlinck). THE GIRL WHO FOUND THE
BLUE BIRD. *Hodder and Stoughton* 1914. Translated by Alexander Teixeira de
Mattos. A sentimental, high-flown book by a woman who knew Helen Keller
well and included a few interesting facts in her adulation.

Peare, Catherine Owens. THE HELEN KELLER STORY. *T. Y. Crowell* 1959. With
a foreword by Peter J. Salmon, administrative vice president of the Industrial
Home for the Blind, New York.

Samms, Esther. HELEN KELLER: SUCCESS IN DARKNESS AND SILENCE.
Women of Renown. *Newnes Educational* 1953. With photographs. This pamphlet
puts an emphasis on the way Helen Keller was taught and her own contacts
with the blind-deaf. There are interesting photographs of deaf children in
modern schools.

Sullivan, Anne. THE RELIGIOUS EDUCATION OF HELEN KELLER, THE BLIND
DUMB AND DEAF GIRL. London, *Arthur C. Fifield* 1905. A valuable source
book, which Anne Sullivan was persuaded to write by the Rev. Phillips Brooks,
for some years Helen Keller's friend and spiritual adviser.

Tibble, J. W. and Anne. HELEN KELLER. Lives to Remember. (*A. and C. Black*
1957) *Putnam* 1958. Illustrated by Douglas Relf.

Waite, Helen E. VALIANT COMPANIONS (*Macrae* 1959) *Hodder and Stoughton*
1961.

Wymer, Norman. THE YOUNG HELEN KELLER. The Young . . . (*Parrish* 1965)
Roy 1966. Illustrated by William Randell.

4c | *Abraham Lincoln*

... An honest old lawyer, with face half Roman, half Indian, wasted by climate, scarred by a life's struggle.
London journalist, quoted by Meserve in PHOTOGRAPHS OF ABRAHAM LINCOLN, p. 8

4c | Abraham Lincoln

A NATIONAL hero represents not what a nation is but what it would wish to be. The life of Abraham Lincoln, a national hero before his death and a world symbol thereafter, can never be told in moderate terms. His partner William Herndon, who tried to correct what he felt were adulatory portraits by early biographers by an abrasive frankness, was as much of an idolator as his predecessors. But later biographers do not only have to face the fact that Lincoln as a symbol is in essence unassailable. The very nature of the man makes it impossible to present a credible, ordinary human being. Lincoln was not ordinary. His appearance lent itself to caricature, his humour was extreme, his honesty unshakeable. Everywhere he looks the biographer is faced with those photographs – stern, formal and positive. Whatever interpretation he intends, the positive Lincoln is there to confound any suggestion of inconsistency.

The release of the Lincoln papers in 1947 has led to reassessments, fresh detail, a great deal of analysis of primary sources: it has brought no change to the lean-faced man himself. In PORTRAIT FOR POSTERITY (1947), Benjamin Thomas plotted the graph of Lincoln studies like this:

> From these letters the theme of the book emerges as a struggle between two conflicting schools of thought regarding the way to write about Lincoln. One school would depict him as a national hero with all the attributes a national hero was supposed to have. The other school thought he should be represented as he was. At first, public opinion was solidly behind the former view. Gradually it shifted. Now people want the facts. Yet, even those who tried honestly to show us Lincoln as he was, had a feeling of

failure. There was something about the man that the most probing technique could not always penetrate.

PORTRAIT FOR POSTERITY, Preface, x

In terms of biographical studies for children, the position becomes still more difficult. No collection of Great Lives could omit Lincoln. He is the property of the world. Television promotion of Churchill's A HISTORY OF THE ENGLISH-SPEAKING PEOPLES as a paperback serial inevitably included "Lincoln speaks at Gettysburg" among its examples. Children will almost always meet Lincoln first as a symbol, and it may sometimes be hard for them to achieve any broader view of the man, especially in the United States. Jerrold Beim's little tale, THE BOY ON LINCOLN'S LAP (1955), shows the man who "helped to free the slaves" as a father figure. When the good boys have cleaned up the statue that has been defaced by anti-social Danny, a press photographer records their action on the commemorative day "and Alan was sitting on Abraham Lincoln's lap".* Most of all, for the young, it is a case of "From log cabin to White House". This approach has, obviously, been favoured in America since the first life of Lincoln for children was published. In a symposium of 1959 containing memorial essays, poems and sketches by hundreds of American pupils in the 'teens, the dominant note was "his is the greatest of the 'rags to riches' stories", with the corollary "Lincoln is a stirring example, in these days of relative ease, of what can be done under the most difficult circumstances if one has the will to do it."† Now that a comparable career is socially more possible in England than it has been in earlier centuries, children who thirty years ago might admire but not aspire may now, like their fellows in America, think of Lincoln as a model and an encouragement to their efforts to rise in the world.

But if Lincoln is to be an example of the good and the powerful citizen, it stands to reason that he must be presented wholly in a good light – or in what educators would regard as a good light, which is not necessarily to be accepted. Nobody denies Lincoln's

*THE BOY ON LINCOLN'S LAP, p. 46
†Jean D. Grambs (ed.). ABRAHAM LINCOLN THROUGH THE EYES OF HIGH SCHOOL YOUTH (1959), pp. 7–8

honesty, but children of intelligence could be asked to accept that
an honest man spurred by ambition might indulge in political
manoeuvre. Young people today are at the least more obviously
discerning and critical of moral propaganda than they were a
generation or two ago. They could make Lincoln their hero in an
acceptable way if they could get nearer to him as a person. Beside
the customary generalisations and examples of his generosity and
scrupulousness as a lawyer – to take one example – I would like to
see quoted the comment of Henry Clay Whitney, who travelled
the Springfield circuit with him:

> In a clear case of dishonesty he would hedge in some way so as
> not, himself, to partake of the dishonesty. In a doubtful case of
> dishonesty, he would give his client the benefit of the doubt, and
> in an ordinary case he would try the case, as far as he could, like
> any other lawyer, except that he absolutely abjured technicality
> and went for justice and victory, denuded of every integument,
> and Lincoln's honesty was excellent stock-in-trade to him, and
> brought success and victory often.
>
> LIFE ON THE CIRCUIT WITH LINCOLN (1892), quoted in
> PORTRAIT FOR POSTERITY, pp. 169–70

We shall see how far the search for a pattern and an exemplum in
juvenile lives of Lincoln has led to banality, lack of balance, even
misrepresentation and inaccuracy.

Readers from nine or ten deserve not only the truth but also the
whole truth and nothing but the truth. For younger children, who
lack historical perspective and are not as a rule interested in complex
questions of character and motive, simplified stories of the great
will inevitably take on the nature of legend, even of fairy-tale. The
stiff figure of Lincoln, seemingly unsuited to fairy-tale treatment,
is seen in the role of younger son turned prince. As Esther Moorhouse remarked, "there was no great difference between the
cobbler's son who became a prince and the backwoods boy who
became President of the United States of America."*

The writer who introduces a very young reader to Lincoln may
legitimately stress this aspect of the story, but he has a responsibility

*THE YOUNG LINCOLN (1944), pp. 103–4

in that he is establishing a base on which later knowledge will rest. His portrait may be simple, but it must not be silly or trivial. Most obviously in the fairy-tale style is the disarmingly large and prettily coloured picture-book, ABRAHAM LINCOLN (1957) by Ingrid and Parin d'Aulaire. Submitting to the picture-book form, the author-artists have chosen episodes with a suitable atmosphere. Looking at a picture of little Abe and Sarah after their mother's death, standing tearfully hand in hand in front of a stylised forest and log cabin, a child might be forgiven for confusing the story with "Hansel and Gretel". What is offered of truth in the text is annulled, up to a point, by the prettiness of the pictures. Words may inform a child that Abe's childhood was hard, that he wielded an axe and carried water at an age when most children were playing, but the double spread of the Pigeon Creek dwelling hardly suggests a hard childhood. Here in a smooth forest enclave the child Abe chops at a tree in the foreground, father ploughs in the background, mother tends the fire in front of the half-faced camp; horse, cow and calf are neatly aligned in a lean-to, and Sally is glimpsed on her way to the spring with a yoke and buckets – all placed like figures in a toy village set. Similarly the picture of Lincoln saving the old Indian during the Black Hawk campaign suggests nothing more serious than a charade.

If there is nothing so ludicrous in the illustrations of Lincoln's later life, the choice remains a picture-book choice. We see the clerk finding Blackstone in a barrel, the President seized by grateful Negroes in the streets of Richmond. Since it fits the atmosphere of the book, the legend of Lincoln's tragic love for Ann Rutledge is perpetuated and gives rise to the first mention of his melancholy mood:

She was sure he would become a great man some day, if he would just go on with his studies. And then they would be married, and be happy ever after.

But one day Ann Rutledge took sick and nothing could be done to save her life. From that day on it was as if there were two Abes. The one was gay and full of funny stories, the other was so sad and sorrowful that no one dared to approach him. But he did his work and finished his studies, and one morning he took leave of his friends in New Salem. He borrowed a horse, and sad

and penniless he rode off to Springfield, the capital of Illinois,
to become a lawyer.

The implication here is that Lincoln rode off to Springfield almost
on impulse to "become a lawyer"; no mention is made of the
encouragement of his friends or the visits to local courts and "his
studies" seem of brief duration. In a picture-book time and event
are naturally telescoped and one cannot really quarrel with the
concluding sentences, which accompany a portrait of Lincoln on
the balcony of the White House listening to the band playing Dixie:

> . . . he sat down on his rocking chair to rest.
>   He had done what he should do. He had held together the
> great nation brought forth upon this continent by his forefathers.
> ibid.

The purpose of the book – to establish early in life the figure of the
greatest American – is a fair one. It may only be doubted whether
this purpose is best served by making use of a picture-book form
which constrains serious material.

How far *can* Lincoln's life be simplified for young readers? The
Lincoln scholar Earl Schenk Miers has made a more acceptable
simplification in THAT LINCOLN BOY (1968). Written in story form,
the book opens, "Abe remembered nothing of his first home . . ."
and ends as he leaves New Salem for Springfield:

> He still wore his pants fastened by one suspender. And no one
> could have guessed then that he would become the sixteenth
> President of the United States. Or that he would be the com-
> mander-in-chief responsible for saving the Union in the bloodiest
> civil war the world ever had known. Or that he would be the
> author of the Emancipation Proclamation. Or that with the
> exception of Jesus of Nazareth more books would be written
> about him than about anybody who ever lived.
>   Yet this, honestly, is what happened to Abe Lincoln, the
> shirt-tail boy.
>   Every word of it is true.
> THAT LINCOLN BOY, pp. 140–1

The bold claim in the last sentence needs some qualification and there is, in fact, a disclaimer in the "Author's note" that follows, admitting that "Occasionally conversation has been invented. The incidents, as described, occurred."

The creation of dialogue indeed is implicit in the mere fact of dramatising contemporary record as narrative. Once a biographer decides to tell a story, he has to do the best he can to make that story vivid without falsifying the facts. In THAT LINCOLN BOY, which is as close to fiction as biography can get, certain key scenes are described in active form – the Indian attack in which Abraham's grandfather died and his father escaped; the building of the log cabin at Hurricane township; the hiring of Abe by Gentry and his visits to New Orleans. These events are "true" in the broadest sense; but the author gives no indication of where strict fact ends and the embellishment of imagination begins. Perhaps this is allowable when a domestic scene is concerned which sets background rather

Lincoln christens his stepmother's newly-whitewashed wall. Drawing by Kurt Werth from THAT LINCOLN BOY (World).

than suggesting character, but no scene should be built on scanty evidence.

In THAT LINCOLN BOY, four pages are devoted to Abe's first visit to New Orleans with Allen Gentry, two to his second with Denton Offutt, and in each scene the author puts significant words into Abe's mouth. On the first occasion we see him reading the New Orleans *Argus*:

> With a quiet ominousness Abe folded the paper. "It ain't right!" he growled.
>
> Allen shrugged. "You can't argue with custom, Abe."
>
> "Customs can be changed."
>
> "With that bloody gash over your right eye, what do you care about slaves?"
>
> "Would you want to be led around in chains or see your wife sold to some stranger who might take her to a plantation where you might never see her again?"
>
> "No."
>
> "Nor would I," Abe said. "Or would I ever want to own a slave."
>
> ibid., p. 87

Describing the second visit to the slave-trading town, the author falls further into hindsight. Offutt asks, "If you could strike slavery down, you would?" and adds "Just maybe, if you put your mind to it, you may."* It is a fact that Lincoln was present in New Orleans on these two occasions; he can hardly have escaped seeing advertisements concerning slaves or witnessing a slave auction. But there is not enough direct and reputable evidence to support a deduced scene containing so much feeling and such plausible speeches. It may be that Lincoln was touched deeply; it may be that at this particular time he viewed the scene with something of the backwoods hardness that is so evident in the brief sketch he wrote of his life. We do not know. We know that he wrote to Horace Greeley in 1862:

> If I could save the Union without freeing *any* slave I would do it, and if I could save it by freeing *all* the slaves I would do it; and
>
> *ibid., p. 115

if I could save it by freeing some and leaving others alone I would also do that. What I do about slavery, and the colored race, I do because I believe it helps to save the Union; and what I forbear, I forbear because I do *not* believe it would help to save the Union.
Letter to Greeley from Washington, 22 August 1862, quoted in Roy P. Basler. LINCOLN (1961), p. 125

and we know that in another letter, to Joshua Speed, he recalled a river-boat journey they took together from Louisville to St Louis when "there were on board ten or a dozen slaves shackled together with irons". Lincoln continues, "That sight was a continued torment to me, and I see something like it every time I touch the Ohio or any other slave border." That letter was written in 1855, and from the historical point of view it would have been a safer instance to cite than the certainly more dramatic scene in Lincoln's youth which depends on a disputable late testimony from John Hanks.

The celebrated phrase which Lincoln possibly never used – "I'll hit it hard" – was used by Cecil Northcott as the title of a book which produces the following flight of imagination:

As the bidding started and quickly mounted higher and higher, the two young men from Indiana looked on with a growing sense of horror. The coarse face of the auctioneer disgusted Lincoln; the thought of the young girl in such hands nauseated him; the sight of the old worn-out slaves meekly waiting their fate aroused his compassion. As he strode away from the sale-yard with his cousin he felt himself growing hot and angry.

"Dreaming again, Abe?" asked John Hanks that night when they lay silently side by side on the raft.

"No, just thinkin' about them slaves," answered Lincoln. Then, his voice betraying his depth of feeling, he said, "If ever I get a chance to hit this thing *I'll hit it hard!*"
I'LL HIT IT HARD! (1943), p. 7

Apart from the fact that John Hanks was not in fact with Lincoln on this particular occasion, the sentimental rendering of what Lincoln *might* have felt and said transgresses the elementary obligation of anyone who uses historical material.

I'LL HIT IT HARD! is a deliberately popular pamphlet deriving from the English comic *Eagle* and intended for readers of average or below-average tastes and intellects; it is not a book to be discussed in the same breath as THAT LINCOLN BOY. All the same, both books face a common problem, and one that is deeper than that of invented dialogue, Any book on Lincoln, particularly any book written in the last thirty years or so, is bound to be affected by modern ideas of racial integration and discrimination. It is easier to describe the physical background of Lincoln's life with historical imagination – the backwoods, the horseback journeys, the meetings at the New Salem store – than it is to keep hindsight out of any discussion of his personal and political views. It is this difficulty of writing within an historical context that makes me feel it would be better for children not to read any extended account of Lincoln until they are old enough to be given, if not the whole truth, at least nothing but the truth. But it is clear that books will always be provided for all reading ages on this particular subject and, for the earliest reader, THAT LINCOLN BOY makes reasonable provision.

Certainly English children of nine or so would find in it a more balanced idea of Lincoln's position in American and world history than they would in the many Hall of Fame summaries accessible to them. All of these make slavery their central point, and three of them start in the slave-market. A brief essay by Peggy Chambers has a subtitle "The President who freed the slaves", and begins dramatically, "New Orleans on a humid day in the spring of 1828"!*; the author seems confident that the scene she describes really happened in just this manner. J. Walton's MAKERS OF THE U.S.A. (1943) has an "indignant young Westerner" exclaiming, predictably, "If ever I get a chance to hit that thing, I'll hit it hard."† Rhoda Power's more scholarly account in GREAT PEOPLE OF THE PAST (1932) is headed "How a backwoods boy became a President", but the emphasis is still on slavery. Walton is over-positive in his statement:

Millions of men in the North and West loathed slavery and were determined that it should be confined to the States where it

*Eric Duthie (ed.). CHILDREN'S BOOK OF FAMOUS LIVES (1958), p. 239
†op. cit., pp. 51–2

already existed. A national disgrace, it must be curbed and as soon as possible abolished. Abraham Lincoln now stood forth as the champion and leader of these men, and was chosen a candidate for the Presidency.

MAKERS OF THE U.S.A, p. 56

Outlines like these are by their nature biased or misleading. The pity is that an unenterprising boy or girl who skims through a Great Lives compendium may never go any further, feeling he has "done" Lincoln, rather as he might say he had "read DAVID COPPERFIELD" when he had read an abridged or retold version. Can we really afford to make dead-ends like these available without some attempt to lead children further?

The Hall of Fame treatment is dangerous because of its extreme compression of fact. It is also, almost always, painfully dull. Severe limitations of words means that the dramatic element must give place to solid exposition, and for readers between eight and eleven an element of dramatisation is perhaps always desirable. Certainly it can be helpful in historical biography. The advantage of this form for the young is that a series of historical events which could be confusing if it were offered straight may be given shape and clarity when events, causes and principles illustrate the life of a key figure. There is obvious value in introducing children to the American Civil War by means of a biography of Lincoln.

Any biography is in a sense a "story", but we can make a formal distinction between dramatic narrative and plain explanation. In the former the writer will use conversation and descriptive detail and will tell his tale in a way calculated to make the reader feel he is witnessing the scene himself: the latter, more remote from the event, we receive as something past and, as it were, static. The distinction may be conveniently illustrated in three passages describing a single incident during the flatboat journey down the Mississippi which Lincoln made with Allen Gentry when he was nineteen.

In the first passage the author has allowed herself a considerable degree of licence to invent in order to make the scene immediate:

A rough hand on his shoulder awakened Abe. His training through years of sleeping in the forest had taught him to waken instantly.

"Allen!" he yelled. "Allen! Watch out!" As he shouted, Abe twisted free and flung the intruder head over heels into the river. His long arms flailed around in the darkness; he caught two more thieves and tossed them into the water. By then, Allen was up and fighting. They grabbed clubs, which they kept handy, and chased four men to shore.

. . . Abe cast off and took the place at the wide sweep. Only then he noticed that he had a deep cut above his right ear. He bound it up the best he could, but he carried the scar all his life.
Clara Ingram Judson. ABRAHAM LINCOLN, FRIEND OF THE PEOPLE (1954), pp. 60–1

At the opposite end of the scale we have a plain but vivid *account* of what happened:

One night near the end of their run, as Abe and Allen slept on the flatboat, which was tied up at the shore near a Louisiana sugar plantation, a gang of seven homeless Negroes crept on board to kill them and steal the cargo. Abe and Allen fought the thieves with clubs and drove them off in a battle during which Abe knocked several into the water. He received a cut over the eye that gave him a scar for life.
May McNeer. AMERICA'S ABRAHAM LINCOLN (1957), p. 26

The third extract shows how immediacy has been lent to a straight-forward account by the use of quotation:

. . . at a place described as "the plantation of a Madame Duchesne, not far from New Orleans", a band of Negro brigands armed with hickory clubs attacked the craft. The watchful crew fought desperately to save their cargo. Both parties were bleeding when the battle ended, but Abe and Allen had managed to beat off their marauders. Then they "hastily swung into the stream and floated down the river till daylight".
Earl Schenk Miers. ABRAHAM LINCOLN IN PEACE AND WAR (1964), p. 22

None of the passages quoted departs from the truth, though the first one has extended known fact. Very little addition has in fact

Photograph of Lincoln in 1846 from ABRAHAM LINCOLN IN PEACE AND WAR
(American Heritage), by courtesy of the Library of Congress

been needed, for the incident is well authenticated. Not unnaturally
it is this type of incident which is most often chosen for dramatised
treatment; there is more danger in expanding events for which
only a hint or an outline are available. Lionel Ruby has summarised
the position of the junior biographer when he writes about the
historian in general:

When we read Carl Sandburg's ABRAHAM LINCOLN, or a
history of the Civil War, we assume that the historian has received

a substantial part of his information from other historians. But somewhere along the line we find the "first historians" of an event, and these are based upon the testimony of witnesses, and circumstantial evidence.

THE ART OF MAKING SENSE (1969), p. 176

We should be grateful indeed if we could feel that writers for the young had consulted Sandburg at least. Too often the lack of vitality in their books seems traceable to the habit of taking material from each other or from a line of school-books from earlier generations, while it hardly seems to occur to anyone to go to Lincoln himself for material. This is certainly not because his own brief autobiography, and his speeches, are not accessible. More probably the reason lies in the basic motive for junior biography – its purposive character. Lincoln must be offered to the young as a hero. But Lincoln did not attitudinise, did not regard consistency of opinion as a virtue, retained to his last days a certain backwoods hard-headedness. This kind of man is not easy to flatten behind glass to hang on the wall as a sampler. The author who wants to frame him has to select, from his life, scenes that will fit the pattern and ignore the rest.

I have suggested in discussing THAT LINCOLN BOY how Lincoln's life can be arranged to suggest certain points. In THE STORY OF ABRAHAM LINCOLN (1952) by Nina Brown Baker we find an infinitely less scholarly manipulation of fact. In order to domesticate her subject and to draw morals from his life, the author more than once resorts to actual invention. For instance, as the family journeys towards Indiana the seven-year-old boy and his sister converse on the border:

He looked at the Kentucky shore. He looked around him at Indiana. "They don't look no different to me. This state business is just something somebody made up. You can see a river, or a hill. You can't see a state nohow. It's all just land. What's the sense calling it something you can't see?"

THE STORY OF ABRAHAM LINCOLN, p. 12

It cannot be positively stated that such a conversation never took place, nor can it be positively stated that the anecdote told by Herndon is authentic, which describes how Abe and his step-brother John Johnston, tired of being betrayed when they crept out at night by the barking of Thomas Lincoln's yellow coon-dog, killed a coon and sewed the dog into the hide, with the result that the other dogs tracked the animal home and destroyed him. Herndon winds up the story:

> The next morning old Thomas Lincoln discovered lying in his yard the lifeless remains of yellow "Joe", with strong proof of coon-skin accompaniment. "Father was much incensed at his death", observed Mr Lincoln, in relating the story, "but as John and I, scantily protected from the morning wind, stood shivering in the doorway, we felt assured little yellow Joe would never be able again to sound the call for another coon hunt."
> HERNDON'S LINCOLN (1889), vol. i, p. 22, footnote 3

Herndon's anecdotes are not always gospel truth, but he tells them to show Lincoln as a human being; he does not manipulate events to deliver a message to his readers. Fortunately a great many children are protected against evasive writing by native shrewdness.

Nina Baker's book belongs to the fairy-tale category. She perpetuates many stories (the legend of Ann Rutledge, Lincoln's fierce words in New Orleans on the slave question) which are not confirmed by historical scholars. Being over-anxious to put herself on a level with her readers, she gives most of her space to Lincoln's early life, saying little about his career as lawyer and politician and dealing with vital issues in a spirit as domestic as that in which she describes the family in the backwoods. Lincoln is seen writing the Emancipation Proclamation when his son Tad comes to fetch him for a walk. "Just a minute, Tad," says the President, and reads aloud, "and henceforth shall be, free." The little boy asks questions which are answered with jocularity. The scene ends ludicrously:

> "Don't say a word about this, Tad . . . My Cabinet knows about it, and a few other people. You must help us keep it a secret until the right time comes."
> THE STORY OF ABRAHAM LINCOLN, pp. 158–9

Surely a child as young as eight or nine deserves to be given the actual words of at least part of this document, to think about in his own time. But a book as cosy as this would have fallen apart if reality had been allowed to get near it.

Unfortunately this is the only story biography for the middle years that is available in England at the present time. We could with advantage import THAT LINCOLN BOY or, for children ready to tackle something slightly longer and more detailed, May McNeer's AMERICA'S ABRAHAM LINCOLN (1957). This attractive, profusely illustrated book opens with an almost fairy-tale scene:

> Wilderness trees stood thick along the rough roads of Kentucky in 1816. In the pale dawn of an October day stars winked out of sight as two small children walking in the ruts of wagon wheels glanced back at the sight of fire flicker through a cabin door. Then they turned their faces towards Muldraugh's Hill, where Knob Creek rushed over the stones.
>
> The boy was called Abraham, and he walked to school with his sister Sarah. Although he was tall, thin, and big-boned for a seven-year-old, he wore nothing but a homespun shirt that came down below his knees, for he was still young enough to be just a "shirttail boy."
>
> AMERICA'S ABRAHAM LINCOLN, pp. 3–4

The book is pictorial and vivid throughout, and at moments when abstract statement might flatten the narrative, the author resorts to a legitimate extension of facts:

> Even so, most people did not believe that war would last long. In the North people talked in country stores, and on street corners in towns, saying, "Well, if war comes it won't last more than a few weeks." In the secession states young men boasted, "We'll have the Yankees licked in a month, or before." But older men in the South looked grave, and said little, for many of them understood better what was ahead, and many did not want division of the Union.
>
> ibid., pp. 92–3

The balance of narrative and explanation in the book is dictated by its purpose. The title is AMERICA'S ABRAHAM LINCOLN, and the book belongs to a series which is designed to show the part played by certain individuals in the making of a nation (other subjects being Paul Revere, Ethan Allan and Robert E. Lee). Simple and clear as the story is, the emphasis is on the *shaping* of a man. Inevitably hindsight cannot be entirely avoided: it is easy to see why the author should permit herself licence in a passage like the following:

> Among the visitors Abe heard much talk of land deeds. There was the right kind and there was the wrong kind of deed – the pieces of paper that enabled rich men, who had large plantations and many Negro slaves, to get possession of the farms of poor men. He heard his father tell how he had been brought before the law judge as a "trespasser." What was a trespasser?
>
> When Abe heard his father talk about the law, he wondered. Laws could be used against a poor man, who couldn't read and didn't know that he had the wrong kind of papers. Yet laws could protect Tom Lincoln, who had the right kind of deed. His father told him that the United States was built on laws. Laws were important.
>
> ibid., pp. 10–11

The domestic note suitable in this section about a small boy has deepened when the description is of a young man grasping his opportunities:

> He had been part of the village during most of its lifetime, for he came soon after it was built, and now it looked as if the village would not long outlast his leaving. The tall youth with the sad eyes and humorous mouth, who had wrestled, played marbles with children, clerked, and read books here, was now a man on his way to a law practice. He had mastered, on his own, the difficult profession of lawyer.
>
> ibid., p. 50

Exposition is clearly more suitable here than the inventing of an actual scene. Whatever method the author chooses, the facts she uses are carefully chosen to further her theme. Of all the junior studies of Lincoln, this one seems to me to give the best idea of his *development*. His political career is described in the clearest possible terms, and we can see how one office led to another. He appears unmistakeably as a great man, but he is never represented as a miracle; we see how he became great.

Through the proper study of her material, May McNeer has been able to link Lincoln's actions and his principles. She is wary of describing his feelings – words can tilt very easily towards sentimentality – but she relies to some extent on illustration to add the warmth of emotion to her book. Lynd Ward's pictures never go beyond known fact (though in street and crowd scenes they expand and extend fact, obviously) yet they awake the past in a special way which words could less easily accomplish. That February day in 1861 when Lincoln left Springfield to take up his Presidency is one of those scenes that catch out an unwary writer. Confining herself to plain statement, May McNeer records that Lincoln stood "in a misty rain on the rear platform of his train", and that he wore his usual black broadcloth with "a woollen shawl over his high shoulders". Feelings are just suggested in the last sentence of the relevant paragraph:

> The tall gaunt man in his high stovepipe hat stood looking silently at the city of Springfield, and the brown prairies of Illinois, as they disappeared from his sight.
> ibid., p. 90

In the coloured picture of the scene, Lincoln's posture, the hand gripping the rail, the melancholy, attentive face, help the reader's imagination without impeding it.

Very occasionally the artist is persuaded into emotion which most scholars would consider unjustified – as, for instance, when she portrays Lincoln leaning on his axe mourning the death of Ann Rutledge. Most of her pictures are firmly based on fact and on the numerous photographs of Lincoln, so that we are invited to look not at an idealised figure but at an acceptable image of the man as he was, in scenes active enough to interest the young.

Clara Ingram Judson's ABRAHAM LINCOLN, FRIEND OF THE PEOPLE (1954) also owes a good deal to illustration, although in appearance this is less of a picture-book and more of a serious study than May McNeer's. Apart from Robert Frankenberg's pen drawings, which provide minor decorations in the shape of head and tail pieces and occasional insertions in the text, the chief illustrative material consists of kodachrome representations of fourteen from the set of twenty dioramas made for the Chicago Historical Society. These dioramas are far more than running commentaries on a text; indeed, the author uses them as the skeleton of her narrative. This is appropriate because a diorama is essentially a scene combining event and character with background, and the author's library research has been augmented by a conscientious journeying to all the places where Lincoln lived, worked and spoke. A strong emphasis on place, both in words and pictures, makes this a delightful book for English children, who can hardly picture Illinois or Washington for themselves. If May McNeer's aim was to display Lincoln as a man making his mark, Clara Judson's might be said to be to bring the man to life in his environment. Hers is a biography rather than an historical study.

In this biography the dramatic approach is consistent and strong. The opening sentence shows us the four-year-old following his father over a ploughed field, reaching into a bulging sack "at regular intervals for kernels of corn which he dropped into the open furrow"; the book closes with an as-it-were eye-witness account of the scene at Ford's Theatre. The restraint imposed by the form of historical biography is relaxed considerably in this book – not always forgiveably. The over-elaborate account of Sarah Bush Lincoln arriving to take over the motherless household; the sentimentalised scene when Abe rescues his dog from the ice-jammed river ("Jest give me time, Old Fellow", he said quietly, "I'm comin'!"); the scene of Ann Rutledge's death which, though lightly sketched, goes far beyond proven fact; scenes like these spoil the control and veracity of the book as the author tries too hard to humanise the historic figure of Lincoln.

On the credit side there is an amount of apt quotation unusual in a book for juniors and due partly to the author's strenuous perusal of contemporary newspapers as well as of more obvious reference sources. On one or two points she gets nearer to the truth than most writers for the young. The impression usually given of the Gettysburg speech is one of rapid composition, even of improvisation, Clara Judson fills out the picture accurately:

The next day the President and a large party went from Washington to Gettysburg by special train. In his pocket he had the paper he had read to William Slade. On the train he took it out to make a slight change. Men nearby saw him writing and thought that he had carelessly left writing his speech until this last minute.

ABRAHAM LINCOLN, FRIEND OF THE PEOPLE, pp. 189–90

This is a scholarly basis for the story technique.

In AMERICA'S ABRAHAM LINCOLN and ABRAHAM LINCOLN, FRIEND OF THE PEOPLE the techniques of the story-teller and the teacher are used alternately as they are appropriate. These are not historical novels because the story line is not invariable. In any discussion of the treatment of historical fact in historical fiction, Aileen Fisher's MY COUSIN ABE (1962) is especially relevant, since the author's care for accuracy is as marked as the vitality, movement and atmosphere of her story. She has achieved this by putting the story into the mouth of Abe's cousin Dennis Hanks. "We were always together until he was twenty-one years old", Hanks told Herndon, and he went on, "I am the only relative living that was always intimate with him from Birth until his Assassination."* In a preface to MY COUSIN ABE, the Lincoln scholar Paul Angle wrote:

In the statements he made to Herndon, Dennis was not always accurate. Doubtless he exaggerated the intimacy of his relationship with his young cousin, and gave himself more than merited credit for influencing Lincoln's life. But he knew the environment in which he himself had grown up in Kentucky and Indiana, and by recalling it vividly, enabled Herndon to present an imperishable picture of Lincoln's surroundings in his formative years.

MY COUSIN ABE, Foreword by Paul Angle, vii

The author of this outstanding fictionalised biography is well aware that the memories of Dennis Hanks have to be edited. She allows only the barest mention of Ann Rutledge, and will have nothing to do with the popular "scene" in the slave market. Her reconstructions are plausible, built up with discrimination and good

*Dennis F. Hanks, Paris, Illinois, 1877, as communicated to William Herndon

taste and with a carefully controlled imagination. Paul Angle's sensible comment on the novelist's treatment of history applies to this book and to those story biographies I have already discussed:

> Admittedly, Miss Fisher cannot know that when Dennis Hanks unexpectedly appeared at the Lincoln cabin in Indiana young Abraham called out: "Denny! We purt near gave up thinking you'd ever come!" and a few minutes later boasted: "Feel my muscle! I can chop, Dennis. I've been a-chopping ever since we came to Indianny."
>
> But the point is not whether these words were actually spoken, but whether they accord with what we know of Lincoln, Dennis Hanks, and their circumstances at the moment. I think they do. I also think that by this test Miss Fisher's book comes off with a very high mark.
>
> ibid., vii–viii

Aileen Fisher's story is valuable for the immediacy which good fiction can give to historical event; it is also valuable for its moderation. There is no sentimentality, no straining after effect. Dialect is skilfully used and the utterances of Lincoln are confined as far as possible to reported remarks. The oblique viewpoint of Dennis Hanks is preserved all through the book, in the context of his lifetime. He utters no forced prophecies of Lincoln's greatness. He watches his cousin grow in stature as a man of his capacity would do, commenting on it with the freely expressed admiration and criticism of a blood relation. It is a portrait in depth which illustrates the particular advantages of fiction in the right hands.

Lincoln's life abounds in the kind of anecdote which can bring the past alive for children with limited historical knowledge. As Paul Angle remarked in the preface already quoted, "Austere historians" use imaginative reconstruction "more often than most readers realize". At the same time there are books on Lincoln for the eight to eleven age-group which are strictly expository, and one that is available in England, THE REAL BOOK OF ABRAHAM LINCOLN (1951) by Michael Gorham, is almost painfully so. If some of the story biographies run the risk of being too chatty, the *Real* book seems determinedly didactic. Not at first sight, however. The contrary impression seems to be intended, judging from chapter headings like "Longshanks finds jobs" or "Abe talks about slavery"; and the material selected, especially for the early years of Lincoln, is consistently trivial and domestic in character. Abe falls in the river, gets sunburned, fights Jack Armstrong, romps on the floor with his children.

Oddly contrasting with this element is the author's flat style and his awkward way of encompassing a subject. He writes of Lincoln's youth:

> Abe was busy with serious things as well as funny stories. Once when he was not going to school he wrote an article on preserving the Constitution. He was already interested in that. He showed it to a lawyer friend from whom he had borrowed lots of books, and the lawyer said, "The world couldn't beat it." The lawyer liked the article so much that he wanted to take Abe into his office to study law. Abe would have liked that, but he said his family were too poor to spare him.
>
> THE REAL BOOK OF ABRAHAM LINCOLN, p. 52

Far from building up incidents with invented dialogue, the author, here and elsewhere, has kept his subject at arm's length. The book seems a collection of facts connected by no very strong feeling in the writer and no particular theme or principle behind it. Neither has it the advantages of full documentary detail which a detached biography has the space to give. Various sources have been used – some reputable, others (like Herndon and Helen Nicolay) to be used with caution; but the author has not classified the items in his book-list and he seldom makes it clear when he is using known fact, when he is deducing, expanding or accepting legend.

In simplifying, he telescopes events into passages as vague as this:

> Back in New Salem he wondered what to do, and as he wondered he thought of a job that appealed to him. He knew he would like to be a member of the Illinois State Legislature. He could make a living by making speeches and by knowing things and by thinking clearly. Abe counted all the friends he had in New Salem and close by, and he decided to stand for the legislature.
>
> ibid., p. 84

No mention of Lincoln's ideas on river transport which he wanted to use, none of the humour of his canvassing or his disclaimers about his ambitions; nothing, either, of what "the legislature" precisely means. English readers at least would need some specific detail in this kind of account, and any detail would make it less flabby. There is plenty of evidence of Lincoln's views at the time and the position he was aiming at. Moreover, for English children, again, a further point has to be made:

> The obvious road for the ambitions of a young man of abilities was that of local politics. Public office would have seemed wholly out of the question for a person of such modest background at that time in Britain; but in America, especially in the new West, it was an everyday matter. Leaders in politics sprang up from among the people, they were not imposed upon them from a higher order of society. So that, in 1832, Lincoln decided to chance his luck by standing as a candidate for the legislature of the state of Illinois.
>
> J. R. Pole. ABRAHAM LINCOLN (1964), p. 7

The books by May McNeer and Clara Judson mentioned earlier both explain Lincoln's ideas of the needs of the locality he knew so well, not only to illuminate the immediate political aspect of the matter but also to show the kind of local knowledge Lincoln accumulated in the course of his daily life. This practical side of his genius is of far more value than the generalised adulation deemed necessary in so many books for the young. Lincoln's entrance into the political arena is often so drastically simplified that it seems as though he reached the House of Representatives on a magic carpet.

It is very obviously the duty of a biographer to plot in clear terms the *evolution* of his chosen subject. Manuel Komroff in his ABRAHAM LINCOLN (1959), an account with little story-telling in it, offers to readers from ten or so upwards enough fact and quotation to enable them to see just how Lincoln emerged from obscurity. You do not "explain" a man like Lincoln; in a sense he is outside biography, even. But much can be done to explain some of the outward aspects of his life and Komroff does this, in particular, by emphasising how the course of Lincoln's life brought him in touch with *people*, and shows that this contact – closer and more intimate than usual, in a small community – was an essential factor in his political career. Far from suggesting that he was eccentric in his love of cracking jokes (as writers feel obliged to do now and then), he describes the kind of occasion in which the man's peculiar sense of humour could be stimulated and satisfied:

> John T. Stuart became Lincoln's sponsor in Vandalia. They shared a room in a local tavern, and because of Stuart's experience as a lawyer and his previous term of office in the same Legislature, this room became unofficial Whig headquarters. Lawyers and legislators as well as office seekers and politicians gathered there, and Lincoln, with his friendliness, humour and endless stories, soon became very popular. In this way, and during his very first term, Lincoln made many friends and established many connections which were to prove of help to him in the following years.
> ABRAHAM LINCOLN, p. 48

An author writing for adults could take for granted that this way of rubbing off the corners and preparing for a political career would be immediately understood in terms of modern life: for children, something of the point must be spelled out. All through Komroff's book, the sequence of event and of illustrative fact is ballasted by cool, sensible generalisation of this kind, directed to bringing out the character of Lincoln on broad lines.

Any life of Lincoln must be by definition historical biography, but if it is intended as biography and not as history, the end product must be the man and not the surrounding events – Lincoln and not the Civil War. The distinction may be illustrated by comparing Komroff's book with the excellent volume in Methuen's *Outlines* series, LINCOLN AND THE AMERICAN CIVIL WAR (1966) by Audrey Cammiade. The balance here is totally different. The author outlines Lincoln's attitudes rather than his personality, her task being to explain his part in the Civil War from beginning to end. Comment is brief and to the point:

> Lincoln disapproved of slavery. His basic objection to it was simply that it was wrong. Even so, he was not in sympathy with

the abolitionists, who wanted to make a clean sweep of it at once throughout the Union. He could see that that would ruin the slaveowners, and furthermore it would ruin the slaves. They would be turned loose in hundreds of thousands, without any idea of self-discipline and without any place prepared for them in any community. Finally, it would be unconstitutional. Lincoln's reverence for the Constitution went very deep.

LINCOLN AND THE AMERICAN CIVIL WAR, p. 14

Any child who is really interested to build up a picture of Lincoln beyond junior biography would be well advised to add this crisp and well documented account to Komroff's biography; the two together will get him into training for books like Bruce Catton's broad histories for the general reader.

English and American readers alike need a proper domestic and social background to a life of Lincoln, for any age. Komroff has assessed the relative value of his sources and has assimilated them so well that he writes with something of the enthusiasm and imagination of an historical novelist as he sets a scene. In certain circumstances, though, nothing is better than quotation from contemporary sources. The deadness of so many biographies comes from their reliance on secondary rather than on primary sources. Even when a writer has consulted contemporary documents, we are all too seldom allowed to share these with him.

Why, for instance, are children not shown Lincoln through his own words, in his autobiographical sketch, or shown his background in the words of his friend and law-partner William Herndon? Certainly Herndon is not always to be trusted. It was he who started the proliferation of romantic absurdities about Lincoln's love for Ann Rutledge; lawyers examining transcripts relating to Lincoln's legal career have come to question some of his remarks on his partner's qualifications and practice; biographers have come to criticise his over-ready psychological purple patches. All the same, we have no special reason to doubt the truth of the following anecdote, which Herndon heard from James Matheney, a lawyer on circuit with Lincoln, and which tells us as much of Lincoln's environment as of his personality:

Near Hoffman's Row, where the courts were held in 1839–40,

lived a shoemaker who frequently would get drunk and invariably whipped his wife. Lincoln, hearing of this, told the man if he ever repeated it he would thrash him soundly himself. Meanwhile he told Evan Butler, Noah Rickard, and myself of it, and we decided if the offense occurred again to join with Lincoln in suppressing it. In due course of time we heard of it. We dragged the offender up to the court-house, stripped him of his shirt, and tied him to a post or pump which stood over the well in the yard back of the building. Then we sent for his wife and arming her with a good limb bade her "light in". We sat on our haunches and watched the performance. The wife did her work lustily and well. When we thought the culprit had had enough Lincoln released him; we helped him on with his shirt and he crept sorrowfully homeward. Of course he threatened vengeance, but still we heard no further reports of wife-whipping from him.

HERNDON'S LINCOLN, vol. I, p. 189, footnote

Local history doubtless contains its share of exaggeration and misreported fact, but it contains also an atmosphere uniquely true. When Herndon tells the story of the yellow coon-dog; when he gives, again as Lincoln's statement, the motives of prudence and common sense that led him to re-enlist in the Black Hawk campaign, discarding "pure patriotism" as a "comfortable view" based on sentiment; when he describes in his rough and ready way the society of New Salem or remarks "Mr. Lincoln used to tell me that when he had a call to go to the country to survey a piece of land, he placed inside his hat all the letters belonging to people in the neighbourhood and distributed them along the way"; when he passes on this homely scene:

I lived next door to the Lincolns for many years, knew the family well. Mr. Lincoln used to come to our house, his feet encased in a pair of loose slippers, and with an old, faded pair of trousers fastened with one suspender. He frequently came to our house for milk. Our rooms were low, and he said one day, "Jim, you'll have to lift your loft a little higher; I can't straighten out under it very well."

Statement by James Gourly, given to Herndon 9 February 1866, quoted in ibid., vol. 2, pp. 589–90, footnote then we have, not the debunking of a national figure but a necessary corrective to the sycophantic portrait supposed to be more seemly for the young. Herndon's idiom, his homely details, his forthrightness, are in tune with Lincoln's own words about himself, and for this reason occasional extracts from Herndon could bring children nearer to Lincoln the man.

Ultimately Herndon's anecdotes and descriptions lie behind such literary reconstructions as Paul Horgan's ABRAHAM LINCOLN, CITIZEN OF NEW SALEM (1961). This polished piece of prose, commissioned by the *Saturday Evening Post* for the centennial of Lincoln's first inauguration, is described as "an essay in biography devoted to Lincoln's formative years as a young citizen of New Salem, Illinois". The picturesque style of the piece is matched with fine lithographs and an elegant production; it is an acceptable way of filtering the rough-edged records of Lincoln's own time, for the particular occasion, and its debt to those records may be seen in pictorial passages like this:

> The hungry-minded storekeeper came to his teacher with a taste for reading already well developed. He was never without a book, walking by the river or through the woods or along the single street. A boy who watched him said that when night came, "he read by the aid of any friendly light he could find". Sometimes he would go to Onstot the cooper's shop and scrape up shavings and other scraps of wood lying about and make a fire, "and by the light afforded read until far into the night" . . . What he learned made him more of a companion, not less of one lost to them in superior knowledge. He talked about what he was reading, and Caleb Carman wrote it down that the storekeeper would "Refer to that Great man Shakespeare allso Lord Byron as being a great man and Burns and of Burns poems and Lord Nellson as being a Great Admarall and Naval Commander and Adams and Henry Clay Jackson George Washington was the Greatest of them all of them and was his Great favorite . . ."
>
> ABRAHAM LINCOLN, CITIZEN OF NEW SALEM, pp. 56–7

I have mentioned elsewhere the impression that any critical study is bound to give, that children will read more than one book on any subject that interests them. Young readers who meet Lincoln

once and for all in a junior biography would do so with advantage
through Earl Schenk Miers or May McNeer, with Manuel Komroff
or Clara Judson. All the same, it may be suggested that a boy or
girl of twelve and over with some grounding in the facts of Lincoln's
life might find it pleasurable to review their knowledge in another
form. They could not do better than the American Heritage volume,
ABRAHAM LINCOLN IN PEACE AND WAR (1964), in which Earl
Schenk Miers offers an extended essay that is compressed but
immensely lively in the reading. Facts and ideas are brought
together so simply that a schoolboy or girl, helped by the particularly
fine and varied set of pictures – ranging from portraits and photographs to posters and caricatures – would find no difficulty in
following the text. Writing for the general reader, the author has

Frank Leslie's Illustrated Newspaper, FEBRUARY 2, 1861

Cartoon by G. P. A.
Healy, from ABRAHAM
LINCOLN IN PEACE
AND WAR (American
Heritage)

wasted no words; but if he assumes some knowledge in his readers, he is still ready to allow them the pleasure and aid of a visual description.

Here, for example, is a picture to bring to life Lincoln's first entrance into politics, at Vandalia in 1834:

> He took his seat on the first floor of the rickety capitol building where the House of Representatives met. Occasionally a speaker would have to shout over the din of falling plaster. Long tables were provided as desks for the legislators, and they were most convenient for resting legs upon.
>
> ABRAHAM LINCOLN IN PEACE AND WAR, p. 35

Here, again, is a legitimate dramatisation of an historical event whose importance has in foregoing paragraphs been carefully explained:

> As January 1, 1863, drew near, the public asked another question: would Lincoln really sign the Emancipation Proclamation? That muddy, dismal New Year's Day, Lincoln shook hands for three hours with callers at the White House. When he reached his office in midafternoon his right hand was limp and swollen.
>
> Only a few dignitaries were on hand to witness the signing. Never, Lincoln said, had he been more certain of doing right and he hoped a trembling signature would not be interpreted as showing hesitancy. "But anyway it is going to be done!" he declared. Slowly he signed his full name.
>
> ibid., pp. 123–4

Which do children deserve, a scene drawn with immediacy, based on contemporary record, or the piece of meandering sentiment quoted on page 381.

Concrete fact and abstract thought work together in Earl Schenk Miers's study of Lincoln for this pictorial volume. The junior coffee-table book has its dangers. Far too often publishers rely on a generous and spectacular sequence of pictures to commend a book to the public; that the text may be dreary, slipshod or pedagogic hardly seems to matter. The American Heritage series for the young is notable for an intelligent balance of illustration and text, of scholarship and literary alertness; this is the right kind of book to help children to co-ordinate random pieces of knowledge.

Let us assume that our young reader of twelve or upwards, who has read a junior life of Lincoln and enjoyed the above-mentioned volume, now wants to read a more substantial, specialised biography. He may be best served by Carl Sandburg's ABRAHAM LINCOLN GROWS UP (1931). Sandburg, better known in England as poet than as historian, combined imagination and scholarship strikingly in two books – ABRAHAM LINCOLN, THE PRAIRIE YEARS and THE WAR YEARS (1955) – built on a mixture of reverie and documentation. The first twenty-six chapters of THE PRAIRIE YEARS were rewritten and condensed for ABRAHAM LINCOLN GROWS UP, so that classrooms should be supplied with authentic Lincoln material. In his Dedicatory Preface, Sandburg wrote:

> To my younger friends
> When I began writing *Abraham Lincoln, The Prairie Years* I had young people in mind. It seemed to me that Lincoln was a great companion and a beautiful neighbor who should be known to boys and girls as a living friend. I hoped he would be so real and alive that sometimes while reading about him, young men and women might say in Kentucky and pioneer lingo, "Why! I feel as if I knowed him myself!"

Setting aside the purposive note (which is less obtrusive in the book than it might seem from this preface) we can find in this book a great deal of description of places, local custom, small-town worthies, and a modicum of talk "based word for word on sources deemed authentic". Sandburg in a remarkable way retains the homely flavour of Herndon while he does not conceal his own emotional involvement with Lincoln's early years. One of his few deviations from truth is his acceptance of the Ann Rutledge legend, which allows him to lend a passion to his portrait of the young man.

Since his books for adults are long and detailed, a young reader may have to be content to leave Sandburg's Lincoln on his way from New Salem to Springfield. It is a pity that no junior version exists for the later years, and that the spectacular, close-packed Frith-like portrait by Margaret Leech, REVEILLE IN WASHINGTON (1941), which covers the war years 1860–1865, is also beyond most readers under sixteen. Still, it must be said here, and will be said again, that readers in those lively reading years of eleven to fourteen or so are being consistently underestimated in their power to accept close detail and searching analysis in the biographies they read. Sandburg in full should certainly be available for them, together with Bruce Catton and other historical narratives about the Civil War period. Junior biographies have only done half their job if they do not lead young readers to forage widely in other fields of information.

The choice of reading in the 'teens must depend on need, background and degree of competence and adventurousness. Books on Lincoln written in a school context can hardly be classified as biography, perhaps not even as historical biography, yet in their very nature there is less risk of falsification than in a "life" which looks at the man first and his times afterwards. In any "story" of Lincoln, whether for young or adult readers, the selection of material will more often than not be dictated by human needs. One might illustrate this by pointing to the way Lincoln's acquaintance with Ann Rutledge has been elevated to a grand passion, basically because there is a sentimental wish to see Lincoln in the atmosphere of romantic love, if only to balance the very practical (and far more natural) course of his stormy married life. The distinction between the historian and the popular writer has seldom been better shown than in the popular treatment of this tavern-keeper's daughter of New Salem, the analysis of Lincoln's states of mind offered as fact, the touching description of the girl's deathbed, all based (as J. R. Randall crisply remarks in LINCOLN THE PRESIDENT) on "one person reporting what another person had written him concerning what that person recollected he had inferred from something that Ann had casually said to him more than thirty-one years before."* A book written mainly for the classroom may have a better chance of producing a balanced study of Lincoln.

Ideally an historical study would aim at the truth without any particular platform; it would present a man, not an abstraction or an illustration of a principle or a movement. For English readers at least, however, Frank B. Latham's ABRAHAM LINCOLN (1968) is too closely in the spirit of its series title, *Immortals of History*,

*LINCOLN THE PRESIDENT (1945), p. 328

to be a true portrait. This is the picture of an ideal, not of a great man. English readers in the 'teens would probably feel more at home with M. R. Ridley's ABRAHAM LINCOLN (1965) (in Blackie's *Famous Lives* series) as being more obviously cast in a simple form, or with Herbert Agar's ABRAHAM LINCOLN (1952) in the series of *Brief Lives* published by Collins. The approach of these last writers is stated clearly in the introduction to Agar's book:

> Lincoln is a secular saint for millions of people, world-wide, who believe in human dignity; but he has often been canonized for the wrong reasons. He was not, in fact, the Great Emancipator. He freed very few slaves, and he would have been content to free none at all if that had been the price of saving the American Union. He deplored slavery, of course; and he knew that if he saved the Union the slaves would one day be free. But he put first things first.
>
> ABRAHAM LINCOLN, p. 7

These are no doting portraits but forthright, well-documented books in which Lincoln is seen in the context of history. M. R. Ridley is especially concerned to describe Lincoln as a *lawyer*, and all through his study he stresses the importance of law in giving a direction to his life. Where writers have to cast round or to invent in order to fit Lincoln's views on slavery to the present day, Ridley has no difficulty in establishing his point by quoting from Lincoln's own speeches and from the opinions of his contemporaries. The evolution of Lincoln from a backwoods boy to a small-town lawyer and thence to the leader of his country is so clearly developed that it gives, through quotation and illustration rather than in direct comment, a definite idea of an individual, although the author spends relatively little time discussing Lincoln's personal and domestic life.

Among all the books on Lincoln for secondary school readership, Ridley's also seems the most scrupulous in seeing the man in context. He constantly stresses that we have to regard him and his circumstances *as they were*. This historian's view is well expressed when he compares Lincoln's two inaugural speeches and summarises the difference between the man he was in 1861 and in 1865:

The Lincoln who delivered the great Second Inaugural in 1865
was a very different man from the Lincoln who delivered the
well-considered, clear, and balanced Inaugural of 1861, and
almost beyond recognition a greater man. He knew beyond
question in 1865 that he was a great leader – he had always a
clear eye for facts and not even his profound and genuine
humility could blind him to them. He had stood at the helm of a
rather crank craft for four very stormy years; he had been beaten
upon by tempests of derision and abuse; he had had to deal with
something like mutiny among his crew and with dangerous
ambition and disaffection among his subordinate officers; from
all his trials he had learned how to set a course and hold it, and
at last the ship was beating up for harbour.

This was Lincoln in 1865. But what was he in 1860? He was a
man who had risen from the humblest beginnings to be a competent Middle-Western lawyer; he had been fighting for a bare
living for as long as he could remember; such education as he
had he had managed to get by sheer dogged determination; he
had been a not very distinguished member of Congress, and
been later defeated by Douglas for the senatorship; he was well
practised in local and state politics, but very little practised in
anything outside them; on the credit side he had gained a vast
deal of practical wisdom by contact with all sorts and kinds of
men, a wisdom which might, in some circumstances, be far more
valuable than book-learning; he was dead honest, and he had a
most penetrating eye for the things that really mattered in any
problem that confronted him. He had no illusions about himself.
His mind moved slowly, but surely. He would ask for, and listen
to, advice from anyone whose opinion he respected. He would
use the advice to help him in making up his own mind about the
situation, but when he had made up his own mind, he was
inflexible. He was completely courageous.

ABRAHAM LINCOLN, pp. 84–5

This kind of general statement could co-ordinate accurately for a
boy or girl the miscellaneous anecdotes and impressions gleaned
from books of a more junior kind.

Ridley's history contains a shrewd idea of character. Herbert
Agar's is more warm, comments more directly, contains less

quotation. It is essentially a political history, with much detail of
Lincoln's career in the Senate; but for all that, it gives a sense of
Lincoln's presence and the accumulation of small facts add up to
a considerable portrait. The author writes with complete lack of
sentiment, but the warmth of his writing pervades the book, and
that feeling of commitment which any biographer must have if his
work is to awake response is very evident in his final paragraph:

> Thus he went home to be buried in the little prairie-town. That
> cruel land, "watered by the tears and enriched by the graves of
> her women", had given him steadiness and patience and a
> natural piety. Grierson in his memoirs describes a pioneer
> woman of Illinois: "Moulded and subdued by the lonely days,

The last photograph of
Abraham Lincoln, taken by
Alexander Gardner on
April 11 1865, shows the
effect of the war and its
responsibilities on a
compassionate and
determined man. From
ABRAHAM LINCOLN IN
PEACE AND WAR
(American Heritage), by
courtesy of the Meserve
Collection.

the monotonous weeks, the haunting hush of the silent nights, and the same thoughts and images returning again and again, she appeared as one who had conquered the world of silence."

If a genius should arise in such a land it is fitting that he should be thoughtful in the manner that all great men from lonely places have been thoughtful, and that he should make simplicity more beautiful than the brave show of kings.

ABRAHAM LINCOLN, pp.139–40

Herndon said of Lincoln, "he never revealed himself entirely to any one man, and therefore he will always to a certain extent remain enveloped in doubt."* Intelligent readers who have already explored the limited supply of junior books on Lincoln need a handbook† in which they could find a selection of his speeches (not only the great speeches most often quoted) and a transcript of Lincoln's "Sketch of the present subject", written in June 1860 in connection with his nomination as Republican candidate for the Presidency.

This last document, which is modestly factual and precise, may surprise someone brought up on fairy-tale versions of his life, but it could do nothing but add to his stature in the eyes of an intelligent boy or girl. In this sketch Lincoln described how on his second flatboat journey to New Orleans with Offutt he helped to sew up the eyes of thirty hogs which they were having difficulty in driving on to the boat. The description of this curious expedient‡ (which was not successful) was omitted from the campaign biographies for

---

*HERNDON'S LINCOLN, vol. 2, p. 585

†Roy P. Basler's LINCOLN provides such material, but with comment that may be inadequate for English school-children unless they have directly studied Lincoln and his times. More comprehensive collections like Basler's ABRAHAM LINCOLN: HIS SPEECHES AND WRITINGS (1946) or Paul Angle's THE LINCOLN READER (1947) and the later book of extracts edited by Paul Angle and Earl Schenk Miers, THE LIVING LINCOLN (1955), would be useful for reconnaissance for anyone undertaking a junior collection of first-hand material, with suitable editorial comment; the definitive edition of Lincoln's writings would be available as the primary source. There is room for a junior biography written in admiration, with full scholarship, that will be at once inspiring and clear-eyed, a biography that would offer Lincoln as the kind of hero the young look for today, rather than the kind of hero their elders would like them to need.

‡ See also pages 150–1.

which Lincoln had prepared his biographical sketch, and the
original manuscript of the first four chapters of the official life by
Lincoln's secretaries, John Nicolay and John Hay, has a marginal
note "leave out(?)" and, underneath, a direction by Lincoln's son
Robert "I say leave out – R.T.L." It is understandable that Lincoln's
early biographers should have been squeamish about this kind of
frontier incident, just as it is understandable that Lincoln should
have included it without embarrassment.

This and other examples of censorship remind us of the general
difficulties of biography upon which Lincoln himself has left a
shrewd comment, which he made after reading a life of Burke:

> It's like all the others. Biographies as generally written are not
> only misleading, but false. The author of this life of Burke makes
> a wonderful hero of his subject. He magnifies his perfections – if
> he had any – and suppresses his imperfections. He is so faithful
> in his zeal and so lavish in his praise of his every act that one is
> almost driven to believe that Burke never made a mistake or
> failure in his life . . . History is not history unless it is the truth.
> Quoted in PORTRAIT FOR POSTERITY, p. 163

If biography for the young is intended to communicate to them
some general principle (and I believe it almost always is so intended)
then the life of Abraham Lincoln can surely do something more
than summarise the attributes of greatness. In the broadest sense
it could show the young the value of *thought* and reason as applied
to a democracy. Abraham Lincoln directed and disciplined his
emotions by the deliberate, slow process of thinking out his attitude
to life. He forged his personal independence of spirit through
intellect. Herndon wrote:

> Clocks, omnibuses, language, paddle-wheels, and idioms never
> escaped his observation and analysis. Before he could form
> an idea of anything, before he would express his opinion on a
> subject, he must know its origin and history in substance and
> quality, in magnitude and gravity.
> HERNDON'S LINCOLN, vol. 2, p. 594

Young people engaged in seeking personal independence with

hot emotion could do well to examine the life of a man who educated
himself in the way of power by examining the tools of power, by
the deliberate logic of law and by an equally deliberate and powerful
self-determination. With an honest biographer they might also
glimpse a man compounded of mirth and melancholy, whose
mystery is the mystery of all human personality.

Reading List

Agar, Herbert. ABRAHAM LINCOLN. Brief lives. (*Collins* 1952) *Shoe String* 1952.
With photographs and a map.
Alington, A. F. THE STORY OF THE AMERICAN CIVIL WAR. Men and Events.
Faber 1964. Illustrated by photographs and prints. A short, reliable account for
children from twelve or so.
Allt, A. H. THE AMERICAN CIVIL WAR. Then and There. *Longman* 1961.
Illustrated by photographs and prints. A useful, well arranged summary,
intended for use in schools, for the middle 'teens. Very well illustrated.
Angle, Paul. THE LINCOLN READER. New Brunswick, *Rutgers University Press*
1947.
Angle, Paul and Miers, Earl Schenk. THE LIVING LINCOLN: THE MAN, HIS
MIND, HIS TIMES AND THE WAR HE FOUGHT, RECONSTRUCTED FROM HIS
OWN WRITINGS. *Rutgers University Press* 1955.
d'Aulaire, Ingrid and Edgar Parin. ABRAHAM LINCOLN (*Doubleday* revised edition
1957) *Cambridge University Press* 1957, revised edition 1964. Illustrated by the
authors.
Baker, Nina Brown. THE STORY OF ABRAHAM LINCOLN. Signature biographies.
(*Grosset and Dunlap* 1952) *Marston Low* 1960. Illustrated by Warren
Baumgartner.
Basler, Roy P. LINCOLN. Profile Books. (*Grove Press* 1961) *Evergreen Books* 1961.
With photographs, prints and maps.
Basler, Roy P. (editor). ABRAHAM LINCOLN: HIS SPEECHES AND WRITINGS.
Grosset and Dunlap 1946.
Beim, Jerrold. THE BOY ON LINCOLN'S LAP. *Morrow Junior Books* 1955.
Illustrated by Tracy Sugarman.
Cammiade, Audrey. LINCOLN AND THE AMERICAN CIVIL WAR. Outlines.
(*Methuen* 1967) *Roy* 1967. Illustrated by photographs and prints. Maps by
R. R. Sellman.

Catton, Bruce. THIS HALLOWED GROUND (*Doubleday* 1956) *Gollancz* 1957. With maps and photographs.

Catton, Bruce. THE AMERICAN CIVIL WAR (*American Heritage Pub. Co.* 1960) *Penguin* 1966. Illustrated by photographs, prints and maps.

Coy, Harold. THE FIRST BOOK OF PRESIDENTS. First Books. (*Franklin Watts* 1952) *Bailey and Swinfen* 1958. Illustrated by Manning De V. Lee. The clear though brief explanation of the role and election of presidents could be useful also for English children from about nine.

Drinkwater, John. THE WORLD'S LINCOLN. New York, *Bowling Green Press* 1928.

Duthie, Eric (editor). CHILDREN'S BOOK OF FAMOUS LIVES. *Odhams Press* 1958. With drawings.

Fisher, Aileen. MY COUSIN ABE. *Thomas Nelson* 1962, U.S.A. Drawings by Leonard Vosburgh.

Foster, Genevieve. ABRAHAM LINCOLN'S WORLD. *Scribner* 1944. Quotations, anecdotes and narrative setting the scene for Lincoln's life; little on Lincoln himself.

Gorham, Michael. THE REAL BOOK OF ABRAHAM LINCOLN. Real Books. (*Doubleday* 1951) *Dobson* 1959. Illustrated by Elinore Blaisdell.

Grambs, Jean D. (editor). ABRAHAM LINCOLN THROUGH THE EYES OF HIGH SCHOOL YOUTH. Washington 1959

Herndon, William and Weik, William. HERNDON'S LINCOLN: THE TRUE STORY OF A GREAT LIFE (*Belford and Co.* 1889) *Sampson Low* 1893. The history and personal recollections of Abraham Lincoln by William H. Herndon, for twenty years his friend and law partner, and Jesse William Weik, A.M.

Horgan, Paul. ABRAHAM LINCOLN, CITIZEN OF NEW SALEM (*Farrar, Straus* 1961) *Macmillan* 1961. Illustrated by Douglas Gorsline.

Judson, Clara Ingram. ABRAHAM LINCOLN, FRIEND OF THE PEOPLE. *Follett* 1954. Pen drawings by Robert Frankenberg. Kodachromes of the Chicago Historical Society Lincoln Dioramas.

Komroff, Manuel. ABRAHAM LINCOLN. Lives to remember. (*Putnam* 1959) *A. and C. Black* 1961. Illustrated by Charles Beck.

Latham, Frank B. ABRAHAM LINCOLN. Immortals of History. *Franklin Watts* 1968. With photographs, and a map by Dyno Lowenstein.

Leech, Margaret. REVEILLE IN WASHINGTON (*Harper* 1941) *Eyre and Spottiswoode* 1942.

McNeer, May. AMERICA'S ABRAHAM LINCOLN. *Houghton Mifflin* 1957. Illustrated by Lynd Ward.

Meserve, Frederick Hill. THE PHOTOGRAPHS OF ABRAHAM LINCOLN. *Harcourt, Brace* 1944. Introduction, "The face of Lincoln" by Carl Sandburg. This wonderful collection of photographs is interesting for the odd uniformity of pose and expression, mainly due to long exposure technique.

Miers, Earl Schenk. ABRAHAM LINCOLN IN PEACE AND WAR. *Harper & Row* 1964. Illustrated with photographs and prints.

Miers, Earl Schenk. THAT LINCOLN BOY. *World* 1968. Illustrated by Kurt Werth.

Moorhouse, Esther (afterwards Meynell). THE YOUNG LINCOLN. *Chapman and Hall* 1944.

Northcott, Cecil. I'LL HIT IT HARD! Eagle Books No. 50. True Stories of Real People. *Edinburgh House Press* 1943.

Pole, J. R. ABRAHAM LINCOLN. Clarendon Biographies (*Oxford University Press* 1964 U.K.) *Oxford University Press* 1964 U.S.A. With portraits.

Power, Rhoda. GREAT PEOPLE OF THE PAST (*Cambridge University Press* 1932 U.K.) *Cambridge University Press* 1932 U.S.A. With photographs and prints.

Randall, James G. LINCOLN THE PRESIDENT: SPRINGFIELD TO GETTYSBURG. *Dodd Mead* 1945.

Ridley, M. R. ABRAHAM LINCOLN. Famous Lives. *Blackie* 1965. With photographs, portraits and a map.

Ruby, Lionel. THE ART OF MAKING SENSE: A GUIDE TO LOGICAL THINKING (*Lippincott* 1968) *Angus and Robertson* 1969.

Sandburg, Carl. ABRAHAM LINCOLN GROWS UP. *Harcourt, Brace* 1931.

Sandburg, Carl. ABRAHAM LINCOLN: THE PRAIRIE YEARS. THE WAR YEARS (*Harcourt, Brace* 1926) *Cape* 1955.

Tausek, Joseph. THE TRUE STORY OF THE GETTYSBURG ADDRESS. *Dial Press* 1933.

Thomas, Benjamin. PORTRAIT FOR POSTERITY: LINCOLN AND HIS BIOGRAPHERS (*Rutgers University Press* 1947) *Eyre and Spottiswoode* 1953. See also his excellent biography, ABRAHAM LINCOLN (*Knopf* 1952) *Eyre and Spottiswoode* 1953.

Walton, J. MAKERS OF THE U.S.A. Living Names. *Oxford University Press* 1943.

5 | *Careers*

If you're the sort of person we want, you want a career . . . not just a job!
Advertisement of the Scottish Equitable Life Assurance Society, in *The Times Educational Supplement*, 13 March 1970, p. 55

5 | *Careers*

CAREER books occupy a narrow band in the spectrum of books about human society – biographies and real-life adventure, histories of institutions and public services, technological handbooks and studies in the arts and a host of others. The first impulse towards a life's work might come to a boy after he had read the apologia of a craftsman, like Doreen Brookshaw's POTTERY CRAFT (1967) or the enthusiastic introduction to design or modelling by an inspired teacher like Tony Hart. He might be fired by the authoritative personal commitment of Theodore Savory's INTRODUCTION TO ZOOLOGY (1968) or Martin Ballard's THE STORY OF TEACHING (1969) or one of Hans Baumann's electrifying stories of archaeological discovery. He might catch something of the practical

Among factors which put people off are prospects of involvement in the rat race and loss of identity.

Cartoon from The Times Educational Supplement, 6 November 1970

enthusiasm of Carol Odell's A LINER GOES TO SEA (1969) or of
EXPLORING MAPS (1962) by Patrick Moore and Henry Brinton
or of Barbara Smalley's WORKING WITH HORSES (1961) or of
Bernard Ashley's admirable history of the lifeboat organisation,
THE MEN AND THE BOATS (1968) or of Alan Jenkins's first-hand
anecdotes of a trawler in THE SILVER HAUL (1967). He might
ponder over the general ideas suggested by Garry Hogg's ENGIN-
EERING MAGIC (1966) or one of the *It's Made Like This* series
from John Baker or the *How They Were Built* series from Oxford
or C. H. Doherty's lively studies of men at work, SCIENCE ON
THE BUILDING SITE (1962) and SCIENCE AND THE TUNNELLER
(1967). He might move on from the sceptical standpoint in E. W.
Hildick's "Close look" (1969) books on advertising, newspapers,
television and so on. None of these books is a career book as such,
but some extend their account by suggestions of training and
apprenticeship and all of them in a rounded description of a
profession, trade or craft at least imply that new blood is always
welcome.

The pointer to a career will not necessarily come from books.
It may stem from family tradition, the suggestion of a careers
adviser, a school tour, the sight of a recruiting poster, a television
programme or an incident in the street. In a discussion at Broms-
grove County High School, the principal careers officer for
Worcestershire, Mr C. P. Walton, made the following point:

> Bromsgrove breeds highly articulate boys and girls who are easy
> to interview. Most of them are able to assimilate ideas through
> reading. I think that if one gets children who are less competent
> in manipulation of words one has to find new ways of educating
> them in the opportunities that are available; a careers room with
> visual material available; films, slides and filmstrips.
>
> "Conversation piece", in *The Times Educational Supplement*,
> 13 March, 1970, p. 42

On the face of it one might wonder whether with the interview
system and visual aids provided by most secondary schools today,
books are needed at all in this business of choosing a career. They
could be defended on negative grounds, certainly. A careers officer,
or a group of individuals discussing their particular jobs, are not

always regarded by the young in the way they would choose. A good many sophisticated boys and girls in the middle 'teens look upon careers meetings as a kind of circus arranged by their elders for reasons best known to themselves. Alternatively, direction from teachers and other interested adults can provide an excuse for a less intelligent child to continue in the submissive role of a pupil and abandon any idea of thinking for himself. Books can be picked up and put down as time and mood dictate; they can be argued with and cannot answer back or accuse one of being impertinent; their vested interest is not pressed too hard; and they leave room for the reader to investigate his own point of view. Can we allow career books more than this grudging advantage?

Another question must be answered first. Do young people *want* to read books on careers? I would guess that very few want to read books of a theoretical, general kind. To read in general terms about choosing a career is a little like reading the Highway Code; the generalisations are either utterly obvious or they are meaningless until they are put into practice. A great deal of the advice given in general career books (on how to prepare for an interview, how to make the best of your education, why we distinguish between a job and a career, how important pay is) could be communicated by word of mouth in two or three sentences and, given sensible parents and teachers, would have reached a child probably long before he got to the stage of thinking about his future.

Part of the difficulty lies in the deadness of abstract words and ideas. Who would willingly submit to this kind of voice:

> Continued education is not recommended solely because it gives you the knowledge required for passing examinations. The world of work gets more complex all the time and the stresses imposed upon people at all levels tend to increase so that adaptability is rapidly becoming one of the most valuable qualities since it is easier to retrain a worker who has had a good general education than one who has merely acquired the necessary skills to do a particular job.
> Catherine Avent. WHICH CAREER? (1965), p. 35

Written by a highly qualified careers officer, this book comes to life only when the author discusses particular careers. Her chief purpose is to persuade young people to stay longer at school, but persuasiveness is the last quality one would claim for her prose. Here, perhaps, is someone at the mercy of her position. In every branch of the world of information books, people who express themselves forcibly and clearly in direct conversation are required to translate their views into the written word when they may be neither trained nor gifted as writers. The only hope for general careers books is surely to simulate the natural tone of voice which could, in an interview or meeting or discussion group, stiffen the diffident, spur the undecided and enlighten the confused. A book with the breezy, socially conscious, downright tone of George Pattison's THE WORKADAY WORLD (1966) would stand more chance of catching the attention of a boy or girl of today than a more orthodox work: a 'teenage magazine might well come even closer to the reader's needs.

In the end, such generalised advice as "Everyone wants to be useful and to feel needed,"* or "While accepting all the information and advice we can give you, you must still do the hardest thinking yourself,"† savours of what we called in my school-days "a glimpse of the obvious". There is much that is shrewd in books of this general kind but most of them give the impression that they have been written by adults not so much for the young as for other adults; the consciously friendly "you" approach is not always consistent with the way advice and information are phrased. It is rare to find a writer who can keep his dignity and his distance and still seem to identify himself with his young readers. Clifford Allen decries psychologists' questionnaires, but accepts that they will scorn more amateurish efforts to give advice on careers:

> Then my retort will be that when we are hungry we do not refuse to buy a piece of cheese, roughly weighed on the rusty scales in the village shop, although we know that the weight will not be very accurate. All that the young man I am addressing wants is to find some indication of a suitable career in which he is likely to succeed; not statistical odds of his possible success or failure.
> PLANNING A CAREER, pp. 113–14

---

*Catherine Avent and Eleanor F. Fried. STARTING WORK (1965), p. 11
†CAREERS FOR SCHOOL LEAVERS (1969), p. 10

In this matching game played between school and pupil or between parent and child. both job and child will necessarily be presented as typical. It wilı depend on the writer's honesty how far or how little they are represented as ideal. Career books of a specific kind approach their material in one of three ways. They tell what *I* do, what *they* do or what *you* may do. Of these methods the first, the career autobiography, is the most approachable because it is the most informal. The man who writes directly about his job has at least the opportunity to be personal and so to escape from the insidious generalised treatment that leaves a frustrated reader asking "But what *exactly* do you have to do?" Even if he is commissioned to introduce his particular avocation to the young, he can avoid a hortatory note by concentrating on particular circumstances, good or bad, congenial or disappointing, and can let these circumstances speak for themselves. A book as urbane and wise as Philip Unwin's BOOK PUBLISHING AS A CAREER (1965) is a great deal more to the point than many a handbook, but it is a book to read for sheer enjoyment, whether or not you happen to want to go into publishing, and this is the best kind of encouragement to the boy or girl bewildered by leaflets, advice and an apparently limitless choice for the future.

In the series *My Life and my Work*, Educational Explorers have cast a wide net. Among the authors of these career autobiographies are a dentist, an artist, a Wren officer, a chef, a teacher, a statistician, a sailor in the Merchant Navy, clergymen, journalists, an architect and a personnel manager in a large store. The books are easily recognised by a neat uniform format and somewhat forced punning titles (the most gruesome is CHEW THIS OVER, for the life of a dentist). They are welcome for their candour and their particularisation of training, but they are not all equally personal. Children might well use them to check a particular enthusiasm, but I do not think all of them would actually arouse enthusiasm in the first place.

Informative they certainly are, but not often truly aubiographical – that is, flavoured by individuality. I remember as exceptional the dedicated feeling in Francis Hoyland's A PAINTER'S DIARY (1967) and the practical zest of the man; the insouciance of Rodney Bennett's account of a career in radio and television, THE INFORMING IMAGE (1968); the racy hyperboles of Julian Morel's AT YOUR SERVICE (1968), describing life as a *commis* waiter at the

Savoy and as a power in the Pullman service; the undogmatic sincerity of Ray Billington, giving his individual life and aims as a Methodist minister (1967).

It has been remarked that:

.... one might argue that with a lot of children the comment of an external person sometimes has a sort of halo round it simply because it is external. It carries more weight.

"Conversation piece", in *The Times Educational Supplement*, 13 March 1970, p. 42

As with personal confrontations, so with books. When a successful and famous couple like Dulcie Gray and Michael Denison write of their own experience within the general framework of THE ACTOR AND HIS WORLD (1964), or when Owen Summers and Unity Hall review their struggle towards fame and fortune in DATELINE: FLEET STREET (1969), a very live relationship grows between writers and readers. Possibilities spring to mind, ambitions are born. They may never come to anything, but life has opened up for one more boy or girl.

Perhaps career autobiography is for inspiration rather than for information, however practical it may be. The style may be dégagé and colloquial, but each author means what he says about a way of life which he has chosen and pursued with determination. At the opposite end of the scale we may place career novels, in which each story (whether told in the first or third person) is really told from the point of view of a young hero or heroine. Such stories vary in quality from skilful light fiction to potential pulp, but they have one thing in common. The success of the chief character at least is by custom assured, and to some extent this detracts from the value of practical detail, however accurate and up to date it is. If a good career autobiography can inspire a boy or girl with a desire to emulate, career novels inspire daydreams which may do no harm to the strong-minded and the sophisticated but could certainly lead simpler souls into mistaken paths if this were the sole source of careers information available to them. Mercifully this is not so, and the career novel is probably most often read as agreeable unexacting fiction with an obvious but slight relevance to real life.

Autobiography and fiction offer active pictures of a career in motion; if they begin to seem distant and impersonal it may be because the story element has been dominated by the fact-finding element. The books that tell a reader what "they" do have a special function to summarise the hard facts, to place a particular profession, trade, craft in its place in society, to suggest by implication how a young person can find a job but, still more, how he can find a place in the world that will really suit him. From the earliest years a child will meet books which put his neighbours into their social context; the numerous books on the Postal Service already discussed (see pages 49–75) may serve as examples.

At twelve or so, the finding of a career might be incidental to the kind of personal reading that can bring the complexity of the world into some kind of order. James Derriman's DISCOVERING THE LAW (1962) is not specifically a career book, but the author is so skilful in using cases to explain the intricacies and principles of the law that if he does not put ideas into a reader's head, he will at least ensure that the head is not filled with misapprehensions. A profession even more difficult for the young to understand, or even to identify, is presented by John Carswell so lucidly in THE CIVIL SERVANT AND HIS WORLD (1966) that the pattern of society must seem far more definite than before; and who would not warm to a man who introduces the difficulties of diplomacy by advising "never try to negotiate in a foreign language, however well you think you speak it, and never enter into competition with Bulgarians in the drinking of vodka, however genially the offer is made."*

Books like this do not only place a particular job in a present-day context. John Stroud's CHILD CARE OFFICERS AND THEIR WORLD (1965), a book full of the warmth of dedicated work, describes the history of a system as it has evolved with certain needs in mind. Professions with a longer history are studied in depth in Martin Ballard's THE STORY OF TEACHING (1969) and THE STORY OF NURSING (1965) by Desirée Edwards-Rees and in other books in a series from Longman which need to be read and savoured at leisure for the tradition they foster and the ideas they throw out. The aim of every good careers officer is to find a suitable niche for the pupils who consult him; he may find part of this job

*op. cit., p. 122

done for him if books of this degree of intelligence are offered to them.

Finally, what "you" can do. Here we have the advertising leaflets, the recruiting pamphlets, the official handbooks and the more flexible symposia – the essential reference books for career advisers and for the young person who has made a decision or at least wants to follow up a definite subject. It would be easy to suggest that ministerial directories and management publications were all that were needed and that no private individual or educational body need be concerned – as so many are – to add their own careers dictionaries and commentaries to the growing pile of available literature. But official pronouncements can be daunting in their brevity, their lack of qualification and the impersonality of their approach: each such publication is sufficient to itself. There is seldom room for the psychological approach indicated, for instance, in the publisher's foreword to Hale's *Target* series:

> This library of books was started in order to help the younger generation to settle the increasingly difficult question: "Where do the finest opportunities lie?" By this we do not necessarily mean where can the highest pay be found but rather where and how can youngsters develop harmoniously in an environment that will suit their character and outlook so that they can employ their best qualities in the service both of their family and their fellow men.
>
> In an age when the machine tomorrow may do the work of hundreds of men today, where atoms generate electricity, where businessmen fly across the world in a few hours, where nervous exhaustion is almost an epidemic, it is more than ever important that a youngster should know as much as possible about a job before he settles to it.

This very obvious but necessary point may of course be shrugged off by a boy or girl impatient at the long-term view of advising adults. This difficulty may be avoided by something as simple as a change of format – a change, for instance, from the drab quarto pages of most general books on careers to the slick appearance of Margaret Baker's TOP GIRL (1966). The magazine appeal of this book is matched by its direct, conversational manner:

Yours is the first generation of girls to begin work in the knowledge that this is not just a stopgap between school and marriage.
You have to think in terms of training, a period of work before
and during the first years of marriage, then a gap if you have a
family, and a return to work in middle age.

It is difficult when you are still at school to visualize yourself
at eighteen, or twenty-one, let alone as a married woman with
children, but you must make the effort to do this, however
improbable it seems, so that you can plan your working life
properly and make sure that you are doing a job that you like
and which makes full use of your potentialities. At the moment
work seems unreal and as a result you may drift into a job that,
although it pays well, does not demand anything from you, and
so you don't care. Not caring is the disease of our time, and you
don't want to catch this disastrous attitude if you can help it.
TOP GIRL, p. 97

Again, in a symposium like CAREERS AND VOCATIONAL TRAIN-
ING (15th edn. 1967) edited by Margaret Fuge, the advantage
of articles by different people is obvious. While a careful index
and repeated revision make a book like this useful for reference,
it can offer also the personal angle. THE PEACOCK BOOK OF
CAREERS FOR GIRLS (1966), edited by Ruth Miller, a particularly
lively compilation, excels in its summary of the kind of person
needed by a certain kind of job – a gambit in the matching game
that is sometimes neglected.

To some extent I would regard the Peacock book as a successor
to Jeanne Heal's CAREERS FOR GIRLS (1955), a book published
sixteen years ago which is now out of date in some of its facts but
which must have appealed to the young for its interviews with men
and women who have made a success of their chosen career –
among them Eileen Joyce, Norman Hartnell, Flora Robson and
Dame Laura Knight. More especially geared to boys, the interesting
OUTLOOK (1963) by Robin Guthrie and its sequel OUTLOOK
TWO (1965) by Robin Guthrie and Tony Watts, contain articles
on various careers including medicine, business, veterinary work,
engineering – each one a straight piece of autobiography and each
one implying the comment "I want a job that will be a way of life."

For intelligent girls, perhaps the best series of handbooks available at present is the *Career Guides* from Bodley Head, now appearing one by one in paper-covered editions from Evans. These books have the hallmarks of efficient guides. Each one covers a multiple subject – fashion, the theatre, nursing, writing and so on – and each one is so arranged that qualifications and training, addresses, reading list and other essential details are to be found with every sub-division. In this way the reader can easily discover what she might do in a particular field. She will also discover what "they" do – what a job consists of – partly through direct description and partly through brief quotations from recorded interviews that give a very immediate and personal aspect to a general picture. Authors like Barbara Brandenburger, Elizabeth Grey and Joan Llewelyn Owens have brought to these books an expertise in arranging facts and a knowledge of the kind of fact a young person needs to know if she is to decide whether a certain career is suitable for her or not.

It is perhaps natural, though I think it is regrettable, that books on particular careers tend to be on the professions or, very occasionally, on the skilled crafts – the implication being, perhaps, that potential dockers, taxi-drivers, waitresses, typists and miners would rather find their facts elsewhere than in books and perhaps, even, that these are not "careers". This seems a pity for many reasons, one of them being the monotony of the existing books en masse. Career books are in a special sense born out of a demand and do not exist in their own right. They ought to earn their right to exist by being better written, more interesting and, above all, more vitally keyed to what the young are really like and really need in the way of written guidance. No reluctant reader is going to get through a book unless it is interesting. He or she may positively want a book on hairdressing or the police force. Let us be sure there is one available that is interesting but not melodramatic, realistic but not cynical, clear and simple but not banal.

In this section I shall discuss in detail various career books available about Nursing and Journalism. I shall try to show in particular how far any of these suggest to the reader that his job or career might not only satisfy him but also make him a useful and intelligent citizen.

Reading List

Allen, Clifford. PLANNING A CAREER: FOR PARENTS, TEACHERS AND SCHOOL-
LEAVERS (*Macmillan* 1965) *St Martin* 1965.

Ashley, Bernard. THE MEN AND THE BOATS. Serving our Society. *Allman and Son*
1968. Illustrated by photographs, prints and drawings.

Avent, Catherine. WHICH CAREER?: GUIDANCE FOR THE UNDECIDED. Target
for Careers. *Robert Hale* 1965.

Avent, Catherine and Fried, Eleanor L. STARTING WORK: A GUIDE FOR YOUNG
PEOPLE LEAVING SCHOOL. *Parrish* 1965.

Baker, Margaret. TOP GIRL. *Lutterworth* 1966. Illustrated by Belinda Lyon.

Ballard, Martin. THE STORY OF TEACHING. *Longman Young Books* 1969.
Illustrated with photographs and prints.

Barker, D. W. (editor). BEGINNINGS: AN ANTHOLOGY OF APPRENTICESHIP
AND SUCCESSFUL VENTURES. *Macmillan* 1953. Quotations from works by
Phyllis Bentley, Neville Cardus, John Moore and others, well chosen to support
the subtitle.

Baumann, Hans. THE LAND OF UR (Germany 1968. *Oxford University Press* 1969)
Pantheon 1969. Translated by Stella Humphries. Drawings by Hans Peter
Renner, and photographs in colour. See also LION GATE AND LABYRINTH
(Germany 1966. *Oxford University Press* 1967) *Pantheon* 1967, and other works.

Bennett, Rodney. THE INFORMING IMAGE: A CAREER IN RADIO AND
TELEVISION. My Life and my Work. *Educational Explorers* 1968. Illustrated by
photographs.

Billington, Ray. REV. *Educational Explorers* 1967.

Brandenburger, Barbara. WORKING IN TELEVISION. Career Guides. *Bodley Head*
1965. Illustrated by photographs.

Brookshaw, Doreen. POTTERY CRAFT (*Warne* 1967 U.K.) *Warne* 1968 U.S.A.
Illustrated by Doreen and Drake Brookshaw, and with photographs.

Central Youth Employment Executive. CAREERS GUIDE. *Her Majesty's
Stationery Office* yearly. The standard reference book.

Carswell, John. THE CIVIL SERVANT AND HIS WORLD. *Gollancz* 1966.

Derriman, James. DISCOVERING THE LAW. Discovering . . . *University of
London Press* 1962. Drawings by Jennifer Miles, and some photographs.

Doherty, C. H. SCIENCE ON THE BUILDING SITE. World of Science.
Brockhampton 1962, revised edition 1970. Illustrated by Gerald Wilkinson.
SCIENCE AND THE TUNNELLER. World of Science. *Brockhampton* 1967.
Illustrated by Michael Baker.

Edwards-Rees, Desirée. THE STORY OF NURSING (*Constable Young Books* 1965) *Verry* 1965. Illustrated by photographs and prints.

Fuge, Margaret (editor). CAREERS AND VOCATIONAL TRAINING. *Arlington Books* 15th edition 1967.

Gray, Dulcie and Denison, Michael. THE ACTOR AND HIS WORLD. *Gollancz* 1964.

Grey, Elizabeth. CAREERS IN FASHION (1963). CAREERS IN BEAUTY (1964). Both *Bodley Head* Career Guides, illustrated by photographs.

Guthrie, Robin. OUTLOOK: A CAREERS SYMPOSIUM. *Macdonald* 1963.

Guthrie, Robin and Watts, Tony. OUTLOOK TWO: A CAREERS SYMPOSIUM. *Macdonald* 1965.

Hart, Tony. THE YOUNG DESIGNER. How it is Done. (*Kaye and Ward* 1968) *Warne* 1968. Drawings by the author, and photographs. See other books in this series.

Heal, Jeanne. JEANNE HEAL'S BOOK OF CAREERS FOR GIRLS. *Bodley Head* 1955.

Hildick, E. W. A CLOSE LOOK AT TELEVISION AND SOUND BROADCASTING (1969). A CLOSE LOOK AT ADVERTISING (1969). Both *Faber*, illustrated by photographs. See also page 465.

Hogg, Garry. ENGINEERING MAGIC: GIANT PROJECTS TO CHANGE THE WORLD (*Abelard-Schuman* 1966) *Criterion* 1966. With photographs and maps.

Hoyland, Francis. A PAINTER'S DIARY. My Life and my Work. *Educational Explorers* 1967. With pictures by the artist.

Jenkins, Alan C. THE SILVER HAUL. The World we are Making. *Methuen* 1967. Illustrated by photographs, diagrams and drawings.

Leafe, M. BRIDGING THE GAP. 1. CHOOSING YOUR JOB (1968) 2. GOING OUT TO WORK (1969). *Cassell*. A book of classroom exercises in the use of English using the theme of the world of work. An interesting idea which should stimulate practical and personal discussion.

Miller, Ruth (editor). THE PEACOCK BOOK OF CAREERS FOR GIRLS. *Penguin* 1966.

Moore, Patrick and Brinton, Henry. EXPLORING MAPS. Exploring . . . (*Odhams Press* 1962) *Hawthorn* 1967. Illustrated by Cyril Deakins.

Morel, Julian. AT YOUR SERVICE: A CAREER IN THE HOTEL AND CATERING INDUSTRY. My Life and my Work. *Educational Explorers* 1968. Illustrated by photographs.

Odell, Carol. A LINER GOES TO SEA (*Tri-Ocean* 1968) *Angus and Robertson* 1969. Illustrated by photographs.

Owens, Joan Llewelyn. WORKING WITH CHILDREN (1962). TRAVEL WHILE YOU WORK (1963). WORKING IN THE THEATRE (1964). All *Bodley Head* Career Guides, illustrated by photographs. See also page 438.

Pattison, George. THE WORKADAY WORLD: A GUIDE FOR YOUNG PEOPLE TO
   LIFE AFTER SCHOOL. *Barrie and Rockliff* 1966.

Savory, Theodore H. INTRODUCTION TO ZOOLOGY. *Newnes* 1968. Illustrated
   by Melchior Spoczynski.

Smalley, Barbara. WORKING WITH HORSES. *Museum Press* 1961. Illustrated by
   Tom Chapman.

Stroud, John. CHILD CARE OFFICERS AND THEIR WORK. *Gollancz* 1965.

Summers, Owen and Hall, Unity. DATELINE: FLEET STREET. My Life and my
   Work. *Educational Explorers* 1969. Illustrated by photographs. See also page 460.

Unwin, Philip. BOOK PUBLISHING AS A CAREER (*Hamish Hamilton* 1965)
   D. White 1967.

—— CAREERS FOR SCHOOL LEAVERS. *Cornmarket Press* 1969, revised regularly.

—— CAREERS: AN ANNOTATED LIST. *National Book League* 1966.

—— WORKADAY WORLD: A CAREERS BOOK LIST. *Leicestershire County Library*
   1968

5a | Nursing

When a careers adviser arrived recently to talk at a girls' school and asked if there were any careers the girls particularly wanted her to talk about she received the negative reply: "Please talk about anything but teaching and nursing."
Eleanor Brockett. CHOOSING A CAREER, p. 52

Nursing – surely the most rewarding job in the world.
Cover of a recruiting pamphlet issued by the Department of Health

5a | Nursing

WHEN small children play Hospitals the girls dress up as nurses and the doctor has to be a man, if only in costume. Progressive educationists in Sweden and elsewhere are busily adapting children's picture-books so that they comply with current views on sex discrimination; it must not always be a little girl who tucks the dolls up in bed or a little boy who holds the stethoscope. But traditional attitudes die hard. As far as career books are concerned, nursing is for girls. Sections on male nursing (usually in connection with mental illness) are brief and almost incidental. Womanliness is the key to the profession. Matters have hardly changed since, a century or so ago, that most professional of nurses Florence Nightingale remarked that "until the last ten to twenty years people in England thought that every woman was a nurse by instinct."*

Florence Nightingale herself dispelled this illusion once and for all by forcing the public to accept nursing as a profession, demanding strict and serious training. But no matter how downright and domestic her NOTES ON NURSING (1860) may be, they rest on the assumption of service, which was demonstrated once and for all at Balaclava and Scutari. The nurse serves humanity in a particular way which art, industry and science do not match. She is concerned vitally and deeply with people in crisis. An experienced S.R.N. puts it bluntly:

> If you do not like people (and this is no crime), if you prefer books, figures or tools, then I don't think you should choose nursing as a career. There are many other jobs you will enjoy far more.

Peggy Nuttall. NURSING AS A CAREER (1960), p. 13

*Quoted in J. McK. Calder. THE STORY OF NURSING (1954), p. 65

However specialised the training of nurses may become, the basic fact of wanting to help people will not change. Nowadays career advisers tend to stress the scientific interest that the nurse's training holds for the academic type of girl, but the human element remains essential. The principal sister tutor at a London hospital, interviewed by Joan Llewelyn Owens for a careers handbook, made the following significant point:

> In the introductory course there has been an alteration in emphasis. The previous concept was to learn the normal in a year and the abnormal in two years. The present concept is – nursing is looking after people. Therefore nursing is looking after people with disturbed normality. The emphasis is on the whole patient, and you don't look upon him as a disorder – talk about him as "the appendectomy", for instance – because the disorder is only part of him.
> HOSPITAL CAREERS FOR GIRLS (1961), p. 89

This is of course not a new point of view. Florence Nightingale laid it down that a patient was "not merely a piece of furniture, to be kept clean and ranged against the wall, and saved from injury

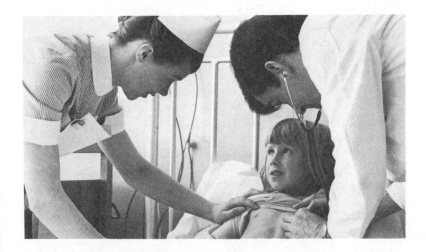

A persuasive photograph from the recruiting pamphlet, A GIRL LIKE YOU (H.M.S.O.)

and breakage", adding that "to judge from what many a nurse does and does not do you would say he was".*

Every career book or official leaflet stresses that in nursing girls will find a unique opportunity for service. In this context the word "vocation" becomes important. Semantically it seems to be embedded in two separate concepts, as it is applied to nursing. It reflects the idea of service basic to the profession and central to the International Nursing Code of Ethics:

> Service to mankind is the primary function of nurses and the reason for the existence of the nursing profession. Need for nursing service is universal. Professional nursing service is therefore unrestricted by considerations of nationality, race, creed, colour, politics or social status.
>
> Inherent in the code is the fundamental concept that the nurse believes in the essential freedoms of mankind and in the preservation of human life.
>
> Quoted in THE STORY OF NURSING, p. 97

The word has also attracted to itself a social implication which is less lasting. In the past, middle-class women, with few respectable ways of earning open to them, could without embarrassment join their richer sisters, for whom nursing was a form of philanthropy, if the word "vocation" were invoked. For a gentlewoman, dedication to nursing could satisfy frustrated emotion, it could be profoundly rewarding to the personality but it could also neatly solve a financial dilemma. Like many other words connected with morality, "vocation" is seen to be somewhat ambiguous.

Modern career books on nursing show a very necessary change from the attitude of fifty years ago. In the past, vocation in a more or less religious sense was stressed so consistently that girls must often have hesitated to commit themselves to such positive dedication. Pamela Bright comments on the dictionary definition of "vocation" as "The action of God in calling a person to exercise some special (usually) spiritual function, or to fill a certain position"†; she believes that for the majority of girls "there is

---

*NOTES ON NURSING, quotation from rev. ed. 1952
†THE NURSE AND HER WORLD (1961), pp. 11–12

little divine influence or guidance towards their choice of this
this career", and Claire Rayner's sensible comment should reassure
the most hesitant schoolgirl:

> Many nurses nowadays agree that while it is obviously good to
> have a deep interest in other people, and a healthy curiosity about
> illness and how it can be cared for, the sort of intense vocation
> that used to be considered necessary for a nurse just is not required
> any more. Any reasonably intelligent kindly person with an
> interest in the welfare of other people can train to be a nurse
> and be a very successful one at that. The work demands certain
> qualities of mind and heart, admittedly, but they are not the sort
> of qualities that are found only in a few rare individuals; most of
> us have the ability and interest in other people that would make
> us into perfectly successful nurses.
> SHALL I BE A NURSE? (1968), p. 92

The decision to train as a nurse none the less remains a considered
and a personal one. All career advisers urge young people to look
dispassionately at their characters and capabilities before they
embark on this particular career, and although in the climate of
today the inducements to become a nurse may be less idealistic
and more practical than they were, there is no intrinsic difference
between Evelyn Pearce's description of 1953:

> Those setting out on this career need not be discouraged for
> everyone can acquire these basic qualities:
> The *goodwill* to accomplish with interest, kindness and con-
> sideration what is just and right.
> The *good nature*, which includes good humour, and excludes
> pride, fear, self-regard, those common sources of unhappiness.
> The *good* or *common sense*, bringing intuition and the ability
> to put the art of nursing into practice simply and naturally.
> The *good manners*, which put people at ease, and have a definite
> value in creating a therapeutic atmosphere.
> NURSE AND PATIENT, p. 76

and the more matter-of-fact character sketch in the Peacock careers
book:

A genuine desire to be of service; sympathy for the sick without sentimentality; an interest in medicine without morbid curiosity about illness; sensitivity coupled with a certain amount of toughness so as not to get too emotionally involved; patience; a sense of humour to put up with the inevitable occasional short tempers and difficult people; ability to know when to be firm – and how to be firm but not rude; powers of observation; initiative; ability to take responsibility one moment and to do exactly as told the next.

THE PEACOCK BOOK OF CAREERS FOR GIRLS, p. 254

When a little girl plays nurses and hospitals, she is not really trying on a career for size so much as acting out a stage of her progressive defining of the world she lives in. A nursery book from America, Carla Greene's I WANT TO BE A NURSE (1957), is advertised as being "designed to encourage independent reading on beginner level. The concepts – broad as a child's imagination – bring pleasure to early reading experience and better understanding of the world." The last phrase is the one that most nearly concerns the book. With very few words to a page, the author contrives to fit a good deal of information into the chatter of Jane and Jack, who appeal to a nurse for help when Jane's doll falls ill. The two of them hear about children's wards, dispensing, the nurse's uniform. Besides placing hospitals and nurses in the scheme of life, the book reassures children about hospital; some of the details in the last picture, which shows the doll in bed surrounded by Get Well cards, would certainly help.

It is, I suppose, a matter of taste whether cute, self-consciously comic pictures best suit this kind of domestic text, but the content of the book is sound and well-presented, and it shows an advance in sophistication from THE HOSPITAL NURSE by E. M. Phillips, a book published twenty years ago, in which the fictional formula is rather ponderously used. Uncle, just out of hospital after breaking his leg, is pleased when Joyce says she wants to be a nurse, but warns her ". . . to be a Nurse you must pass exams., and that means working hard even when you are quite small. Later you would go to a school for Nurses"; he continues with simple facts about the nurse's duties in taking temperatures, doing night duty, bandaging, making beds and attending casualty patients.

In the climate of today this kind of fictional framework in a book designed to be read by a child may be less congenial than a simple collection of straight facts. THE NURSE (1963) by Vera Southgate and J. Havenhand in the Ladybird *Easy Reading* series is full of good sense. Here is the nurse within the hierarchy of the hospital; her world and her status, described very briefly, are described *together*, so that right from the beginning the child sees her working in a team, with her own particular contribution to make. This book and the somewhat similar DOCTORS AND NURSES, WHAT DO THEY DO? (1963) by Carla Greene offer selected facts in simple statement and help to lay the foundation of knowledge of how society works.

For rather older children, facts are also very easily and agreeably assimilated from John Chillingworth's STUDENT NURSE (1960), which has a picture-book format and consists of a series of photographs taken at the Royal Free Hospital in London, each one being fully captioned. This is more specifically a career book in that it invites readers directly to think about nursing:

> Nursing is a career which requires physical, mental and spiritual strength, but its all-embracing demands also mean that a girl who becomes a good nurse also becomes a mature person who has made full use of all her gifts.
> STUDENT NURSE, no page numbers

These are all books which could be used one way or another in the junior or middle school. Even STUDENT NURSE is simple enough in its approach for a child of ten or so to find it stimulating. In a broad sense the various books for younger readers about hospitals account for another step forward. Just as an outline like the Ladybird THE NURSE can show a child where this particular profession fits into the social pattern, so a book like HOSPITALS (1970) by Alan James or Charles King's book of the same title (1969) or Norman Wymer's BEHIND THE SCENES IN A HOSPITAL (1965) can show him where the various people concerned – nurses, doctors, technicians, workmen and of course patients – fit into the special pattern of the hospital world. Books like these introduce children to the hospital routine from the point of view of the work, whereas Claire Rayner's WHAT HAPPENS IN HOSPITAL (1963)

and Mary Cockett's MARY ANN GOES TO HOSPITAL (1961)
describe, through the story of one child's tonsillectomy, what it is
like actually to be in hospital. The picture is the same, the angle is
different, and the facts are there for a child to assimilate and to
remember later in the more specific context of career advice.

A great many girls become nurses without reading a word about
the profession; there are doctors or nurses in the family or they are
fired by a film, an older friend or a careers talk. At secondary
school, though, thoughts of a possible future will be in the air and
a girl accustomed to using the printed word will turn to the career
library, for ideas probably rather than for particular information.
Her head may well become filled, or may already be filled, with the
picture of a glamorous nurse resembling Helen Dore Boylston's
Sue Barton or Laurence Meynell's *Nurse Ross* or Constance White's
Sally of St Patrick's or Shirley Darbishire's *Nurse Carter*. With
any luck, common sense will have suggested already that no single
nurse could hope to meet so many enthralling emergencies, and
that the patients in fiction suffer nobly, never vomiting or incontinent
and seldom more than mildly irritable. Most career fiction about
nursing is designed to entertain, and the stern dose of training is
hidden in a liberal allowance of jam. Claire Rayner's SHALL I BE
A NURSE? is exceptional, as one can see from the forthright opening:

> They arrived at the Royal Hospital at three o'clock on a sunny
> April afternoon. One by one, they made their way across the
> wide courtyard, bustling with doctors, nurses, ambulances,
> wheelchairs and patients – all of them rather over-awed by the
> sheer size of the place.
> op. cit., p. 7

The eight characters in this book are at conveniently different
stages of their education. Emily Jennings has "A" levels and has
been working in an office. Jennifer Brown has three "O" levels
and was working in her father's shop when her mother suggested
nursing as a more interesting life. Heather wants to be an air
hostess and thinks a nurse's training may help her. John Peterson
wanted to be a doctor but his talent for science proved inadequate.
Susan and Barbara have been working in a children's home and
Susan at least genuinely loves children. Jane and Frances, who have

the C.S.E. exam to their credit, lack the academic ability for the State Registered training but Frances, who likes people but is bad at exams, is a natural for the State Enrolled system. In following the fortunes of young men and women with varied personalities and social backgrounds, the author is able to construct as it were a calendar of a nurse's training and to introduce useful facts about pharmacy, physiotherapy, theatre work, hospital administration, social medicine, midwifery, overseas service, district nursing, factory and school nursing, health visiting and the duties of a receptionist.

For a girl whose ideas of a career are vague, the fictional form of this kind of book is likely to appeal more than a general, abstract explanation of the stages of a nurse's training. This is not yet the time for a serious specialised book on the subject. Recognising this, M. Carver presents THE NURSE (1965) in Ward Lock's *Going to Work* series in the context of history, summarising the service aspect of nursing with examples from the past beginning, engagingly, with Moses in the bulrushes. An interesting choice of event is supported by a far better choice of pictures than is usual in such books; they include a photograph of St John's Ambulance men dealing with a jockey and a fallen horse, Elizabeth Fry reading to prisoners in Newgate and the Matron of St Thomas's surrounded by the probationers of the class of 1881. A girl who is attracted by the lively continuous tradition described in this book is advised to look to a Youth Employment Officer for further information. The author suggests that the Red Cross or St John's Ambulance can provide valuable practice until the intending nurse is old enough for training. She offers sensible comments on the behaviour expected of a nurse, and succinct information about grants and about the various types of training open to girls and boys. As a general book THE NURSE is unusually practical. A chapter on "A day in the ward", for example, really does give a concrete picture of the way a ward team gets to work and – a novel touch – the author describes the nurses in the casualty department as a patient would see them.

This is not a dogmatic book, but at one point the author confines herself to a single point of view. She is in favour of young people entering upon some form of training related to nursing, before they reach the statutory age of eighteen. The latest official pamphlet

Want to be a nurse? issued by the Department of Health recommends a pupil to "stay at school and take as good a leaving certi-
ficate as you can get"; while specifying how to find out about
hospital cadet schemes, pre-nursing courses and voluntary nursing
bodies, it also advises the school leaver that "any job which enables
you to know people or widen your horizons would be useful", and
suggests "You would be wise to read widely and if possible take
further education classes and study for 'O' level G.C.E. passes."
Most general books on nursing offer a choice of opinions, but they
will usually lean towards the conclusion expressed in simple terms
by Peggy Nuttall:

> Whilst there may be someone at school who will be able to teach
> you these subjects for your preliminary examination, when you
> get to hospital there will be no one who will have the time or
> opportunity to teach you English, history, geography, or civics.
> They will be too busy going over the ground you have already
> covered. So think it over carefully. Later in life I think you will
> find you would rather have a better knowledge of other subjects
> than of the anatomy and physiology that you will have to do,
> some time or other, in any case.
> NURSING AS A CAREER, p. 27

However individual a careers book may be, however much it is
flavoured by the personality of the author, it is an obligation on that
author, if she gives a particular point of view, to indicate that there
are others. Few young people are going to read four or five books
to get an average view of a subject: in the careers library they
should be able to find a broad view and a complete one in any
book they consult.

It is for general points like this about further education, in which
an adult may be thought qualified to advise, that a general careers
book may be valuable. They will all give a more or less adequate
summary of the course of a nurse's training and the kinds of career
it can lead to. Girls coming up to school leaving age can in any case
find out the immediate facts most readily from an official leaflet or
a careers meeting, and the Department of Health's leaflets are
particularly clear and attractive. A careers book on nursing has
other kinds of help to offer. It can, for example, help a girl to decide

whether or not she has the right temperament to be a nurse. Harry Gaston's A GUIDE TO HOSPITAL CAREERS (1962) provides a practical questionnaire which could be useful to the indecisive. Among the questions are:

> Are you prepared to accept a degree of discipline which, in the light of your growing maturity, may seem more rigorous and irksome than anything you experienced at school, and which your friends who take up some other career might regard with incredulity?
>
> Are you prepared to work long, awkward hours, day and night, high days and holidays, sometimes arranged or altered at short notice?
>
> ... Are you prepared to earn less than some of your friends for two or three years, remembering that it is almost inevitable that at times you may regard them a little enviously in this respect?
>
> A GUIDE TO HOSPITAL CAREERS, p. 103

This is facing facts in a more direct manner than usual; young people will only be able to mean the "honest, unhesitating 'yes'" which Harry Gaston demands if they have the question put to them straight.

The attitude of nurse to patient is not easy to explain in general terms. Most young people accept advice most easily when it is practical and do not welcome a tone of moral uplift. Nobody would deny the truth of Joy Burden's generalisation "Taking time and trouble regardless of personal convenience is the sign of a giver, and nurses are in hospital to give freely", but it would carry less weight if it were not preceded by the comment: "Picking up Mrs. Jones's knitting, dropped for the umpteenth time, and returning it good-naturedly, is all part of the nursing service . . ."* Dr Hubert Thomas's GOING INTO NURSING? (1964) is overtly religious in its approach, but the sincerity of the book redeems it. Besides, the author touches on points seldom mentioned in this kind of book. He warns young people that they will need to consider their own opinions on abortion and euthanasia, and he is prepared to discuss

---

*WHAT ABOUT NURSING? (1959), p. 12

more frankly than most writers the difficulty of coming to terms with pain and its effect on people. Accepting the fact that a student nurse is bound to be anxious about responsibility, he offers the kind of direct statement that could be very reassuring to a girl thinking about nursing as a career:

> The very background of professional co-operation is of enormous help to the nurse, especially the younger one, when she is confronted as never before by the prevalence of pain and suffering. There is nothing pleasant about either, but it is good to realize that she is not alone in the effort to lessen and eliminate them. The new nurse will soon see that pain does actually serve as a warning that something is wrong or out of order. Like an alarm bell it gives the signal that something should be done about it. The nurse is there, not to feel sorry but to deal with what the pain indicates, not forgetting that sometimes the wisest action is to do nothing. She will soon learn that the hospital ward is no place for panic.
>
> GOING INTO NURSING? p. 15

and again:

> As in the case of the doctor, the nurse's fundamental human concern can be taken for granted. If that were not so she would never have gone in for nursing. The efficient nurse will always be deeply concerned but never openly or even inwardly *worried* about a patient, and her patient will often gain as much from her conscientious but detached manner as from the medication administered.
>
> ibid., p. 18

In this context, girls might also find Helen Anthony's career autobiography, MEDICAL SOCIAL WORK (1968), particularly reassuring to read. In this account of an almoner's training, the author is very open about her feelings and in particular about the struggle to come to terms with the personalities of the people she had to deal with. However strong the desire to serve, many girls doing some kind of pre-nursing training must at one time or another feel distaste and doubt in their contact with people, and there are books which can at least assure them that they are not alone in feeling guilty about sliding back from the first glowing ideal.

Most boys and girls would probably prefer to read books which discussed this aspect of the nursing services among others than to be given a clear, concise account like L. M. Darnell's NURSING (1959), which hardly mentions the fact that this is a career where individuals work with individuals, and which makes no allowance for any apprehensions about crises in the wards.

Peggy Nuttall's attitude is bracing and realistic. "You *do not*, repeat *do not* see blood spurting all over the place," she assures her readers, and tells them that most people are unconscious when they die and that it *is* possible to accept the fact of death without becoming dehumanised. She is well aware of the alarming way certain aspects of work in a hospital must present themselves to a nurse in training, or someone preparing to start training:

> Every night nurse is in a dilemma. She must create an atmosphere of peace and quiet so that the patients may be able to sleep undisturbed, but she and her colleagues must be constantly on the alert. This is not always easy.
>
> NURSING AS A CAREER, p. 48

A sense of humour helps this author through a masterly summary of all the branches of nursing and an unusually detailed description of training, ward routine and hospital hierarchies. But for a thorough and thoroughly human treatment of nursing, which could confirm many an ambition, the outstanding book for the careers library is undoubtedly Pamela Bright's THE NURSE AND HER WORLD (1961).

This book was published in 1961 and drew on twenty-six years of nursing experience. Apart from the wage situation (played down in all career books on nursing), there is little to suggest that the book was written so long ago. The author has a crisp prose style and organises her material admirably, dividing it into one section on general training and another on more specialised kinds of nursing. Addresses, a book list, good classification make it a useful reference book, but it is also entirely readable, coming over in a voice neither detached, dictatorial nor effusive. The author puts herself very much in the position of a young person who wants to know what it is really like – not only what she will be asked to do but what it will feel like. Experience counts for much, but it is not everyone who can communicate experience, as Pamela Bright does, for instance, when she offers a necessary warning:

> To escape from fatigue in nursing is a difficult thing. I do not mean purely physical tiredness, which leads to sound sleep and good appetite and gives zest to the work on the wards. I mean the nervous strain which causes fatigue without the nurse really being aware of it. From the very beginning of her training, the nurse has been constantly aware of someone in authority over her. The fear of doing the wrong thing or of making a tactless remark, the fear of reprimands, the hurry to get things done in time, often resulting in indigestion, the suppression of emotions – all these have added consciously or unconsciously to the strain. However sympathetic the Sister in charge of the ward, however helpful the Staff Nurse, the student may still have taken her worries to bed with her, and in the hours of the night, when she should have been gaining fresh strength to cope with the morrow's work, she will have been turning over and over in her mind problems which at the moment she could do nothing about.
>
> THE NURSE AND HER WORLD, pp. 59–60

A junior nurse might fancy herself above such qualms, but human nature does not change and the analysis still holds good; moreover, although the author seems to be addressing herself to a girl already embarked on a nurse's training, her words are equally useful to answer the unspoken questions of much younger girls thinking about the future.

The information in this very full, thorough book is lightened because the author is thinking all the time in particular rather than in general terms. "I think a sense of humour is important", she says, and changes at once to a particular instance – "It is more than easy to get annoyed . . . with the difficult or irrational old lady who wants to go home to see her canary rather than get into bed."* She can laugh at her profession too and her categorising of the

*ibid., p. 15

type-specimens whose example she hopes the young will not follow
– the Brick, the Angel of Mercy, the Ray of Sunshine and others –
is invigorating.

Pamela Bright writes out of a knowledge of what it means to be a
nurse and her book seems as sane and sensible now as it was when
it was published in 1961, yet for today it is incomplete. Today
the hospital hierarchy is being questioned – the "benevolent
paternalism" as one doctor puts it that exists between nurses and
doctors and that allows some doctors to continue to regard nurses
as "little dedicated sisters of mercy" who submit to being exploited.
Traditions of rank and privilege are difficult to explain, but if it is
understandable that writers of career books should accept them,
or appear to do so, it is equally understandable that young people
who have friends or relations actually working in hospitals should
regard the omission with some scepticism. The camaraderie of
television programmes like *Emergency Ward 10* probably deceived
few members of the younger generation.

Still more likely to be criticised is the omission of the simple
and essential fact of wages. There is grim humour in the words of a
surgeon who thirty years ago lectured to nurses in training:

> It is sometimes said that nurses' hours of work are too long, that
> their pay is poor, that they are badly housed, and that they are
> often badly fed. Such conditions occasionally exist, but in recent
> years great improvements have taken place, and those in charge of
> the interests of nurses are active in speeding up reforms where
> necessary. No young women need have any hesitation in entering
> on training on account of such statements for there is now little
> fear of encountering such conditions. But, when they do occur
> they can usually be traced to the days, not long ago, when mainly
> voluntary and charity organizations undertook the care of the
> sick, and when women without thought of gain were eager to
> sacrifice all personal interests to the calling.
> E. Drybrough-Smith. DO YOU WANT TO BE A NURSE? (1941),
> p. 9

The nurses' strike of 1969 provoked distaste and disapproval in
the public because the tradition of service seemed to be outraged.
Individual stories of hardship, widely reported, might be believed,

but it was still felt that there was something wrong in dedicated people holding the public to ransom.

Complaints and answers might well be quoted in career books written today and no career book can be considered truly useful unless it is as firm about the material rewards of the profession as about the psychological satisfaction (whether you call it emotional, intellectual or spiritual) which can be promised to the right kind of student nurse.

There is one more gap, I feel, in career books. Inevitably, but unfortunately, when they are concerned with a single career they tend to regard it in isolation. A hospital is a little world and it may seem task enough to deal with its ramifications without going outside it. But a hospital is an essential part of society, urban or rural, and a nurse is serving society when she serves individuals. One of the best ways for a girl to see her prospective career in a wide context is to read a really good history of the nursing services or of medicine in general. Nobody could put down Mary Stocks's humane and

An aspect that career books tend to ignore; article by William Breckon from the Daily Mail, 14 November 1969.

wise survey, A HUNDRED YEARS OF DISTRICT NURSING (1960), without seeing the nursing career in a better perspective than before. The value of a hospital career could only be enhanced by the reading of Jean Calder's THE STORY OF NURSING, with its emphasis on service, or Desirée Edwards-Rees's book with the same title (1965), which drives forward to the firm conclusion that the status of nurses has not been allowed to keep pace with their achievements. Nor would any intending nurse be anything but encouraged and uplifted, as well as amused now and then, by Cecil Woodham Smith's LADY IN CHIEF (1953), with its candid speaking likeness of Florence Nightingale.

Boys and girls should be made aware of what nurses have done in the past and how their work has marched with the march of civilisation. They should, just as much, be well informed, before they undertake this fine career, about the place of hospitals and nursing homes in the world of today. Where is the career book that explains the present system of hospital boards, that gives any indication of the various ways in which hospitals are financed, that touches on the effects of publicity (good and bad) on the public image of the nursing profession, that discusses the opening of Women's Institutes and other organisations in mental homes, that pursues the possible effect on families when one member enters upon nursing? Girls and boys who enter upon the nursing career pledge themselves to far more than simply hard work. General career books rightly stress that young people have a duty towards the world they live in, but the books available for them – on nursing as on other professions – do not give them enough encouragement to regard themselves as citizens or enough advice to help them to make themselves useful as well as contented citizens.

Reading List

Anthony, Helen. MEDICAL SOCIAL WORK. My Life and my Work.
    Educational Explorers 1968. Illustrated by photographs.
Baker, Margaret. HOSPITAL CAREERS. Picture Career Books. *Lutterworth* 1966.
    Photographs by Patrick Ward. The excellent photographs, taken at the
    Middlesex Hospital in London, help the reader to understand something of the

many kinds of medical, technical, administrative and social work available in a hospital.

Bright, Pamela. THE NURSE AND HER WORLD. Young Persons' Guides. *Gollancz* 1961.

Burden, Joy. WHAT ABOUT NURSING? *S.P.C.K.* 1959. See also her ADVENTURES IN VOCATION. Wells, *St Andrew's Press* 1961.

Calder, Jean McKinlay. THE STORY OF NURSING. Outlines. *Methuen* 1954, 4th revised edition 1963. Illustrated by Roy Spencer.

Carver, M. THE NURSE. Going to Work. *Ward Lock* 1965. Illustrated by photographs.

Chillingworth, John. STUDENT NURSE. *Lutterworth* 1960. Illustrated by photographs.

Cooper, Lettice. THE YOUNG FLORENCE NIGHTINGALE. The Young . . . (*Parrish* 1960) *Roy* 1961. Illustrated by Denise Brown. A lively fictionalised biography for the middle years, closely derived from Florence Nightingale's diaries and writings.

Darnell, L. M. NURSING. Target Books. *Robert Hale* 1959.

Drybrough-Smith, E. DO YOU WANT TO BE A NURSE? *Simpkin Marshall* 1941.

Edwards-Rees, Desirée. THE STORY OF NURSING (*Constable Young Books* 1965) *Verry* 1965. Illustrated by photographs and prints.

Gaston, Harry. A GUIDE TO HOSPITAL CAREERS. *Museum Press* 1962.

Greene, Carla. I WANT TO BE A NURSE (*Childrens Press* 1957) *W. and R. Chambers* 1963. Illustrated by Becky and Evans Krehbiel.

Greene, Carla. DOCTORS AND NURSES, WHAT DO THEY DO? I Can Read . . . (*Harper & Row* 1963) *World's Work* 1964. Illustrated by Leonard Kessler.

James, Alan. HOSPITALS. Learning Library. *Blackwell* 1970. Illustrated by Laszlo Acs.

King, Charles. HOSPITALS. People at Work. *Blackie* 1969. Illustrated by the author.

Miller, Ruth (editor). THE PEACOCK BOOK OF CAREERS FOR GIRLS. *Penguin* 1966. See page 419.

Nightingale, Florence. NOTES ON NURSING (First published 1860. *Duckworth* revised edition 1952) *Lippincott* replica edition 1957.

Nuttall, Peggy. NURSING AS A CAREER. Batsford Career Books. *Batsford* 1960.

Owens, Joan Llewelyn. HOSPITAL CAREERS FOR GIRLS. Career Guides. *Bodley Head* 1961. *Evans* revised edition 1967, Summit Career Guides. Illustrated by photographs.

Pearce, Eveleyn C. NURSE AND PATIENT: AN ETHICAL CONSIDERATION OF HUMAN RELATIONS. *Faber* 1953.

Phillips, E. M. THE HOSPITAL NURSE. Question Time. *Macmillan* 1951.

Rayner, Claire. WHAT HAPPENS IN HOSPITAL. *Rupert Hart-Davis* 1963. Illustrated by Katharine Hoskyns.

Rayner, Claire. SHALL I BE A NURSE? *Wheaton* 1968. Illustrated by Denis Wrigley.

Smith, Cecil Woodham. LADY IN CHIEF: THE STORY OF FLORENCE NIGHTINGALE. Story Biographies. *Methuen* 1953.

Southgate, Vera and Havenhand, J. THE NURSE. Ladybird Easy Reading series. *Wills and Hepworth* 1963. Illustrated by John Berry.

Stocks, Mary. A HUNDRED YEARS OF DISTRICT NURSING. *Allen and Unwin* 1960.

Thomas, Dr Hubert. GOING INTO NURSING? *Epworth Press* 1964.

Wilkins, Frances. SIX GREAT NURSES. Six Great . . . *Hamish Hamilton* 1962. With reproductions of portraits. Interesting accounts of Louise de Marillac, Florence Nightingale and Edith Cavell, with others.

Wymer, Norman. BEHIND THE SCENES IN A HOSPITAL. Behind the Scenes . . . *Phoenix* 1965. Line drawings by Laszlo Acs, and photographs.

Relevant Stories

Cockett, Mary. MARY ANN GOES TO HOSPITAL. *Methuen* 1961. Illustrated by Shirley Hughes.

Darbishire, Shirley. YOUNG NURSE CARTER (1951). NURSE CARTER MARRIED (1955). Career Novels. *Chatto and Windus.*

Kamm, Josephine. STUDENT ALMONER. *Bodley Head* 1955. A pleasantly written career novel, stressing hospital etiquette and offering many case-histories.

Martin, Nancy. CALL THE NURSE. *Macmillan* 1966. Illustrated by Jackie Grippando.

Martin, Nancy. TERESA JOINS THE RED CROSS (1968). RED CROSS CHALLENGE (1970). *Macmillan.* Illustrated by James Hunt. Topical junior novels with firm characterisation and much useful fact.

Meynell, Laurence. NURSE ROSS TAKES OVER (1958). NURSE ROSS SHOWS THE WAY (1959). NURSE ROSS SAVES THE DAY (1960). NURSE ROSS AND THE DOCTOR (1962). GOOD LUCK, NURSE ROSS (1963). *Hamish Hamilton.*

White, Constance. SALLY OF ST PATRICK'S. Jet Books. *Cape* 1966.

5b | Journalism

Journalism's my scene. After all it's a compromise between being a dropout and a lawyer.

From a G.C.E. "O" level essay on ambition, quoted in *The Times Educational Supplement*, 14 August 1970, p. 1

... those who serve journalism serve one of the great professions of the world. The allegiance it properly commands is absolute.

Those who give it that allegiance need stand in no man's shadow.

Francis Williams. DANGEROUS ESTATE, p. 291

5b Journalism

MOST of the current career books on journalism could be subtitled "How to make an interesting subject as dull as ditch-water"
– and I do not mean just by writing clichés. This is only partially
explained by the fact that career books are required to generalise
about a subject which defies generalisation. No matter how strong
the strait-jacket of editorial policy, it is the individualists who get
to the top, but I have yet to find an author with the honesty to
start a careers book on journalism with the words "Only egotists
need apply", or, for that matter, by saying "Egotists had better
think twice about applying".

All writing is an act of display which needs as much nerve as
talent to carry it through. Authors of career books do warn the
reader who is thinking of journalism that he will be writing under
severe limitations of time, space, subject and interpretation; only
rarely do they mention the emotional effect of this highly specialised
kind of writing or suggest that a journalist is required to keep his
egotism but also to harness it.

A well-founded library shelf labelled Journalism will probably
include some sociology, newspaper history, polemic and handbooks that could be used by practising as well as intending journalists. It might also be extended backwards to take in the kind of
junior topic book that can and occasionally does wake a latent
ambition. The advantage of such junior books is that because they
are simple they can be inclusive. Even an infant school pamphlet
like Kenneth Nuttall's NEWS FOR ALL (1964) begins and ends with
the finished newspaper and mentions printing press, teleprinters
and compositors as well as stating roundly, "All the time, all over
the world, newspaper men are collecting news."*

*op. cit., p. 9

At the primary school level, children will be ready to be interested in newspapers or the people who produce them, or both, and the wider the picture they are given, the better. Carla Greene's brisk and rather cute I WANT TO BE A NEWS REPORTER (1958) starts with a boy commenting on the headlines of a paper on a newsstand, "I wonder if Uncle Jack wrote that story", but by the time the book has ended Don has not only been to the Zoo to help find out about a baby elephant and to a shipyard to get news of a fire, but his uncle has shown him some of the workings of a newspaper office and has suggested that he might do a little amateur reporting at school. Nicholas Fisk's lively LOOK AT NEWSPAPERS (1962) makes very clear the journalist's responsibility towards finding and using news, and in discussing the layout of a newspaper and the way its news items are balanced, he implies a good deal about the discipline within which a journalist has to work. Humour and panache are rare in information books of any kind; here is an author who offers proof that a happy-go-lucky style can convey fact as easily as a portentous one. Two children are watching Hank the copy-taster:

"Look – here's a piece of copy that's just come in. I read it" . . . (and he read it through in a matter of seconds) . . . "I decide that it won't do, it's not our sort of news, I don't like its taste – and so I SPIKE it! There!" And he jammed the paper on to a spike already loaded with other bits of rejected copy.
LOOK AT NEWSPAPERS, pp. 64–5

It is occasionally suggested that journalists write primarily for other journalists, and certainly few people read newspapers more assiduously than those who write for them. It would be absurd and useless to enter upon any career without some knowledge of the medium you are going to work in, and would-be journalists have to train themselves as readers, among other things. Geoffrey Smith's NEWS AND NEWSPAPERS (1962) is written from the point of view of newspaper readers – in this case, top primary and middle school children whose interest will be satisfied by brief but careful accounts of the history of newspapers, the hierarchy of a newspaper office and the processes of production and distribution. Beyond this, the author explains with exceptional clarity how the presentation of news changes from one editor to another and from one paper to another. He discusses the Royal Commissions on the Press of 1949 and 1961, challenging his young readers to respond to his argument, and he emphasises their particular responsibility:

> . . . it is the readers themselves who determine the standards of newspapers . . . If we want good newspapers we must be discriminating readers. That is one reason why we should choose our paper carefully, and judge it critically but fairly. In addition, that is the best way to enjoy a daily newspaper and to look forward with pleasure to its arrival every morning.
> NEWS AND NEWSPAPERS, p. 95

The question of slanting the news is not often aired with much conviction in books about journalism – sometimes, perhaps, because the authors are still in the business. Intelligent boys and girls in the 'teens will hardly need telling that newspapers do not often leave the news to speak for itself, but E. W. Hildick in A CLOSE LOOK AT NEWSPAPERS (1966) puts general scepticism to particular use when he uses programming techniques to analyse the processes of news reporting and to suggest how boys and girls working in the classroom can literally cut a newspaper to pieces and see the way it has been put together and what house style emerges. It is not the purpose of his book to explain directly how a journalist goes to work, but facts are sometimes remembered better if they insinuate themselves into a reader's mind, and there are plenty of facts to be noted here. Further, a book as sardonic and candid as this is likely to create or to encourage the kind of atmosphere in which a boy or girl with a vague desire to "write" might recognise a specific ambition to become a journalist.

THE BOYS' BOOK OF THE PRESS by Derek Hudson (1964) is not noticeably broader in its explanation of the workings of a newspaper than other information books, but this and companion books in the series are popular with eleven-plus readers because of their workmanlike and efficient format. The simple layout with double columns, broken up with paragraph and section headings and freely sown with illustrations, leads the reader from point to point and makes it easy for him to find particular facts. Authors writing in this series set themselves to satisfy the taste of boys for actualities,

A page from A CLOSE LOOK AT NEWSPAPERS (Faber); an invitation to use eyes and wits

for learning how cars or aeroplanes or newspapers work *now* in the world they know.

Actuality does not wholly account for the popularity of THE BOYS' BOOK OF THE PRESS. Although the author does not set himself to discuss a journalist's career as such, he directs the

attention emphatically to its social aspect. This is too sensible a
book to suggest that journalism is a matter of chasing scoops and
polishing purple passages. Because this particular series is concerned
with the world of today, the newspaper and the journalist are
connected specifically with that world:

> . . . journalism can give young people the chance to play their
> part as citizens. The standing of the Press as the purveyor of
> news is not, admittedly, quite what it was in the recent past,
> before the arrival of on-the-spot television. There are now many
> fewer newspapers published than thirty years ago; for economic
> reasons, newspaper power has been concentrated in a small
> number of hands, which inevitably raises anxiety as to the free
> expression of individual opinions. Even so, the well-run enter-
> prising newspaper still has its opportunities. And on the level of
> serious exposition and argument the influence of the written
> word will remain extremely powerful and sometimes decisive.
> A recent distinguished editor declared that he chose to become a
> journalist as "a way to get things done," and if a young man is
> concerned about the integrity and quality of life in Britain, as he
> should be, he will find ample scope in journalism to expose, and
> to seek to remedy, the abuses of our time.
> THE BOYS' BOOK OF THE PRESS, pp. 143-4

This may be a somewhat idealised picture of the press, but the
point needs to be made, even if an apprentice journalist has to suffer
some disappointment when things turn out to be rather different
from the generalised picture. The author has tried, rightly, to make
his readers look beyond newsprint to its function. Duff Hart-Davis
in BEHIND THE SCENES ON A NEWSPAPER (1964) has a different
object in view. His aim is suggested in the title of his book. This is
literally a look behind the scenes; what does this or that member
of staff do, and why? A crisp, concise way of writing helps to take
the reader along to a scene which is made actual also by the plan of
"a day in a newspaper office".

The author has borrowed enough of the technique of fiction to
catch its immediacy:

The final edition is printed at four o'clock. At four forty-five the

presses slow down and stop for the last time. Outside it is already
light as the vans roar off on their final journey. Another day in
the life of the newspaper is over. A hush falls over the building,
and once more the fire-guard's footsteps echo round the empty
rooms.

But although most people in England are asleep, at this very
moment some journalist on the other side of the world is settling
down to send in his report. In the wire-room on the second floor
a teleprinter starts to chatter. Tomorrow's news is already
beginning to come in.

BEHIND THE SCENES ON A NEWSPAPER, pp. 88–9

He is undaunted by having to clarify the exact functions of so many
different people. Who would not prefer to take information in
this active form:

A sub-editor has a great deal to remember, and, to add to his
problems, he is nearly always working against the clock. As the
time approaches for the first edition to go to press, the pace
grows rapidly hotter, with copy piling up on his desk. As the
pressure builds up, it becomes more and more difficult to think
clearly, but the sub-editor must never become harassed: even
though a messenger may be standing at his shoulder, waiting to
rush the copy to the printer, he must keep cool and make certain
that everything is exactly right before he hands the story over.
ibid., p. 43

rather than in Richard Wiggan's more generalised sentences:

Speed is essential in all sub-editing; there is no time to waste
when copy arrives on the sub-editor's desk in batch after batch.
He must be able to deal with it swiftly and efficiently, all the time
taking care to see that no errors slip through.
SO YOU WANT TO BE A JOURNALIST (1963), p. 103

BEHIND THE SCENES ON A NEWSPAPER should command plenty
of readers who are not necessarily looking for a career book, but it
provides, none the less, the kind of information about the job as it
is to confirm a vague ambition.

There are almost as many motives for turning to journalism as
there are journalists. Among the boys and girls who want to write,
who thirst for fame, who enjoy people, who would like to travel,
there may be some who are fascinated by the communications
industry as a whole and by the way news is circulated now and has
been circulated in the past. Certainly one way to ensure that no
young person thinks of journalism as a narrow or self-sufficient job
is to offer him books like Nelson Davis's THIS IS THE NEWS (1965)
when he is still new to the skill of absorbing facts from books, or
the very simply organised compendium from America, ABOUT
NEWS AND HOW IT TRAVELS by Willma Willis Simpson (1961),
or Frank Jupo's READ ALL ABOUT IT (1962), which makes good
use of comic pictures to stress a point, or FROM DRUMBEAT TO
TICKERTAPE (1960) by Edward Osmond, which deals with the
subject in a more sober and mature manner.

An intelligent child who reads books with the general theme of
communications will sooner or later be struck by the variety of
media through which news is transmitted today; but if he is firm
in wanting to work with the printed word, he may take heart from
reading one or another of the current histories of the Press and
absorbing something of the tradition that lies behind the newspaper
of today. For junior reading one could hardly do better than Betty
Williams's lively KNOW ABOUT NEWSPAPERS (1963), an expert
piece of simplification that covers under one brightly coloured
umbrella facts about production, staffing and distribution, the tone
and temper of various national papers, and their development from
early news letters. One of the attractions of this little book is the
variety of illustrative matter; here are type-facsimiles, a page from
an office diary, headlines, a pamphlet of 1607 and many other
visual samples from an enormous subject. There is variety also in
Elizabeth Grey's THE STORY OF JOURNALISM (1968), a book
conceived in a more literary style and offering more concentrated
material. This is a book that abounds in lively detail, like the
following example of methods of carrying news:

During the American Civil War . . . there was enormous competition to be first with the outcome of battles. To begin with,
Reuter and *The Times* both chartered special fast steamers to
meet the mail-boats as they came into Southampton. The

American mail was put into wooden cylinders, these were thrown overboard and picked up by the newspaper boats, which then raced each other to the shore. Waiting for them there were fast horses which carried the dispatches to the nearest telegraph office.

THE STORY OF JOURNALISM, p. 45

This book traces the line of the fight for the freedom of the press. Brian Inglis makes this the chief point of his book on THE PRESS (1965); his account of censorship and of Press prejudice, past and present, is an important commentary to bear in mind as an addition to less specialised books. Besides, he invites his readers to participate, in a very pertinent way:

Form yourselves into a Press Council. Your job is to draw rules by which all members of the press, journalists, reporters, columnists, must abide. Your rules should cover some, or all, of the following: individual privacy; the need for people to be well

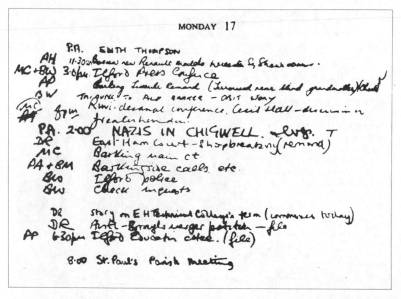

A page from an office diary specifying reporters' assignments, from KNOW ABOUT NEWSPAPERS (Blackie)

informed as to the state of the country; foreign affairs; the use
of the press as an instrument of propaganda; conduct when
interviewing people; what should or should not be printed; how
far news is more important than, say, a nation's happiness. You
will find, as you discuss, that many more points than those
printed above will need to be thought about.

THE PRESS, p. 52

Denis Thomas's THE STORY OF NEWSPAPERS (1965) gives
unusually full attention to the early news sheets and intelligencers
and their influence on newspapers now. But to convince a child of
the responsibility of a journalist, perhaps the best book would be
Marjorie Wilkerson's NEWS AND NEWSPAPERS (1970), for its
broad sociological theme and its persuasive plan.

Reporters told: You've no special rights

NEWSPAPERS have no legal privilege to refuse to disclose sources of information if ordered by a judge.

This ruling was given yesterday by Lord Denning, Master of the Rolls, in the Appeal Court.

He was dismissing the appeals by two Fleet-street reporters against their conviction and jail sentences for contempt in refusing to disclose sources of information to the Vassall spy tribunal.

Mr. Brendan Mulholland, 29-year-old *Daily Mail* reporter,

as his justification the pursuit of truth. It is in the public interests, he says, that he should obtain information in confi-

Mr Foster and Mr Mulholland yesterday

judge is the person entrusted on behalf of the community to weigh these conflicting interests.

Daily Mail article from THE PRESS (Blond Educational), by courtesy of Associated
Newspapers Ltd

NEWS AND NEWSPAPERS does not offer history for history's
sake nor for the sake of defending a tradition. The series to which
the book belongs is entitled *Past-into-Present*. Balancing sociological
and technical detail, the author shows how the role of newspapers
in the world today has grown directly from the past. The relevance
of her facts to the lives of her readers makes it likely that they will
understand what she is saying about their function as newspaper
readers and even, perhaps, as workers on a paper.

The freedom of the Press is no idle phrase, even if we cannot
accept nowadays without demur the optimistic statement of a
quarter of a century ago:

> The public attitude towards journalists in the eighteenth century
> and today differs as widely as the popular opinion of a snake
> and a fox terrier. In the course of this book we shall consider
> some of the men who were responsible for bringing about this
> change from distrust to confidence – from Dr. Johnson's verdict
> that journalists were "without a Wish for Truth, or Thought of
> Decency" to Mr. Churchill's declaration in 1943 that "our vast
> influential newspaper press has known how to combine inde-
> pendence and liveliness with discretion and patriotism."
> Derek Hudson. BRITISH JOURNALISTS AND NEWSPAPERS
> (1945), p. 7

What is a journalist? This is a question that is more easily
answered negatively:

> One thing the journalist today is *not*: He is not a fast-talking, hard-
> as-nails guy with a press card in his hatband and a bottle in his
> desk drawer who can lead the cops through their own misjudged
> clues to the criminals' hideaway and stop the presses in time to
> get the story on page one. He is almost none of the stereotypes
> you have seen in the movies or in television's situation dramas,
> and he does very few of the cliché things you may have seen him
> do.
> Leonard Eames and Bernard Ryan. SO YOU WANT TO GO INTO
> JOURNALISM (1963), p. 12

This lively survey is as relevant to Britain as it is to America, its country of origin, in its description of "an exciting, lazy, frustrating, demanding, sloppy, rewarding way of life". In order to defend their contention that a "journalist" as such hardly exists, the authors offer descriptions of imaginary interviews by imaginary reporters who take various standpoints and make all the classic mistakes.

I do not imagine that many young people seriously expect to enjoy the good fortune of Laurence Meynell's young reporter, Robin Weston, who at the beginning of his career rounds up an escaped convict, goes on to help defecting Russian scientists and wins a newspaper competition that takes him to an island full of drug smugglers. These are thrillers, not career stories. But, allowing for the good luck that necessarily attends a fictional hero, career stories can usefully show in actual rather than in general terms what a journalist actually does.

It is not impossible, for example, that a youth in his probationary period on a local paper should be on hand when a fire starts in a large department store, and not at all unlikely that such a youth would make the mistakes that John Robb's novice Colin does and be as observant and willing to learn as he is. FRONT PAGE STORY (1960) naturally centres round one unusual event rather than round the endless sequence of small happenings that make up the greater part of a novice journalist's work, but the drama of the fire does not prevent the author from describing exactly how Colin finds a telephone, how the news editor reduces him to coherence and indicates what kind of facts he should be collecting, how the older reporter sent to help him introduces himself to police, firemen and members of the public, and how the story is dealt with, piecemeal, at the desk.

It is difficult to imagine how this kind of detail, which could well be a decisive factor in the choice of a career, could be effectively put over in general terms, without a specific instance. Many generalised career books, indeed, make use of fictional inter-polations. Betty Williams's KNOW ABOUT NEWSPAPERS opens with the much-used hypothetical situation of a reporter at a fire. Roy Perrott starts DISCOVERING NEWSPAPERS (1961) with the story of Bob Chalmers taking the chance of working on a weekly paper in a Sussex market town during the school holidays. By great good luck Bob is able to observe how an experienced reporter, who is also local correspondent for a London daily, deals with such incidents as a bull running amok at a show and a ship in distress. Moreover, because Bob chances to find the ship's boy nursing the ship's cat at a refugee centre and has the acumen to ask him some questions, he is able to add an exclusive to the story of the wreck and on the strength of this is invited to the *Gazette* in Fleet Street for a week as a messenger boy.

Strictly speaking this is not a career book but a survey of newspapers and how they work; all the same, the factual part of the introductory story, because it is kept sensibly within bounds, has an inspiring effect. In the same way, the general background of F. Huggett's THE TRUE BOOK ABOUT NEWSPAPERS (1955) is enlivened by a chapter describing how a factory robbery is dealt with from the moment when the first news is collected to the sub-editor's release of the finished story.

Because they must carry at least some conviction, stories about journalism usually place their young heroes (or, occasionally, heroines) on a provincial paper, where they are more likely to be able to play an active part in events that must be chosen to make a good story as well as to introduce salient facts about work on a paper. Both background and fact can be helped if the author uses a large cast of characters. One of the best career stories of journalism, James Leasor's THE MONDAY STORY (1951), introduces three friends at a grammar school who have differing ambitions; Paul wants to learn to be a journalist in the best way possible, Bill wants to "write" and Mervyn has his eyes on fame in the Street.

In the course of a year only Paul succeeds, by applying himself to the duty of reading copy in a provincial paper and by seizing every chance to go out with "long, shaggy, tobacco-stained Isaiah Dunkley" who "pedalled hundreds of miles every month in rain or frost or sunshine, combing the villages about the town for news".* One can discern in Dunkley the usefully knowledgeable Uncle of so many information books, but his rambling speeches contain useful facts and general truths:

> "Monday's paper is the worst to fill. Nothing much ever seems to happen on Sundays . . . The Monday Story is the hardest of all to write. You may have to make bricks with straw – like writing

*op. cit., p. 58

on the length of sermons these days, with the views of octogenarian rectors, and so on. Dead stuff, agreed, but I've seen it trotted out time and time again. Or maybe your page one lead will only be an account of a storm . . . If I had my way, I'd have all new recruits to daily journalism start on a Sunday. Then they'd see a newspaper office at its worst."

THE MONDAY STORY, pp. 126-7

Stories like these can convey ideas to young people about the kind of jobs they may have to do and, more usefully, the qualities they will need – of curiosity, alertness, confidence, cheerfulness and sheer physical energy. They may suggest, too, something of the opportunism which is sometimes called a "nose for news". Perhaps the village where the young hero lives in JONATHAN ENTERS JOURNALISM (1956) is above average in its quota of eccentrics and perhaps Granville Wilson allows the boy to be on the spot too invariably for real life, but Jonathan's news stories, however bizarre – one is about a man who sings to his pigs when they are ill, another about a musical-comedy-type Brigadier and his lost swan – serve to illustrate the diversity of raw material which a young journalist could deal with if he learned to find it for himself. "A reporter," wrote Francis Williams, "is a man who never knows what will turn up but always hopes something exciting will," (p. 65) but he also says, still more pertinently:

The first essential quality any journalist must have is curiosity. He must be interested in all kinds of things and all kinds of people. He must be constantly curious about what is happening both immediately around him and in the world at large.

It is no good becoming a journalist if you easily get bored or if you are rather contemptuous about many of the things that ordinary people enjoy. A lot of your time, particularly if you start in journalism on a local weekly, which is the usual way, will be spent reporting small happenings, little local meetings, bowling matches, cricket matches, local fetes, flower shows, all the sort of things that, if you are a rather superior and intellectual kind of person, you may tend to feel rather dull and beneath your notice.

JOURNALISM AS A CAREER (1962), pp. 35-6

What is this composite character, "the journalist"? He is not to be identified by a uniform, but he may still be said to have certain field-characters as a species. A consciously provocative article by Nicholas Tomalin suggests that "the only qualities essential for real success in journalism are ratlike cunning, a plausible manner, and a little literary ability."* A milder prescription calls for "the best qualities of a detective (as an investigator), of a psychologist (for handling and summing up people), and of a lawyer (for drawing logical inferences for fact)."† According to an up-to-date edition of the DIRECTORY OF OPPORTUNITIES FOR SCHOOL LEAVERS, journalism demands "in addition to the ability to write, a high sense of responsibility, sustained effort, a lively mind and an adaptable personality", and suggests that the rewards in this career are "creative and often exciting work, travel, contact with people from all walks of life and the real possibility of wide executive authority carrying a good salary at an early age."‡ The Central Youth Employment Executive's official leaflet offers a more specific and searching list of requirements:

> Success or failure in journalism depends upon the individual journalist's personality far more than in most professions. The personal qualities required are many and various. Academic brilliance alone is no indication of an aptitude for journalism.
>
> The ability and the urge to write are essentials and must be accompanied by a wide general knowledge of everyday affairs and a consuming interest in people and things. A healthy and lively curiosity which can be developed into that necessary but intangible quality, a "nose for news", is also required.
>
> . . . When writing a story or an article he must identify himself with his readers, and present things in a way they can understand and appreciate.
>
> JOURNALISM AND PRESS PHOTOGRAPHY, p. 2

The lack of friendly invitation in this passage suggests a basic difference between official career information and the more per-

---

*Nicholas Tomlin. "Stop the Press, I want to get on." *The Sunday Times* magazine, 26 October 1969, p. 63

†John Dodge and George Viner. THE PRACTICE OF JOURNALISM (1963), p. 44

‡DIRECTORY OF OPPORTUNITIES FOR SCHOOL LEAVERS. TODAY'S PROFESSIONS (1969), p. 36

This cartoon by Calman headed an article by Nicholas Tomalin, "Stop the Press. I want to get on", which appeared in the Sunday Times colour supplement of 26 October 1969. Although Tomalin argued with perverse brilliance against the present system by which journalists must undergo a training scheme approved by the National Council for the Training of Journalists, his article breathed professionalism as surely as Calman's grotesque men illustrated every kind of irresponsible approach to a career on a newspaper. A picture like this can hide very shrewd advice in its back-handed humour; to a young aspirant the cartoon could be worth pages of abstract Do's and Dont's.

suasive introductions to careers with an individual standpoint: both, obviously, are needed by the young.

One thing they should be able to gather even from the most woolly and idealistic book on journalism – that the word "writing" carries a rather different meaning from the one they were used to at school. One hopes, too, that by the time a boy has become serious about his future he will have stopped using give-away phrases like "taking up" or "going in for" and will have developed a healthy suspicion of books that are "designed to introduce young writers to the exciting sport of writing daily".* He may have gathered from the definitions most commonly applied to sub-editors (at least in books written by reporters) that his most carefully worked para-

*Carl N. Warren. NEWS REPORTING (1929), p. 4

graphs will not necessarily be received with acclaim or printed as they stand. He will perhaps have been made to think about the particular kind of writing he proposes to attempt by reading W. T. Stead's advice to a putative journalist:

> Don't waste time over mere phrases. Sail right into the heart of your subject. When you have written your masterpiece, imagine that you have to telegraph it to Australia at your own expense. Cut out every superfluous word – above all, the adjectives. Then, if anything remains, try it on an editor and see what happens.
> F. J. Mansfield. THE COMPLETE JOURNALIST (1962), p. 161

or he may have faced another harsh truth through the sensible words of Francis Williams:

A style for a journalist must always be conditioned by the fact that he is seeking to convey information in comparatively short space. It is also conditioned, of course, by the newspaper in which it is to appear. A newspaper, . . . is the product of a team effort. Everything in it must have relationship to the newspaper's personality as a whole.

JOURNALISM AS A CAREER, p. 97

Career books are able to pronounce with authority on this kind of point, and a good English teacher can very soon persuade a boy that the craft of writing depends on constant practice. Few career books suggest that writing can really be "taught", although occasionally a writer will make specific suggestions – for instance, Richard Wiggan in SO YOU WANT TO BE A JOURNALIST gives advice on how to choose between words like "begin" and "commence" with a pedantry which perhaps accounts for the pedestrian character of his book, and E. H. Butler in AN INTRODUCTION TO JOURNALISM (1955) more usefully explains the pyramid-technique of arranging news to make an impact.

But advice in suspension is not likely to have much lasting value, and perhaps the career writer does best to allow that writing, even under newspaper conditions, is an intensely personal business, and to try to accustom the young reader to the fact that while his words could have an influence on somebody – and therefore must be carefully chosen – he will be happier in the profession if he adopts the wry attitude of Robert Harling's feature writer, who commented that "dried old women with hapless eyes, doomed old men with falling jowls, painted typists and brassy clerks, scrub-faced soldiers and minders of machines. All for a penny could have my words."*

Advice on how to look for news and how to develop techniques for collecting it may seem premature for readers still at school, but the more clearly they can envisage the job, the better. How and when to approach a police officer in court; how to prepare the ground for an interview; how to cut and still have a coherent story left; how to sharpen what you write ("The traffic jam is more interesting than 'the problem of road congestion in the conurbations'. The restaurants which serve only egg and chips are more

---

*Robert Harling. THE PAPER PALACE (1951), p. 71

interesting than 'the lack of eating facilities in small towns'.")*;
the best kind of advice on the broad matter of style is given in
practical terms.

Looking for specific illustration of the problems any journalist
faces, a young reader will do better to avoid the correspondence-
course type of book and look for something written by a journalist
with experience and style. The symposium from which I have
quoted above, THE PRACTICE OF JOURNALISM, contains articles
ringing with the unmistakeable sound of experience. Maurice
Fagence on the nature of "news", Harold Evans on reporting
techniques, L. A. Dicker on the duties of restraint and severity which
a sub-editor has to reconcile – these are articles not written specifically for the young, and for that reason all the more useful. A
similar symposium, FLEET STREET, edited by Vivian Brodsky
(1966), which was published in aid of the rebuilding of the Press
Club, contains a good deal of idle reminiscence but also "Non-stop
story" by John Williamson, which is the best short explanation I
have found of the working of the Press Association, and a forthright
view by William Redpath, in "Top secret: source of information",
of the ethic of journalists in their use of facts. PRACTICAL NEWS-
PAPER REPORTING by Geoffrey Harris and David Spark (1966)
offers less anecdote but has an admirably candid tone. Any boy who
has committed himself with trepidation to a journalist's training
should be encouraged by the sensible way these authors describe
the assignments a beginner might be given and what kind of facts
he may elicit, if he behaves suitably, from an undertaker, a local
councillor or a shop steward.

From two outstanding journalists come the clearest and most
humane discussions of the journalist's work. In JOURNALISM AS
A CAREER, Francis Williams set himself to be as precise as possible.
Each chapter starts with a question – What is journalism? What
qualities do you need? What sort of training? What sort of future?;
and in each the answer reveals an urbane, optimistic attitude to the
function of the press. Geoffrey Moorhouse's THE PRESS (1964)
is planned on a broader base, with a good deal of speculation on
the way people read newspapers and an exceptionally interesting
explanation of the law of libel and the freedom of comment in their

* THE PRACTICE OF JOURNALISM, p. 110

application to newspapers and magazines. Perhaps this book might lead readers to see themselves as feature writers in the making. If so, why not? At least the book should restore their faith in themselves as writers, a faith that is likely to be somewhat shaken by other more matter-of-fact books.

If it is encouraging to read about those who have made a name for themselves, it is perhaps even more so when you can follow their careers from the beginning instead of accepting it at its highest point. The career autobiography DATELINE: FLEET STREET (1969) by Owen Summers and Unity Hall does to a certain extent make journalism sound easy because of the blithe anecdotal manner in which the husband and wife duet is conducted. They make its rigours sound exhilarating just by their style. Here is Owen Summers on work with a morning daily:

A morning newspaper is a fresh as paint commodity for a newsagent to sell, an article which starts its brief life neatly folded and pressed – and ends as a crumpled castaway.

A morning newspaperman is equally a highly marketable commodity whose daily existence works along the same lines. During the fifteen hours plus of his sustained effort, energy, enthusiasms and the carefully charted confusion which terminates in the birth of the newspaper itself, he loses his freshness, grows tired, his clothes sag and he dies a little.

DATELINE: FLEET STREET, p. 31

For all their ebullience, the writers do enlarge on the stages of their careers, the one from provincial reporter to crime reporter for a national paper, the other from magazine journalism to the Pacesetters page in the *Sun*. While these two lively writers emphasise the humour and clubability of their calling, they are also emphatic about the obligation of a journalist to be accurate and honest and the power of the Press in correcting injustice and revealing abuse.

Here again is an optimistic attitude, suggesting that the young journalist can make his job what he wants it to be. Neil Stephen's JOURNALISM (1963) supplies a healthy corrective, starting as it does with a chapter on "What's wrong with journalism" which asserts that "the people have turned their backs on public affairs, and the Press has reacted by trying to transform itself into a branch of the entertainment industry." But this is not a negative book, harsh though it is. Besides giving sound, detached advice on the kinds of jobs available on a newspaper, the author makes clear a very active standpoint:

> Fundamentally, a journalist needs to be able to use his mind, and the policy of his own newspaper is as appropriate a subject for critical thought as anything else. There are time-servers enough in the business already. What is needed now is the type of recruit who is prepared to stand back and look at journalism against a wider system of values. If he is still satisfied with his choice, then is the time to begin discussing his qualifications for the job.
> JOURNALISM, p. 18

This is perhaps the most optimistic, as well as the most challenging, statement that young people are likely to meet in what is sometimes termed a "pre-career book".

Should career books encourage and invite? How far should they discourage? The careers handbook comes into its own when the reader has made up his mind and wants to start in the direction of his goal. Joan Llewelyn Owens in WRITING AS A CAREER (1967) varies the list pattern of her information about references and qualifications, methods of applying and so on with extracts from interviews with employers and with students. The latter sometimes regard their work with a lively scepticism – like the girl who confessed "I am a very nosey person . . . One of the reasons why I took up journalism is that it gives me an excuse to find out what is going on. I don't take anything at its face value." Dudley Barker's extremely informative THE YOUNG MAN'S GUIDE TO JOURNALISM (1963) takes the line that "It is not easy to become a journalist", but gives an exhaustive summary of facts on existing papers and magazines, types of work, training schemes, hours of work, wages and so on. While the more general aspects of this book are still valid, it is out of date in some of its facts about training and has largely been superseded by the very practical volume from Pergamon, Bernard J. Hall's BASIC TRAINING IN JOURNALISM (1968), which has, incidentally, one or two unusual features, like a glossary of technical terms and some examples of teleprinter messages gradually built into a news story.

It seems obvious that for the young person who is set on this
particular career the best course is to digest the facts in an official
publication such as the H.M.S.O's pamphlets for the Central Youth
Employment Executive and to rely for guidance on the official
leaflets from the National Council for the Training of Journalists,
through which body any intending journalist must apply for a
place in the compulsory training scheme. "Compulsory" is a dirty
word, and national newspapers still sometimes "quietly recruit
outside the ranks of provincial trainees" as Nicholas Tomalin put it.
His summing up of the situation is hardly as irresponsible as it
sounds, nor as revolutionary:

> The trouble is that journalism in Britain is crucially divided.
> Half, or three-quarters, or perhaps even seven-eighths of it, is a
> service industry, shovelling out perishable facts and names
> just as the United Dairies deliver milk. The other half, or frag-
> ment, is a collection of wayward anarchistic talents responding
> to, and usually opposing, the society they are supposed to
> report.
>   It serves no purpose to pretend that these two traditions aren't
> in many ways opposed to each other. No one denies life is tougher,
> and more *real*, for foot soldiers and general practitioners than it
> is for generals and specialists. No one denies this is so for the
> yearly batch of 600 trainees. But it really is a nonsense, born of a
> vague egalitarian urge to improve the public relations image of
> an unjust world, to pretend that they are cleverer, or even man
> for man more valuable, than the men who try to be brilliant on
> their wits alone.
> "Stop the Press, I want to get on", p. 66

It would certainly be good training for prospective journalists to
meet points of view various and unreconcileable, but they are not
likely to meet them in career books, which by their very nature must
speak to the average reader. The un-average one will already,
perhaps, have found the books which the average one should be
encouraged to try – books like the sour and stimulating THE SUGAR
PILL (1957), in which T. S. Matthews asks "Does journalism
actually do more harm than good?" or MADE FOR MILLIONS
(1947), a critical study of "the new media of information and

entertainment", in which Henry Durant, writing on the Press, makes the sober comment:

In the United States the newspapers still refer to themselves as "The Fourth Estate". So far as Britain is concerned we would like to see them doing their job of reporting the world and at the same time acting as the mentor and the conscience of the other three.

MADE FOR MILLIONS, p. 74

This above-average school leaver will perhaps have discovered Robert Hornby's forthright THE PRESS IN MODERN SOCIETY (1965) which does much to correct the parochial nature of so many career books in suggesting what an informed press could do for society and, incidentally, what education could do to prepare the young to contribute actively to that society. Certainly, if our young reader really wants to be a journalist, he will have plunged into Francis Williams's exhilarating and committed DANGEROUS ESTATE (1957), which is second to none in its resolute statement of a journalist's right to his own opinions.

On the theoretical side, career books on journalism are almost uniformly dull: on the concrete side nearly all project a disappointingly trivial image. It could be confidently stated that they are useless for any intelligent boy or girl of fifteen and over; if they are seriously thinking about a career in journalism they will already have come to question newspapers and those who work for them in a way that makes most career books otiose. A discussion with sixth formers from four London schools (published in *The Times Educational Supplement* 22 March 1968) shows the kind of questions young people ask – questions about the moral responsibility of a reporter towards his public and the people he interviews, about the intellectual quality of newspaper reporting, about the implications behind "Woman's Page" selection, about political bias.

For such readers, a careers shelf need contain nothing but an official statement of the facts about training as well as outstanding general books on journalism and associated subjects. It is not given to many journalists to be acknowledged legislators of society, but it is given to every young person to believe in himself. A school leaver will already have been conditioned by his home background, his school and his reading. Career books may have something to do with the conditioning that gives him his particular approach to the future. The higher the aim suggested in a career book, the more likely the reader is to aim high – not because he wants to be important or to do good but because he wants his work to be necessary and useful in the society in which he finds a place.

Above all, he wants to satisfy himself. Career books in general express the hope that young people will look further than a "job", but books on particular careers do not as a whole offer a particularly inspiring picture. Journalism is consistently represented as something you *do*. Only very occasionally do career books try to indicate the intellectual pleasure of manipulating words, the satisfaction of communicating facts, ideas and opinions. They are, in short, usually guilty of presenting as a "job" what is in fact a "career".

Reading List

Barker, Dudley. THE YOUNG MAN'S GUIDE TO JOURNALISM. Young person's Guide . . . *Hamish Hamilton* 1963. Illustrated by photographs.

Boston, Richard (editor). THE PRESS WE DESERVE. *Routledge and Kegan Paul* 1970.

Brodsky, Vivian (editor). FLEET STREET. *Macdonald* 1966.

Butler, E. H. AN INTRODUCTION TO JOURNALISM. *Allen and Unwin* 1955.

C.Y.E.E. JOURNALISM AND PRESS PHOTOGRAPHY. *Her Majesty's Stationery Office,* yearly from 1958.

Cutforth, René. ORDER TO VIEW. *Faber* 1969. A lively autobiographical travelogue concerned with radio news reporting.

Davis, Nelson. THIS IS THE NEWS. Walrus Books. *University of London Press* 1965. Illustrated by photographs and prints.

Dodge, John and Viner, George. THE PRACTICE OF JOURNALISM. *Heinemann* 1963.

Durant, Henry. "The Press" in MADE FOR MILLIONS: A CRITICAL STUDY OF THE NEW MEDIA OF INFORMATION AND ENTERTAINMENT edited by Frederick Laws. London, *Contact Publications* 1947.

Eames, Leonard and Ryan, Bernard. SO YOU WANT TO GO INTO JOURNALISM. *Harper and Row* 1963.

Fisk, Nicholas. LOOK AT NEWSPAPERS. Look at . . . *Hamish Hamilton* 1962. Illustrated by Eric Thomas.

Greene, Carla. I WANT TO BE A NEWS REPORTER (*Childrens Press* 1958) *W. and R. Chambers* 1965. Illustrated by Frances Eckart.

Grey, Elizabeth. THE STORY OF JOURNALISM (*Longman Young Books* 1968) *Houghton Mifflin* 1969. Illustrated by photographs.

Hall, Bernard J. BASIC TRAINING IN JOURNALISM (*Pergamon Press* 1968 U.K.) *Pergamon Press* 1968 U.S.A.

Harris, Geoffrey and Spark, David. PRACTICAL NEWSPAPER REPORTING (*Heinemann* 1966) *Verry* 1966. Illustrated by photographs.

Hart-Davis, Duff. BEHIND THE SCENES ON A NEWSPAPER. Behind the Scenes . . . *Phoenix* 1964. Illustrated by photographs.

Hildick, E. W. A CLOSE LOOK AT NEWSPAPERS. A CLOSE LOOK AT MAGAZINES AND COMICS. *Faber Educational* 1966. See also page 417.

Hornby, Robert. THE PRESS IN MODERN SOCIETY. *Muller* 1965.

Hudson, Derek. BRITISH JOURNALISTS AND NEWSPAPERS. Britain in Pictures. *Collins* 1945. Illustrated by photographs and prints.

Hudson, Derek. THE BOY'S BOOK OF THE PRESS. Boys' Book of . . . *Burke* 1964. Illustrated by photographs.

Huggett, F. THE TRUE BOOK ABOUT NEWSPAPERS. True Books. *Muller* 1955. Illustrated by F. Stocks May.

Inglis, Brian. THE PRESS. Today is History. *Blond Educational* 1965. Illustrated by photographs and prints.

Jupo, Frank. READ ALL ABOUT IT: THE STORY OF NEWS THROUGH THE AGES (*Prentice-Hall* 1957) *World's Work* 1962. Illustrated by the author.

Mansfield, F. J. THE COMPLETE JOURNALIST. *Pitman* 1962.

Matthews, T. S. THE SUGAR PILL: AN ESSAY ON NEWSPAPERS. *Gollancz* 1957.

Moorhouse, Geoffrey. THE PRESS. *Ward Lock Educational* 1964.

Nuttall, Kenneth. NEWS FOR ALL. Services we Use. *Longman Educational* 1964. Illustrated by W. G. Morden.

Osmond, Edward. FROM DRUMBEAT TO TICKER TAPE. *Hutchinson* 1960. Illustrated by the author.

Owens, Joan Llewelyn. WRITING AS A CAREER. Career Guides. *Bodley Head* 1967. Illustrated by photographs.

Papas, William. THE PRESS. *Oxford University Press* 1964. Illustrated by the author. A firework of a book for adults and sophisticated school-children. Brilliant cartoons and a compressed text provide a broad view of newspapers and the people concerned with them.

Parsons, Tom. FIND A CAREER IN JOURNALISM. *Putnam* 1959.

Perrott, Roy. DISCOVERING NEWSPAPERS. Discovery Reference Books. *University of London Press* 1961. Illustrated by Moire Hoddell.

Simpson, Willma Willis. ABOUT NEWS AND HOW IT TRAVELS (*Melmont* 1960)
Muller 1965. Illustrated by Jaroslav Gebr.

Smith, Geoffrey. NEWS AND NEWSPAPERS. Johnston's Bookshelf. *Johnston and
Bacon* 1962. With photographs.

Stephen, Neil. JOURNALISM. *Robert Hale* 1963.

Summers, Owen and Hall, Unity. DATELINE: FLEET STREET. *Educational
Explorers* 1969. Illustrated by photographs. See also page 420.

Thomas, Denis. THE STORY OF NEWSPAPERS. Outlines. *Methuen* 1965.
Illustrated by photographs.

Warren, Carl N. NEWS REPORTING. *Harper and Row* 1929. Illustrated with
photographs and prints.

Wiggan, Richard. SO YOU WANT TO BE A JOURNALIST. *Colin Venton* 1963.
Illustrated by photographs.

Wilkerson, Marjorie. NEWS AND NEWSPAPERS. Past-into-Present. *Batsford* 1970.
Illustrated by photographs and prints.

Williams, Betty. KNOW ABOUT NEWSPAPERS. Know About . . . *Blackie* 1963,
revised edition 1969. Illustrated by photographs, prints and collages.

Williams, Francis. DANGEROUS ESTATE: THE ANATOMY OF NEWSPAPERS.
Longman 1957.

Williams, Francis. JOURNALISM AS A CAREER. Batsford Career Books. *Batsford* 1962.

—— DIRECTORY OF OPPORTUNITIES FOR SCHOOL LEAVERS. TODAY'S
PROFESSIONS. *Cornmarket Press* 1969, and regularly revised.

Relevant novels and stories

Harling, Robert. THE PAPER PALACE. *Chatto and Windus* 1951.

Leasor, James. THE MONDAY STORY. *Oxford University Press* 1951. Illustrated by
Evadné Rowan.

Meynell, Laurence. SCOOP (1964). THE SUSPECT SCIENTIST (1966). SHADOW
IN THE SUN (1968). *Hamish Hamilton*.

Robb, John. FRONT PAGE STORY: THE DRAMA OF NEWSPAPERS. *Hutchinson*
1960. With photographs.

Trease, Geoffrey. FOLLOW MY BLACK PLUME (*Macmillan* 1963) *Vanguard* 1963.
A THOUSAND FOR SICILY (*Macmillan* 1964) *Vanguard* 1966. Illustrated by
Brian Wildsmith. Mark Apperley, a schoolboy and later a cub reporter, follows
Garibaldi's fortunes between 1849 and 1860.

Wilson, Granville. JONATHAN ENTERS JOURNALISM. Career Novels. *Chatto and
Windus* 1956.

Wood, Andrew. TICKET TO FLEET STREET. *Macmillan* 1960. A lively tale of a
group of friends on a provincial paper.

6 | *Epilogue*

Go on now, and read other good Books diligently, and thou shalt become learned, wise and Godly.
John Amos Comenius. ORBIS PICTUS (1959), p. 309

6 | *Epilogue*

THE system of publishing information books in series is by now firmly established, and each writer finds his own way of conforming to a pattern without losing his individuality. Certain series seem to have remained static over the years – the *True Books*, for example – though changes in style and format are long overdue. Others have changed with a changing outlook or have broadened from a simple beginning; the American *Let's-Read-and-Find-out Science* books and the English *Stand and Stare* series have an inner dynamism that must be as welcome to writers as it is to readers. New ideas for information books are conceived in an individual mind, born in consultation and reared, for the most part, in the shelter of a series. The types of books offered to the young in the wide category of non-fiction are constantly and healthily changing.

Perhaps the most noticeable trends today can be seen at the two extremes of the reading public – in books for the pre-school child and for the older 'teens. It is to some extent a new departure to design information books expressly for children under five, and it is not always easy to define their difference from story-books already existing. The immediate aims of these "books of awareness" vary considerably, though their basic purpose of instruction is plain enough. First and simplest are the organised books of recognition. These are hardly new in essence, though possibly they may be new in their mode of presentation. Instead of identifying a saucepan as and when it appears in a picture-book – for instance, in a folk-tale illustrated by Margot Zemach or William Stobbs, or in an alphabet under the letter S – the child might identify it in Pat Albeck's BEN IN THE KITCHEN (1970), where it appears side by side with other utensils and objects likely to be associated with kitchens in the child's mind.

This associative grouping of objects can be comforting by its very orderliness; infants may find it reassuring to see, as Hans Andersen put it, "a place for everything and everything in its place". On the other hand, they may need and enjoy the anarchy of a sauce-pan in the sand-pit or used as shelter for a robin's nest. Small children need to meet familiar objects in and out of context, in picture-books of purposive and fantastic character, and it would certainly be a pity if the particular kind of logic shown in association books were elevated to a self-conscious principle of pre-school education.

The sorting element in Pat Albeck's *Ben* books does not differ essentially from the casual sorting in the most elementary rag-book of kittens and puppies. The child is at this stage learning words more than anything else; books give him practice in the naming which he has been doing from the moment he began to speak. There are books being produced today, however, in which the logical sorting of objects goes a stage further. The child is induced to learn something about these objects, accepting them as related, and absorbing information about them as objects in a group. Again this is nothing essentially new but the learning aspect is more deliberate today than it has been in the past. In the *Look Around* series recently imported into England from France, Alain Grée has used the basic plan of his earlier *Keith and Sally* books in small compact volumes for very young children.

Keith and Sally were lively children of seven or thereabouts whose curiosity was exercised in the woods, at the seaside, in the garden, in a television studio and elsewhere. The omniscient Captain Simon listened to their questions and supplied answers suitable to their years. In the *Look around* books, the role of Captain Simon falls to Rufus the fox, who helps little Jake and Tina to put names to the various things they see and to define them very simply. The elementary facts the children discover about a daisy, a motor-car, the effect of mixing blue and yellow, are facts they could have learned in other ways. They learn them here from books with several attractive characteristics – they are full of bright, striking pictures, they are small, square and friendly in shape, and because they are in a series they can be collected. These points are likely to make them popular with organisers of play-groups and nursery schools as well as with small children, and this is certainly

a cogent reason for their appearance as an apparently new type of
information book.

The words used in Alain Grée's books amount to little more than
labels; the few points that are made are still labels – indicating, for
instance, the difference between a child's clothes on the Equator
and in a European country, or naming the parts of a flower. Play-
books or information books – it hardly matters which term we use
to describe them. Their common denominator is their appearance;
they are brightly coloured and they are the right shape to go in
a treasure-box or a miniature satchel. For this reason it is possible
that the *Stand and Stare* series (Methuen), started in 1964 for
children who can already read, might be commandeered by younger
brothers and sisters simply as picture-books. These pleasant little
pocket-books present simple illustrations of animals in their proper
habitats or of vehicles and buildings familiar to children in everyday
life. A child not yet at school could learn to identify from these
books. He might learn a few useful facts as well – about the materials
used in building a house or a sparrow's nest, for instance – from
looking at the pictures. A series like this is not new, but it gives a
new look to old material.

In the past it has seemed natural to offer facts to young children
mainly in the framework of a story, but in the last few years the
concept books prepared for the early school years have been
extended backwards to the pre-school child. To give an example,
the *Things I Like* books are basically list books, illustrating simple
objects as backgrounds to the actions of children, but they contain
by implication concepts which provide a new way of sorting
these objects. The commentary on the suavely coloured pictures in
these books is arranged like free verse, with an occasional concealed
rhyme. The contrast displayed in ROUGH AND SMOOTH (1971),
for example, includes this set of definitions:

> Cooking salt
> an angry voice
> chapped hands
> and a tall brick wall,
> these are rough.
>   But
> a baby's skin

snow and ice
the soft
grey coats
of rats and mice.
Licked lollipops
and chocolate drops
satin cushions
gooseberry fools, copper pots
and clean new tools,
these are very smooth.

This kind of book can lead on to something like Charles Hatcher's WHAT SHAPE IS IT? (1963) and WHAT SIZE IS IT? (1964), which present concepts and techniques more directly for children already at school. Certainly the difference between heat and cold need not necessarily be conveyed to an infant in such literal terms, but elementary concept books do not exclude the more familiar folk-tales from which he can also learn basic facts.

As information books grow with the growing child, their emphasis changes. A simple list will stretch to include a clinching idea. The sorting of a group of animals will broaden to include exceptions. Gradually the child will realise that no book is complete in itself and that he can go further to find out more. Nowadays participation is an important aspect of information books, especially for the middle school years.

This may be seen if we compare the history text-book of thirty years ago with its modern counterpart, a mixture of political and social history, psychology, geography, art, economics and other subjects and no longer cast in an exclusively classroom style. Nowadays source material is provided far in advance of the quotations that used to break up pages of solidly packed information in lesson books. The bias towards social history in our century is noticeable in a series like the *Wayland Documentary Histories*, books consisting of relevant extracts with the briefest explanatory links. The volume on the Plague and Fire of London already mentioned on page 253 shows the usefulness of this kind of book. Another volume, Patrick Rooke's THE AGE OF DICKENS (1970), offers extracts from letters and diaries, government publications, bills, advertisements, public notices and so on as a background to

Dickens's life and work; but a boy or girl interested in the pattern of life in the last century may find material here on trades unions, Darwinism, the Ragged Schools and a host of other subjects through which he can add to his impression of the Victorian age as a whole. Still closer to "what happened in history", the *Jackdaw* portfolios provide not quotation alone but also facsimiles of historical documents, cut-out models and other reconstructions of the past.

A *Jackdaw* portfolio cannot make a child into an historian but it could set his foot on the right path. At the very least, to look at contemporary documents is to move towards a sense of period. With this end in view the Brockhampton *Picture Reference Books*, started in 1965, provide carefully selected pictures of weapons and armour, vehicles, domestic objects, portraits of various periods, using no text other than the necessary labels for identification. The resources of graphic art are being called upon in numerous ways to provide visual aids to the study of the past and individual artists have set their seal on books where illustration is paramount – for example, Christine Price in her beautifully illustrated MADE IN THE MIDDLE AGES (1962) and MADE IN THE RENAISSANCE (1963), which draw on museums and galleries all over Europe, and Alan Sorrell's fine reconstructions of settlements and buildings in PREHISTORIC BRITAIN (1968) and ROMAN LONDON (1969). Perhaps the most original device in this sphere is the jigsaw method by which Ian Ribbons arranges short extracts (from books, newspapers, letters, dispatches and so on) and small coloured pictures to give an impression of two days momentous in history – the day of Trafalgar and the day when World War I was declared. Illustrated books like these are a means to an end and we are likely to have more of them – particularly, I hope, more collections of source material – if education holds to its aim of helping children to learn for themselves.

The duplication of original sources does not inhibit an historian from putting forward his own views. Can a writer expect the same freedom when he is writing of the problems of modern society – pollution and over-population, the situation of minority groups, crime and drug addiction, power politics and social change? Subjects like this have naturally found a place in junior novels with contemporary settings and they are being considered more and more often in information books specially written for the 'teens. The

spread of readership for books on such controversial subjects could
be very wide, starting at twelve or thirteen and with an upward
limit of sixteen or seventeen, though at any time during this period
young people will begin to look to adult books for the information
they want. Assuming that they do also, during this time, need books
tailored for their years, these may justify their existence for several
reasons. They may supply food for thought which can be digested
slowly, where the impact of television and the Press is likely to be
quicker and more superficial. On the other hand, books on topical
subjects will necessarily become out of date very quickly, so that
they can never be used as an exclusive source of information. A
writer may compensate for this by establishing a collecting point
for current facts. For example, D. J. Williams's STRIKE OR
BARGAIN? (1965) provides a brief and non-partisan history of the
rise of trades unions from the last century, leading to an outline of
the situation at the time of writing. The book is designed to be used
as a basis for discussion in school; it does not pretend to be complete,
but it invites its readers to extend it by their own observations. In
the same way Katharine Savage's THE HISTORY OF THE COMMON
MARKET (1969) offers a summary of events and points of views
which a young reader could not easily accumulate for himself, and
leaves him, as it were, extra pages on which he can add notes of the
present situation.

Books like this serve their purpose better if the author takes an
impartial view of his subject, but to be objective does not mean to be
negative. Some of the widely known series dealing with other
countries show a reluctance to deal with difficult issues. In LET'S
VISIT PAKISTAN (1966) by John C. Caldwell and LET'S VISIT
RHODESIA (1970) by Guy Winchester-Gould, the facts are so
cautiously selected that the books give little more than a tourist's-
eye view of countries whose problems boys and girls at school should
be considering seriously. A notable exception to the evasions in this
series, LET'S VISIT CHINA (1966), the work of a Chinese graduate
of Oxford and her British husband, offers a clear-sighted view of
the development of Maoist China, with a good deal of practical
evidence to back it. In any case, we may have reached the point of
no return in regard to this kind of one-country book; the young
are making demands for an international outlook which writers of
information books can hardly afford to ignore.

One of the justifications for books on controversial subjects is surely that they can offer their readers a collection of facts upon which to base a judgment, an opinion or a theory. In this case, should we not expect books to be a good deal broader in their outlook than they are? A book on pollution, for example, as well as illustrating the evil effects of releasing effluent in rivers, should also explain fairly and honestly some of the economic reasons why this is done; nor should any such book be so specialised that it omits to set some such broad pattern of ecosystems as the Darlings set in their admirable book, A PLACE IN THE SUN (1970). There is a case for producing books on subjects like drug addiction, apartheid, the Hungarian Revolution, which are not written by an individual but which are a symposium of opinions – responsible and fully documented opinions – from people of different ages, backgrounds and nationalities.

Books written specifically for young people on such subjects may quickly change from being books of persuasion to being out-and-out propaganda. This tendency must be carefully watched. We have to consider how far it is right to use books to direct the opinions of readers who are still prepared to accept what is in print as necessarily true and complete. It would be a disaster, too, if pre-digested surveys of social philosophies or economic pressures should be offered to the young as in any sense a *substitute* for adult books containing the mature, committed statements of men and women in positions of power and responsibility, whether such power and responsibility is exercised inside or outside the existing norm of society.

An information book must communicate facts and ideas to its readers, of whatever age or capacity, in such a way that they will develop the will and the mental equipment to assess these facts and ideas. In the broadest sense, an information book is a teacher, and the role of a teacher is to lead his pupils towards a considered independence of thought and action. Instruction is important, but freedom of thought is more important still.

Reading List

Albeck, Pat. BEN IN THE GARDEN. BEN AT THE SHOP. BEN IN THE KITCHEN. BEN AND HIS TOYS. *Methuen* 1970. Illustrated by the author.

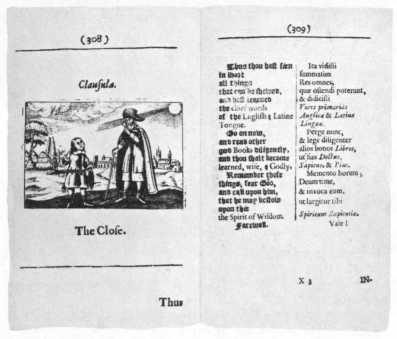

Spread from ORBIS PICTUS by John Amos Comenius, by courtesy of The Trustees of the British Museum

Blakeley, Peggy. BIG AND LITTLE. FAST AND SLOW. HOT AND COLD, and other volumes. Things I Like. (International Copyright Institute 1966) *A. and C. Black* 1968. Illustrated by Philippe Thomas. MY HOME AND YOURS. FIRST AND LAST. SUNSHINE AND SHADOW. ROUGH AND SMOOTH. Things I Like. (International Copyright Institute 1971) *A. and C. Black* 1971. Illustrated by Henry Branton.

Caldwell, John C. LET'S VISIT PAKISTAN. Let's Visit . . . (*John Day* 1960) *Burke* 1966. Illustrated by photographs.

Darling, Lois and Louis. A PLACE IN THE SUN. (*Morrow* 1968) *World's Work* 1970. Illustrated by the authors.

Grée, Alain. KEITH AND SALLY AT THE SEASIDE. KEITH AND SALLY GO ABROAD, and other stories. (France 1963) *Evans* 1965. Adapted by Annemarie Ryba. Illustrated by the author.

Grée, Alain. I KNOW ABOUT CLOTHES. I KNOW ABOUT CARS, and other volumes. Look Around Books. (France 1968) *Methuen* 1970. Illustrated by the author.

Green, Barbara. PREHISTORIC BRITAIN. *Lutterworth* 1968. Illustrated by Alan Sorrell.

Hatcher, Charles. WHAT SIZE IS IT? (1963). WHAT SHAPE IS IT? (1964). *Brockhampton*. Illustrated by Gareth Adamson.

Liao, Hung-Ying and Bryan, Derek. LET'S VISIT CHINA. Let's Visit . . . *Burke* 1966. With photographs.

Lucas, Angela. TELEPHONES. BUILDING A HOUSE. Stand and Stare, nos. 25 and 26. *Methuen* 1970. Also other volumes. Illustrated by Derek Lucas.

Price, Christine. MADE IN THE MIDDLE AGES (*Dutton* 1961) *Bodley Head* 1962. MADE IN THE RENAISSANCE (*Dutton* 1963) *Bodley Head* 1963. Illustrated by the author.

Ribbons, Ian. MONDAY 21 OCTOBER 1805 (*Oxford University Press* 1968) *D. White* 1968. TUESDAY 4 AUGUST 1914 (*Oxford University Press* 1970) *D. White* 1970. Illustrated by the compiler.

Rooke, Patrick. THE AGE OF DICKENS. Wayland Documentary History series. *Wayland Press* 1970. Illustrated by photographs and prints.

Savage, Katharine. THE HISTORY OF THE COMMON MARKET (*Longman Young Books* 1969) *Walck* 1970. Drawings by John Miles, and some photographs and diagrams.

Sorrell, Alan. ROMAN LONDON (*Batsford* 1969) *Arco* 1969. Illustrated by the author. See also under Green, Barbara.

Williams, D. J. STRIKE OR BARGAIN? THE STORY OF TRADES UNIONISM. *Blond Educational* 1965. With photographs and prints.

Winchester-Gould, Guy. LET'S VISIT RHODESIA. Let's Visit . . . *Burke* 1970. Illustrated by photographs.